THE RATLINE

Also by Philippe Sands

THE
RATLINE

LOVE, LIES *and* **JUSTICE**
on the **TRAIL** *of a* **NAZI FUGITIVE**

PHILIPPE SANDS

First published in Great Britain in 2020 by Weidenfeld & Nicolson
an imprint of The Orion Publishing Group Ltd
Carmelite House, 50 Victoria Embankment
London EC4Y 0DZ

An Hachette UK Company

3 5 7 9 10 8 6 4 2

A CIP catalogue record for this book is
available from the British Library.

ISBN (Hardback) 978 1 4746 0812 1
ISBN (Trade Paperback) 978 1 4746 0813 8
ISBN (eBook) 978 1 4746 0815 2

Typeset by Input Data Services Ltd, Somerset

Printed and bound in Great Britain by Clays Ltd, Elcograf S.p.A.

www.weidenfeldandnicolson.co.uk
www.orionbooks.co.uk

For Allan, Marc and Leo,
fathers and sons

and

In memory of Lisa Jardine

'Their bows will slaughter the young men;
they will have no mercy on the fruit of the womb;
they will not look with pity on the children.'

Isaiah, 13:18

'It is more important to understand the butcher than the victim.'

Javier Cercas

CONTENTS

Note to the Reader

The story in this book takes place across a period of time in which boundaries, the exercise of power and names of places often changed. For example, through the nineteenth century, the city today known as Lviv was generally known as Lemberg, located on the eastern outskirts of the Austro-Hungarian empire. Soon after the First World War, it became part of newly independent Poland and was called Lwów until the outbreak of the Second World War, when it was occupied by the Soviets, who knew it as Lvov. In July 1941, the Germans unexpectedly conquered the city and made it the capital of Distrikt Galizien in the General Government, when it was known once more as Lemberg. After the Red Army vanquished the Nazis in the summer of 1944, it became part of Ukraine and was called Lviv, the name that is generally used today. Lemberg, Lviv, Lvov and Lwów are the same place.

What to call the city, and other places the names of which changed across the years, in the pages of this book posed a number of difficulties. I have generally sought to use the name by which the place was referred to by those who controlled it at the time of which I am writing.

Principal Characters

Wächter Family

Otto's family

Josef Wächter, b. 29.12.1863, Hawran, father
Martha (Pfob) Wächter, b. 23.9.1874, Vienna, mother
  Hertha (Wächter) Chaterny, b. 1898, sister
  Ilse (Wächter) von Böheim-Heldensinn, b. 1900, sister
  Otto Gustav, b. 1901
    m. Charlotte (Bleckmann) Wächter, b. 1908
      Otto Richard, b. 1933
        Otto, b. 1961, a nephew of Horst
      Lieselotte (Liesl), b. 1934
        Dario, b. 1969, a nephew of Horst
      Waltraut, b. 1937
      Horst Arthur, b. 1939
      Heidegund (Heide), b. 1940
      Sieglinde (Linde), b. 1944

Charlotte's family

August von Scheindler, b. 1852, grandfather
Henriette (Schwippel) von Scheindler, b. 1856, grandmother

Carl Walther Bleckmann, b. 1868, father
Margarete (Meta) (von Scheindler) Bleckmann, b. 1878, mother
  Hanne (Sterz) Bleckmann, b. 1902, sister
  Helene (Küfferle) Bleckmann, b. 1903, sister
  Heinrich Bleckmann, b. 1904, brother
  Charlotte (Wächter) Bleckmann, b. 1908
  Wolfgang Bleckmann, b. 1909, brother
  Richard Bleckmann, b. 1914, brother

Horst's family

m. Jacqueline (Ollèn) Wächter, b. 1951
  Magdalena Wächter, b. 1977, daughter
    m. Gerlot Galib Stanfel, b. 1968

Otto's Comrades (1930–45)

Otto Bauer, deputy head of Otto's office, Lemberg, 1942–4

Hanns Blaschke, *Deutsche Klub*, July Putsch, Mayor of Vienna, 1943–5

Martin Bormann, private secretary to Adolf Hitler, 1943–5

Josef Bühler, Secretary General, General Government of German-occupied Poland, 1939–45

Josef Bürckel, Gauleiter of Vienna, 1939–40

Eugen Dollmann, German diplomat, SS member, Ambassador to the Holy See, 1939

Georg von Ettingshausen, Viennese lawyer and party member
  Helga Ettingshausen, his wife

Hans Fischböck, Reichsminister for the Netherlands, 1940–5
  Trudl Fischböck, his wife, Charlotte's friend

Ludwig Fischer, Governor of Warsaw, 1941–5

Hans Frank, Governor General of German-occupied Poland, 1939–45
  Brigitte Frank, wife of Hans Frank
    Niklas Frank, son of Hans Frank, b. 1939

Alfred Frauenfeld, July Putschist, Nazi Gauleiter in Vienna, 1930

Odilo Globočnik (Globus), Gauleiter of Vienna, 1938, SS and Police Leader, 1939–43

Reinhard Heydrich, Director of Gestapo, 1934–9, Director Reich Main Security Office, 1939–42

Heinrich Himmler, Reichsführer SS and Chief of Police, 1933–45

Wilhelm Höttl, SS Sturmbannführer and intelligence officer, colleague in Italy

Ernst Kaltenbrunner, *Deutsche Klub*, SS Leader Austria, Chief of Reich Main Security Office, 1943–5

Friedrich (Fritz) Katzmann, SS police chief, Lemberg

Albert Kesselring, Generalfeldmarschall, Luftwaffe

Erich Koch, Reichskommissar for Ukraine, 1941–4

Friedrich-Wilhelm Krüger, Higher SS and Police Leader, General Government of German-occupied Poland, 1939–43

Karl Lasch, Governor of the District of Galicia, 1941–2

Ludwig Losacker, head of Otto's office, Lemberg

Kajetan Mühlmann, art historian and SS officer

Hermann Neubacher, Mayor of Vienna, 1938–40

Rudolf Pavlu, July Putschist, Otto's friend and colleague, Mayor of Kraków, 1941–3

Walter Rafelsberger, SS Leader and fellow State Commissioner, Vienna, 1938–40

Burkhardt (Buko) Rathmann, 24th Waffen Mountain Division of the SS Karstjäger, 1943–5

Walter Rauff, SS officer, Reich Main Security Office, chief of secret police (Italy), 1943–5

Alfred Reinhardt, engineer, party member

Baldur von Schirach, head of the Hitler Youth, 1931–40, Reich Governor of Austria, 1940–5

Albert Schnez, Wehrmacht officer

Arthur Seyss-Inquart, Chancellor of Austria, 1938, Reichskommissar of the Netherlands, 1940–5, Horst's godfather

Karl Wolff, SS-Obergruppenführer, commander SS and police forces in Italy, 1943–5

Otto's Contacts

Stefan Brassloff, Professor, University of Vienna, Otto's teacher, 1925

Emmanuel (Manni) Braunegg, close friend of Otto, Vienna

Engelbert Dollfuss, Chancellor of Austria, 1932–4

Luise Ebner, friend of Otto, Bolzano

Reinhard Gehlen, SS intelligence officer

Friedensreich Hundertwasser, artist for whom Horst worked

Josef Hupka, Professor, University of Vienna, Otto's teacher, 1925

Herbert Kappler, SS police chief, Rome, 1940–4

Georg Lippert, architect, Vienna

Nora Oberauch von Hösslin, friend of Otto, Bolzano

Ferdinand Pawlikowski, Bishop, friend of the Bleckmann family

Erich Priebke, SS officer, Rome, escaped to Argentina via the Ratline

Dr Franz Rehrl, Governor of Salzburg, owner of a house in Thumersbach

Franz Hiernonymus Riedl, journalist, South Tyrol

Lothar Rübelt, photographer, Vienna

Franz Stangl, Commandant of Treblinka, escaped to Brazil along the
  Ratline

Hansjakob Stehle, historian and writer, acquaintance of Charlotte

Josef Thorack, sculptor, neighbour of the Wächters, Thumersbach

Melitta Wiedemann, journalist

Simon Wiesenthal, Nazi hunter

Karl-Gustav Wollenweber, German diplomat in Rome, 1940–4

PROLOGUE

Rome, 13 July 1949

The condition of the man in bed nine was grave. An intense fever and acute liver condition meant he was unable to eat, or focus on the matters of ambition and desire that propelled him throughout his life.

The notes at the end of the bed offered scant information, and much of it was inaccurate. 'On July 9th 1949 a patient by the name of Reinhardt was brought in.' The date was right, the name was not. His real name was Wächter, but it's use would alert the authorities that the patient was wanted for mass murder, a senior Nazi. He once served as a deputy to Hans Frank, Governor General of occupied Poland, hanged three years earlier in Nuremberg for the murder of four million human beings. Wächter too was indicted, for 'mass murder', the shooting and execution of over one hundred thousand people. The estimate was low.

'Reinhardt' was on the run in Rome. He believed himself to be hunted by Americans, Poles, Soviets and Jews, for 'crimes against humanity' and 'genocide'. He hoped to get to South America.

His father was identified in the notes as 'Josef', which was correct. The space to record his Christian name was blank. 'Reinhardt' used the name Alfredo, but his real name was Otto.

The patient's occupation was described as 'writer', which was not entirely wrong. Otto Wächter wrote letters to his wife and kept a diary, although the entries were few and, as I would learn, written in a shorthand or code that made them difficult to decipher. He also wrote poems and, more recently, to fill the empty hours of a man in need of distraction, one film script and a manifesto on the future of Germany. He gave it the title *Quo Vadis Germania?*

When he was powerful and free, the patient put his name to documents of a kind that would cause a man to be hunted. His name appeared at the bottom of important letters and decrees. In Vienna he ended the careers of thousands, including two of his university teachers. In Kraków he authorised the construction of a ghetto. In Lemberg, he prohibited Jews from work. It would be more accurate, therefore, to describe the patient's occupation as a lawyer, a governor, an SS-Gruppenführer. For the last four years his main focus was survival, a man who hid and sought escape, and who believed he had succeeded.

The notes stated his age as forty-five. He was three years older, and had recently celebrated his birthday.

The notes described his marital status as single. Actually, he was married to Charlotte Bleckmann, identified as Lotte, or Lo, in his letters. She called him *Hümmchen*, or *Hümmi*, a term of endearment. They had six children, although it could have been more.

The notes offered no address in Rome. In fact, he lived secretly, in a monk's cell on the top floor of the Vigna Pia monastery, on the outskirts of the city, tucked in a bend of the River Tiber. He liked to swim.

The notes did not mention that the patient was brought to the hospital by two monks who lived at Vigna Pia.

As to his condition, the notes stated:

The patient indicates that he has been unable to eat since July 1st; that he developed a high fever on July 2nd, and showed symptoms of jaundice on July 7th. The patient is diabetic, and the clinical examination revealed a liver condition: acute yellow liver atrophy (*icterus gravis*).

From other sources, we learn that 'Reinhardt' received three visitors during his stay at the Santo Spirito Hospital. One was a bishop, once close to Pope Pius XII. Another was a medical doctor who served at the German embassy in Rome, during the war. The third was a Prussian lady, married to an Italian academic, with whom she had two children. She visited him each day, once on Sunday, the day after he was admitted, twice on Monday, once on Tuesday.

This day, Wednesday, 13 July, was the fifth visit. Each time she brought a small gift, an item of fruit, or a little sugar, as the doctor suggested.

It was difficult for the Prussian lady to enter the Sala Baglivi, in which he lay. On the first visit she was questioned intently by a guard. 'Not enough specifics,' he told her. Be discreet, she has been warned, say only you are a friend of the church. She repeated the words, the guard relented, and now they recognised her.

The visitor was impressed by the scale of the Sala Baglivi. 'Like a church', she would tell the patient's wife who, according to the notes, did not exist. She appreciated the coolness of the vast space, a refuge from the heat of the day, as she walked from her home, past the Piazza dei Quiriti and the fountain which caused Mussolini to declare that four naked women should never be present in a park.

. She entered the Sala Baglivi, passed the small chapel, turned right, approached the patient's bed, lingered. She greeted him, spoke a few words, cooled him with a damp cloth, changed his shirt. She took a little stool from under the bed and sat, to offer conversation and comfort. A new patient in the neighbouring bed meant less privacy, so she took care with her words.

The patient had little to say. He was on penicillin – intravenously – to treat the infection, and the drug lowered the fever but left him weak. He was told to consume little, coffee with milk, a few drops of orange juice, a tablespoon of dextrose. The doctors cautioned him to protect his stomach.

On each visit the lady noticed a change. On Monday he was weak and spoke little. On Tuesday he seemed fresher and more talkative. He enquired about letters he expected to receive, and shared the hope that his oldest child, also called Otto, might visit before the summer was over.

Today's words were encouraging, even if the body seemed weaker. 'It's getting much, much better,' the patient said. She fed him a teaspoon of orange juice. His mind was clear, his eyes luminous.

The patient managed a longer thought. 'If Lo can't come now, it doesn't matter, because I felt so very close to her these past long nights, and I am happy that we are so closely united. She understands me fully and everything has been as it should be.'

Inside he burned, but felt no pain. He seemed calm, lay still, held the lady's hand. She told him about her day, life in Rome, the children. Before she left she stroked his forehead, gently.

He spoke a few final words to her. 'I am in good hands, I will see you tomorrow.'

At half past five the Prussian lady bade farewell to the patient known as 'Reinhardt'. She knew the end was near.

Later that evening, the patient received the bishop. At the final moment, on the account of the bishop, in whose arms it was said he lay, the patient spoke his last words. He alleged that his condition was caused by a deliberate act, and identified the poisoner. Many years would pass before the words he was said to have spoken to the bishop, in the presence of no one else, would come to be known by others.

The patient did not see the next day.

A few days later the lady visitor wrote to Charlotte Wächter, the widow. Ten handwritten pages described how she met Wächter, a few weeks earlier, soon after he arrived in Rome. 'From him I learned about you, the children, everything he held dear in life.' 'Reinhardt' told the lady visitor about his work before and during the war, and in the years that followed, spent high in the mountains. The letter described a state of restlessness, and alluded to a weekend trip he made outside Rome. She did not share the name of the place he visited, or the person.

The letter ended with a few words about the diagnosis. The doctor believed death was caused by 'acute liver atrophy', a form of 'internal poisoning', possibly caused by food or water. The lady offered thoughts about the future, how Charlotte would miss her 'optimistic, friendly comrade'. Think only of the children, she added, they needed a courageous, happy mother.

'It is especially that brave cheerfulness, your two feet firmly on the ground, that your husband loved so much about you.'⁶ She ended the letter with those words, which passed in silence as to the true name of the patient.

The letter was dated 25 July 1949. It went from Rome to Salzburg, where it was delivered to the home of Charlotte Wächter and her six children.

Charlotte kept the letter for thirty-six years. Following her death, in 1985, it passed to her eldest child, Otto junior, with other personal papers. After Otto junior died in 1997, the letter passed to Horst, the fourth child. He inhabited a vast, dilapidated, empty, magnificent castle in the ancient Austrian village of Hagenberg, between Vienna and Brno, in the Czech Republic. For years the letter remained here in private obscurity.

Then, after two decades had passed, on an extraordinarily cold day, I visited Horst in the castle. Introduced to him a few years earlier, I was aware of the thousands of pages of his mother's personal papers. At a certain point he asked if I would like to see the original of the Prussian lady's letter. Yes. He left the kitchen, climbed the steep stone steps, entered his room and approached an old wooden cabinet with glass windows, near his bed, close to the photograph of his father in an SS uniform. He retrieved the letter, brought it down to the kitchen, placed it on the old wooden table, and started to read aloud.

His voice faltered, and, for a moment, he wept.

'It's not true'.

'What's not true?'

'That my father died from an illness.'

The logs in the stove crackled. I watched the condensation of his breath.

I had known Horst for five years. He chose this moment to share a secret, a belief that his father was killed.

'What is the truth?'

'It is best to start at the beginning,' Horst said.

AUSTRO-HUNGARIAN
EMPIRE, 1901

0   100   200
Kilometer

Leipzig   Breslau   Lodz
Frankfurt   (Wroclaw)   RUSSIAN EMPIRE

GERMAN EMPIRE

Havran
Prague   GALICIA   Lemberg (Lviv)
BOHEMIA   Kraków
Hagenberg   CARPATHIAN MOUNTAINS   Dniester
Munich   Danube   Vienna
Zurich   Salzburg   Mürzzuschlag   Budapest   Iaşi
                TYROL   AUSTRO — HUNGARIAN EMPIRE
Milan   Bolzano
Venice   Drave   Maros
                                Zagreb   TRANSYLVANIA
                Trieste   ROMANIA
                                Save   Belgrade
                DINARIC ALPS   Bucharest
ITALY   Zara   Danube
                (Zadar)   BOSNIA-   Sarajevo   SERBIA
                                HERZEGOVINA   Niš   Sofia   BULGARIA
CORSICA   Rome   Adriatic Sea   MONTE-
(FRANCE)   NEGRO
                                ALBANIA

Elbe Weser Oder Vistula Tisza Po Aluta

I

LOVE

'I never knew the old Vienna before the war, with its Strauss music, its glamour and easy charm . . .'

Graham Greene, *The Third Man*, 1949

1

2012, Hagenberg

The beginning was the visit to Horst Wächter, in the spring of 2012, when the fourth child of Otto and Charlotte Wächter first welcomed me to his home. I crossed a disused moat and passed through the large wooden doors of Schloss Hagenberg, to encounter a musty smell, the incense of burning wood that clung to Horst. We drank tea, I met his wife Jacqueline, he told me about his daughter Magdalena, his five brothers and sisters. I learned too about his mother's papers, although many years would pass before I would see them all.

The visit was an accident. Eighteen months earlier, I travelled to the city of Lviv, in Ukraine, to deliver a lecture on 'crimes against humanity' and 'genocide'. Ostensibly, I went to visit the law faculty, but the true reason for the journey was a desire to find the house where my grandfather was born. In 1904, Leon Buchholz's city was known as Lemberg, a regional capital of the Austro-Hungarian empire.

I hoped to fill gaps in Leon's life story, to discover what happened to his family, about which he maintained a discreet silence. I wanted to learn about his identity, and mine. I found Leon's house, and discovered that the origins of 'genocide' and 'crimes against humanity', legal ideas invented in 1945, could be traced to the city of his birth. The journey caused me to write a book, *East West Street*, the story of four men: Leon, whose large family from Lemberg and its environs was obliterated in the Holocaust; Hersch Lauterpacht and Rafael Lemkin, also from the city, two jurists who put the terms 'crimes against humanity' and 'genocide' into the Nuremberg trials and international law; and Hans Frank, Governor General of German-occupied Poland, who arrived in Lemberg in August 1942 and gave a speech which was followed by the extermination of the Jews of the region known as Galicia. The victims of Frank's actions, for which he was convicted and hanged at Nuremberg, were four million in number. They included the families of Leon, Lauterpacht and Lemkin.

In the course of the research I came across a remarkable book by Niklas Frank, entitled *The Father*, about Hans Frank. I sought out Niklas, and one day we met, on the terrace of a fine hotel near Hamburg. In the course of our conversation, knowing of my interest in Lemberg, he mentioned Otto Wächter. One of his father's deputies, Wächter, served as Nazi governor in Lemberg from 1942 to 1944, and Niklas knew one of the children, Horst. As I was interested in the city, and as it was during Wächter's time in Lemberg that Leon's family perished, Niklas offered to make an introduction. It came with a mild warning: unlike Niklas, who harboured a negative view of his parent – 'I am against the death penalty, except in the case of my father,' he said within an hour of meeting – Horst embraced a more positive view of his father. 'But you will like him,' Niklas said, with a smile.

Horst responded positively to the introduction. I flew from London to Vienna, rented a car, headed north across the River Danube, past vineyards and hills, to the tiny, ancient village of Hagenberg. 'I'll dance with you in Vienna,' the radio sang, 'I'll bury my soul in a scrapbook.' During the journey I felt a sense of anxiety, as Otto Wächter most likely played a role in the fate of Leon's relatives in and around Lemberg, all but one of whom perished during his rule. His name seemed to have been airbrushed out of the historical narrative for that period. I gleaned that he was Austrian, a husband and a father, a lawyer and a senior Nazi. In 1934 he was involved in the assassination of the Austrian chancellor, Engelbert Dollfuss. After the Nazis arrived in Austria in March 1938, following the Anschluss, he had a senior position in the new government in Vienna, where my grandparents lived. Later he was appointed governor of Nazi-occupied Kraków, and then, in 1942, governor of Lemberg. After the war, he disappeared off the face of the earth. I wanted to know what happened to him, whether justice was done. For that I would leave no stone unturned. The journey began.

I need not have worried about Horst. He greeted me with enthusiasm, a tall and attractive man, genial in a pink shirt and Birkenstocks, with a twinkle in his eyes, and an embracingly guttural, warm, hesitant, gentle voice. He was delighted I had travelled to the dilapidated baroque castle that was his home, constructed around an internal courtyard, imposing and square, four storeys high, with thick, stone walls and a moat covered in a vibrant undergrowth.

A famous actor just visited, he enthused, with an Italian director.

'Two Oscar winners at my castle!' They were filming *The Best Offer*, a tale of love and crime set across Europe, in Vienna, Trieste, Bolzano and Rome. Little did I know, back then, the relevance of these places to the Wächters.

Accompanied by a cat, we entered the schloss, a solid building that had seen better days. We walked past a workshop, filled with tools and other implements, drying fruit and potatoes and other vegetables, and met the dog. Horst found the building in the 1960s when it hosted a colony of artists. A place of 'secret festivities', he explained. Two decades later he bought it with a modest inheritance left to him after Charlotte's death.

He shared the basics of his life. Born in Vienna on 14 April 1939, he was named after the 'Horst Wessel Song', a Nazi anthem. His parents chose Arthur as his middle name, in honour of Arthur Seyss-Inquart, his father's comrade and friend, and Horst's godfather. He was a lawyer with tortoiseshell spectacles who sat at Adolf Hitler's top table, who served briefly as chancellor of Austria, after the Anschluss, and governor of Ostmark, as Austria was known in the Third Reich. Shortly after Horst's birth, Seyss-Inquart was appointed minister without portfolio in Hitler's cabinet, and soon after that given the task of governing occupied Holland. Hitler's last will and testament, written in 1945, appointed Seyss-Inquart to be foreign minister of the Reich. Within a few months the lawyer and godfather was caught, tried at Nuremberg and hanged by the neck for the crimes he committed.

I was somewhat surprised, therefore, to see a small black and white photograph of Seyss-Inquart near Horst's bed. It was tucked into the frame of a photograph of his father Otto, near an oil painting of his grandfather, General Josef Wächter, a military man who served in the imperial army during the First World War. A photo of Charlotte taken in 1942 hung on another wall of the bedroom. Horst slept close to the family.

Horst introduced me to his wife Jacqueline (Ollèn), who was Swedish. They occupied two cosy rooms on the ground floor of the castle, heated with a large wood-burning stove, although their relationship did not seem so tender. He made tea and talked more affectionately about his parents than did Jacqueline. It was immediately apparent that they continued to occupy a special place in his heart. He seemed especially close to his mother, for whom he cared during the last years of her life, a woman who, I would learn, loved him as her favourite. Charlotte's relationship with Horst's four sisters was more difficult, and when they grew up three of them moved abroad.

During that first visit, Horst impressed upon me that he hardly knew his father, who was often absent during the war years, in faraway places. With the family in Austria, he might be in Kraków, Lemberg or Italy, or in Berlin. I learned that he was a 'lady's man', that he disappeared after the war, then died in Rome.

That was all Horst said on that first visit. Somehow, in an indirect way, he explained, the castle was a gift from Otto, a place of refuge and solace. 'I dropped out of normality,' he said, when he was in his thirties. He left behind a regular life, because of his father's story, hoping to find an alternative way.

Normality ended for Horst in 1945, six years old when the war was lost. 'I was raised like a young Nazi boy, then from one day to the next everything was gone.' It was a trauma, national and personal, as the regime broke down and life around the family collapsed, a happy childhood punctured. He evoked a memory of his birthday party in April 1945, sitting outside the family home in Thumersbach, looking across Lake Zell. 'I was alone and knew I should remember this moment for all my life.' His soft voice cracked as he recalled British and American planes dropping unused bombs into the waters. 'The house started to shiver, yes, I remember . . .' His voice trailed off, his eyes moistened, I felt the shiver. He cried, softly, for a brief moment.

Later, Horst escorted me around the castle, a place of many rooms, large and small. We settled in his bedroom, on the first floor, under the gaze of Josef, Otto, Charlotte and godfather Arthur. He brought out Charlotte's photo albums, we sat together, the images perched on our knees. He alluded to an extensive family archive, many letters between his parents, his mother's diaries and reminiscences, written for the children, for posterity. I did not see these materials, that day, but they left a memory that intrigued.

I did see a few pages from one diary, from 1942, a tiny volume filled with his mother's busy writing. I was interested in 1 August, the day Hans Frank visited the Wächters in Lemberg to announce the implementation of the Final Solution across the District of Galicia, a speech that offered a sentence of death for hundreds of thousands of human beings. The diary entry for that day told us that Frank played chess with Charlotte.

We returned to the photographs from the albums, a story of family life, of children and grandparents, of celebrations and holidays in the mountains. The Wächters together, a contented family. There were lakes, and a photo of Otto swimming, the only one I would ever see. 'My father loved to swim,' Horst said. Over the page a man with a smile and a chisel carved a swastika into a wall, 1931. A man stood outside a building, greeted by a line of arms raised in Nazi salute. *Dr Goebbels* it said under the photograph. Three men in conversation, in a covered yard. Two letters under the photograph, *A.H.* This was Otto's angular writing. Adolf Hitler with Heinrich Hoffmann, I would learn, his photographer, and a third man. 'Not my father,' Horst said. 'Maybe Baldur von Schirach.' This was a reference to the head of the Hitler Youth, also convicted at Nuremberg, whose grandson Ferdinand was a fine writer.

We turned more pages. Vienna, autumn 1938, Otto in his office at the Hofburg Palace, in a distinct SS uniform. Poland, autumn 1939, a burnt-out building, refugees. A crowded street, people dressed against the cold, an old lady in a headscarf, a white armband. A Jew photographed by Charlotte, in the Warsaw ghetto. A photograph of Horst, with three of his four sisters. 'March 1943, Lemberg', Charlotte wrote underneath. A day of bright sun, with long shadows. A note

from Horst to Otto. 'Dear Papa, I've picked you some flowers, kisses, yours, Horsti-Borsti.' He was five back then, in 1944.

We danced around more delicate subjects. He asked about my grandfather, listened in silence to the details. I enquired about his parents and their relationship. 'My mother was convinced that my father was right, did the right things.' She never spoke a bad word about

him, not in Horst's presence, but he came to recognise there was a
dark side. 'Of course, I felt guilty about my father.' He knew about the
'horrible things' the regime had done, but it was only later that they
intruded into daily life. The period after the war was a time of silence.
No one in Austria wanted to talk about the events, not then, not now.
He alluded to difficulties with the family, with his nephews and nieces,
but no details were offered.

We passed to other matters. Charlotte wanted Horst to be a successful lawyer, like his father, but he chose another life. No more studies, he
told Charlotte, he would disappear into the woods. 'Bye-bye mother.'
She was deeply disappointed that he found his own path. In Vienna,
in the early 1970s, he was introduced to a painter, Friedensreich
Hundertwasser, and the two men connected. 'I knew Hundertwasser
would need me, we would get along, because he was a shy person,
like me'. Horst worked as the artist's assistant, sailed his boat, the
Regentag – 'rainy day' – from Venice to New Zealand, accompanied
by his new wife, Jacqueline. During that voyage their only child was
born, a daughter, Magdalena. That was 1977.

'Somehow, that Hundertwasser was Jewish was good for my feelings,' Horst continued. 'Perhaps also with you, Philippe, because you
are Jewish, somehow this is attractive for me.' The artist's mother
feared Horst. 'She knew my father's name, who he was, with her
experiences in the war, running around with a Star of David . . .' As
he spoke his fingers danced across his arm, where an armband might
have been.

Yet, he explained, the historical responsibility of his father was a
complex matter. Otto was against the racial theories, didn't see the
Germans as supermen and all others as *Untermenschen*. 'He wanted
to do something good, to get things moving, to find a solution to the
problems after the first war.'

That was Horst's view. His father as a decent man, an optimist,
who tried to do good but who got caught up in the horrors occasioned
by others.

I listened patiently, not wanting to disturb the atmosphere of our
first meeting.

A few days later, back in London, I received a message from Horst.
'I appreciated your visit to Hagenberg, to learn of the tragic story of
your grandfather's family in Lemberg.' He offered the address of a
man from Lemberg whose life he said his father had saved, a Polish

Jew. Back then, he added, the 'deplorable situation of the Jews was generally accepted as "*Schicksal*".' The word meant fate.

As to his own situation, he said that his solitude had been relieved by my visit. Other members of the family did not wish to talk about the past, and were critical of his endeavours. They did not wish for a spotlight on the life of Otto von Wächter.

I left our first encounter curious and fascinated. I could not help but like Horst, gentle and open, seemingly with nothing to hide. He was a son who wanted to find the good in his father. At the same time, he was unwilling to countenance the idea that Otto Wächter bore any real responsibility for terrible events that occurred on the territory he ruled. I wanted to know more about his parents. Details matter.

2

1901, Otto

Otto Gustav Wächter was born in Vienna on 8 July 1901. His father, Josef Wächter, was an ardent monarchist, an officer of Emperor Franz Joseph's imperial Austro-Hungarian army. Of Czech origins but German-speaking, he came from the small Sudeten town of Havran, on the outskirts of the empire, north of Prague. He was also a nationalist and a virulent anti-Semite, and married Martha Pfob, from a wealthy family in Vienna, who had three children.

Otto had two older sisters, Hertha born in 1898, Ilse in 1900, yet he was beloved as the only son, and the youngest child. An early image of the family was taken by an imperial and royal court photographer, when Otto was just a few months old. Martha with Josef in uniform and a striking moustache, who holds Otto gingerly, with pride. The portrait was formal, a mirror of a life devoted to monarchy and empire.

Otto spent his early years in Vienna, a city at the peak of its power, a time of wealth and intellectual creativity. Gustav Mahler directed the State Opera House, Sigmund Freud developed new ideas on psychoanalysis, Josef Hoffmann and Koloman Moser ran the Wiener Werkstätte, a progressive community of artists and designers. Mayor Karl Lueger ruled with an iron fist and a strong anti-Semitic authority. Otto attended the Volksschule, a local school on Albertgasse, in Vienna's 8th district. Reports marked his academic progress as 'very good'.

When he was seven the family moved to Trieste, on the Adriatic coast, where he enrolled at the Deutsche Volksschule, on Via della Fontana, near the central rail station. He learned Italian, developed

a facility for languages and made 'com-
mendable' progress, except for writing,
which was only 'satisfactory'. He took
his first Holy Communion, entered
high school and learned to swim at the
Militärschwimmschule, the military
swimming school. He was purposeful
and confident, already comfortable in a
uniform.

The family was in Trieste when war
broke out in the summer of 1914. As a
major in the *kaiserlich und königlich*
(*k.u.k.*) imperial army, Josef was posted
to Galicia, and later promoted to com-
mand its 88th Infantry Regiment, near Lemberg. Otto moved with
his mother and sisters to Budweis, in southern Bohemia, today in the
Czech Republic, with a year spent in nearby Krumau. His history
studies touched on Caesar and the Gallic wars, and lessons in physical
education focused on the basics of armed and unarmed combat.

Emperor Franz-Joseph died in 1916, after a reign of nearly sixty-
eight years. Two years later the war ended and four centuries of
Habsburg reign came to a close, Austria reduced to a rump of its former
glory. These were impoverished times for the Wächter family, which
returned to Trieste. Josef had invested the family assets in government
bonds, which lost all value in the financial collapse that followed the
war. He had, however, been awarded the Order of Maria Theresa, for
bravery, a presentation that was filmed for posterity and saved, which
meant I could watch the moment he became a nobleman. This honour
allowed him – and later Otto – to use the title of *Freiherr*, or baron.
The Wächter men became von Wächters.

Otto graduated from high school in the summer of 1919. A leaving
certificate allowed him to join the faculty of law at the University of
Vienna, where he started on 18 October 1919, a time of unrest, stoked
by the end of empire and the Russian Revolution. Among the refugees
who streamed in from the lands of the former empire, in the east, was
Hersch Lauterpacht from Lemberg, who enrolled with Otto at the law
school and would, a quarter of a century later, come up with the legal
concept of 'crimes against humanity' with which his fellow student
would become embroiled.

Otto's student card portrayed a purposeful young man, the aquiline profile topped with a good head of hair above a large bow tie. He spent

five years and nine semesters at the law faculty, studying with renowned professors, including Hans Kelsen, who offered classes in constitutional law, and Alexander Hold-Ferneck, a virulent nationalist who believed that a million years would pass before 'international law proper' would come into existence. Stephan Brassloff, specialist in Roman law, and Josef Hupka, expert in trade and exchanges, were among his Jewish teachers.

A fine athlete, Otto joined the *Donauhort*, the Vienna Rowing Club, on the Danube, and became a national champion of Austria, in an eight-man boat. In 2017 the club would publish a pamphlet to celebrate its 150th anniversary, which singled out Otto as a 'very successful, very popular' member. He was active in the mountains, climbing and spending weekends at a ski resort near Vienna. A large circle of friends surrounded him, including women who appreciated his energy and tactile sensitivities.

At law school Otto became politically engaged, encouraged by his father's politics, a nationalism rooted in the German-speaking Sudetenland. Josef was an early member of the *Deutsche Klub*, a conservative all-male society whose members favoured pan-Germanism and opposed the influx of Jews and other refugees from the lands of the former empire. 'Buy Only from Aryan Businesses!' the *Klub*'s newsletter advised members.

In March 1921, shortly before his father was appointed minister of defence, Otto participated in a large anti-Jewish protest in central Vienna. Organised by the *Antisemitenbund*, founded two years earlier, 40,000 participants called for Jews to be stripped of basic rights of citizenship and property, and the expulsion of all who arrived after September 1914. Jewish shops and streetcar passengers were attacked. Otto was arrested, charged and tried at Vienna's District Court, then convicted and sentenced to fourteen days in prison, suspended for a year. He was identified in the press as a 'monarchist'. Not yet twenty, he crossed the line of criminality for the first time.

The experience fuelled a taste for politics. In an archive in Vienna I found a copy of his National Socialist Party of Austria membership card, from 1923. At twenty-two, he was an early supporter of Adolf Hitler, former resident of Vienna. Anti-Marxist, anti-Semitic and ambitious, the young law student joined the Austrian branch of a political party, a connection with Germany. A year later Otto graduated from the law faculty, impecunious but titled. With a visiting card that identified him as Dr Otto Freiherr von Wächter, he started traineeships at various courts, to hone courtroom and advocacy skills. In December 1925 the Vienna Court of Appeal certified his practical approach, legal knowledge and 'impeccable behaviour'.

In 1926 his mother died unexpectedly, and he moved into a small apartment at number 3 Bräunerstrasse, near St Stephen's Cathedral in the heart of Vienna. He got himself a new letterhead – a gilded 'W' topped with a *Freiherren* crown, an indication of nobility – and began a series of traineeships in commercial law. By the spring of 1929 he was working for a Dr Völkert in a nineteenth-century building in Vienna's 4th district. On Saturday, 6 April, politically active and socially engaged, the national rowing champion-cum-trainee lawyer went to the Südbahnhof to spend a weekend skiing at the nearby Schneeberg. Accompanied by a man and a woman, he got on the train to Puchberg, entered a compartment and sat down. Seated opposite him was an attractive young woman with brunette hair.

The moment introduced him to a new world, of industry, money and even greater ambition.

3

1908, Charlotte

The young woman with brunette hair was Charlotte Bleckmann, a twenty-year-old student of art recently returned from a year in England. She was on a weekend trip to the mountains, hoping to meet a suitor.

Seven years younger than Otto, Charlotte was born in 1908, in Mürzzuschlag, a hundred kilometres south-west of Vienna. A small town nestled in the lower Alps of Styria, in a valley coursed by the gentle River Mürz, it was renowned as the last stop on the Semmering railway line, the world's first mountain railroad, opened in the mid-nineteenth century. Today the town is somewhat obscure, celebrated as the place where Johannes Brahms wrote his Fourth Symphony and the birthplace, after the war, of writer Elfriede Jelinek, winner of the Nobel Prize in Literature.

Charlotte was the fourth of the six children of Walther Bleckmann, a prosperous, evangelical Protestant, and Meta, his Catholic wife. The family owned a steel mill founded by Charlotte's grandfather, celebrated for the quality of its product, used in the manufacture of fine blades and tools. The mill employed two thousand workers, a quarter of the town's population.

A century later, almost no trace of the Bleckmanns remained. The steel mill was owned by others, and the *Herrenhaus* (the 'manor house'), the fine villa and gardens at the entrance to the mill where Charlotte was born and lived with her five siblings, was long gone. Nearby Villa Luisa, where her cousins lived, was the site of a high school named in honour of Hertha Reich, one of the twenty-nine Jewish residents driven out of Mürzzuschlag after March 1938 when the Nazis took over. The photographs in Charlotte's albums offered a sense of Charlotte's world, and of what was lost: wood-panelled rooms, hand-crafted furniture, oil paintings, books, a wooden horse, and Charlotte's immense doll's house.

A photograph recorded the Bleckmann family in February 1914, after the birth of the sixth and final child. Charlotte, aged six, had the air of a confident child, one who looked into the camera. Upright and nonchalant, a flower tucked into her hair, she was adored by austere Walther and gentle Meta, and a strong-willed child. The Bleckmanns stood on the cusp of change and wealth, as war increased demand for steel for armaments and the manufacture of steam engines for the local lines. In 1916, the firm of Orenstein & Koppel built the *Lotte*, a locomotive in honour of Charlotte, to run on the narrow-gauge line between factories in Mürzzuschlag and Hönigsberg.

The war ended in November 1918. Chancellor Karl Renner told the Austrian parliament that the Austro-Hungarian empire was prostrate, with national humiliation and economic distress pointing to a union with Germany, to avoid servitude to foreign capitalists. Instead, the treaty of Saint-Germain-en-Laye, signed in September 1919, imposed upon Austria an obligation of independence and immutable borders. Bolzano and south Tyrol were handed to Italy, the German Sudeten lands became part of Czechoslovakia, and large parts of Styria and Carinthia attached themselves to Yugoslavia. Mürzzuschlag found itself at the eastern end of tiny Austria, close to a new kingdom of Slovenes and Croats.

Amid the political mayhem, daily life went on. On her thirteenth birthday, Aunt Auguste gave Charlotte a notebook, a *Stammbuch*, as she called it, the book of the tribe. She recorded daily happenings and kept it for the rest of her life, pages that gathered inscriptions, ditties and drawings, memories of family and friends. The entries reflected a world of plenty, divided between the large family apartment in Vienna, on Belvederegasse, and Mürzzuschlag, with frequent holidays across Europe. A friend of the family, a renowned radiologist, sketched an ink drawing of 'Gala Peter', the Swiss milk chocolate adored by the young girl. An English suitor offered a line by the poet Robert Browning ('all's love, yet all's law'). One admirer sketched her in a bright-yellow dress, holding a delicate posy of deep-red flowers, another offered the prospect of a journey by train.

As a daughter of the steelworks, Charlotte enjoyed a happy, prosperous childhood, with parents who were strict but fair. Initially educated at home, by a private tutor, she later moved to a small *Realgymnasium* in Vienna, and then to the Catholic *Realgymnasium* on Wienhauptstrasse. Shy but sociable, Charlotte was a fierce and loyal friend, and many whom she met in the early years would remain constant to the end of her life.

She was close to her maternal grandfather, August von Scheindler, a classical philologist and school inspector who wrote Latin textbooks, translated Homer's *Iliad* and *Odyssey* into German, and enjoyed strolls with his granddaughter around the Belvedere gardens. 'Yes, this tall, old man, already retired, with a slight stoop, hands behind his back, walked proudly with my grandmother . . . punctual like a clock,' she recalled many years later. The gardens became a locale for meetings with young men.

At seventeen Charlotte moved in with Aunt Auguste, in Vienna, her parents hoping the classical singer would soften their daughter's rebellious edges. She started a daily diary, a practice that would be maintained for the next quarter of a century after the first entry, on 1 January 1925, describing New Year's Eve with her parents. She proceeded to record a life of school and luncheons, English lessons, hair appointments, piano, visits to the opera, travels around the countryside with friends like Vera and Pussi, holidays in Zell-am-See, sporting activities on the tennis court and in the mountains. A rich life meant that Charlotte was among the first women in Mürzzuschlag to drive an automobile.

In September 1925 she travelled to England, with her parents and brother Heini. The monotony of the 'incredibly boring' journey across Europe was broken by occasional flirtations. 'Exchanged glances with a Jew who was quite dashing', she recorded on the train between Nuremberg and Frankfurt. Her parents deposited her at Granville House in Eastbourne, a boarding school for young ladies. She spent the academic year in the sixth form, improving her English under the guidance of headmistress Mrs Ida Foley, the sister of Arthur Conan Doyle, inventor of Sherlock Holmes. Fido, as she called her, became a friend.

At Granville House, Charlotte played hockey and became an accomplished horse rider. Letters home described attendance at a local Catholic church, elocution lessons and trips to the theatre, including *Julius Caesar* ('quite good, Brutus not so special') and *The Merchant of Venice* ('exciting'). She developed a passion for opera – Wagner and Tchaikovsky in particular – and appreciated the poetry of Rupert Brooke and William Wordsworth. Lessons in photography catalysed an interest in galleries and art, and she spent much of the Christmas holidays in London, visiting museums, like the National Portrait Gallery ('wonderful'), the Tate ('fabulous'), the National Gallery ('I couldn't see enough'). At the British Museum she adored the ground-floor library.

Charlotte was intensely social, a people-watcher ('tea on the Strand, saw a fabulous man') and wanderer of streets ('wonderful'). She sought out hairdressers, attended balls (masked or not), went to the cinema, theatre and opera (*Rosenkavalier*, *Carmen*, *The Flying Dutchman*, *Tristan and Isolde*, all in a month). In the spring of 1926 she took a motoring holiday around southern England, with her friend Lieselotte Lorenz, unaccompanied by a male chaperone. She knew it would be refused, so didn't ask permission of her parents. 'I was a really terrible child,' she confessed. The two drove to Dorchester, Exeter and Totnes, then Cornwall and back via Oxford. A second trip, to Paris, was cancelled because of the General Strike.

The names of many friends with English names were entered into the *Stammbuch* – Cynthia Cottrell, Joyce Smith, Bette Clarke, Ruth Bennett. There were a few German ones too, including Mizzi Getreuer, whose name I found on a list of those who perished at the Stutthof concentration camp in Poland, just two decades later.

At the end of July her time in England came to a close. She enjoyed a farewell lunch with Fido and took a boat to Denmark. She stood on the deck, 'till my dearest England, the lights vanished', feeling low. 'I could have cried,' she recorded, 'but didn't.'

In Vienna in the autumn, Charlotte returned to the family apartment on Belvederegasse and enrolled at the *Wiener Frauenakademie und Schule für freie und angewandte Kunst* (the Vienna Women's

Academy and School for Free and Applied Art), located on Siegelgasse, in the 3rd district. Along with three hundred fellow women pupils, she took courses in drawing and design offered by renowned artists, mostly men. Introduced to the designer Josef Hoffmann, of the Wiener Werkstätte, she developed a fine eye.

Out of school, she socialised, took walks around Vienna with her grandfather August, attended concerts at the Vienna Philharmonic, spent holidays in Mürzzuschlag, skied and climbed in the nearby mountains. In May 1927, at the *Herrenhaus*, the family celebrated the golden wedding anniversary of her maternal grandparents, the Scheindlers. The ceremony was blessed by a local dignitary, Bishop Ferdinand Pawlikowski, a powerful family friend with excellent connections to the Vatican.

Charlotte gave no hint of being politically engaged. She was, however, much occupied with the vital task of finding herself a decent husband.

4

1929, Vienna

On the morning of Saturday, 6 April, Charlotte awoke in the family home on Belvederegasse. As the clock of the Catholic Church of St Elisabeth struck eight times, the telephone rang, a friend wondering if she'd like to spend a weekend on the Schneeberg, a nearby resort. An accomplished and competitive skier, she knew the mountain well, but the caller didn't offer other attractions. Sensing her hesitation, he said they'd be joined by Herma Szabo, a world champion figure skater and Olympic gold medallist. Distantly related to Charlotte, Herma was always surrounded by attractive young men.

At the Südbahnhof, none of Herma's eight male companions were of immediate interest to Charlotte, who decided to sit in a separate compartment of the train to Puchberg. Three good-looking young people entered, a girl and two men. 'I particularly liked the tall, blond one,' Charlotte recalled, but he was with a girl so she decided to ignore him. The tall, blond man was introduced to her as 'Baron Wächter', and she chatted amiably with Otto von Wächter, about matters of no importance.

By the time the train reached Puchberg, Charlotte learned the young woman was merely Otto's sister Hertha, so she allowed an interest to be sparked. 'My new "Baron" was tall, slender, athletic, with delicate features, very beautiful hands,' she recorded. 'He wore a diamond ring on the little finger of his right hand and had a noble appearance, one that any girl would notice.' Charlotte ended up spending the weekend with the group, sharing a room with Hertha. They skied – she teased Otto when he waxed her skis, 'what no gentleman had done before' – and lunched at the Fischerhütte. With each hour Otto's attractions grew.

They were joined by Emanuel – Manni – Braunegg, Otto's closest friend at university, from whom she learned more about a national rowing champion who wanted to be an important lawyer. They returned together to Vienna. Otto promised to call, but as she didn't trust him she took the precaution of obtaining his phone number. That evening, she wrote his name in her diary, and underlined it. Baron Wächter. Years later, she recalled, that was the day 'I fell in love with good-looking, cheerful Otto'.

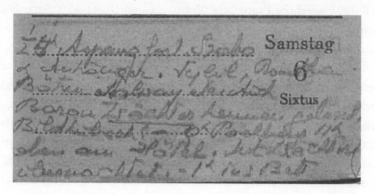

*

She offered no details about their conversations. Whether they talked about her art studies, or his political activities, his criminal conviction or membership of the Nazi Party in 1923, is not known.

Two weeks passed without contact, then Charlotte had a run-in with a horse-drawn carriage. The need for a lawyer offered a pretext to contact Otto, and he visited her the next day, at art school, to offer advice. They saw each other three weeks later, after she returned from a holiday in Italy. From Rome, on 4 May, she sent him a postcard of Castel Sant'Angelo, with the dome of St Peter's Basilica in the Vatican visible in the background near the Santo Spirito Hospital. 'I always keep my promises', she wrote, 'back on Monday', but did not share another concern. 'Who knows which girl would seduce Otto in the meantime?' she recorded privately. The fear would last for many years.

Two weeks later they went dancing. Otto drove her home and tried to kiss her. She did not object, but the next day he apologised and asked: 'By the way, do you want to marry me?' She laughed and declined, not sure if he was serious, but also committed to her art studies and with no desire to become a dull housewife. Secretly she was thrilled. 'How beautiful was our young and blossoming love, how happy I felt.'

She learned more about ambitious, joyful, jokey, flirtatious Otto. He was proud of his father Josef, sad about the unexpected death of his mother, from the prosperous, Viennese Pfob family. The family money was lost when Josef invested in war bonds at the end of the war, he told her, 'for love of country'. Otto might come with a title but there would be no dowry.

During that long, first summer they spoke often, took walks in the City Park, visited the Prater, sat on benches on the Heldenplatz, boated in Tulln. On his twenty-eighth birthday she watched the 'rowing rascal' compete on the Danube, a minor celebrity who won competitions. She said nothing of Otto to her parents, as he was surrounded by other women, often flirting with them in her presence. He was, she noticed, unusually tactile and liked to hug and touch those around him, acts which planted a seed of jealousy that left deep roots. She sulked when he gave a rose to her friend Anita, so she kept other options open, responding to invitations, like the one from a stranger she met on a train. She even allowed Viktor Klarwill, known as Zybil, who she described as *ein halb Juden* ('a half Jew'), to continue his futile pursuit of her.

That summer, she and her mother took a motoring holiday across Europe with Bishop Pawlikowski and his portly, middle-aged friend Monsignor Allmer, who liked to flirt with her. They drove across Switzerland, through France, to Spain. Lourdes left 'a terrible impression', hundreds of people on crutches in a procession to the main square. In Barcelona they attended the World Fair, drank moscato wines, enjoyed the Sagrada Familia, saw a bullfight at Castell de Mar, and visited the 'romantic rock' of Montserrat. At Figueres, Monsignor Allmer's silly jokes caused Charlotte to wet herself.

Charlotte and Otto, who was canoeing on the Rhône, exchanged postcards and letters, all of which were kept. At the end of the summer Otto visited Mürzzuschlag, but the relationship remained a secret. 'I was in love with him, but couldn't show my feelings to my parents.' Mutti, as Charlotte referred to her mother, would have been bowled over by the idea of a dashing baron. In the autumn, when school resumed, Charlotte drove Otto – 'Tschaps', she called him, a form of the English word 'chap' – from one courtroom hearing to another. He had little interest in opera or concerts, so they went to the cinema. Charlotte marked a success in the bar exams with a vase fashioned in clay, engraved with images of their activities.

At Christmas Otto skied in Kitzbühel, without her. She begged to join him but her father refused permission, so she stayed home, 'very sad'. They talked each day by phone, one call lasting an hour and nine minutes, at huge cost.

*

Otto blew hot and cold as 1930 brought new suitors buzzing around Charlotte. In January they attended a ball, she magnificent in a yellow evening dress, crepe de Chine with little volantes. They danced so late into the night that she permitted herself to be hopeful, but then silence for three days. Another ball, a trip to the Schneeberg, a ski competition in the Altenmarkt. Otto turned his attentions towards Melita, a former flirt, and didn't call Charlotte for days. 'I never could be completely sure about him,' Charlotte recalled. 'His behaviour, hugging girls as soon as he met them, made me doubt again and again if he really was serious about me.'

In late spring things seemed to pick up. They took a hiking trip, up the mountain on foot, down with skis. One morning they left at four to climb to a mountain hut with memorable views over the Königsspitze. One avalanche after another, thundering noises, 'unforgettable', Charlotte recorded. Then up to the Schöntaufspitze, to 3,000 metres, where they hugged. Three hours up, ten minutes down, then to a castle with amazing views of Merano. An intimate night in Bolzano, but she did not give herself to him completely.

As the relationship progressed, more slowly than she wanted, Charlotte's career began to take off. She set up an atelier at the family home, and her fabric designs started to sell ('1,350 schillings in the first year, a lot for a beginner'). She took trips to Dresden and Hanover armed with books of drawings, which brought sales and flirtations, but she remained faithful to Otto.

In the autumn they took a three-week trip to Italy, without telling her parents, accompanied by Manni Braunegg, boats, a squashy air mattress and three tents. In Verona they attended a performance of Modest Mussorgsky's *Boris Godunov*, and on Lake Garda they slept in an olive grove near Sirmione. 'Beautiful signorinas' buzzed around Otto, causing her to wonder if she would ever get used to the attention he drew. In Venice they spent a night at a hotel on the Grand Canal, their skins so darkened by olive oil that someone described them as *I Negri*, 'the Negroes'. 'The best holiday of my life', she recalled, 'totally carefree and full of young love'.

In Vienna, Charlotte fell ill with jaundice. Otto visited; she hoped for a proposal of marriage but it didn't come. No interest in marrying a rich girl, he told her. Christmas brought new hope. 'I truly belonged to him, and loved him more than anything', a man who could enforce his will on her. 'I liked that', and that he was right in everything he said.

It was around this time that Otto rejoined the Nazi Party. His membership number was 301,097.

The year 1931 was dominated by the death of Charlotte's beloved grandfather, Dr Scheindler, the school inspector, from pneumonia. Only to him did she confide the secret of her love for Otto and the hope of marriage. 'Marry and bear 10 children,' her grandfather advised her.

Life fell into a routine. Art school, slalom competitions on the Schneeberg, evenings with old friends, encounters with new ones, like the Fischböcks, Hans and Trudl. Otto's persistent interest in other women, like her wealthy cousin Paula – small, blonde, 'nigger lips', who would irritate Charlotte for another four decades – continued to jar. Charlotte got rid of Paula by outskiing her, and she outclimbed all the other competition, literally: on one occasion, she and Otto took four hours to reach the peak of the Zuckerhütl, 3,505 metres of sugar-loaf, using only a rope and two pickaxes.

In March 1931, in keeping with the times and his interests, Charlotte offered Otto a gift, a copy of Adolf Hitler's *Mein Kampf*. Black cover, no title, a gilded eagle astride a swastika. 'Through struggle and love,' she wrote on the flyleaf, 'to the finish.' Many years later, the book hid on a shelf in Horst's castle, and I would pick it out at random. 'I didn't know I had that!' Horst chuckled, excitedly. He had lost the copy given to him by his godfather, Arthur Seyss-Inquart.

Two months after the gift, Charlotte joined the party. That was 28 May 1931, member number 510,379. Her diary rarely referenced Otto's political activities, and made no mention of his Nazi membership, or that he had risen to the upper echelons of its Viennese chapter. As district chief of the Nazi Party in Vienna, he followed his father into the *Deutsche Klub*, becoming a member of the board in January 1932. Here he met members who would play a significant role in his life, like the writer Franz Hieronymus Riedl, lawyers Hans Fischböck, Arthur Seyss-Inquart and Ernst Kaltenbrunner, and Hanns Blaschke, future mayor of Vienna. Wilhelm Höttl and Charlotte's brother Heinrich Bleckmann also became members of the *Klub*, which offered lectures and concerts at its offices in the Hofburg. In January 1931, Hans Frank visited from Germany to deliver a special lecture, well attended because he worked as a lawyer for Adolf Hitler. The *Klub* became a hub for plotting and intrigue by Austrian Nazis.

That summer, Otto spent five weeks in Munich at the Reichsführerschule, a summer school for aspiring Nazis. 'I'm ever so busy', he wrote to Charlotte, 'elected as the scribe' to a group of ninety Nazis bonded by a 'wonderful feeling of camaraderie'. The day was divided in military fashion – 'waking, morning gymnastics, bathing, breakfast, lecture 1, lecture 2 etc., eating, etc.' – with singing and games at night, exercises and marches during the day. 'The whole thing is very interesting and informative – we're listening to the big names in the party, even Hitler spoke to us, it was wonderful.'

He returned with photographs to be pasted into the family album, the one that Horst showed me on that first visit. The album did not, however, include a copy of a famous photograph, one that I came across elsewhere, of the participants at the summer school. Taken by Heinrich Hoffmann, Hitler's photographer, Otto stood in the second row, just to the left of Hitler.

'Tschapsli telephoned again after five weeks,' Charlotte recorded in her diary, which also noted political developments: two weeks after he returned she scribbled '*Heimwehr putsch*' into the diary, a reference to an abortive coup attempt by a nationalist group. Many of its members would, in due course, join Otto in the National Socialists.

In September she spent time in Mürzzuschlag, working on fabric designs, enjoying the mountains and receiving visitors. Everything was 'so lovely' away from Vienna, 'all those Jews, wherever you go – they make me completely despair'. If her radicalism developed any further, she warned Otto, she'd 'soon be going around with a dagger'. One visitor was Alfred Frauenfeld, recently appointed as Nazi Gauleiter in Vienna, who offered to introduce her to Hitler and accompany her on her travels. 'You always say that England is very important and that we should direct as much propaganda there as here,' she told Otto. Frauenfeld raised her self-confidence, which he'd 'beaten down', she implied, teasingly. 'All I hear on Bräunerstrasse is how silly and ugly I am, with a Jewish nose and small feet, too fat, etc.'

In October, she travelled to England to sell fabric samples. The journey allowed a conversation with a Frenchman, in which she argued for an *Anschluss* – 'joining' – with Germany. A union between Germany and France was impossible, she told him, and talk of international cooperation was 'a Jewish ploy'. Delighted to be back in London, she attended a concert at the Austrian embassy and celebrated her birthday with brother Heini, the local representative of the family steel mill. In Manchester she was introduced to Mr Caswell of the Calico Printers' Association, who purchased samples for a decent sum, fell in love with her, and invited her to Paris. She declined, as he was married with two sons.

The visit coincided with a general election campaign in the United Kingdom, and her own political awakening. She welcomed the mood, a country where most firms refused to buy foreign steel, even Heini's. 'You can breathe easily in a country where the inhabitants almost to a man have such a nationalistic feeling,' she wrote to Otto, although they'd failed adequately to 'emphasise the Jewish question'. Many she met were open to ideas about national socialism, so she 'spread the word'.

The British election was won by a National Government, led by the Conservatives, with support from Labour and Liberal politicians. 'Everyone believes in a better future thanks to nationalism,' she informed Otto, on 28 October. Hopefully the Germans would follow suit, set aside their differences, and 'join hands under the flag that A. Hitler will hoist'. Those who believed such ideas were impractical should travel to England. A week later she planned her return to

Austria, via Munich. 'You could pick me up from there, my love, and tie it in with your visit to Hitler.'

The trip to Britain was a success, and with the money earned – over 10,000 schillings – she was able to buy a small house with a garden at number 5 Anzengrubergasse, on a hill at Klosterneuburg Weidling, a Viennese suburb with fine views over the Danube. It served as a studio and a place to host events, like a children's party at which she offered gifts 'under the sign of the swastika'. National Socialism was now a full part of daily life. In the diary she noted a meeting attended with Otto, inscribed with a swastika that danced across the page.

The following year, 1932, opened with no proposal of marriage. Charlotte travelled across Germany and then back to England to sell more fabric designs. Otto completed his training and set up a law office of his own, with Dr Georg Freiherr von Ettingshausen, a friend and comrade in the party, at 47 Margarethenstrasse, in Vienna's 4th district. Otto practised mostly in commercial law, and in the first month earned 8,000 schillings, which compared favourably with the 14,000 schillings Charlotte earned in the previous year. His cases were varied, and included an appearance before the Regional Court of Vienna in a copyright case. He acted for the photographer Lothar Rübelt, who claimed infringement of his rights by the writer Karl Kraus, for the unauthorised publication in *Die Fackel*, the satirical magazine, of a Rübelt photograph of Baron Alfons von Rothschild.

He also had another line of work, offering legal advice to party members in difficulty, and to the party itself, which chimed with his political engagement. In April 1932 he joined the *Schutzstaffel* – the SS – the paramilitary force created as an elite bodyguard unit for Adolf Hitler, as SS member 235,368. As a member of the *Verband deutscharischer Rechtsanwälte Österreichs* (Association of German-Aryan Lawyers of Austria), he spent ever more time at the *Deutsche Klub*, from where Charlotte would often collect him.

In the spring they took a boating holiday, and in June sailed on the Neusiedler See. Charlotte returned to England in the summer, where she met brother Heini's rich, beautiful girlfriend, whose father refused to let his daughter marry an Austrian. In Dublin, with her mother and Bishop Pawlikowski, she attended the thirty-first International Eucharistic Congress, held in Phoenix Park, to celebrate the 1,500th anniversary of St Patrick's arrival in Ireland.

Back in Vienna, on 8 July they celebrated Otto's birthday at his small apartment, with wine, schnapps and love. After three and a half years of 'persistent and tenacious restraint', unable to resist, she offered herself to him completely. That night, as she put it, she revealed to him 'the biggest secret'.

With no offer of marriage, Charlotte's doubts rose. She worried about his closed and cautious character, the shy disposition, the 'child-like' way he conducted himself. He was ambitious and unable to show his feelings; she loved him.

A month later, after a canoe trip, she started to feel unwell. After a doctor told her she was pregnant, she broke the news to Otto in a small café on Margarethenstrasse, near his office. He did not offer to marry her, and she spent the evening alone, weeping.

Two days later Otto relented, under pressure from Manni Braunegg. He wanted a quick marriage, and offered her his late mother's wedding ring. They travelled to Mürzzuschlag to tell her parents, who consented instantly. Proud to have a baron as a son-in-law, Mutti made no enquiries as to the haste. A day later the couple visited General Josef Wächter at the Hotel Straubingher, in Bad Gastein, where he was taking the waters. He almost toppled over on hearing the news, Charlotte recalled, then hugged her tight. He too consented.

The wedding took place on Sunday, 11 September, in the Basilica of Mariazell. Bishop Pawlikowski officiated, Manni Braunegg and Charlotte's brother Heini acted as witnesses. Few guests were invited, barely enough to make it an event, as Otto wanted a discreet ceremony. She wore a traditional Styrian dirndl dress, to hide the pregnancy; he donned a bespoke Styrian suit. 'I could not wait for the ceremony to end, as a fly sat on my arm, itching,' Charlotte recalled.

A feast followed, and the newlyweds spent the night at a small inn near Leopoldstein. The next morning they returned early to Vienna, as Otto had a court hearing. Whether it concerned a commercial matter, or representation of the party, Charlotte did not record.

5

2013, Hagenberg

After the first visit to Hagenberg, Horst and I continued to exchange friendly emails. Horst wrote in detail about the castle, built by Heinrich von Hakkenberg, a Knight Templar, who joined the thirteenth-century German crusade to the Holy Land. The ground plan was modelled on elements of the Temple of Solomon, Horst explained, and in the late seventeenth century the gardens were transformed and the interior reconstructed. A large, two-storey main hall was added, a temple to honour Hermes Trismegistus – Hermes thrice-greatest, supposed author of the sacred texts of hermeticism. Horst liked to invoke the name and the connection.

He wrote with thoughts about his parents, and sent clippings from Austrian newspapers. One came with a photograph, a 'demonstration of beautiful girls for the SS-Division my father created there', as Horst put it. This was a reference to the Waffen-SS 'Galicia' Division, created by Otto in the spring of 1943. His father was not responsible for any crimes, he assured me. Rather, he was an 'endangered heretic' in the National Socialist system, opposed to the racial and discriminatory actions applied in the German-occupied territories of Poland and Ukraine.

At this time, Ukraine was once more in the news, pulled between Russia and the European Union. History went round in circles, it seemed. A century earlier, in September 1914, Tsar Nicholas's army occupied Lemberg, a city Horst hoped to visit. The thought prompted a commission to write a profile of him for the *Financial Times*. I returned to Hagenberg with a photographer, in the bitter cold of midwinter.

Horst greeted us in a large coat and a bright-red, woollen hat. We spent two days in front of a large fire in the two-storey grand hall, or in his bedroom, barely warmed by a large, wood-burning stove, the white tiles blackened by decades of use. The flames danced as Horst told stories, seeking to persuade me of the decency of his father, as I pushed him to reflect in a more critical way about Otto. It was a game of double advocacy, one that would run for years.

Horst sat in a large armchair, peering at the family photo albums. Occasionally, he went to another room, to return with a document or two from Charlotte's papers. Now and then he caught my glance across the room, towards the portrait of his grandfather Josef, or the photographs of Otto and Seyss-Inquart, or an ancient print of Kraków. 'Maybe my mother stole the picture,' he suggested. Once, he explained, he had tried to return certain items to Poland, but without success. No subject was off limits.

We spoke of his childhood, but he recalled little. Memories were coloured by photographs pasted into albums, or by Charlotte's home movies, since lost. The disappearance was 'terribly unpleasant' and he still hoped they might turn up, maybe in his sister-in-law's basement. He blamed his brother Otto, who died many years earlier, for the 'debacle', a desire to keep the father and the family under wraps, a form of 'panicked secrecy'. His nephew Otto, the son of Otto junior, counselled against engaging with me. 'They don't want to know anything,' he said of the family.

Family life never was easy. Years ago he would have two dinners, an early one with his mother, a later one with his wife. The close attachment to Charlotte was a problem which caused Jacqueline to leave him. When Charlotte fell ill, he nursed her, and after she died, in 1985, Jacqueline returned. Tall and wispy, strong and sharply intelligent, Jacqueline's family was imbued with 'progressive' values, her father a distinguished journalist in Sweden. There was no love lost between the two families, and at a certain moment, when Jacqueline and I were alone, drinking black tea, she said she divorced Horst because of his excessive devotion to Charlotte. 'We got back together only after she was gone,' she said. She was 'a Nazi until the day she died', Jacqueline whispered. As we left she said the same thing to the photographer who accompanied me.

Horst shared a memory about the last time he saw Otto, in 1948, at Christmas. He didn't realise it was his father, at home in Salzburg, a man with a moustache who visited his room at night. A distant relative, Charlotte told him, a time when he didn't know his father was on the run, or even alive. He recalled no conversation with Otto, no real connection. 'I did not love my father,' he said bluntly, 'our contact was too limited'. Yet Otto's reputation dominated his life.

After the war, in Salzburg, Horst recalled an ostracised family. 'Was my father really a criminal?' he began to wonder. His mother didn't think so, and he came to an understanding that allowed a softer light to be cast on Otto. It turned on a distinction, the father as an individual, a mere cog in a powerful system, part of a larger criminal group. Horst did not deny the horrors, of a holocaust, of millions of people murdered. It happened and it was wrong, period. 'I know the system was criminal, that my father was part of it, but I don't think of him as a criminal.'

Others spoke well of Otto, a good husband and father, a decent man who lived up to his responsibilities. True, he followed orders, and the oath to Hitler. Yet he was an idealist, an honourable man who believed the system could be improved, and who tried to improve it. He couldn't leave the system, Horst explained, and he saved Jews, didn't kill them. When I asked for details or names, Horst mentioned Erwin Axer, the distinguished Polish theatre director, who sent him a letter, in German. 'I didn't meet your father,' Axer wrote, although he recalled, as a locksmith, unlocking a box for Charlotte, the baroness. 'I never forgot Otto's adjutant Stasny,' he added, who 'helped to save my life'.

I sensed that the attachment to Otto was a form of deflected love, for Charlotte, or Josef. 'I cannot say I love my father, although I do love my grandfather' – whose portrait hung above the bed. There was something else, too, the love of a parent as a matter of duty. 'I have a responsibility for him, to see what really happened, to tell the truth, and to do what I can do for him.' More than once Horst invoked the

Fourth Commandment – 'honour your father and mother' – in a version translated by Martin Buber. He wanted to focus on the positives,
not merely to condemn. Terrible things happened, but others were
responsible, the General Government, the SS, Himmler. Only in that
sense did Otto bear an indirect responsibility, and even those words
were spoken with trepidation. They brought moisture to his eyes.

During that second visit I heard a little more about Charlotte's
papers, but not much. On this occasion, for the first time, Horst spoke
of Otto's death in Rome. In the summer of 1949, unexpected, he said,
but no more, and no details.

In the weeks that followed, Horst wrote often to me. He did not doubt
the honesty of my approach, and recognised that his father was 'a
leading part of an horrifying machinery that caused so much death
and misery', but worried about the consequences of the article I was
writing. There were many 'fanatics' around, looking to heap revenge
on Nazi criminals and their descendants. 'I am confident that you will
never really blame me for anything,' he added, that I would eventually
acknowledge the reality of his father's 'situation', the essential probity
of a man who did the best he could in trying circumstances.

Horst too was an advocate. He directed me to extracts from the
memoirs of Dr Ludwig Losacker, one of his father's colleagues in
Lemberg, with translations into English, which showed Otto in a
favourable light. Perhaps we should visit Herr Losacker's widow? An
article in *Die Zeit*, written twenty years ago by a noted historian,
offered a different perspective. Losacker was characterised as a known
anti-Semite, one who was 'a central figure in the murder of Jews in the
District of Galicia'.

Horst wrote again – on Hitler's birthday, he noted – with a different
theory of innocence. The Government General was divided into two
parts: one was run by Hans Frank, the civil government; the other by
the SS government, under the control of Heinrich Himmler and his
underlings. Two parallel governments with separate responsibilities.
Otto bore no responsibility for the 'maniacal actions' of the SS government. The real culprit in Lemberg was SS-Obergruppenführer Fritz
Katzmann, Horst explained, the local SS chief. Yes, his father knew
about the horrors, including the 'death camps', and such knowledge
would have given rise to a 'tremendous pressure', but he never visited
the 'death camps'. Because, Charlotte once told him, he knew he was

powerless to do anything about them, or to help anyone.

In Washington, doing research for the portrait of Horst, I visited the US Department of Justice. In response to my enquiry as to what material they had on Otto, they shared three documents which were said to show his involvement. Two were documents that addressed the resettlement and employment of Jews, written in 1942, one of which he signed. A third letter, dated 25 August 1942, indicated that Otto wished to remain in post in occupied Poland, to carry on with his work, and not return to a desk job in Vienna. I showed the documents to Horst. Yes, they referred to 'sad and restrictive' measures taken against Jews in Lemberg, but since they made no explicit mention of 'extinctions' or killings they offered no proof of his father's culpability. He mentioned another letter, one written by Otto to Charlotte on 16 August 1942, which showed he could not be responsible. He would send it to me, but I should bear in mind that Otto knew the letters were being monitored by the SS, so he took care in what he wrote.

In May 2013 the *Financial Times* published the profile of Horst. It came with the title 'My Father, The Good Nazi', and included a full portrait photograph of Horst, in coat and red hat, seated serenely in the large hall.

The article provoked a variety of reactions. The Austrian ambassador in London complained that Horst's failure to condemn his father did not reflect current views in Austria. Others saluted Horst's courage, the son's effort to find the good in his father. One reader thought Horst's attitude was 'slightly noble', a reflection, in the reader's view, of a son's love for his father.

Horst was not happy with the article. He said this not to me but in a few words posted on the newspaper's website. 'I do not really like your article,' he wrote. I had left out much, like the esteem with which Otto was held by many in Lviv today, including Poles, Ukrainians and Jews. Jacqueline thought the article portrayed him as a madman, blind to overwhelming facts. Nevertheless, Horst concluded, our time together left him feeling sedate and stout-hearted.

I thought the relationship might draw to a close, but it didn't. Horst kept me updated on the reactions of others. His nephew Otto told him he'd been selfish in giving the interview, ignoring the consequences for him, an Austrian lawyer who worked for a law firm with an office in New York, with many Jewish colleagues. 'Maybe you could talk to him?' Horst suggested. 'It is my legal right to work up the history of my father,' he added. 'If he had lived until the Cold War, he could have become a key figure for the West.'

Over time, Horst's disappointment with the article dissipated. 'I have already benefited a lot from your intervention,' he wrote a few months after it appeared. He understood and accepted my position, and some people had written to express their approval. 'Waves of gratitude,' he called them, which might assist with the efforts to restore the castle. I want to be positive, he added, 'to understand the past, why and how things happened'.

Horst would step up his efforts to persuade me that his assessment of his father was right, that Otto's true character was decent, that he was not implicated in matters that could give rise to any criminal liability. By now we had been in touch for nearly two years, and I assumed the communications would become less frequent, that they would fade into silence. I was wrong. A seed was sown, the relationship took a new direction, nourished by a steady flow of information and unexpected points of detail.

6

1933, Vienna

Otto's true character was about to be tested. A few months after the wedding, on 30 January 1933, the *Machtergreifung* occurred, the Nazi seizure of power, with Adolf Hitler installed as chancellor of Germany. This changed the status of the Nazi Party in Austria, where opinion as to developments in the Third Reich was bitterly divided. Bishop Pawlikowski, who had expressed opposition to Nazi doctrine, circulated a pastoral letter written by a colleague, which rejected Nazi views on race as 'totally irreconcilable with Christianity'. To scorn, hate and persecute Jews on the basis of heritage was 'inhumane and anti-Christian', the letter declared. However, it continued, every staunch Christian had a duty to fight the harmful influence of the 'Jewish, international world spirit' embraced by those estranged from God, which promoted both 'mammoth capitalism' and served as an 'apostle' for socialism and communism, precursors to Bolshevism.

With the change in Germany, Otto embraced the 'forbidden party' even more fully. He spent ever more time at the *Deutsche Klub*, plotting with comrades and fellow Nazis, as Charlotte waited patiently at home, a pregnant foot soldier who embroidered swastikas onto garments. 'I always was a bit of a revolutionary,' she recorded, a keen supporter of 'the movement', hoping the Nazis would bring tranquillity and an end to chaos in Austria and Europe. On 5 March the Nazis won the German federal elections, a moment marked by Charlotte with a postcard of a smiling Führer sent to her friend Helga Ettingshausen. On 21 March, Otto travelled to Potsdam to attend the opening of the new Reichstag (the old building was destroyed by a fire), and it was on this occasion that, according to Charlotte, he met Hitler for the first time. Two days later Hitler passed legislation to give himself absolute power.

A few days after her husband's return from Potsdam, Charlotte went into labour. Early on the morning of 2 April, she made her way alone to the Rudolfinerhaus clinic, where Otto junior was born. Sheepishly, Otto visited with a bunch of flowers, having stayed in bed at home,

Charlotte recorded, 'clueless' and with a visceral dislike of hospitals and the smell of germicide. Charlotte was home ten days later, and Otto junior was baptised by Monsignor Allmer.

In May, the Austrian chancellor, Dollfuss, banned several political parties, including the National Socialists. Otto took his politics underground, actively supported by his father and Charlotte, and soon found himself in difficulty. In the summer, the *Abend* newspaper reported a police raid at a 'Secret Nazi base', operating undercover as a central European press office. Propaganda material was found and twenty-five people were arrested and taken into custody, including 'Nazi lawyer Otto Wächter'. Police proceedings were initiated against him, for 'continued activity' with the banned Nazis, and maintaining illegal contact with German counterparts.

Once again the brush with the law merely reinforced Otto's political direction, and Charlotte's active support. In September the couple travelled to the Venice Lido, to attend a meeting of party officials from Germany and Austria. Convened by his father Josef, the participants included Rudolf Weydenhammer, a German industrialist, plotting for Nazi rule in Austria.

In October, Otto appeared for the defence of Rudolf Dertil, a party member and former Austrian army soldier, indicted for the attempted assassination of Chancellor Dollfuss. Dertil was sentenced to five years in prison.

In December, Charlotte returned to London to sell more fabric designs. She stayed at the Bonnington Hotel, on Southampton Row, but this time the trip was not a success, barely covering her expenses, although she did meet several people of 'value'. Former acquaintances thought she looked 'stunning' but didn't notice the new wedding ring. 'I was still considered Miss Bleckmann.' She was pregnant again, so the trip was not easy.

In 1934, Charlotte got herself a new diary, 'Housewives' Notebook'. 'I love everything you do,' Charlotte wrote of Otto. 'If you are faithful to me, and continue to be, if you look into another's eyes, I trust you like you trust me.' In the spring Otto travelled to Berlin to meet Theodor Habicht, Hitler's point man in Austria, expelled from Vienna a year earlier. On this visit, it seems that Otto met Hitler for the second time. This I learned not from Horst, or Charlotte's papers, but from an academic article that included a grainy photograph of Otto in uniform, standing between the Führer and Alfred Frauenfeld, his comrade in Vienna with an eye for Charlotte. Otto was invited to the Reich Foreign Ministry, to report on the situation in Austria, where he met Gerhard Köpke, a career civil servant, who prepared a note. 'Austrian lawyer Baron Wächter came to me, to pass on good wishes,' Köpke recorded, a 'fresh and young' man, with 'clear judgement and an articulate, determined and energetic disposition'. Otto offered an account of the situation in Austria that was 'darker and more serious' than previously reported, as Austrian Nazis turned to acts of terror. Worried that the *Sturmabteilung* – the SA – was out of control, Otto reported that Austrian Nazis needed effective leadership, and encouraged Hitler to intervene. 'A change is needed,' Otto proposed, and requested a meeting with Hitler. Köpke said his views would be communicated to the new foreign minister, Konstantin von Neurath.

Köpke's report of the meeting lingered in a Berlin filing cabinet for many years. In 1945 it emerged as an item of evidence in von Neurath's trial, at Nuremberg. In due course, I found a photograph from that time, with a caption that showed Alfred Frauenfeld shaking Adolf Hitler's hand, with Otto between the two men, in a uniform.

In June Otto travelled to Zurich to meet Habicht, Fridolin Glass (the leader of the SS Vienna Standard 89, for which Otto served as legal adviser) and Rudolf Weydenhammer, his father's contact. The illicit meeting discussed the toppling of Dollfuss. A division of responsibilities was agreed: Otto would lead political efforts, Glass would direct the military side, and Weydenhammer would act as liaison between the two men. Anton Rintelen, Austria's ambassador to Italy, was identified as a replacement chancellor.

That month Charlotte gave birth to their second child, a daughter, Lieselotte Hertha Margarete Marta. Charlotte developed a blood clot and thrombosis. Critically ill, she was still in hospital in late July, when her sister gave birth to a son, and she became an aunt. That day, 25 July 1934, was significant for another reason. As Charlotte lay in hospital, Otto led an effort by Austrian Nazis to overthrow the Dollfuss government. The July Putsch began with a group of armed men breaking into the Ballhausplatz, the government offices, to confront the chancellor in his office. Matters spiralled out of control, and Oskar Planetta, a discharged army sergeant, shot Dollfuss dead. Whether by accident or intention was not clear, nor was the matter of the involvement of Berlin and Hitler. 'Ask Mussolini to look after my wife and children,' were the dying Chancellor's last words.

The plot failed. Some of those involved were arrested, tried and convicted, and sentenced to death and hanged. Rintelen was charged with treason, and sentenced to life imprisonment. As others fled, Otto, who never reached Dollfuss's office, disappeared. Some reports suggested he was being held at the Imperial Hotel, others that he escaped. Charlotte would later piece together the day's events from a conversation with Otto's former client, the photographer Lothar Rübelt, who had in the meantime worked on Leni Riefenstahl's film *The White Ecstasy*.

Tipped off about the plot, Rübelt hoped to photograph the coup. He arrived too late and returned home, for lunch with his mother, when Otto turned up unexpectedly. He was highly agitated, fearful of being caught and executed, and looking for a place to hide. Otto joined the Rübelts for lunch, made a single phone call, and was collected by an unknown man. Rübelt asked no questions of Otto, but picked up rumours that he'd taken refuge in an apartment owned by the German ambassador. Rübelt did not see Otto again until their paths crossed in 1936, at the Olympic Games in Berlin.

The authorities, camped outside her room at the clinic as she recovered, questioned Charlotte. She told them she knew nothing. Yes, Otto visited the day before the attempted coup, but she was so unwell she barely recalled the conversation. She noticed nothing unusual in his behaviour, but would have supported him if she'd known what he was up to. After all, Chancellor Dollfuss was hanging Austrian Nazis.

Decades later, she told historian Hansjakob Stehle that Otto was not the brains behind the July Putsch, which was planned by Austrian SS members, incompetently and without proper leadership. Otto did try to gain access to the Ballhaus, at least three times, but wasn't able to get in. To her aunt Lola Matsek, however, in another conversation, Charlotte offered a different account. Yes, Otto was 'mixed up' with the plot, and only a string of unfortunate circumstances conspired to prevent him from entering the Ballhaus. The death of Dollfuss was unintended. 'If you have a pistol and see somebody running away, you shoot.'

Otto crossed the line of criminality for the third time. Indicted by the Austrian state for high treason, he became a hunted man and disappeared, leaving Charlotte alone with two young children.

7

1934, Berlin

As the wife of a man on the run, Charlotte's life in Vienna came under intense scrutiny. She remained in hospital for several days after the July Putsch, repeatedly questioned by police. Formally interviewed, she was shrewd and standoffish. 'I know nothing,' she told the authorities, as she learned what it meant to be an 'illegal', a *persona non grata*. The police seized the house in Klosterneuburg, a car, clothing, her passport and 5,000 schillings in cash.

By back channels, Charlotte learned that Otto was safe. After several days without news, word arrived that he was in Germany. She picked up details, that he hid on the banks of the Danube, scrambled onto a coal barge disguised as a shipman, and travelled downriver, arriving in Budapest on 28 July. He was met by a dishevelled journalist with a monocle, Herr Kornhuber, who helped him to Germany and a new life. The government and party offered full assistance to an SS man on the run. Over the next four years, he completed military service, was offered 'special employment', became a naturalised citizen of the Reich, and qualified as a German lawyer. He would rise quickly through the SS ranks, promoted within a short time to Hauptscharführer, then Untersturmführer, then Obersturmführer.

He learned what it meant to be a fugitive, to take care. Letters home offered coded instructions to Charlotte, on his needs, including clothes and linen, and the gravity of his situation and the dangers his wife faced. 'It seems you are being watched, or rather your surroundings are being spied on,' he warned, instructing her to take care. He sent the children drawings in ink, stories without words. Horst had showed me a few photographs from that time, pasted by Charlotte into a family

album. Otto at a military barracks, on a training exercise. Otto in a black SS uniform. Otto on a tranquil residential street, bearing an armband that carried a swastika. Otto outside his new home, a 1930s villa in a Berlin suburb. Otto leaning nonchalantly on his car, a 'good Steyr', confident and proud, in a dark suit and hat.

The images did not give the impression of a man on the run from Austria. Kurt von Schuschnigg, who succeeded Dollfuss as chancellor, was a conservative of the Christian Social Party, firmly committed to Austrian independence from Germany, a supporter of the death penalty for men like Otto. A virulent anti-Nazi, he maintained the ban on the Nazi Party in Austria.

In Otto's absence, Charlotte recovered, left hospital and went to Mürzzuschlag with Otto junior and Liesl. They occupied two rooms on the ground floor of the family home, the *Herrenhaus*, although her parents were mostly in Vienna. Her father was now retired, so there was less income, but enough for a car and chauffeur, and a maid to assist Charlotte. She recalled the period as one of weariness and despair, of limited contact with Otto, in conditions of utmost secrecy. Her diary carried coded references to furtive phone calls with her husband, and she later told the children that the cunning she learned in that time would stand her in good stead.

Mutti was her lifeline, drawing on experience of wounded soldiers at the rehabilitation home she ran in Mürzzuschlag during the Great War. By the end of 1934 Charlotte got back the house in Klosterneuburg and her passport, which allowed her to travel to Davos, the Swiss ski resort, at Christmas. During the illicit reunion with Otto, they used a false name, the 'Wartenbergs', and were accompanied by the Ettingshausens, who had also fled Austria and lived in Munich.

Charlotte's 'thrombosis leg' made skiing difficult, and she complained he was inattentive until he injured himself on the slopes. From Davos they went to Berlin, then headed south. 'Evening in Berchtesgaden', Charlotte noted in her diary on 12 January 1935, the small town near the Austrian border where Hitler had bought a retreat, the Berghof, with the proceeds of *Mein Kampf*. Otto returned to Munich, and Charlotte made her way to Salzburg, Vienna and Mürzzuschlag, to look after the children, play chess and receive visitors, including the Fischböcks. She was required to report regularly to a police station in Vienna, attended the trial of Anton Rintelen, and followed the trial of Hanns Blaschke, another comrade, in which Otto's role in the attempted putsch was highlighted. 'Dr Wächter's character was beyond doubt,' Blaschke told the judge. 'I had no hint of any plan for a putsch.'

In Germany, the Nuremberg decrees were passed, to protect the purity of the Aryan race and strip Jews of citizenship and the right to be employed as a lawyer, doctor or journalist. Otto signed up for military training. He served at Dachau, as photographs of him and the barracks attested, the ones I saw in the family album.

At Christmas the couple met in the Czech Republic, at a hotel on the Schneekoppe, the highest point in the country. Charlotte registered under her maiden name, Bleckmann, Otto as Wartenberg. They were joined by the monocled journalist Kornhuber and his girlfriend, who pretended to be married, as Charlotte and Otto pretended they weren't, which amused her greatly. 'A lovely time', Charlotte recalled, but it passed too quickly. She decided that the following year, in 1936, the family would be reunited.

Early in the new year they met in Garmisch, at the Winter Olympics, to work out the details of the move. 'Ski jumping with Hitler', Charlotte noted in her diary, on 13 February. In March, she noted the German occupation of the Rhineland, followed by 'evening, cinema'. They decided she would move to Berlin once Otto's military service in the Wehrmacht was completed, in the autumn.

Charlotte stayed in touch with Otto's friends and comrades. She saw Rudolf Pavlu, after he left prison for his role in the July Putsch, until he moved to Berlin, to join the party's *Flüchtlingshilfswerk*, the refugee agency established by Rudolf Hess, Hitler's deputy, for persecuted Nazis. She met with Arthur Seyss-Inquart and Theodor Habicht, who served as go-betweens for her and Otto, and Otto's best friend Manni Braunegg. He lived on Obere Donaustrasse, I learned from her diary, in the Leopoldstadt district. I knew the street because it happened to be the one to which my great-grandmother, Amalia Buchholz, was banished in 1939, after being evicted from her home, a point of transit on the way to Treblinka, where she would be killed three years later.

In the summer, Chancellor von Schuschnigg signed an agreement with Hitler's government. This brought another colleague of Otto's – Edmund Glaise-Horstenau – into the Austrian government, and gave Seyss-Inquart a role as liaison between the banned Austrian Nazis and the Austrian chancellor.

In the autumn, Otto completed his military service in Freising, near Dachau. He applied to work for the SS, emphasising his experience in Austria and the Reich, and committing himself to the SS as the guarantor of party unity and strength, crucial to German foreign policy. 'I have had close ties with the SS since the time of the struggle,' he wrote in his application letter, and 'have always prioritised my ties to the SS over my duties as a lawyer'. The head of the Nazi refugee agency supported him, as a 'superb national socialist'. Another referee, a former SS colleague from Vienna, described the work he did as legal adviser of the 11th SS Standard in Austria as having been performed with diligence, loyalty and energy. On multiple occasions, the referee reported, Otto risked his reputation by putting the commitment to the SS above all professional and ethical duties.

In the autumn, Charlotte finally brought the family to Berlin after two years apart. She and the children collected Otto from the barracks at Freising, and together they drove to Berlin, where they moved into a flat at Höhenweg 12, a single floor of a villa on the western outskirts of the city, rented by a 'fun-loving' landlady. They had three bedrooms and a garden that overlooked Lake Havel. 'At last the family was together', Charlotte noted, after two years apart.

Otto was offered a new job at the Hauptamt (Main Office) of the *Sicherheitsdienst des Reichsführers-SS*, known as the SD, the intelligence agnecy of the SS. His character was recorded in his file as open and intelligent, a perfect fit for the 'office of spying and surveillance services', as Charlotte referred to it. He worked in the SD's Criminal Division, at no. 8 Prinz-Albert-Strasse, a building shared with the Gestapo and the SS.

It was here that Otto came into the orbit of Reinhard Heydrich, the SD head, and Heinrich Himmler, recently appointed by Hitler as Chief of the German police service. The SD was a place of work for distinct and highly qualified individuals who would, in due course, reach the upper echelons of power across the territories occupied by the Reich. In the Berlin federal archive I found the Staff Directory for the SD Main Office for January 1937, in which Otto's name appeared. His colleagues, in a small and tightly focused organisation, included SS-Hauptscharführer Adolf Eichmann and SS-Unterscharführer Karl Hass.

There was no indication that Otto was anything other than delighted to be working here, although Charlotte would later assert that he never really liked the work, a place where 'he surely saw things he couldn't change, which were decided against his principles'. Yet ever contradictory, she described the period as one of the greatest happiness and harmony, a perfect combination of family reunited, Nazis in control, and Berlin on the

rise around the world. There was even time for trips together to the mountains.

The period was not entirely free of personal tensions, however, as Charlotte discovered that Otto was having an affair, this time with a young German woman called Traute. It was not the first such development, or the last. Pregnant again, she responded ferociously, forcing an end to the relationship and determined to punish Otto, which she did by terminating the pregnancy. The decision was tough, she concluded, but necessary, to avoid losing her husband.

Early in the new year, 1937, Otto was promoted to SS-Obersturmbannführer, and took other necessary steps to smooth the path to the top table. In his SS personnel file I read a letter he wrote in April, by which he committed himself totally to the service of the Führer. 'I hereby report that I completed my resignation from the Roman Catholic church on the 15th of this month.' He signed off with a 'Heil Hitler! Wächter'. He declared himself *gottgläubig*, committed to a life of piety and morality without affiliation to any formal religious denomination. The idea had been promoted by Heinrich Himmler to reflect a total dedication to the ideals of the SD and the SS, and the Führer.

Otto spent several months at the SD criminal division, then transferred to the party's refugee relief agency, to work with Rudolf Pavlu. The job allowed him to travel across Europe, to Belgrade, Trieste, Zagreb, Dubrovnik and Venice, making contacts for the future. He passed the state bar examination. His personnel file described him as an SS man with an 'upright and open' character, well-educated, with common sense, and perfect 'racial characteristics', namely 'tall, slender, with Nordic appearance'.

The family planned for an extended stay in Berlin. Charlotte made brief forays into Austria, to Mürzzuschlag and Vienna, sold the house at Klosterneuburg, and retrieved other property confiscated after the July Putsch. Back in Berlin, she was pregnant once more, and this time decided to keep the child. In November 1937 she drove herself to hospital for the birth of their third – a girl, much to Otto's disappointment, who dreamt of having six boys. Charlotte needled him further, by insisting that the new daughter be named Traute, in honour of his recent affair. 'That should please you,' she wrote.

As relations between Austria and Germany soured – Chancellor Schuschnigg evoked the 'abyss' that separated Austria from Nazism –

Charlotte made preparations for a lengthy stay in Berlin. She went house-hunting, clipped advertisements and pasted them into her diary. In January 1938, Himmler promoted Otto to SS-Standartenführer. Official portraits were commissioned: Otto on the telephone, reading papers, talking to colleagues. The images projected power and authority, the dark-black SS uniform, the aquiline face lit to emphasise the fine cheekbones, the cap tilted slightly, now bearing a *Totenkopf*, the 'death's head' that marked him as an SS man of power.

Charlotte found a house, in the Kleinmachnow district, near Potsdam. The price was reasonable, the size adequate, the purchase quickly completed. They now had a house with four bedrooms, a library, a 'rather striking' home with a straw roof, built-in cupboards, a fine garden and many 'trimmings'. 'We were absolutely thrilled,' Charlotte recorded. She planned to move in by May.

The move never happened. On 12 February 1938, Adolf Hitler hosted Austrian chancellor Kurt von Schuschnigg at the Berghof, in Berchtesgaden. A little after four o'clock in the afternoon, diplomats handed Schuschnigg a draft agreement prepared by the Germans, one that imposed on Austria the obligation to allow Nazi ideas to flower, release imprisoned Nazis and permit them to return to their former positions in public office. Two senior Nazis would enter the government of Austria, both close comrades of Otto: Arthur Seyss-Inquart ('a good friend from the "*Deutsche Klub*" in Vienna', Charlotte noted) as minister of the interior, and Dr Hans Fischböck, as federal commissar.

Under intense pressure, von Schuschnigg signed the agreement. On his return to Vienna he took steps to implement it, announcing a national plebiscite to confirm the independence of Austria and avoid a union with Germany. Hitler ordered the plebiscite to be cancelled. When von Schuschnigg relented, Hitler demanded his immediate resignation. Under threat of armed intervention, he did so. On 11 March, Otto's friend Seyss-Inquart became chancellor of Austria.

The following morning, 12 March, German troops entered Austria. The moment was known as the Anschluss, the Nazi takeover of Austria, a singular case of annexation, fusion and occupation. Charlotte saw it in her own way: Seyss-Inquart was appointed governor of Austria and he then asked Hitler to occupy, 'so the Austrian government sort of asked our Führer to take over'.

The development changed the lives of Charlotte and Otto. After years in the Austrian wilderness, they would taste absolute power.

II

—

POWER

卐

'Dinner with Wächter, governor of Kraków, just today appointed governor of Lemberg. His wife receives us. Pretty. Wächter too is Viennese . . .'

Curzio Malaparte, Diary, 1942

8

1938, Vienna

Otto and Charlotte did not expect a quick return to Austria, Charlotte recalled. 'Then a single event changed everything, and our wildest dreams, which we never imagined could be realised, suddenly came true.'

She wrote a long account of the events of March 1938, when the Führer entered Austria and occupied the country. Her words were infected with a palpable joy, set to paper forty years after the events occurred, and read by me a further forty years after they were written.

Every Nazi felt such joy about this miracle, we all embraced each other. Yes, it was one of the most decisive moments of our lives, and in those of the hundreds of thousands who had fled to Germany and were living as 'illegals'. They'd been expelled from their dear homeland, living as outcasts, some separated from their families in a country not far from their homeland, but where everything was out of reach for those who had left stealthily. Yes, I was homesick for all those who were dear to me and for the mountains, open fields and woods. I was more reconciled to our fate when Trautchen came, although I was always able to cross the border. But Otto could never dare to.

Now this great event, the Führer at the top of a great Reich – we suddenly forgot all plans about 'building a life for ourselves in Berlin'. We called all our friends and relatives. Initially there was chaos, not only in our minds but for all those who, because of this 'dream', had dedicated their lives, left their families and had, to some extent, abandoned everything.

Friends decided to drive from Germany to Vienna, and she accompanied them. They left on the morning of 10 March – a journey 'full of excitement about the great event in our homeland' – and arrived in Vienna that evening, at Belvederegasse 10, where her parents and siblings were living.

The morning after arriving in Vienna I ran like a madwoman from one place to another to try to find any old friends of Otto's who were in Austria, or rather in Vienna, and who could summon Otto from Berlin to Vienna. This wasn't so easy. Seyss-Inquart was away, travelling to meet Hitler, to receive him at the border or meet him in Linz. No one knew anything. It was unbelievably chaotic, even the porters didn't know who was in which building, room, position, seat, etc. The government at the *Bundeskanzleramt* [chancellery] was dissolving, the head of the police had stepped down and no replacement appointed. It was all hither and thither.

Then I heard that Globočnik [Globus], who was the go-between during the illegal time, was in the security building at the court. I rushed there and, after searching the building from top to bottom, I found him in a room on the second floor (I think), enthroned in front of a desk. He recognised me straight away and asked what I wanted. I asked him to call Berlin and get in touch with Otto, to ask him to come to Vienna, so that he could be at the parade on the Heldenplatz on 13 March 1938 as the *Führer* marched in. Globus, who was rather slow and circuitous, said: 'That's not possible! The telephone lines are all blocked and where can I get hold of him and how can I give him an order without consulting . . .'

I slammed my fist onto his desk, made him jump, and said: 'Otto sacrificed everything for the party, which he's been a member of since 1923. He risked his life, he lost everything. And he's not going to be there on 13 March?! What are you thinking, Herr Globus? If this is our reward, that he can't be there for the greatest day in history, then nothing is worthwhile!'

'What do you want me to do?' asked Globus. 'It's a difficult situation and there's only a day to go.'

'Give me the order, that you're happy for Otto to come,' I blurted out.

'If you can do it, please do so,' he said.

'Can I take it seriously?' I said.

'Yes, I order you to let him know,' Globus said.

And so I ran to my parents' in Belvederegasse, with a happy, grateful heart. I immediately picked up the telephone and, although all the lines were blocked, I put in a call to Berlin. I can still remember, it lasted three minutes and cost 90 schillings, a lot of money, but was well worth it. In a couple of hours, I got hold of him in the office of Obergruppenführer Rodenbucher, the most senior supervisor of the 'refugees'. [. . .] He came on the telephone and, full of joy and pride, I said: 'In the name of Globočnik, I hereby order you to make an immediate departure for Vienna, in order to be here when the *Führer* marches in.'

It was quite a surprise! He asked me a couple of times if this could be true? I reassured him that it was, and hoped he'd get to Vienna in good time. I was so happy, because I knew it was a miracle to have been able to get hold of him. I'm sure that Globus thought I'd never be able to make contact so quickly. Maybe he'd have thought twice about it.

And at seven o'clock the next morning there he was, in the doorway of my parents' flat in Vienna, as a *Brigadeführer*, in his black SS coat with white lapels and SS uniform. In spite of the strain and the fatigue, he looked splendid. He washed, had a coffee, made a quick phone call, then we headed straight into town. His chauffeur was ready as well; what a feeling it must have been to be able to see his home town after four long, anxious years. He returned at midday with two tickets for the balcony of the Heldenplatz. There were only a couple of hours until the great event, so we were very excited.

On 13 March 1938, we went into town in the big Mercedes and looked for our friends and the place we'd been assigned. The Fischböcks, the Lehrs and others were all there. Suddenly we heard a loud cry in the distance, which turned into an overwhelming cry of joy, 'Heil Hitler'. It approached like a surging human sea, getting closer and louder. The road to the Heldenplatz was completely full, people standing shoulder to shoulder, all the way up to the Rathaus, around the Ballhausplatz. It took a lot of time and effort to clear the route. The Führer was standing with a raised hand, greeting the crowd, which was shouting excitedly . . . a spontaneous and heartfelt outburst of joy. Everyone was carried along in this feeling of heartfelt joy.

Seyss-Inquart and his wife and a number of others came with the Führer, who slowly climbed the stairs of the Hofburg, up to the balcony. He was standing a metre in front of me, and I could see and hear him well. After a greeting, he began his speech. As an Austrian, he was deeply moved, as though he could hardly believe it himself. It didn't last all that long, but it looked like Otto was talking with Seyss and greeted all our other friends.

For Charlotte, the time with Hitler on the balcony of the Heldenplatz would always be 'the best moment of my life'. After they left, at the bottom of the marble steps that led from the balcony, Otto asked Charlotte if she would prefer that he return to legal practice and make money, or enter public service and accept a position as an official in the new government. Do what interests you the most, she told him, 'we will always have enough to eat'. With this green light he kissed her hand, a pact perfected.

Incorporated into the German Reich, Austria became the Province of Ostmark. The new government was headed by Seyss-Inquart and included comrades from the *Deutsche Klub*. Ernst Kaltenbrunner, Otto's closest friend in the SS, became minister for public security, reporting directly to Himmler; Hans Fischböck was appointed minister for trade and traffic; and Odilo Globočnik became Gauleiter of Vienna. Bishop Pawlikowski, briefly imprisoned for objecting to a colleague's arrest, was released and joined the rapture, as the Church was brought onside.

Reliable officials were introduced from Germany. Josef Bürckel, from Himmler's staff, became Reichskommissar, to perfect the union with Germany, implement the Nuremberg racial laws and resolve the 'Jewish question'. He established the *Zentralstelle für jüdische Auswanderung in Wien* (Central Agency for Jewish Emigration in Vienna), under the direction of Otto's former comrade at the SD, Adolf Eichmann, who installed himself at the Metropol Hotel. The Central Agency expedited the emigration or expulsion of Austrian Jews, and within a few months more than 100,000 had left. One among them was my grandfather Leon Buchholz, deprived of his liquor-making business, made stateless and expelled from the Reich by judicial decision, in November 1938.

Early on, Otto met Seyss-Inquart at the Ballhaus, the building to which he failed to gain access four years earlier, in the July Putsch. He was offered a position as state commissioner, a fact reported in German and Austrian newspapers, and in the *New York Times*:

Dr Arthur Seyss-Inquart, Governor of Austria, has appointed an organizer of the Nazi Putsch of July, 1934, Dr Otto Waechter, to be State Commissioner for matters of personnel. When he learned the Putsch had failed, he fled to Germany.

Hitler returned to Vienna a month later to celebrate the Day of the Greater German Reich. On 9 April, Charlotte joined a gathering at City Hall, had lunch with Otto at Meissl & Schaden, the famed restaurant on Neu Markt, and attended a concert. 'Sat in the second row, marvellous.' The following day, Austrians voted in a plebiscite on union with the German Reich, with Jews and other undesirables excluded from voting. They were urged to vote yes by many, including the leader of the Social Democrats, Karl Renner, and the Catholic Church. Bishop Pawlikowski supported unification and, perhaps softened up by the short stint in jail, added his name to a call to suppress 'the destructive influence of world Judaism'.

'Voted early', Charlotte noted in her diary. She was one of the 99.74 per cent who supported the union, a result that cemented the situation and allowed Charlotte to become a social butterfly, invited to cocktails, parties and receptions for the 'prominents'. A glamour couple, she and Otto attended concerts and operas, and the film premiere of Leni Riefenstahl's *Olympia* and the reception that followed. The Seyss-Inquarts and the Fischböcks became frequent visitors to Mürzzuschlag.

Otto received other positive news, when Himmler informed him that Hitler had abandoned an inquiry into the reasons for the failure of the July Putsch. This freed Otto from the charge of possible responsibility for the embarrassment, an accusation he vigorously denied. 'I faithfully followed the Führer's will,' he wrote. On 8 July Charlotte hosted a lavish dinner party to celebrate her husband's thirty-seventh birthday. The guests included Manni Braunegg and other old friends, comrades from the July Putsch, like Pavlu and Blaschke, and political leaders Ernst Kaltenbrunner, head of the SS and police, and Walter Rafelsberger, a state commissioner charged with Aryanising Austria. Hermann Neubacher, the new Nazi mayor of Vienna, was invited, as was Professor Norbert Gürke, the leading anti-Semitic law professor appointed to Otto's alma mater.

Charlotte attended the Salzburg Festival and went to Bayreuth, with Trudl Fischböck, for Wagner's *Ring Cycle*. 'Marvellous', she wrote on a postcard which showed the *Haus der Deutschen Erziehung* (The German House of Education) draped in swastikas, each day was better than the last. 'The Führer is here, eating with H, up above', a reference to Himmler. 'Trude went to see Frau Göbbels and the Führer', the day before *Götterdämmerung*.

Two weeks later, Charlotte sat in a box at the Vienna State Opera House next to Arthur Seyss-Inquart, for Verdi's *Falstaff*. She did not yet know she was pregnant with their fourth child, conceived during the blissful days of excitement that followed the Anschluss. Nine months later, Horst Arthur Wächter was born in Vienna, on 14 April 1939. Seyss-Inquart agreed to be his godfather, offering a copy of *Mein Kampf* as a gift to his godson. Charlotte was delighted with Horst, a second son, with masses of long black hair. She received visitors on a veranda of their new home, the Villa Mendl, ablaze with spring azaleas. 'I loved nursing him, and he thrived, although he was weak and drooled a great deal.'

9

2014, London

'I was a Nazi child.' Horst so described himself on the occasion of our first meeting, but back then I was not aware of the details, or the extent of the truth he spoke. Now I could understand his comfort with the title of the article published in the *Financial Times*, 'My Father, The Good Nazi'.

In the months after publication, an idea emerged for a possible event in London, a public conversation between Niklas Frank and Horst Wächter, two sons with different approaches to their fathers. Initially, Horst was doubtful. Niklas, my 'fellow in misery', was simply too negative about both fathers, he told me, and the article in the *FT* caused 'difficulties' for his nephew, Otto junior. I doubted the charge, but kept the thought to myself.

Horst soon changed his mind. 'I decided to accept your invitation to London,' he wrote. He was prompted by a sense of duty, a desire to face the issues posed by the past, including the responsibility of his father, and his own responsibility to deal with the truth. In this way he might be able to contribute to a more humane future.

In February 2014 we gathered at the Southbank Centre in London. A few days before the event Horst enquired if his daughter Magdalena, who was in her late thirties and an artist, could join us. Of course, I responded. But, Horst added, she wears a headscarf, a reference to her recent conversion to Islam. No one would be shocked, I assured him, his fears were misplaced, so Magdalena came, as did Niklas's daughter Franziska. The event sold out, coinciding with protests in Kiev's Maidan Square, as Russia sought to prevent Ukraine from signing an association agreement with the EU. 'Everyone to Kiev! Let's support the Maidan,' writer Andrey Kurkov noted in his diary as we assembled in the intimacy of the wood-panelled Purcell Room.

I sat between the two septuagenarians, Horst to my right, Niklas to the left. As we talked, black and white photographs of the fathers and families were projected on a large screen above us. Hans Frank with Adolf Hitler, 1928. Otto Wächter with Heinrich Himmler, 1942. Two couples, the Franks and Wächters, at the Wawel Castle, 1942. The families in Bavaria, at the Franks' country home, 1943. Frank in the dock of Courtroom 600 in Nuremberg, 1945. Frank executed, 1946. Charlotte with Horst and siblings, a photograph she sent to Frau Frank, 1948.

Horst asked that one photograph in particular be shown, 'the one where my father leans on me, in 1944, at the railway station in Zell-am-See'. Otto in uniform, SS cap tilted, with Charlotte, and Traute, and Horst in white socks.

There were film cameras in the Purcell Room, under the direction of David Evans, present because he read the *Financial Times* article and thought the subject – memory and the shadow of responsibility – could make an interesting documentary. We had already filmed Niklas in Bavaria, and Horst at Hagenberg, my third visit to the schloss.

The event ran long past the planned ninety minutes, with no interval. An attentive, silent audience of several hundred Londoners listened to two competing versions of history, of responsibility and family life. 'Electrifying and unscripted', one newspaper reported. Horst's approach was the more difficult, and the questions to him more acerbic, but his warmth and honesty, and the sense of candour he offered, endeared him to many in the audience. He was pleased to be in London, he explained, where one could speak frankly. 'This kind of listening would be impossible in Austria, we don't know anything, and we don't want to know anything.'

Yes, he conceded, his father did play a role in the terrible events in occupied Poland during the war. But no, he bore no criminal guilt for the horrors that occurred, for which he was not and could not be responsible, given his 'decent character'. True, there were incriminating documents from the period of the governorships in Kraków and Lemberg, but Otto's signature did not appear on them. A mention of the three letters shared with me by the Department of Justice, in Washington, was swatted away by Horst.

Niklas responded sharply. 'You told me once I should make peace with my father,' he told Horst. 'I have peace with my father, because I acknowledged his crimes.' Pause. 'And you, you are struggling, for what? The files are also against your father.' Another pause. 'Sorry, dear friend.'

'I see the structure of the whole annihilation of the Jews quite differently,' Horst replied, settled comfortably into the chair. In Lemberg, after Vienna and Kraków, his father was able to be independent, to be close to the Ukrainians. 'He wanted to do something positive, in a former Austrian province.' He could have left, but he chose to stay, I suggested, drawing on a letter sent by Himmler to Berlin, which made clear that Otto declined an offer to leave Lemberg for a desk job in Vienna.

'Because he felt responsible for the people,' Horst retorted.

'For some people'.

'For some . . . the only thing he could do for the Jews was to change the district orders, and that he did, to save Jewish workers.' The actions of the SS left him powerless, and he couldn't leave the system, as he was too involved with 'the people'. Horst invoked Charlotte's papers, documents I had not seen. 'If you read the diaries of my mother, there were always Poles and Ukrainians around him that he tried to contact, and he tried to be nice.'

Horst preferred to focus on the positives, and wasn't looking for peace with his father. 'It's my duty as a son to put things straight with my father, that's all,' he said, a sentiment that will have resonated with some in the audience. He had nothing to hide, after all, and wanted to be open. 'And my dear family was angry, and is still angry.'

Any regret at appearing before such an audience?

'Yes, of course,' he said with a large smile. This provoked a ripple of nervous laughter, one that cut through the tension.

Questions followed, which he engaged with politely, ignoring any hostility.

No, his view of his father had not changed over time.

Yes, Otto's history did trigger his own interest in Jewish wisdom and culture.

No, orders for killings signed by his father did not exist.

Yes, if he was presented with such an order he would condemn Otto, but he could not imagine that such a thing existed. 'For me, it would be impossible that he would have done it.'

No, Otto did not give himself up after the war. Why not? Because if he had he would have been turned over to the Russians and executed immediately. 'There would have been no justice for him.'

No, Otto wouldn't have been sent to Nuremberg. 'There was no indictment after the war, he was four years hidden and there was no indictment against him, no searching.'

The statement required a correction. There was a Polish indictment, reported in the *New York Times*, although I had not yet found a copy. That was 1942, Horst responded, long before the end of the war. Anyway, he had another document, which stated that Otto did all he could to save people. 'I don't think he would have been indicted by the Poles or the Ukrainians.'

His conclusions were based on private papers in his possession, he explained, more than eight hundred letters that Charlotte and Otto wrote to each other, over many years. They supported the positive view he took, even if his parents' relationship wasn't always easy. 'My father was a pretty man, my mother was jealous.' And, he conceded, 'some of the letters are missing', destroyed by Charlotte. He didn't have everything they wrote, but what he did have was positive.

Yes, he understood why some saw Otto as complicit in crimes. 'I never would accept the system,' he added, 'but I accept this father as my father.'

The questions went on. As the evening drew to a close, Horst asked if he could say a few final words. He took the microphone and spoke firmly. 'My father was revered in Lviv and western Ukraine, then and now, because of his firm position against the Soviets and communism.'

That was what he said, and that was how the evening finished.

A few days later Horst sent a gracious note of thanks. He welcomed the chance to speak up for his father, but our engagement must now end. This was because of something I said at lunch the day after the event, at a small Greek restaurant, in the presence of Magdalena. If Otto had been caught he would have been tried, convicted and sentenced, like Hans Frank, was what I said.

Horst did not like that. 'You have put my father on the same level as the executors of the Holocaust,' which in his eyes was gravely wrong. 'I see no sense in continuing this.'

We had reached the end of the road.

10

1938, Vienna

Otto's job as a state secretary offered power and perks, an office in the Hofburg, and a portrait in the *Völkischer Beobachter*, the leading Nazi daily. The Wächters were provided with a new Mercedes and home, following the sale of the recently acquired property in Berlin and Charlotte's house in Klosterneuburg. In July they moved into the Villa Mendl, an official residence made available with the help of Georg Lippert, a friend, architect and recent convert to the Nazi cause. The property came with a park of its own, at 11 Wallmodengasse, in Vienna's plush 19th district, appropriated from the Mendl family, founders of the renowned Ankerbrot bakery.

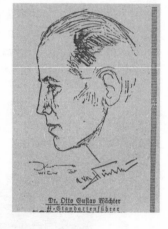

Dr. Otto Gustav Wächter
H-Standartenführer

There wasn't much on the market but Lippert 'obtained the Jewess Bettina Mendl's house for us', was how Charlotte put it. Bettina Mendl, educated at Cheltenham Ladies' College, ran the business founded by her father. As a passionate anti-Nazi and fine equestrian, she had refused to compete at the 1936 Berlin Olympics. She fled Vienna as German troops arrived and ended up in Sydney, Australia. A memoir by her daughter explained that Lippert was one of Bettina's closest friends, a frequent visitor to the villa, where he played tennis and attended concerts and parties. He curried favour with the Nazis, and arranged for the property to be requisitioned and 'become the residence of Dr (Baron) Gustav Otto Wächter'. In the daughter's account, the Wächters looted the Mendl family's treasures, including a fine collection of art and antique crystal glassware. 'In the years after World War II, attempts were made to bring Wächter to justice for war crimes,' she continued, but the efforts failed, as he 'used the loot from Villa Mendl and other similar properties to purchase safe custody'.

Villa Mendl was no doubt 'very beautiful', but Charlotte complained it was in poor condition – only one wing habitable – and too 'old-fashioned, cold and uncomfortable' for her taste. Yet she appreciated the vast living room and fine library, and a veranda that overlooked the elegant gardens, where she could entertain. She retained the Baumgartners as caretakers ('good old sorts' who quickly transferred their loyalties), hired a nanny for the children (a gem, 'soft, warm and plump'), and had a cook.

At the Villa Mendl, in October, Charlotte celebrated her thirtieth birthday, an occasion marked with ten roses from Arthur Seyss-Inquart. The month was filled with concerts and films, *Don Carlos* at the Vienna State Opera, *Under the Roofs of Paris* at the cinema, and the *Chancellor of Tyrol* at the Josefstadt Theatre. In the company of the Seyss-Inquarts, she was introduced to Reichsmarschall Hermann Göring, on a visit from Berlin.

Otto's work brought travel around the Reich and Europe. In September he and Charlotte went to Nuremberg, and spent four days at the Tenth National Socialist Party Congress, a 'Rally for Greater Germany'. Three quarters of a million people attended, the largest such gathering but also the last. In her diary Charlotte noted the daily themes: 'Friday 9th, in honour of political leaders; Sunday 11th, celebration of the S.A.; Monday 12th, eulogy for the Wehrmacht'. On the final day, Hitler spoke to the joy of the Anschluss, a welcome for his Austrian 'fighters'. He declared: 'Today you stand among us, as *Volksgenossen* and citizens of the German Reich', after a lengthy period of suffering caused by the nefarious Versailles Treaty, victims of the duplicity of the 'democracies' and the Bolsheviks in Moscow, and of the Jewish parasites who sucked the lifeblood out of Germany. Charlotte placed a photograph into the family album, a night shot.

A few days later she noted the Sudetenland crisis. 'Chamberlain with Führer', she wrote, 'scary situation'. Seyss-Inquart assured her that war would be avoided, but she took the precaution of buying gas masks for the family.

Otto's long working hours, and the fear that he was once again engaged in extramarital dalliances, caused Charlotte's mood to plummet. On 8 November, she bought a picture and had a ghastly, upset evening alone. On the 9th, she went to Otto's office to confront him, describing her own behaviour as 'nasty'. In the evening she attended the premiere of *Cromwell* at the Burgtheater, a new play to celebrate 'strong leadership in the service of a united nation'. If, on leaving the theatre, she noticed the events of *Kristallnacht* on the streets of Vienna, they passed without mention in the diary. Party members roamed Vienna, ransacked Jewish businesses, destroyed synagogues, beat up Jews and then arrested them.

The next morning she returned to Otto's office. 'I was cross and nasty, again,' she recorded of the renewed confrontation. Back in the villa at noon, she spent the day waiting for him to come home. They spent a 'fearful' evening together. Within a week, however, her spirits improved and calm was restored. She attended a concert of Mozart and Beethoven, conducted by Furtwängler, and a performance of *Die Fledermaus*. New Year's Eve was spent at the Volkstheater, at the *Opernball*. 'Afterwards home and waited for midnight alone', she recorded. Still, 1938 was a 'glamorous year which brought big changes to our lives! . . . We are now a big country, and we have the Führer.'

Otto's work took him ever more deeply into the heart of Nazi power. He travelled frequently to Berlin, often with Seyss-Inquart, or his colleague Walter Rafelsberger who, by the end of 1938, had Aryanised and seized more than 26,000 Jewish small and medium-sized enterprises.

As state secretary, Otto's office was in the Ballhaus, and the family album held several photographs. 'Back in Vienna!' he wrote on the back of one. Interior shots, a stairway, the Congress Hall, a portrait of Otto in the *Neue Freie Presse*, views of his office and Seyss-Inquart's, a large map of Ostmark, a meeting room, a waiting room. 'View from

my room, in the Viennese spring', he
wrote on another. His work was assisted
by fresh legislation imported from
Germany. Within a week of the
Anschluss, a new constitutional provision allowed for the reform of public
bodies. A special ordinance restructured the Austrian civil service, a
Berufsbeamtenverordnung, or 'BBV',
which empowered Otto to remove any
civil servant from his position. Section 3
operated more or less automatically, to
dismiss all Jews and *Mischlinge*, part
Jews. Section 4 gave Otto the power to

dismiss or 'retire' others, because of 'prior political behaviour' that
might undermine the Nazi cause. Otto's decisions were final, without
appeal to any court.

He was empowered to remove vast numbers of public officials
from their posts, because they were Jewish or politically unreliable.
Decisions were recorded in correspondence and other documents,
carefully archived. I was not able to find a single example of his use
of an exception in the legislation, or any act of leniency. Examples
of the individuals he targeted were not hard to find. He removed
Viktor Kraft, a teacher of philosophy and chief state librarian of the
University of Vienna, from his positions because he had a Jewish wife
and was once a member of the *Wiener Kreis* (Vienna Circle). Friedrich
König was another target in the university library, a volunteer with the
imperial army who lost a leg and an eye. On 5 June 1939 Otto wrote
to inform him he had lost his job. 'Because you are a *Mischling*, First
Grade,' he wrote.

The precise number of individuals subjected to Otto's
Säuberungsaktion ('cleansing action'), as his work was known, was
difficult to ascertain, as many of the files sent to Berlin were lost. On
the basis of archives in Vienna, however, it seems that Otto dismissed
or reprimanded at least 16,237 civil servants, 5,963 of whom were
classified as 'high ranking'. The numbers included 238 working in the
federal chancellery, 3,600 in the security service, 1,035 in the judicial
sector, 2,281 in the educational sector, 651 from the financial sector,
and 1,497 from the postal service.

Otto's 'cleansing actions' were implemented with single-minded purpose, and had significant consequences. 'A number of times I tried to put in a good word for my old comrades with Wächter,' a senior colleague reported, 'but succeeded only very rarely.' Those who 'were hit or brushed by Wächter's sword couldn't even get a job on the side'. In some cases Otto's actions had fatal consequences. He wrote to the 64-year-old former procurator-general, Robert Winterstein, who had served as minister of justice in von Schuschnigg's government: 'In light of § 4 para. 3 of the Ordinance on the Restructuring of the Austrian Civil Service of 31 May 1938, RGBl.I S.607 you are dismissed. Your dismissal enters into force on the day this notice is delivered. The dismissal cannot be appealed. Signed: Wächter.' The former minister was arrested on *Kristallnacht*, as Charlotte attended the Burgtheater. Deported to the Buchenwald concentration camp, he was dead within eighteen months.

Otto even targeted some of his former teachers at the law faculty of

Vienna University. Professor Josef Hupka, for example, on the left, who taught him trade and exchange law, and signed his university graduation certificate, was one victim. Professor Stephan Brassloff, who lectured him in three courses, including Roman criminal law, was another. Removed from their university positions in the summer of 1938, within six

months both lost their pension rights. In due course both professors would be deported to camps, where they perished.

The task of cleansing the Austrian civil service – only a 'temporary position', Seyss-Inquart indicated – was not without challenges. 'I remember Otto being very unhappy in this job,' Charlotte recalled, although the diaries written contemporaneously offered no hint of unhappiness. He was forced 'to "clean" the civil service of the people who weren't Nazis or were against the Nazis', she told photographer Lothar Rübelt. In other words, to paraphrase her thinking, he had to purge, didn't really want to.

Still, she recognised the position did allow him to give full expression to his love of politics, even if it gave rise to intrigue and, when things went wrong, blame. Otto was 'stuck' in the job and often got into 'hot water'. 'The Nazis said he wasn't tough or thorough enough, the opposition complained he was too strict!' He became ill, his teeth rotted. A dentist recommended the removal of ten teeth, another offered a less draconian solution, root canal treatment. Such were the travails faced by Otto Wächter.

Then, unexpectedly, Seyss-Inquart was replaced as governor of Ostmark by Josef Bürckel. 'A German, from the Palatinate', Charlotte recorded, small, fat, rude, a drinker, with no hint of sensitivity or tact. Otto wanted out, and the arrival of war saved him. In August 1939, Germany and the Soviet Union signed the Molotov–Ribbentrop Pact, with a secret protocol to divide Europe into 'spheres of influence'. On the morning of Friday, 1 September, Germany found a pretext to attack Poland, causing Britain and France to declare war, to Charlotte's great disappointment. Two weeks later, as the Red Army moved into Poland from the east, Germany and the Soviet Union agreed to divide Poland and create a new frontier.

On 8 October Hitler annexed large parts of western Poland, with a view to making them part of the Greater German Reich. A few days later, he declared the establishment of a Government General to run parts of German-occupied Poland, naming Dr Hans Frank as his personal representative, the governor general. Arthur Seyss-Inquart was appointed as deputy, and Josef Bühler as state secretary, the number three. The territory of German-occupied Poland was divided into four districts – Kraków, Lublin, Radom and Warsaw – each with a governor who reported to Hitler and Dr Frank.

On 17 October, on the recommendation of Seyss-Inquart, Otto was appointed chief administrator for the District of Kraków. He was delighted, as was Charlotte. 'Full of joy to change posts, hoping to get a better task', she recorded.

He did not have to wait long for the better task.

11

1939, Kraków

'Poland was taken, Seyss-Inquart made *Gouverneur* of Krakow,' Charlotte noted. Horst's godfather appointed Otto as his deputy, a post he accepted with 'pleasure', as his father served in the area during the First World War. Having cleansed the Austrian civil service of Jews, he needed a new challenge.

In October 1939 Otto took up his post as chief administrator in the District of Kraków. Within a month Seyss-Inquart was moved on, and Otto appointed governor of Kraków, a safe pair of hands to serve under Dr Frank. He established his office in the Potocki Palace, on Kraków's main square, marked the occasion with a new *ex libris* slip for his books, a happy melding of his name, the family crest, the tower at Kraków town hall, and a fluttering swastika flag. The family remained in Vienna. 'Otto came home rarely,' Charlotte noted, but wrote often. His letters described life in Kraków and the palace, and encouraged Charlotte and the children to join him on the new adventure. Sooner rather than later, he hoped.

The family arrived a year later, in the winter of 1940, the children enrolled at the German school in Kraków. Charlotte rejoiced in her husband's new work, and the 'humane and sympathetic' way he exercised power. Others too held that view, she believed, including university professors and members of the Polish intelligentsia, who respected him as a 'decent man, of good character'. The Wächters occupied a large villa outside Kraków, while Otto's cousin, an architect, worked on a new palace on the other side of the River Vistula. Staff included a cook, scullery maid, parlour maid, nanny, gardener, coachman, a chauffeur and two bodyguards for Otto, and a housekeeper called Helena Scharkow.

As the family settled in Kraków, Otto discovered that working life with Dr Frank was not always easy, although Charlotte adopted a more positive attitude. 'Very intelligent', she recorded, 'I was very fond of him, because he was an excellent musician and well-versed in history', but also 'intuitive, volatile – an artistic sort'. She enjoyed his parties at Haus Kressendorf, a nineteenth-century palace requisitioned as a summer residence, and became a confidante to his wife, Brigitte. Otto rarely attended such events – no time or inclination – but Charlotte became a 'lady of the court', always available to converse with Frau Frank, or play chess with the governor general.

'Well, Frau Wächter,' he liked to say, 'fancy trying your luck again?' She did, and won often, which did not go down well. Frau Frank, older than her husband, larger and shorter than Charlotte, was prone to jealousy about her husband. 'She had no cause on my account,' Charlotte would tell the children. 'She knew how much I cared for my Otto, so she was never jealous of me, but often told me her most intimate thoughts and experiences.'

One weekend visit to Kressendorf, in the spring of 1940, remained in Charlotte's memory. As she prepared to return to Kraków, on the Sunday afternoon, Dr Frank enquired if she might like to accompany him and Brigitte to Vienna, on a 'special train', the night sleeper. She was not inclined to accept the invitation, but the governor general persisted, Otto encouraged her, so she accepted. On the train, they played several rounds of chess, which Charlotte won, then retired to a lavish sleeping compartment. She awoke at seven in the morning, as the train rolled into Vienna.

'My heart leapt for joy at being in my much-loved home city.' The governor general invited her on a stroll through the city, dusted with fresh snow, as Brigitte retired to a hotel. On a clear, fresh winter's day she and Frank strolled out of the Ostbahnhof, stood before the Stephansdom, visited the Schwarzenberg Palace and its gardens, and admired the skyline of Vienna and the large wheel on the Prater, which 'peeped out, with an air of curiosity'.

'What could be more lovely than the past?' she wrote. On they went, together, to the Karlskirche, which she'd never visited, where her parents were married. Frank talked animatedly about design and construction and insisted they visit the Habsburg graves in the imperial crypt. 'A long row of rulers, laid to rest for eternity, ephemeral memorials bearing witness to their existence and absolute power, offering a direct connection to the past.' They visited Beethoven's house, opposite the university, then walked to the Hotel Bristol on the Kärntner Ring for tea with her parents. 'Mutti was thrilled, chatted excitedly, everyone got on splendidly.' That evening they went to the opera,

Der Rosenkavalier, with music by Frank's friend Richard Strauss. Charlotte returned alone to Kraków, on the governor general's train.

Frank remained in Vienna, with other matters on his mind. He returned to Kraków a few days later to announce a decision to make it 'the city in the entire General Government that was the most free of Jews'. A month later the necessary orders were drawn up and signed, to be implemented by Otto. Most Jews would be expelled, and only a quarter of the Jewish population – about 15,000 people – allowed to remain.

Charlotte made no mention of such matters in her diary or letters. Occasionally, she referred to the challenges of working with Frank, or the power struggle with SS-Obergruppenführer Friedrich-Wilhelm Krüger, the SS and police leader in the territory. Once, she recorded, Otto even told Frank and Krüger – 'directly to their faces' – that their differences would be settled only when they were 'faced with the guillotine'.

In times when they were apart, the letters or postcards that passed between Charlotte and Otto tended to focus on the positives, a stream of warm and loving sentiments. They offered no hint of personal difficulty, or any suggestion of unease about any aspects of the work in which Otto was engaged. Nor did his SS file offer any indication of hesitation concerning his professional tasks. Life was good, Otto was on a fine, upward trajectory.

That too was how Charlotte saw things, looking back many years later. She characterised his term of office as governor in Kraków with a single word: humanity. 'He refused to shoot innocent people,' she recorded. 'He would always say: "You have to try to understand the people and govern with love."'

Charlotte was engaged in her own act of cleansing. The details about Otto's work lay elsewhere.

Otto became governor of Kraków a few days after the notorious *Sonderaktion Krakau*. In response to a public display of banned posters to commemorate Poland's national day of independence, reported by Otto to the governor general, Frank ordered him to have one male inhabitant taken from every house where the poster was hung, and for them to be shot. As a 'precautionary measure', Otto detained 120 'hostages'. Professors, lecturers and doctors were summoned to a meeting at the Jagiellonian University, where they were arrested, then deported, to the Sachsenhausen concentration camp, near Berlin, or to Dachau, near Munich. Some did not return. Otto's association with the action, and apparent support for it, coloured his reputation among locals. He was seen then, and still today, as a man of 'brutality'.

It was not the only such action. On the first day as governor he signed an order with the title 'Marking of Jews in the District of Kraków'. The order required Jews over the age of twelve to wear a visible marking, a blue Star of David on a white armband, precisely ten centimetres wide. It came into effect on 1 December, and those who failed to comply faced 'severe punishment'. The order was widely circulated, in German and Polish, on a poster that bore Otto's signature, 'Wächter, Gouverneur'.

Around this time, Otto wrote an effusive letter to Charlotte, in Vienna, delivered personally by Hanns Blaschke, the mayor of Vienna, who had recently visited Kraków. 'A lot is going on here,' Otto informed Charlotte. Several prominent comrades visited him, including Baldur van Schirach, head of the Hitler Youth, and Walther Funk, the minister for economic affairs. The Vienna Philharmonic visited and performed. 'All a great success', Otto reported. Frank was 'very delighted' with progress during his first days as governor.

There were, however, some 'not so nice things' to report. He mentioned acts of sabotage and shootings, as well as car bombs and an assassination attempt on 'G.G.', the governor general. Such matters required an immediate and brutal response. 'Tomorrow, I have to have 50 Poles publicly shot,' he wrote in the letter to his wife, so it was not a good time to visit. 'Wouldn't it be reckless to put you at risk?' He would remain in Kraków for the *Volksdeutsche* Christmas celebrations, and return to Vienna on the 22nd, in time for family celebrations. 'Much love and all the best to you and the "Hunkus",' he wrote. 'Your *Hümmi*!'

The execution of the Poles was a notorious act, the first such reprisal in German-occupied Poland, one that is still marked today with an annual event. The order came directly from Berlin, to set an example, as it followed an attack by the 'White Eagles', a partisan group, on a police station in Bochnia, a town near Kraków. Two German police officers, said to be Viennese, were killed, and the two perpetrators were caught, to be hung from street lamps.

On 18 December 1939, a pristine, cold morning, around fifty men from Bochnia – the number was not precisely recorded – were rounded up. Scantily clothed, they were led across a snow-covered field, gathered up in smaller groups, made to stand in freezing conditions, and shot by a line of twelve German soldiers, to be buried in a mass grave prepared by local Jews. One man escaped, it was said, who was later caught and survived a stay at Auschwitz before he made a new life in America.

I found reports which suggested that Otto attended the execution, forty kilometres from the Potocki Palace in Kraków. In one account, by an eyewitness, he was said to have intervened to advocate the release of five more men, spotted by Seyss-Inquart, 'leaning against a well, starved and half frozen', as they drove across the town square. Charlotte never mentioned the matter. I also came across information that the killings may have been recorded by a photographer, and the images collected in an album said to have been reproduced in four copies, one each for Hitler and Reichsmarschall Hermann Göring, and for the widows of the two assassinated Germans.

Charlotte was now pregnant with their fifth child, although this did not stop her from skiing on the Schneeberg. She fell and broke a leg – 'Five hours screaming, spiral fracture, bone burrowed so far into the flesh that I could hear the angels sing' – which required weeks of recuperation, mostly spent at a newly acquired farmhouse in the small town of Thumersbach, on Lake Zell. The family knew the area well, as Otto's father once hoped to buy a property there – Schloss Prielau – but lost the family's savings on war bonds. Once owned by the widow of Hugo von Hofmannsthal, writer and librettist of Richard Strauss's *Rosenkavalier*, Schloss Prielau was now inhabited by Josef Thorak, a sculptor favoured by Hitler and Albert Speer. He became the Wächters' neighbour.

The farmhouse in Thumersbach was 'bought' with money from the sale of the house in Berlin. 'A small summer house', Charlotte called it, sixteen hectares, a farmer's cottage, stables and the Schifferegger family as tenants. The larger and more desirable places had already been 'snapped up'. She glossed over its provenance, offered by the local party leader – 'old comrade, kind fellow' – after Ernst Kaltenbrunner appropriated it from Dr Franz Rehrl, the former governor of Salzburg, who swapped the farmhouse on the lake for a wooden bunk at the Ravensbrück concentration camp. 'Anti-Hitler', Charlotte explained, nonchalantly, having fought off interest from Herr Porsche, of the VW works. Only later, long after the war, did she suggest any qualms about the acquisition, but those were quickly forgotten. Without the farmhouse, 'how would I get out of Vienna and find some peace and quiet?'

Thumersbach was a place for 'good, healthy, restorative times', one that was 'full of life and happiness'. As she wrote these words, Otto was on a trip to Soviet-controlled Lemberg to arrange a swap of refugees, but agreement was prevented by the desire of 'countless' Jews to return to the Government General or the Reich ('We would rather sit in a concentration camp in the Reich than in the Soviet territory,' he recorded one as saying, as 'the Führer has said he will also resolve the Jewish question'). Otto would not allow Jews to return, as other refugees could, and the negotiations collapsed.

Europe was in a state of turmoil as the Nazis progressed on many fronts. 'Holland capitulates', Charlotte recorded in her diary on 15 May 1940. Three days later, 'Brussels falls'. Then, 19 May, 'Seyss [to] Holland', where Horst's godfather became the Führer's representative in The Hague. And 23 June, 'France peace agreement signed yesterday', a reference to the act of surrender. The victories brought happiness to Charlotte and visitors to Thumersbach, including Josef Wächter and Otto's fervently Nazi sister Ilse von Böheim ('huge help in the kitchen, wonderful comrade, loved by the children, although strict'). At the same time, war approached the homeland, as the Royal Air Force bombed Berlin and Hamburg in September, also noted in the diary.

Heidegund, their fifth child, was born on 16 October, in Vienna, a 'sweet, intelligent thing'. Stuck in Kraków, Otto arrived two days after the birth, detained by war. 'No end in sight', he told Charlotte. Mutti and Josef visited, proud grandparents. Heinrich Himmler sent a congratulatory note, with a gift. 'The Reichsführer has sent us a very pretty candlestick, white porcelain, with a large yellow candle,' Otto enthused. He instructed Charlotte to send him a replacement photograph, as he sent the one of 'Horsti licking his finger'.

As war raged, the family spent Christmas in Zakopane, in the High Tatras, a place with an important Gestapo contingent. They were accompanied by a nanny, which allowed Charlotte to ski with Otto and the two older children. Liesl stayed close to her mother, Otto and Otto junior came 'one after the other'. In Kraków they returned to a new home that was not much to Charlotte's liking, despite the efforts of architect Lippert. Otto tried to revive her spirits with plans to buy a fourth property, a vast castle on the River Vistula, with excellent views of Kraków. He would call it Wartenberg, to honour the name he used while on the run in 1934. He hoped one day to take the title of Otto Wächter von Wartenberg.

Otto threw himself into his work, and stopped using his father's title of nobility, 'von'. As governor, with responsibility for the entire civilian population, including transport, housing and food, he faithfully implemented the decision to expel tens of thousands of the city's Jewish inhabitants into the surrounding countryside. In November

1940 he signed another order, to prohibit Jews from entering Kraków without a special permit. All others were to be expelled, with twenty-five kilograms of possessions, but no more.

In early 1941 he moved to the logical next step. Having required Jews to identify themselves, stripped them of rights and expelled most from Kraków, he prepared an order to force those who remained in the city to be gathered in a single location. On 3 March he signed the decree to create the Kraków ghetto. Around this time, on a trip back to Vienna, Charlotte wrote to say she was being treated for a 'heart deficiency', which required a period of rest. 'It's my destiny to be unhappy,' she told Otto, worrying about his 'youthful vigour' in contrast to her parlous state. She sent instructions for the renovations of the new house: he should move the furniture to the attic, make her a fitted wardrobe to store laundry and clothes, and follow the plan she sent him. She drew a little map of her own.

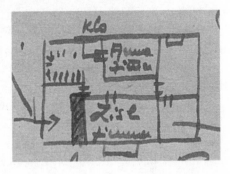

Otto's decree required all the city's remaining Jews to move to the ghetto, on pain of death. Thousands were forced from their homes in the city's Kazimierz district, across the River Vistula, into the Podgorze district. Non-Jewish residents were removed from the ghetto area. Parishioners from St Joseph's Catholic Church, located just outside the ghetto wall, objected, but Otto brushed away the appeals. The pastor was lucky he didn't put the church in the ghetto, Otto told him.

A few non-Jews chose to remain in the ghetto area. Tadeusz Pankiewicz kept open his pharmacy, *Apteka Pad Orlem* ('Under the Eagle'), on Plac Zgody. He witnessed first-hand the consequences of Otto's order. 'Inhuman deportations, monstrous crimes and the constant degradation of human dignity and self-respect of the ghetto's occupants.'

This account reminded me of a passage in a novel entitled *Kaputt*. It was published in 1944 by Curzio Malaparte, two years after he visited occupied Poland with *Corriere della Sera*, the Italian newspaper when, it seems, he met the Wächters. 'Dinner with Wächter', he recorded in his diary, in January 1942. 'His wife receives us', he wrote, in a fine country house on a hill, about eight kilometres from Krakow. 'Pretty' he observed. 'Wächter too is Viennese, went to school in Trieste, speaks Italian.' The journalist's words appeared factual and evocative.

Kaputt is written in the journalist's style, based on first-hand experience, as the diary entry and three articles he published in *Corriere* make clear ('Dr Wächter is Viennese, young, elegant and speaks Italian very well with a sweet accent from Trieste', Malaparte reported). A scene in the novel described a lavish dinner party held in Warsaw's Brühl Palace in February 1942, hosted by Governor Ludwig Fischer, attended by Charlotte and Otto. Over the course of the meal, as wine is served, conversation turned to the residents of the ghetto created by Otto, and Malaparte's account of two Jews he there encountered, an old man and a boy of sixteen. Both were naked. Is this conversation fact or fiction, or an amalgam?

The journalist-turned-novelist proceeds to describe Otto's gentle account of how Jews, being gathered by the Gestapo from the ghetto, would undress and distribute their clothing to relatives and friends, no longer having any use for them. Malaparte's narrator says he has also visited the ghetto, and found it 'very interesting', which prompts a reaction from Charlotte.

'I don't like going into the ghetto,' said Frau Wächter, 'it is very sad.'

'Very sad, why?' asked Governor Fischer.

'So schmutzig – So dirty,' said Frau Brigitte Frank.

'Ja, so schmutzig – Yes, so dirty,' said Frau Fischer . . .

There is no doubt that during the visit to Poland, Malaparte met these individuals. Whether the words and emotions he recorded – including Charlotte's reaction – were actually spoken, however, is not clear.

'In the ghetto of Cracow,' said Wächter, 'I have ordered the relatives of the dead to defray the expenses of the burial. And I have obtained good results.'

'I feel sure,' I said ironically, 'that the death rate dropped overnight.'

'You've guessed right; it has dropped,' said Wächter laughing.

Governor Fischer is reported as recounting the burial of Jews in the ghetto, a layer of corpses and a layer of lime, then a layer of lime and another layer of corpses. 'It's the most sanitary system,' Wächter responds, as they eat.

A few days later, Malaparte attended a second dinner, hosted by Hans Frank at the Belvedere Castle in Warsaw, to honour Max Schmeling, the world champion boxer. Charlotte was present. After dinner the group visited the Warsaw ghetto. 'I was in the first car with Frau Fischer, Frau Wächter and Governor-General Frank', Malaparte writes in the novel, as other guests followed in separate vehicles. The cars stopped in front of a gate in the high red brick wall that surrounded the ghetto, the entrance to the 'forbidden city', where the guests got out.

'In Cracow,' said Frau Wächter, 'my husband has built a wall of an eastern design with elegant curves and graceful battlements. The Cracow Jews certainly have nothing to complain about. An elegant wall in the Jewish style.'

The guests were said to have laughed, as they stamped their feet on the frozen snow. Was Charlotte's presence during that visit to the ghetto, and the pride expressed in her husband's wall, a figment of Malaparte's imagination? Possibly not. Her own diary recorded an earlier visit to the Warsaw ghetto, on 2 April 1941. 'Terrible snowfall and very cold', she wrote. Later that day she went shopping, a search for shoes, but without success. In the evening she attended a concert of classical music.

It is said that a line divides fact and fiction, the real and the imagined. Where it lies, and how it shifts over time, is not always so clear.

12

Bronisława

In the course of writing this book I made several visits to Kraków. I well remember one occasion, when I stood before one of the few fragments of the ghetto wall that remained, imagining Charlotte as she passed through the gate to the space that lay within.

On another occasion I climbed the hill to the Wawel Castle, headquarters of the Government General. In the company of Niklas Frank, I stood before Leonardo da Vinci's *Lady with an Ermine*. Later we stood on the balcony he knew as a child, and looked across the city.

In the Potocki Palace, where Otto signed letters on stationery manufactured by Huber & Lerner of Vienna, I wandered the corridors, lined with cabinets from that period, which might have contained the governor's personal and professional stationery. I sat on an ancient sofa, and stood on the balcony outside his office.

A friend introduced me to Bronisława Horowitz, known as Niusia. She is the last survivor of the group saved by Oskar Schindler, a worker in one of his factories. Niusia was nine years old when Germany conquered Kraków – 'panic, planes and sirens, but everyone said war was coming so we were not surprised' – and Otto became governor. She was a child, too young to recall the moment or his name. She did, however, remember a visit from the Germans, who ordered them to leave their apartment, and one detail stayed with her, as the family possessions were thrown out of a window. 'Many were coloured lilac, my mother loved that colour.'

A mention of the decree signed by Otto, the one that ordered Jews to wear armbands with a Star of David, prompted another memory. 'I remember wearing the short, white armband,' Niusia recalled. 'I didn't feel anything wearing it, but I was scared, I was small.' Her reaction was nothing compared to that of her parents, who transferred their anxieties to the children.

Otto ordered the creation of the ghetto in March 1941, and Niusia lived there from the first day. 'First we lived at Limanovski Street, number 20, then on *Rynek*, the main square, at number 1, near the wall. Later we moved to a single room, filled with many people.' She spent more than a year there, with her brother. In the spring of 1942 her parents learned that the ghetto was to be liquidated, but were unaware of the order for the 'resettlement' of its inhabitants, signed, a few weeks after the Wannsee Conference, by Otto's comrade and friend Rudolf Pavlu. Otto brought him to Kraków, a man described by a secretary who worked in Otto's government as *ein Judenhasser*, a Jew-hater, someone who flew into a mad, furious rage the moment the word 'Jew' was mentioned.

Niusia and her family escaped to Bochnia, where Otto had overseen the public execution of fifty Poles, to another ghetto. Later they were transported to the Plaszow concentration camp, on the outskirts of Kraków, run by Amon Göth. There she saw gallows, starvation and acts of infanticide, small babies and children being killed on the territory of Governor Wächter. 'People arrived in lorries and buses, tried to make children feel better, and within a few minutes the hair of the children was cut, they were put in a large ditch and killed.' This happened two or three times a day, sometimes five times.

Her family worked. She made brushes while her father toiled in a storeroom. Her uncle, a musician, played at Amon Göth's home, where he met Oskar Schindler, who intervened to save the family, invited to join the workforce of his *Deutsche Emailwarenfabrik*. Niusia was one of two hundred women rescued by Schindler from Auschwitz, then taken to another work camp, Arbeitslager Brünnlitz, east of Prague, where Schindler moved his factory.

Niusia survived the war, and later became a beautician. She asked questions about Otto, the man who signed the decrees that required her to wear a white armband and live in a ghetto, and about his family. She seemed numb as I gave answers. The trauma was constant, she said in a weary voice. 'There is pain, drama, suffering, I cannot forget; the sun can shine, or it can be summer, but there is always a darkness.' She was able to sleep only with the help of medication.

'A fragment of the ghetto wall remains,' Niusia said. Each year she joined an annual walk that passed it, a painful act of remembrance. 'I go because they ask me, but if they didn't ask I wouldn't go – it is sad, and for me too difficult.'

I shared with her what Charlotte wrote about the wall, its attractive oriental style. 'Nobody was interested in that,' Niusia responded sharply. 'We were hungry, trying to survive.' The light in her eyes shone bright. 'It's absurd.'

13

1941, Kraków

Did Otto have any qualms about his work in Kraków? If he did they were not reflected in the many cards and letters he sent Charlotte.

One, written shortly after he ordered the construction of the Kraków ghetto, confirmed his commitment to the principles for which his government stood. It was a response to a letter from his father, Josef, which brought to his attention the travails of an acquaintance. Herr Otto Schremmer had a daughter, married to a Jew, and had a young child who was subject to the laws on Jews. Might Otto intervene to assist the child, who resided in his territory?

Otto responded promptly, with affection and firmness. 'Dear Papa!', Herr Schremmer's case was 'complicated and unpleasant', so he passed it to the head of his Ministry of Interior, Herr Engler, who reviewed the matter and concluded, in a written report, that Herr Schremmer's granddaughter was correctly to be 'considered a Jew'. She was not entitled to a normal identity card. The law was the law, Otto told his father, and he hoped the clarification was helpful. Such cases of nationality and race had an 'unpleasant' aspect, but he wanted to be clear: the laws may be 'unfortunate' for the individuals concerned, but they were 'necessary for the public benefit', for the good of the group.

He ended the letter with expressions of filial affection. He hoped the old man was happy to be with his daughter-in-law and grandchildren, and especially 'special protégé Horsti'.

In June 1941, as Charlotte visited the Seyss-Inquarts in The Hague, Hitler launched Operation Barbarossa, a surprise attack on Soviet-occupied Poland. The Wehrmacht headed east at speed, and within a few days the District of Galicia and Lemberg, the capital, were taken and incorporated into the Government General. Karl Lasch became governor of the new territory, a new gubernatorial colleague for Otto, under the authority of Hans Frank.

The development coincided with a difficult moment for Charlotte and Otto, as she learned about yet another affair. 'Otto told me about a Waldtraute that he met and who fell in love with him.' They spent much of the summer apart, he in Kraków, she at the farmhouse in Thumersbach, with trips with the Franks to the Salzburg Festival, the highlight a performance of *Der Freischütz*. Otto visited briefly, and despite her anger Charlotte complained of feeling 'very low' when he was absent. 'I am sad that we are always apart, even though we love each other so much.'

In early September she visited Vienna. 'All is well', she noted in her diary, twice in a single week, except that it was not. She typed out two letters to Otto, furious and bitter, which may or may not have been sent. The first reprimanded him for not having taken her on a trip to Budapest, like Hans Frank and his wife. You've reached a 'certain level of success', she wrote, 'so it seems you no longer need me', a 'hindrance' and an 'idiot'. 'I am no longer willing to be your "maid and nanny",' she declared, and there would be no more children. She declared him to be liberated, free to dally with the many women who wanted to 'possess' a governor.

Within a few days, as often seemed to happen, Charlotte's mood changed. 'I have not felt this good and young for a while,' she wrote in a second letter, and wished him success at work. She would keep her distance if he felt that she and the children were a nuisance. He should reflect on their future. 'Think about it carefully,' she wrote, ending with a 'Heil Hitler!' and signing off as *'Lotte Wächter'*.

She was not able to keep a distance for long. A few weeks later the family was back together in Kraków, a degree of harmony restored, as the final touches were put to their splendid new home. 'Otto hammered the final nail into the beam,' Charlotte enthused at the roofing ceremony of Schloss Wartenberg, which overlooked the River Vistula. That was 15 November, followed by a concert by the Kraków Philharmonic, who performed Brahms' Second Symphony and Beethoven's Seventh, accompanied by pianist Elly Ney.

Otto's long hours involved early starts and late finishes, with many meetings ending after midnight. 'I long for a separate bedroom,' Charlotte recorded, as her husband awoke early to sign orders on housing, food, transport and the creation of a new ghetto, coupled with a decree that imposed draconian penalties on Jews who set foot outside its limits. Conflicts arose, including a bitter one between Frank and SS-Obergruppenführer Krüger, on the allocation of tasks between the civilian administration and the SS.

Otto attended cabinet meetings at the Wawel Castle. An important one took place on 20 October, when the minutes recorded Otto's view that 'ultimately a radical solution of the *Judenfrage* [Jewish question] was unavoidable'. A few weeks later, on 16 December, the governors of all five districts of occupied Poland attended a full cabinet meeting. They were joined by the heads of the SS and police of Lublin and Galicia districts, Friedrich Katzmann and Odilo Globočnik. On the instruction of Heinrich Himmler, Globus was actively engaged in the construction of a first extermination camp on the territory of German-occupied Poland, being built near Belzec, a town with excellent rail connections to Lemberg.

Frank told the cabinet of a new policy, ahead of a meeting to be held in January 1942 in Berlin, at a villa on Lake Wannsee. The 'total elimination of the Jews', the governor general announced. All necessary measures were to be taken in each district of the Government General, in cooperation with the SS and the police. Otto and the other leaders were encouraged to eliminate all feelings of pity for the great 'migration' that was about to begin. 'We must annihilate the Jews, wherever we find them and wherever it is possible,' the official minutes recorded. The decision was unambiguous, without dissent, not from Otto, or anyone else.

Four days after the cabinet meeting, Otto sent Frank warm good wishes for the holiday season and the new year, and for the singular new enterprise on which he was now embarked. 'It will bring me great joy and proud satisfaction, in the coming year, to work as a loyal follower on your project.'

A month later the Wannsee Conference settled the details of the 'great Jewish migration'. Tasks were allocated and responsibilities determined, under the direction of SS-Obergruppenführer Reinhard Heydrich, Otto's former boss at the SD in Berlin. The state secretary of the Government General, Dr Josef Bühler, attended as Hans Frank's representative, to offer the territory of the Government General as a place to which to send the Jews. Conference minutes were taken by Adolf Eichmann, another former SD comrade. The new German living space would be purged of all Jews, by legal means, with 'forced emigration' applied to eleven million Jews across Europe, one quarter of whom lived in the territory of the Government General.

Upon his return to Kraków, Dr Bühler told Governor Frank that

Europe would be combed through, 'from West to East'. The evacuated Jews would be taken to transit ghettos, then transported to the
east, and the 'Final Solution' would begin on his territory, in the
Government General. Transport was good, the administrative agencies of the districts were available to play their role.

The Wannsee Conference concluded on the evening of 20 January,
with a cocktail reception. The following day Otto travelled to Berlin,
then to Kraków where, on 22 January, Frank told him that Karl Lasch
was being removed as governor of the District of Galicia, allegedly for
corruption. Otto was to be named as his successor. That evening the
Franks and the Wächters dined together at the Wawel Castle.

The next day, 23 January, Otto was appointed governor of the
District of Galicia. Incredibly pleased, Charlotte recorded, although
she felt sad. 'What will await us?' she wondered, with yet another
move, although the new location had its attractions. She learned
that Otto was personally selected by Adolf Hitler, as a man trusted
to implement decisions taken at the highest levels, at and after the
Wannsee Conference. 'We need to send our best man to Lemberg, and
I've been advised he is Otto Wächter, Governor of Kraków.' Thus did
Charlotte record Hitler's decision. Two days later, Otto and Charlotte
were in Warsaw for a boxing match with Max Schmeling, the former
world champion.

On 28 January 1942, Otto was driven from Warsaw to Lemberg to
take up the new post, but without Charlotte. 'Very alone', she noted,
and kept a newspaper clipping of his appointment.

14

1942, Lemberg

Otto arrived in Lemberg on 28 January 1942, a return to a medieval city that was, for two centuries, a regional capital of the Austro-Hungarian empire. In November 1918 it was Lwów, in newly independent Poland, then from September 1939 it was Lvov, after the Soviets occupied. In July 1941 Germany occupied the territory and the city was Lemberg once more. With a population of about 420,000, the city was the third largest in the Government General, and the wider District of Galicia had a population of more than a million, a roughly equal number of Poles, Ukrainians and Jews. Within a few weeks Otto had signed a decree prohibiting Jews from certain employment, and a year later most of the Jewish population had been 'liquidated' – more than half a million human beings. With many Poles sent to the Reich, as forced labour, Otto looked to the Ukrainians as potential allies.

Charlotte made no mention of such matters in her writings, which focused on the perks, Otto's sense of liberation from the shackles of Hans Frank, the large villa at number 11 Leuthenstrasse, their new home and intense social activity. Big and beautiful, Charlotte enthused of their new home, a fine place to welcome visitors, from abroad and across Galicia. A lunch party for twenty might be followed by afternoon tea for forty. The city was on the way to the Russian front, so people could drop in, war as a catalyst for social events. Charlotte had a nanny and a large, attentive staff, a cook, a scullery maid, chamber maids, two valets, a coachman and a chauffeur.

Otto spent two and a half years in Lemberg, a time of 'enormous joy' during which, according to Charlotte, he implemented 'his own ideas on humane and good governance'. There was much to be done in the territory, as people retained positive feelings towards Austria and the imperial monarchy. There was also a sense of family connection, as this was where Josef served during the First World War, awarded the Order of Maria Theresa. 'The task is bigger and better and an exceptional accolade,' Otto told his father, but also more difficult, politically and economically, after two years of Soviet rule. He hoped to master the job, as a Wächter raised in Josef's military tradition.

Josef visited in a bespoke lieutenant general's uniform, specially tailored for the trip. Father and son travelled First World War battle-fields, setting off with excitement and a large number of attendants. Otto was delighted to attain the highest rank of his father, by the age of forty, fully in charge of governance. His team included Dr Egon Höller, as personal assistant; *Abteilungsleiter* Otto Bauer, as deputy and head of department; *Chef des Amtes* Dr Ludwig Losacker, as head of the office; and Theobald Thier as SS-Gruppenführer, responsible for liaison with the SS.

The period was not without difficulties. There was some sense of pessimism, caused by problems in the east, Frank's unpredictable and florid leadership style, and tensions between the civilian administration and the SS. In the east, Reichskommissar Erich Koch 'ravaged like a Caesar' in Ukraine, Charlotte recalled. She received personal accounts from Hans Fischböck, who decided to leave his post under Koch and move to The Hague, to work with Arthur Seyss-Inquart on the occu-pation of the Netherlands. Koch's brutality had the merit of casting Otto's approach to governance – 'with love' – in a more generous light. Charlotte recalled a first meeting between Otto, in full SS uniform, and Metropolitan Andrey Sheptytsky. A miracle, the bishop told him, with tears in his eyes, as recorded by Charlotte for the children, although she was not present and never actually met the bishop.

*

She would go to Lemberg in the summer, after a few months apart from Otto in Vienna and Thumersbach, where she enjoyed visits from the family, evenings at the opera and theatre, and an active social life. Otto sent advice from afar, articles on religious studies and musical education that appeared in *Das Reich*, on the education of the young. 'Please read it with regard to our male offspring,' he wrote of one article. 'You can see the hand of Schirach in this' – a reference to his friend, the head of the Hitler Youth.

In the spring, Otto travelled to various parts of the Government General, including Lublin, where Globus was based, and Warsaw. On 9 June he was in Berlin for the funeral of Reinhard Heydrich, assassinated in Prague. He listened to Himmler's funeral oration, declaring a 'sacred duty to annihilate the enemies of our people without weakness'.

In the summer, Charlotte took the children back to Thumersbach. 'In my heart, I'm very much with you in that wonderful place,' Otto wrote. Immersed in occupation activity, he encouraged her to swim and walk, to recuperate from another illness, to enjoy herself. 'I have such a great desire for you,' she responded. 'Visit soon,' she implored, 'and bring Hans Frank!'

She did not explain to Otto why she made the suggestion, keeping her thoughts on a tight hold. The secret truth was that she had fallen in love with the governor general, as her diary made clear.

1 February 1942, 'I wore Frank's boots, sloppily.'

4 March, coffee with Frank in Berlin, felt sad when he left 'for the Führer's headquarters'.

6 March, 'he played the piano, I wrote'. Later, on the special train from Berlin to Kraków 'we sat together as she [Frau Frank] went to sleep'. Late that night they played three rounds of chess, 'he won twice, I once, very nice, it is too nice to be together. To sleep at 11 p.m. When he realised we were alone he got up with a start and left abruptly.'

7 May, at the Wawel Castle, 'I breathed in his air, how much I would like to see him again . . . I don't know what to do, so intensely do I concern myself with my Hansl. I am so in love and long for the moment I will see him again. I have to wait for the moment. How many times a day do I think of him, he is so spirited, so full of zest, thank God no one knows.'

21 June, 'dreamt of Governor General, think of him a lot, must be love'.

I sent a copy of the diary entries to Frank's son Niklas, several years after he first introduced me to Horst. 'Sensational!' he wrote. 'Nobody knew till now that she was in love with my father!' He wondered, jokingly, whether Horst could be his brother.

In August, the governor general's bubble burst. Hitler stripped Frank of various positions, after he gave a series of lectures at universities around Germany to express concern about the rule of law in the Third Reich, and the need for judges to be more independent, albeit in a Nazi sort of way. Frank told his wife he wanted a divorce, because he was in love with another woman, a flame from the past, from his youth. The woman was not Charlotte, however, who was summoned by Brigitte Frank, to pour out her heart and tell her she would never accept a divorce. 'He seems mad, loves another,' Charlotte noted wistfully.

During this period Charlotte and Otto rarely saw each other, but they wrote frequently, mostly about items of local news. In Vienna, their friend Hanns Blaschke had been appointed as mayor, and the tenants were taking good care of the Villa Mendl. Otto wrote vaguely of 'negotiations' in Berlin, causing Charlotte to complain that he'd forgotten about his wife and children. 'Did you even try to call on Lischen's eighth birthday? Everyone remembered, except you!'

In July, Charlotte finally arrived in Lemberg, where she wrote to Otto junior, now twelve, to encourage him about the impending move. A 'very, very nice' place. The house had a big garden, a tennis court and swimming pool, and came with a pony that pulled a little carriage.

She brought a gift for Otto, a portrait of herself, distracted and sad. 'For my love, in remembrance', she wrote on the photograph. Decades later I saw it hanging on a wall of Horst's bedroom. Yes, he told me,

she looked sad. I had still not yet seen her diaries, so knew nothing of her infatuation with the governor general at the moment the photograph was taken. If Horst knew, he did not share the information.

Hans Frank visited the Wächters in Lemberg on Saturday, 1 August, to celebrate the first anniversary of the incorporation of the District of Galicia into the General Government. Charlotte spent some of the day with him, playing chess and eating, until he left with Otto for various meetings. Later in the evening she beat him at chess, which caused him to retire early to bed, angry.

She kept her feelings about Frank to herself, and said nothing in her diary or elsewhere about the speech Frank delivered that day. In the aula of the university, he announced the implementation of the Final Solution in Galicia. The audience applauded him warmly, as Otto sat in the front row.

'Party comrade Wächter! I have to say, you did well,' Frank told him. 'Lemberg is once again a true, proud, German city. I do not speak about the Jews who are still here, we will deal with them, of course.'

'Incidentally,' the governor general continued, 'I don't seem to have any of that trash hanging around here today. What's going on? They tell me that there were thousands and thousands of those flat-footed primitives in this city once upon a time – but there hasn't been a single one to be seen since I arrived. Don't tell me that you've been treating them badly?' The minutes of the meeting noted that Frank's words were received in the aula with 'lively applause'.

On 6 August, after Charlotte left for Vienna, a high-level meeting was held in Lemberg, the subject recorded in a short note with the heading 'Solution to the Jewish question in Galicia'. SS-Brigadeführer Katzmann informed Dr Losacker and Dr Bauer, Otto's deputy and chief of staff, that the Jews would be resettled, expelled or liquidated, so that 'within half a year no free Jew would be left in the General Government'. A few Jewish skilled craftsmen would be retained in special *Judenlager* (Jewish camps) in various districts. Four days later, *die Grosse Aktion* began, as tens of thousands of Jews in Lemberg were rounded up and transported to the extermination camp built by Globus at nearby Belzec.

On Sunday, 16 August Otto wrote a long letter from Kraków, attending a party congress where he played ping-pong with Pavlu during the breaks. 'There was much to do in Lemberg after you left,' he told Charlotte. The harvest data was recorded, workers were transferred to labour camps in the Reich ('already 250,000 have been sent from the District!') and there were 'the current large Jewish operations (*Judenaktionen*)'. After Bochnia, this was a rare reference in a personal letter to matters of a kind that invariably passed in silence. His tone was positive, the progress good, as the party convention went well and everything was 'lovely' at home in Lemberg, even if the house-keeper did cause problems with the Polish staff. Less positive was the suicide of a young soldier, in the house, which gave rise to unfortunate rumours. 'Unrequited love', Otto suggested, 'too weak to live'. 'Lots of love, forever', Otto signed off: 'With Hitler – all or nothing'.

He sent a drawing by Pavlu, who added a few words of reassurance, that Otto was a 'paragon of virtue!!' Pavlu's wife Trude scribbled that Otto was under strict surveillance. Otto returned early to Lemberg, as Himmler – one of the 'big ones' – had decided to make an impromptu visit. 'I arrived just in time at the airport,' Otto told Charlotte. Himmler's official diary recorded the engagements, from the arrival at Lemberg airport on the evening of the 17th, where he was met by Otto, Globus and Katzmann. The four had a 'meeting' – no details offered – followed by dinner. The next morning Otto and Katzmann took Himmler on a 'sightseeing' tour, to see the 'Jewish camps on Durchgangstrasse IV', the road being built to connect Przemysl, Lemberg, Tarnopol and Taganrog, in the east. They visited camps at Jaktorow and Lackie, about sixty kilometres east of Lemberg, had lunch and returned to Lemberg, from where Himmler returned to Berlin by plane.

All went well in the end, Otto reported. So well, in fact, that he felt 'almost ashamed'. The relationship was entirely harmonious, 'very nice and amicable', and Himmler, with only positive things to say about her husband, stood by him on all fundamental matters. Otto felt able to take a break, a trip by canoe down the River Dniester, with two colleagues.

In early September, Martin Bormann, Hitler's closest colleague, received a first-hand, positive account of Otto's work in Lemberg. Wächter had stabilised the situation in Galicia, which was now in a better state than other districts of the Government General, having removed civil servants who lacked character or competence. The report noted that he was assisted by his 'very capable' department chief, Dr Losacker, and noted Otto's views on Hans Frank (sexually dependent on his wife, and more suited to the life of an artist or scholar).

While Otto entertained Himmler, Charlotte's parents and his father visited Thumersbach. Josef took daily walks with Horst, a beloved grandson, while Charlotte attended the Salzburg Festival with the Fischböcks. A day of poetry at Schloss Leopoldskron, Mozart's *Marriage of Figaro* at the Festspielhaus, then a 'simple dinner' for fifty poets and writers, which went on until the early hours. In the days that followed she enjoyed a performance of *Much Ado About*

Nothing, although it left her 'exhausted', and a thrilling performance of Bruckner's Seventh Symphony, her favourite piece of music. It sounded even better when one was seated in the Gauleiter's box.

She stayed with the Lipperts, and visited the nearby Schubert Villa, with Trudl Fischböck, who liked the property and wanted it. It was much sought-after, not least by Herbert von Karajan, who wanted other residents to be removed so it was quiet enough for him to work. 'I'll be interested to see who gets it,' Charlotte told Otto. The children were well, little Horst the 'heart and soul, like Grandpa, very sensitive'. The state of the kitchens at home in Lemberg continued to occupy her. 'What happened with the ovens?' she enquired.

Four days later, on 27 August, Charlotte expressed happiness that Himmler's visit went well, and looked forward to a return to Lemberg. In the meantime, excursions around Thumersbach were 'unbelievably lovely'. They took hikes to the remote Schmittenhöhe, lunched by a pond, swam and lay naked as babies on the moss in the splendid sunshine. She felt 'overwhelmed by the grandeur of nature'. Thank you, thank you, she wrote, a thousand times, from the bottom of her heart, for making possible their 'unspeakably beautiful' home.

As the family enjoyed the mountains, and the *Grosse Aktion* reached its conclusion in Lemberg, Otto took a canoe trip on the Dniester, 180 kilometres of river, a few days of camping, fishing and simple food ('mostly potatoes, corn, always tea'). On his return to Lemberg, auditors arrived from Berlin, as problems in the Government General made it into the local newspapers, and work on the garden slowed. A lack of manual labour, Otto complained. 'The Jews are being deported in increasing numbers, and it's hard to get powder for the tennis court.'

Charlotte hoped the war might be over the following year, although it seemed unlikely. As Otto reported air raids in Kraków and Warsaw, she returned to visit the Schubert Villa once again. '*Mein liebstes Hümmchen!*' she wrote from Thumersbach, with a pencil drawing in colour of the family in movement. 'Could you enquire with the Gauleiter if I might help myself to some of the old furniture?' And, she added, she hoped they'd spend their tenth wedding anniversary together, on 11 September, as he had 'softened' her hard old head. If there were difficult times, it was only ever because they were apart.

Otto was not able to join Charlotte for the anniversary, consumed by problems in Galicia, including food shortages and a negative report from the audit commission in Berlin. A visit by the Interior Ministry offered a ray of light, reporting 'a very positive impression' of Otto's work in Lemberg. He posted a clipping from the *Reich* ('eating fruit before bed is bad for your teeth'), and described a wonderful performance of Mozart's *Die Entführung aus dem Serail* at the Kraków Opera, with visiting Italians. *Hümmi* passed on his best wishes for the anniversary, with love and a heartfelt 'Heil Hitler'.

'The path of life can be mountainous,' Charlotte replied with regard to his travails, so he should take things on the chin. She returned to the Schubert Villa for a third time, with the governor, and visited a nature reserve at Neukirchen, in the company of Josef Thorack, to see some of the forty-eight vultures from the Caucasus being looked after with special care and protection.

As Christmas approached, Otto reported positively to Himmler on the situation in Galicia. The Reichsführer responded with appreciation on 'the beautiful picture from Lemberg', a situation of calm and order. This was to Otto's credit, attributable 'to the harmonious work between you and the competent Katzmann', Himmler wrote, and 'the real cooperation between your administration and the SS and police in your district'. Hoping to return soon to Lemberg, he copied the letter to his deputy, SS-Obergruppenführer Karl Wolff, head of Himmler's personal staff, who Otto knew from the days in Berlin.

Otto may also have been aware of another, less pleasant item of news, which arrived at the end of the year. The *New York Times* reported charges against ten leading Nazis, identified by the Polish government in exile, for crimes committed on the territory of Poland.

Hans Frank was listed as number one, with several of Otto's comrades also named, including Friedrich-Wilhelm Krüger ('terror and executions'), Odilo Globočnik ('Jewbaiter') and Ludwig Fischer ('Warsaw ghettos his speciality'). Otto came in at number seven, his name misspelt. He was 'infamous for the extermination of the Polish intelligentsia'. Under his orders, the *Times* reported, a hundred professors from the university were sent to concentration camps; many died, others went mad.

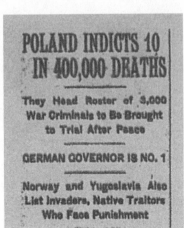

POLAND INDICTS 10 IN 400,000 DEATHS

They Head Roster of 3,000 War Criminals to Be Brought to Trial After Peace

GERMAN GOVERNOR IS NO. 1

Norway and Yugoslavia Also List Invaders, Native Traitors Who Face Punishment

15

Michael

I have often wondered about life in Lemberg, under the 'humane' rule of Otto Wächter. It is a city I have come to know, the place of my grandfather's birth. In writing *East West Street* I learned that Leon's entire family in the region was extinguished, but this turned out to be not entirely accurate. Two years after the book was published, I received a letter from a kindly professor of engineering in Los Angeles. 'Please forgive me for bothering you with this unexpected message,' he wrote, and explained he was surprised to come across the name Natan Flaschner in the book, Leon's uncle. Natan had a son, Henryk, who escaped from Lemberg, he recounted, who was the letter writer's father. Henryk spent the rest of his life in search of other survivors, but never found Leon, his first cousin, who also survived.

A few years ago, in New York, I was introduced to another man who lived through that time of 'good governance' in Lemberg, a rare survivor from the territory controlled by Otto in which more than a million people perished. Today a distinguished paediatrician, his name is Michael Katz. He arrived in Lwów in late 1939, with his parents, after Warsaw was occupied by the Germans, moving into the apartment of his grandparents, on Janowska Street. He recalled how life changed in the summer of 1941 when the German occupation began, and how, a few months later, he was required to wear a white armband with a Star of David.

In February 1942, Otto started work as governor. Michael was fourteen, working at a Wehrmacht garage as a mechanic. He travelled to work on special trolley cars, marked 'For Jews permitted', but soon those were stopped so he had to walk, for about forty-five minutes each way. He recalled the first '*Aktion*', in March 1942, and the deportations that followed. 'I was protected by my papers and an ID, the *Ausweis* that had me working for an important army unit, so I was not vulnerable to being caught.' The *Aktion* coincided with an order that bore Otto's signature, to prohibit the employment of Jews in non-Jewish households. A copy of the order lay in Charlotte's papers, I later learned, with a date written in pencil, possibly by Horst.

The next *Aktion* took place in August, and Michael remembered it even more clearly. 'They took all our IDs, which were returned with extra stamps on them.' He noticed that those of his mother and grandparents were stamped on the inside, whereas his was stamped on the outside. The minor difference had major consequences, a matter of life or death: those with stamps on the outside – 'I was among them' – carried on working, but not the others. 'The stamps were used to segregate, to distinguish between those who would be taken and those who wouldn't, but we didn't know that.'

The *Aktion* took place across the city, within the ghetto and outside. Michael recalled with crystal clarity what happened.

On the day of the *Aktion* my mother, my aunt, her son and my grandparents went to their workplace, the *Städtische Werkstätte*, where they sewed and repaired uniforms. That morning rumours circulated that something was going to happen. My mother wanted me to go with her but I didn't, I went as usual to my workplace, the army garage on Janowska Street. While I was there, somebody ran up and said, 'Something is happening in the city, they are collecting Jews, taking them away by trucks.' I wanted to see my mother, so immediately went to the *Werkstätte*. On the way I was stopped several times, but with my stamp and the ID was let go. When I arrived I found that she was gone, everybody was gone.

Those who were left said terrible things were happening, they were collecting everybody. I went back to the city where my step-uncle, the younger brother of my stepfather, was working in another military establishment, not a garage, more of an office. I found him and by that time my stepfather, his brother, had been killed. He was aware of the fact that something was happening and three of the enlisted men walked in and saw me crying, and one of them said something and the other hit him. What happened was that the other one thought that he'd said something derogatory to me and they were very upset about what I was experiencing, which was an indication of some degree of humanity that prevailed.

He observed people being caught in the streets. Some were let go, including Michael, others were put on trucks that were driven away.

It was called an 'evacuation', or a 'resettlement', words that hid the true meaning of the actions. Who was doing the catching? I enquired. 'Mostly German SS people, there were some Ukrainians as well who were helping them, wearing some sort of khaki uniforms.' This was the auxiliary police force, under the control of Otto.

The *Aktion* went on for several days. Michael ended up at his grand-parents' apartment, where he found his aunt and cousin, and collapsed in despair. The next day he returned to work, and was sent to the Janowska concentration camp, in the heart of the city. 'I never saw my mother again.' He had no details about what happened, but he knew. 'I had no illusions. There was a pseudo story that they would be taken to another place, the excuse being given in all *Aktionen*. They always came and said, "Take one suitcase with you, because you are going to be resettled to work in the east." I knew nothing about Belzec then.'

Back then he was not familiar with the name Otto Wächter. 'Either I forgot it, or I ignored it.' As for the organisation of the *Aktion*, he knew it was run by the Gestapo, with help from Ukrainians, and from the Jewish policemen recruited to assist. Incarcerated in the Janowska camp, he escaped by crawling under barbed wire and hiding in a nearby cemetery. Non-Jewish friends helped him get a fake ID and transport out of Lemberg. 'I took my Jewish armband off and with my new ID travelled to Warsaw.' He left Lemberg on 2 or 3 September 1942, with a new name, Francisek Thaddeus Taletsky.

A few weeks later he returned to Lemberg with a fake birth cer-tificate to collect his cousin, who he brought back to Warsaw, where he rented a bed in a rooming house and found a job. Michael was the only survivor from his Lviv family, although this he would learn only much later. Nor could Michael have known that the 'mass execution' of more than 50,000 Jews on the territory run by Otto Wächter had, by the end of September 1942, been reported directly to the Vatican by President Roosevelt's special envoy to Pope Pius XII. 'I should like to know whether the Holy Father has any suggestions as to any prac-tical manner in which the forces of civilized public opinion could be utilized in order to prevent a continuation of these barbarities,' the US envoy enquired of the Vatican Secretary of State.

16

1943, Lemberg

By the spring of 1943, Michael Katz had left Lemberg and the *Grosse Aktion* was over. Friedrich Katzmann, whose harmonious cooperation with Otto was so admired by Himmler, produced his *Final Report on the Solution of the Jewish Question in the District of Galicia*. The District of Galicia was entirely *Judenfrei*, Katzmann reported, free of Jews, with a total of 434,329 Jews having been 'evacuated'. The city was cleansed, and there was a bonus, a bounty that included 20,952 gold wedding rings, 343,100 silver cigarette cases, 1,257 gold wristwatches, seven stamp collections, and a suitcase filled with fountain pens.

Otto took the opportunity of this success, coupled with growing difficulties for German troops on the Eastern Front, to persuade Berlin to allow him to create the *Freiwilligen-Division Galizien*, or Waffen-SS Galicia Division, comprised of Ukrainians from his territory. This was the first Waffen-SS division composed of non-Germans, one he hoped would bring Germans and Ukrainians closer. 'Why should only our good, German blood be spilt in the field?' he asked Charlotte. He wanted a military draft, prepared recruitment posters, and decided he would personally oversee the division. 'The Galicians are desperate to enlist, and they're reliable.'

Charlotte reported a 'frenzy of excitement' around Lemberg, as young Ukrainians, farmers and sons of the earth, were drafted. They marched through city streets singing enthusiastically, heads covered with flowers. 'They demanded equal rights, which Otto wanted to give them,' she recalled. 'He knew how to govern, with Austrian charm and warmth', and hoped the move would make him popular with Ukrainians. Himmler came to inspect the division, which Charlotte did not mention in her diary. Around this time she obtained a new recording of Bruckner's Fourth Symphony, *Romantic*, which did merit a mention.

There was good reason to expand recruitment, as the war with

Russia was not going well. Catastrophic, in Charlotte's view. 'One of the saddest days of my life', she recorded on 3 February 1943, as word arrived that the assault on Stalingrad had collapsed. 'All the blood that flowed could not be darker.' Otto tried to get in touch with Hitler, to no avail, she recorded for posterity, to warn of the growing dangers of the situation in the east. She also sensed they were being observed, or so she wrote. 'The spying got worse.' Take care, Otto warned, the enemy was listening. They learned once again to communicate in code, by letter and telephone.

From the east, as tens of thousands of wounded German soldiers arrived in Lemberg for treatment, Charlotte volunteered at a hospital on the city's East Street. 'For every hundred seriously injured men we had three nurses, I was the fourth.' She prepared food, penned letters for soldiers who couldn't write, cooked and tended to other needs. She also fell in love, in March, the object of her affections a young lieutenant named Horst Stützen. 'You are too nice today, I love you so much,' he said to her, gently. She entered the words into her diary in English, the language of her secret life, one her husband couldn't read.

She came to like Stützen, she told the young man, as she learned she was pregnant by her husband. In May she had an abortion, but immediately felt it was a mistake. She woke from the anaesthetic and asked the doctor, 'When can I have the next child?' In June, when the young lieutenant departed, she felt sad for her 'lovely' man. She remained in Lemberg until the end of the month, then returned to Thumersbach. On 10 July the Americans landed in Sicily. Two weeks later Mussolini was toppled, and a new Italian government took power. In August she returned to Lemberg, as Otto swore in members of his Ukrainian division, and fought with Krüger about the direction of policy in the occupied countries. As the situation turned, she recorded that belief in the Führer remained 'immeasurable'.

In September, as Germany and Italy signed an armistice which was followed by the division of the country, Lieutenant Stützen visited Charlotte in Thumersbach, to spend a few days at the farmhouse. She collected him at Zell train station, happy to see his bright eyes and boyish looks. They went to the cinema – *Die Stimme des Herzens* (*The Voice of the Heart*), starring tenor Beniamino Gigli – and boated on the lake, late into the evening. 'I like flirting with this child,' she wrote. 'I never forget Otto, but I love this child very much.' She resisted her impulses, however. 'I must take care not to lose myself, I must keep myself together . . .' At the end of the month her feelings changed. 'Now when I know he loves me . . . I am not any more interested in him.' A pity, she added, but 'the only man I love in my life will remain my dear Otto'.

By the end of the year, the young lieutenant had left and once more she felt alone, worn out, exhausted. The situation at home was tense, the children looked after by a nanny, an act for which daughter Traute never forgave her. Charlotte sensed a 'large black death cloud' hovering above their lives, as she and Otto drifted. Again she wondered if he was seeing someone else.

Otto told her that the German war effort was doomed, unless a miracle occurred. Rudolf Pavlu was relieved of his duties as mayor of Kraków for an unspecified act of wrongdoing, and sent to fight on the Eastern Front. From there he wrote with details of the daily horrors faced by a Wehrmacht in tatters, the absence of spare parts and ammunition, men bogged down in a deep winter mud. 'Our soldiers are being mown down like flies, it is a catastrophe.'

By the end of 1943, Charlotte could no longer be positive about the future. They were caught in a trap, personally and nationally. 'We couldn't see a way out.' Otto put his energies into work, and the Waffen-SS Galicia Division.

17

2014, Lviv

Unexpectedly, the Waffen-SS Galicia Division caused the making of the documentary film in which we were engaged to take a different direction. The film might have ended with a conflagration between Horst and Niklas in the Purcell Room, but that didn't happen. The two men disagreed about their fathers, but did so too politely and respectfully to make for good cinema. However, something else happened at the end of the event: Horst took the microphone and explained that his father was still venerated in Ukraine. This sowed a seed, the idea of a trip to Lviv.

'If we are going to travel to Ukraine,' Horst suggested a few weeks after the Purcell Room event, 'we should be there when the commemoration of my father's Waffen-SS Galicia Division will take place.' A re-enactment was staged every year in July, to mark the Battle of Brody, when the division was routed by the Red Army. Why this offered a cause for commemoration was not entirely clear, but it came with an annual ceremony at which newly discovered remains of German soldiers would be buried. Anti-Semitic and anti-Russian statements were 'categorically excluded' from the celebrations, Horst assured, although there may be anti-Soviet references. And, he added, a visit to the region would offer an opportunity to mourn my family, and see for ourselves the veneration of Otto.

Niklas, Horst and I travelled together to Lviv, with David Evans, the director, and a film crew. We stayed at the Hotel George, a return to the inter-war years and the atmosphere evoked by Joseph Roth's novel *Hotel Savoy*. We walked the streets, admired the municipal building that once served as Otto's headquarters, and visited the city archives, in a former monastery. Horst wrote his name in the visitors' book, signing off as 'Son of the Governor'.

We gathered in the chamber of the building that served as the parliament of Galicia during the Austro-Hungarian empire, today the aula of the university. In this impressive room, on 1 August 1942, Hans

Frank announced the plan to exterminate the entire Jewish population of the District of Galicia. He addressed words directly to Governor Wächter, to thank him for doing his work so well. Unexpectedly, Niklas reproduced the moment, leaping onto the stage where his father once stood, and reading out his words. 'You have not done anything nasty to them, have you?' he said, looking at Horst, who was discomfited. Exchanges followed, and I lost my temper with Horst. This was the first and only time that happened, a reaction perhaps to the combination of being in that room and his response to the words of the criminal indictment of his father, a copy of which I had found. The indictment, which was issued by Poland and supported by the United States, charged his father with being a 'mass murderer'. Horst read the document and immediately dismissed it as Soviet propaganda. The uncomfortable moment was caught and made it into the documentary film. My mother-in-law would refer to it as the 'elder abuse' scene.

As calm returned, we visited 133 Ivana Franko Street, where Otto and Charlotte lived. Horst barely remembered the house, a large mansion with plaster filigree above the wooden double front doors and a fine garden, although the swimming pool and the tennis court which could not be powdered were long gone. He remembered where he ate breakfast, as a little boy, and the staircase that led up to the bedrooms. 'I have only a very faint memory, because of the smell' – a house that was never as happy as Thumersbach. From Charlotte's diaries he knew of her work in a hospital, the second abortion, and an event he described as a 'nervous breakdown' of sorts. He rarely saw his mother during that period. 'We had maidens to take care of us while she worked for my father, receiving guests, or at the hospital.'

The next day we travelled by car to the small town of Zolkiew, an hour away. We walked past the spot where Hersch Lauterpacht was born, in a wooden house. We visited the shuttered, ruined synagogue, burned down by German forces in the summer of 1941. There, in the vast, haunted space, Horst spoke even more softly than usual, apparently touched by the columns that rose high, and the ghostlike emptiness. 'Here we confront what happens,' he said mournfully, and 'we feel sad, ashamed maybe'.

Nevertheless, he was unable to connect Otto to the terrible events that occurred in this room, or the town and region. 'I don't think my father ordered this room to be burned down, I don't see him here, walking around in his uniform, saying, "Oh, well done", and things like that.' Horst wanted to be hopeful, not stuck in the past, believing the space would again be full of life. 'I'm not so pessimistic as you,' he said. His voice trailed off.

In the afternoon we walked into a wood, two kilometres from the town centre, along East West Street and onto the sandy path that led to a mass grave for three and a half thousand of the town's residents. Executed on a single day in the spring of 1943, the victims included the families of my grandfather and the Lauterpachts. Otto Wächter wasn't in Zolkiew on that day, but it was part of the territory he governed. Horst took a photograph of a small white memorial, the camera shutter broke the silence.

In this place, under an open sky, Niklas implored Horst to recognise his father's role. 'My father was involved in the system, I know, this is why we are here.' That was as far as Horst could go, without more information. He wanted the exact date, the names of police officers present, details of orders actually given. 'There is death all around us, there must be tens of thousands of Austrians lying around here.' Horst was evoking 1914, when his grandfather Josef fought in these fields, not 1943, unable to accept the notion of command responsibility.

What mattered was the identity of those who actually fired the bullets, and their names. 'My father wouldn't have signed off on much, coming here . . . these people . . . I don't think . . .' As he spoke, his fingers held a tiny white flower, and plucked away the petals, one at a time, allowing each to fall from his hand to the ground.

The following day we took a bus to the countryside, to attend the annual celebration of Otto's Waffen-SS Galicia Division. The scheduled events included the burial of the remains of three German soldiers, recently discovered. There was to have been a re-enactment of the battle, but it was cancelled on the orders of a government department. Such an event would be too incendiary at a time of escalating tensions between Ukraine and Russia.

We arrived at a hillside, seventy kilometres to the west of Lviv, in the direction of Brody, the birthplace of writer Joseph Roth. We stood in a large field, surrounded by white stone crosses to mark the fallen, as three fresh graves were dug, observed by elderly veterans in SS uniforms. 'To hold the mortal remains of Germans and Ukrainians who died fighting the Soviet Red Army, in the summer of 1944,' an old man whispered, with reverence. The sharp, regular sound of metal hitting the earth was accompanied by the lament of a choir, a string orchestra and young women in wispy, red dresses.

Several hundred people assembled on that warm day in July. They included elderly veterans with white hair and walking sticks, wearing medals and ribbons, as well as locals, families with young children, and sympathisers from *Svoboda*, or Freedom, an extreme nationalist party.

Between the event in the Purcell Room and this moment in the military cemetery a new government had taken power in Ukraine. It signed an Association Agreement with the European Union, which prompted Russia to occupy Crimea. War returned to the eastern out-skirts of Europe, a century after Russia occupied Lviv in the summer of 1914. History was circular.

In a tiny white chapel three coffins were draped in the blue and yellow flag of Ukraine. They rested under a mural painted in delicate pastels, religious figures and soldiers in grey uniforms. Men wandered around in battle fatigues and SS uniforms, trying to look serious, some with regimental flags or holding a sub-machine gun. Horst positioned himself outside the chapel, and as each coffin passed he removed his black cap.

Nearby, a man stood in a pale-blue shirt, a large swastika around his neck. The symbol had a different meaning from the one we imagined. He said this with a wry smile.

A man in battle fatigues removed his SS *Stahl* helmet. 'I wore it in Maidan Square, in Kiev,' he told us, showing the damage caused by a sniper's bullet. No, he said to Niklas, he felt no sense of shame to be dressed as an SS soldier.

Young children observed us in conversation. In the distance, earth flew as metal shovels hit the hard, dry ground. Three elderly men, veterans all, with white hair and lined faces, exchanged black and white photographs. Otto's face stood out, in a familiar SS uniform. Another veteran in uniform, wearing many medals, recalled the day Governor Wächter addressed his Waffen-SS Galicia Division. Another veteran, wearing even more medals, spoke with warmth about Otto. 'A fine and decent man.' Horst listened and beamed.

A man in a well-pressed grey uniform of the Waffen-SS, with swastikas and a Ukrainian lion sewn onto the upper arm of the garment, introduced himself. Wolf Sturm was his name. His cap bore a death's head, he wore oversized leather boots and dark glasses, and carried a machine gun, which he offered to Horst, who declined to accept it. Horst was more interested in an old open-topped SS car, a few feet away.

'Please don't get in,' I hoped silently. Horst ambled towards the vehicle. He paused at the back door, opened it slowly, hauled himself in, sat in the back seat, adjusted his cap, leaned back and turned to the passers-by, as Otto might have done. David Evans, the director, beamed. 'I hoped, for the sake of the film, that he would do exactly what he did,' he would later tell an audience.

The silent journey back to Lviv included a detour to a seventeenth-century Jewish graveyard near the town of Brody, where we spent an hour walking amid the ancient headstones. Later we drove to the village of Podhorce, to a baroque, sixteenth-century castle. In the refectory, away from the cameras, at a moment when Niklas was absent, Horst called our group to attention, clinking a glass with his spoon. I have something to say, he announced, as the room fell silent. 'From now on, no one should refer to my father as a criminal, not in my presence.'

The visit to Ukraine caused a rift between Niklas and Horst. In an interview on camera, Niklas intimated that Horst could become 'a new Nazi', that their relationship was no longer endurable. Did he really think Horst was a Nazi? He paused. 'Yes,' he said, with deliberation, 'now I would admit he is really a Nazi.'

Horst only became aware of the exchange much later, when he saw the film, and that would have a consequence that could not have been predicted. In the meantime, he was happy. 'This day was the best for me,' he told us. 'So many people wanted to shake my hand, because of my father, say that he was a decent man. That's all I want, nothing else.'

18

1944, Lemberg

Somehow, Charlotte and Otto pulled themselves together. Perhaps it was the dire military situation, or the fact that Charlotte was pregnant with their sixth child. She decided to keep this child, a means, perhaps, to pull Otto out of his quietude, bring them closer.

The hope was short-lived. In February, Otto's closest colleague and confidant, Dr Otto Bauer, was assassinated outside his home on a Lemberg street. The assassin was a Soviet agent disguised as a German soldier. Otto was deeply shaken, unable to trust even those in a German uniform, although he put on a brave face. 'Despite all difficulties,' he wrote to his father, 'I'm still faring quite well and the work is very enjoyable, especially during this tense time.' Otto Bauer was no true Nazi, Charlotte believed, but he was intelligent, decent and her husband's reliable, loyal colleague. She marked the moment in the diary with his name and a cross. In the family album she pasted a photograph of him, laid out after death. The bullet was meant for Otto, she confided to sister-in-law Ilse.

In these difficult times, as the military front approached Lemberg, bringing the prospect of an 'apocalypse', a form of 'gallows humour' set in. Charlotte refused to allow her social activity to be undermined, taking to horse-riding and fox-hunting in the company of Frau Thier, whose husband Theobald was engaged in closing down the Janowska camp and trying to conceal the many signs of mass murder that had occurred on that site, where Michael Katz was held, and many others in and around Lemberg. An impossible act of cleansing. Otto gave the social activities a miss and stuck to work. 'Too depressed', Charlotte concluded. 'The situation is very bad,' he recognised. 'Let me have some fun,' Charlotte retorted, 'who knows how long it will last?' She wanted to enjoy such time as remained of the life of plenty.

The signs of change were all around, as the German army retreated across Europe and acts of resistance – and measures taken in response, in the style of Bochnia – increased. In the spring, newspapers reported events in Rome, in late March, when members of the SS Police Regiment *Bozen* were attacked by partisans as they sang the 'Horst Wessel Song' while marching along the Via Rasella in Rome. Thirty-three Tyrolean soldiers were killed, and as with Bochnia, five years earlier, Hitler ordered reprisals, ten Italians to be executed for each German victim. A total of 335 Italians were rounded up, taken to the Ardeatine Caves on the outskirts of Rome, and executed. The reprisals in Rome would have reminded Otto of the events in Bochnia, five years earlier.

As the Red Army came closer, Charlotte prepared to leave Lemberg, and organised a farewell tea. Wladislaw, her beloved Ukrainian valet, suggested she take the finest items from the villa, even if they didn't belong to her, to prevent them from falling into the hands of the Soviets. Years later she told Otto junior's son that the suggestion was unacceptable. 'I was strict, and when it came to things that didn't belong to us, I said: "Anything that isn't mine stays in the house."' She couldn't think of taking things with her, she claimed, a stance that disappointed Wladislaw, who adopted a sad look. So devoted to the 'First Lady' of Lemberg, she recalled.

In the spring of 1944 Charlotte and the children left Lemberg and returned to Thumersbach. Otto remained in Galicia but didn't expect to be there for long. 'Tarnopol has fallen,' Charlotte recorded on Monday, 17 April. When the Red Army was less than 125 kilometres from Lemberg, Himmler drafted a new decree to be signed by Hitler. 'I promote the SS-Brigadeführer Dr Otto Wächter (SS-Nr. 235 368) to the rank of SS-Gruppenführer.' A single rank stood between Otto and the Reichsführer. 'I will endeavour to warrant your extraordinary trust through exceptional performance,' Otto assured Himmler, as the Germans retreated, and again pledged his fullest loyalty. 'I will handle the tasks that are given to me . . . and proudly meet them, aware of the special commitment that being a part of the Führerkorps of your SS entails.' Otto sent Charlotte a photograph of Himmler inspecting the Waffen-SS Galicia Division.

On 5 June, the US Army's 88th Infantry and other units entered Rome. The Soviets were fifty kilometres from Lemberg.

In July, Otto received a gift from Himmler, a book inscribed with 'best birthday wishes'. Charlotte expressed the hope that the English might yet be persuaded to join the Germans in the struggle against the Soviets. 'I hope that the English will be fed up and unite with us,' she told Otto. The impediment to that prospect was the Jews, she complained, 'always getting involved, contaminating everything'.

On 20 July, Charlotte noted the failure of the assassination attempt on Hitler, with relief. 'Thank God, nothing happened.' She listened to the Führer on the radio. 'Nice weather, Führer spoke 1 a.m. at night.'

The next day, the house in Lemberg was hit by an aerial attack. The Russians were reported to have surrounded the city, Charlotte wrote to Otto.

On Sunday, 23 July, Charlotte was able to speak to Otto in Lemberg, on the telephone.

On Tuesday, 25 July, Otto found time to write Charlotte a six-page letter, to offer reassurance.

On Wednesday, 26 July, Hans Frank informed colleagues that Governor Wächter had told him that District of Galicia was 'practically lost'.

A few hours later, on the morning of Thursday, 27 July, Otto abandoned the city, as the Red Army entered the outskirts. He drove west towards Tarnow, then took a small Storch plane to Stary Sambir, to visit the staff of the Waffen-SS Galicia Division, then on to Kraków. 'A king without a country,' he told Charlotte. 'My project in Galicia is over.'

She wrote three words in her diary: '*Aufgeben v Lemberg*' – giving up Lemberg. The Red Army marched into Lemberg, and headed on towards Warsaw, Kielce and Riga.

Otto was a hero, she told the children, the last to leave Lemberg, determined to save his beloved Waffen-SS Galicia Division. 'His greatest wish was to ensure that the division would never fall into the hands of the Russians.'

On 30 July Otto arrived in Berlin.

19

1944, Bolzano

In Berlin, Otto was formally discharged from his duties as governor of District of Galicia. Himmler transferred him to Italy, to serve as the head of the military administration in the north of the country. 'He was the liaison man between Hitler and Mussolini's Republic of Salò, under SS-Obergruppenführer Wolff,' Charlotte recorded. Wolff had left his post as Himmler's chief of staff to lead the Wehrmacht in Italy. Otto would be based at Fasano on Lake Garda, where he and Charlotte spent a happy holiday, a decade earlier. He was nearby, she mused, and they could now speak regularly by telephone.

Years later, the journalist Melitta Wiedemann told Charlotte that Otto visited her while he was in Berlin, accompanied by a chauffeur. She suggested to Otto that he might be the one to lead a group of senior officers to 'eliminate' Hitler, to end the chaos and murder. Charlotte was incredulous at the idea that her husband could ever countenance such a suggestion. She was right, he did not. Himmler rightly trusted him. Reliable Otto.

The family remained in Thumersbach, with Aunt Ilse and Grandfather Josef. Charlotte tried to maintain a positive disposition – 'we had a nice maid, so the five children were well looked after' – yet the situation looked bleak. 'Heavy defeats and losses, black clouds on the horizon . . . the failed attack on Hitler.' Curiously, in spite of Otto's absence and the gloomy outlook, she felt 'happy and harmonious'.

In mid-August, Otto managed a brief visit, between trips to Berlin, where he stayed with the Fischböcks, and Italy, where he met General Wolff ('terrific') in Bolzano. 'I'm swimming as much as possible,' he told Charlotte, dividing his time between residences in Bolzano and Fasano. On the 17th Charlotte travelled to Salzburg with Aunt Ilse, for the birth of their sixth child, noting in the diary that the Americans were approaching Paris and the Soviets were on the outskirts of Warsaw. 'Awful.' Sieglinde – the name refers to a shield that protects a victory – was born on 24 August, a healthy, screaming girl, who would be a 'true German Führerkind'. The Americans took Paris the next day.

In early September, Charlotte was back in Thumersbach, on the lake. Otto arrived to meet the sixth child, travelling from Fasano in the Republic of Salò. He arrived with gifts and a telegram from Himmler, warm congratulations on the birth. The Reichsführer enquired as to the name and ended with a rare typographical error. 'Heil Hitzler', he signed off, the 'z' was crossed out in blue ink.

The situation was coming to a head, Otto told Charlotte. The Allies had reached Rome and were heading north. 'Like locusts, by air and by foot', Charlotte noted, accompanied by a vast flow of refugees. 'Being despondent and reflective will get you nowhere,' Otto instructed. 'We can march into the future with our consciences clear and our heads held high, staying true to our conception of this world and this life.' In the past they had enjoyed good and bad days with the Führer, 'we will stand with him in the future'.

In September, somewhat optimistically, Hans Frank confirmed Otto's continued appointment as a governor in the General Government. The decision was ratified by Hitler, who gave him life tenure as a civil servant, with full pension rights.

'My work is fundamentally different from Galicia,' Otto reported. His office was on the western shore of Lake Garda, a few kilometres from Salò, near where Mussolini and the Italian Social Republic had their headquarters. Albert Speer visited, old friends were close by. 'I've just been with Globus, who occasionally also rampages around here.' Globočnik, based in Trieste, seemingly still had energy to round up Jews and Italian partisans, although Otto complained the measures adopted by the Italian authorities weren't 'as drastic as we would like'. As part of the anti-partisan campaign, against the creation of partisan republics, the Germans perpetrated ever more massacres. In Sant'Anna di Stazzema, a village in Tuscany, some 560 civilians were killed, and in Marzabotto, a village south of Bologna, the death toll was even higher, at least 770 civilians. General Wolff's chief of staff noted the order to 'take as few prisoners as possible', to engage in a campaign of 'cold terror'.

Otto made no mention of such matters to Charlotte but sent gifts to Thumersbach. In November, a pair of stockings, which Charlotte passed on to a friend. He wrote most days, details of his 'doings': a visit from Himmler ('in good spirits!'); feeling better about being in Italy ('someone said I'm already in charge of the entire Italian economy'); a visit to Salò for performances of *Cavalleria rusticana* and *Madam Butterfly* (both 'very good'); attacks by enemy aircraft. He still hoped to accomplish something useful, and made sure he stayed fit, swimming often in the lake, even if it was cold. He missed Lemberg, a city he loved with heart and soul.

Globus visited Charlotte for a couple of days at Thumersbach, and Himmler sent her half a kilo of coffee, with a friendly note. A few days later a gift arrived for new-born Sieglinde from the Reichsführer, another candlestick. Neighbours weren't as friendly as before, Charlotte reported, as she worried about putting on weight, after the pregnancy. She wanted to look good for Otto, whenever he next visited. 'I dreamt of your return to Vienna,' she wrote, how he told her he loved her and would never leave her, and how she responded to say that she would let him go if he wished but would keep the children. Brigitte Frank wrote to say that her relationship with the governor general had improved. 'I know your husband better than you do,' Charlotte replied, reminding her that Frank was 'unsteady and jumpy', like many men of genius. In December, she saw the Franks in Vienna, as well as Seyss-Inquart, who visited from Holland.

Despite the difficulties, Otto put on a brave front. He told a friend that he remained 'very optimistic' about the overall situation, and was sure about 'the rightness of our principles'. The actions of the enemy, the Bolsheviks and the Anglo-Saxons, 'cannot be handled through democratic means'. In Fasano he delivered a strong end-of-year lecture to rally the comrades. Germans loved Christmas and never wanted war, he told them. The Germany of Adolf Hitler – nationalist and socialist – wanted 'clean factories, decent housing for workers, mothers and children, improved living conditions created for the masses', not conflict. It had been forced to draw its sword, 'to defend against envious, rapacious neighbours' in a war started by the 'powers of the eternal subversion of capital and Judaism'. Germany wanted 'to help foreign people', to bring progress and make 'the chimneys smoke, the farmers plough, the poor eat'. The enemy – a criminal alliance between Stalin, Churchill and Roosevelt – brought 'hatred and intolerance . . . terror, brutal persecution, conflict, civil war, disintegration, hunger and chaos'. The fight was between 'good and right against the destructive powers of the evil', and a resilient Germany would prevail.

Back in Thumersbach for Christmas, laden with presents for the children, including assorted groceries, he found a wife whose optimism was again on the wane. As British and American bombers flew sorties around Lake Zell, offloading bombs into the waters, Charlotte expressed a different view. 'We knew a victory was not possible any more,' she later recognised, it was simply a matter of survival in a time of chaos. She could not imagine how they could prevail in a 'fight against the English, the Americans, the Russians and the Jews'. Even if the enemy fought among themselves, she noted, 'the Jews would sing with one voice'.

20

1945, Thumersbach

In the new year Otto and Charlotte wrote frequently, letters that evoked daily mundanities to renew spirits that flagged. Christmas was 'a difficult time for a great German celebration', Charlotte wrote gloomily. No, Otto responded, it was a 'fairytale' to be together.

As Allied bomber squadrons flew overhead, Charlotte took the children skiing on the Schmittenhöhe, near Zell. She welcomed the packets of coffee sent by Himmler – a man on whose shoulders much now rested, Otto told her – and her award of a silver *Mutterkreuz* on Mother's Day, to mark the many children she had raised. In northern Italy, Otto, still being driven in an open-top car, complained about the bitter cold. There was much to worry about, beyond the situation in the east, as the General Government would soon fall and Italy too was 'tricky', with frequent Allied air attacks and Mussolini fretting. 'Thank you for putting up with my frailties,' he told Charlotte; he knew he was not ideal. Yes, he supported her idea to donate his work clothes to the *Volksopfer Sammlung* (a campaign to support the armed forces), including the black SS uniform, but not the grey ones, which he wanted to keep.

At the end of January, Kraków fell to the Red Army. 'Our beautiful Reich is destroyed,' Charlotte wrote on the 24th, it was 'unimaginable' that a Polish flag would fly again over the city. Two days later, Brigitte Frank told her that the speed of the fall caught her husband by surprise, and he only just got out, he too a 'king without a country'. On the 30th she welcomed the twelfth anniversary of the *Machtergreifung*, the seizure of power by the Nazis. 'How hopeful and confident we were,' she scribbled, 'it was wonderful and you met the Führer for the first time.' The situation today was gloomy, but so long as the Führer lived there was hope. Listening to another Hitler speech on the wireless, Otto was comforted by the clarity of the message, but concerned by its aggressive tone.

In February, Charlotte visited Salzburg, shocked by the misery she encountered. 'Hundreds of foreign workers, people in ragged clothes, huge craters, destroyed houses, debris, dirt', she wrote, fearful of the crowd of foreigners in her own country. It was now Otto's turn to feel downcast. 'It'll be better when I can go swimming again, a bit of daily movement balances everything out.' Still, he had fresh carnations and roses on his desk, a picture of Lake Garda over the fireplace, and views across the garden and lake to the mountains, which offered 'a bridge to the family in Zell'.

Otto worried about the Allied attacks on Vienna – as 'fate swirls around us' – but refused to accept that the end was approaching. 'It would be too great an injustice for this good, true, constant and brave *Volk*, and too much of a loss for the world.' A work trip revived memories of childhood, reflected in a long letter to Horst, thanking his son for the lovely drawings and letters. 'I loved being in my old Trieste', with memories of the ancient imperial  military swimming school, where he learned to swim, and a visit to the family apartment, on Via Bonomi. The garden of his childhood was now miserable and neglected, and the aqueduct, so huge in his memory, seemed to have shrunk. Stay well and strong, he told the five-year-old, keep doing your Papa and Mama proud. 'Heil Hitler!'

Otto's organisational skills, and continued commitment to the Nazi cause, including a willingness to take brutal security measures, made him a man in demand. After a brief and unsuccessful uprising in Slovakia, the Reichsminister for Bohemia and Moravia, Karl Hermann Frank, suggested that Otto be appointed German ambassador to the Slovak Republic. The current ambassador was insufficiently committed to 'severe security mechanisms'. Nothing came of the suggestion. Instead, Gottlob Berger, chief of the SS Main Office and one of Himmler's closest confidants, requested that Otto be transferred back to Berlin. They were looking for a new deputy head of Group D, which controlled the Germanic SS, a search for an 'outstanding personality'. Wächter was the man, easily replaceable in Italy. Himmler sought the accord of General Wolff, my 'dear Wölffchen'. 'I know that W. is an outstanding employee to you, but the Wlasow-Movement is of high importance for us in Germany.' The reference was to the small army headed by General Andrey Vlasov, leading a group of Russian anti-communists who defected to fight with the Germans against the Red Army.

With General Wolff's support, Otto returned to Berlin at the end of February, not thrilled to leave Italy. He moved into a modern villa, near an office set up for him at Rheinbabenallee 28. The city was changed ('more ruins, even less traffic, people pale and miserable. Women often in trousers [. . .] everyone hauling bags. The offices unheated'), but he welcomed being close to old friends like the Losackers, who visited, with talk about the past, present and future.

As deputy head of Group D at the RSHA/Reichssicherheitshauptamt, Otto had returned to the place he worked a decade earlier, in the Berlin building of Eichmann and Hass. One of his tasks was liaison between an emerging 'Ukrainian National Committee', under the leadership of General Pavlo Shandruk, and General Wlasow's renegade Russians. This made the move to Berlin attractive, offering a platform to work with the Waffen-SS Galicia Division, which was distinct from the Committee, and to save it. At Yalta, in early February, Stalin declared that he wanted all members of the division to be extradited to the Soviet Union, something Otto was determined to prevent. He worked tirelessly to support his former Ukrainian colleagues, 'astonished' that his reputation, enhanced by a policy of treating the population of Galicia 'sensibly', had spread across the Ukraine to the Cossacks and down to the Caucasus. 'Representatives of the various eastern peoples come to me with the greatest respect,' he told Charlotte, except for the Russians, who were aware of his anti-Bolshevik views.

He contacted General Shandruk, and agreed to establish a Ukrainian National Committee (UNC) and a Ukrainian National Army (UNA). The UNC and its army were inaugurated a few days later, with General Shandruk appointed as commander, his remit including the Waffen-SS Galicia Division. In March, an official reception was held in Berlin, attended by Reichsminister Alfred Rosenberg, who welcomed the 'full participation' of the Ukrainians in the coming 'war against Bolshevism'. At the Foreign Ministry, in the presence of just thirteen guests, including Otto, wine and canapés were served.

The Red Army took Vienna on 12 April. A few days later, Otto joined General Shandruk on a visit to the Ukrainian army near Spittal, in Austria, as a representative of the Wehrmacht High Command and Ministry of Foreign Affairs. On the 17th they met in Völkermarkt, to allocate command responsibilities between Germans and Ukrainians, a delicate matter. A few days later, the two visited General Fritz Freitag at field HQ, a much-diminished site on the edge of a wood near a small hamlet. General Shandruk wanted a Ukrainian commander, to replace General Freitag, 'a corpulent man' who didn't make a good impression. Otto supported Shandruk's proposals, and the Waffen-SS Galicia Division was renamed the 1st Ukrainian Division of the Ukrainian National Army.

On 25 April the renamed division was sworn in, in Otto's presence. He wanted the UNA to function as an 'anti-Bolshevik combat unit', working alongside other anti-communist formations – the Waffenverbände of the Cossacks, Caucasians and Georgians – now under American control. Secret negotiations were underway with the Americans, led by General Wolff, and facilitated by Switzerland. The exercise was known as Operation Sunrise. I found no indication that Otto, loyal to the end, was involved in those efforts.

With Germany on the brink of surrender, Otto made a brief trip to northern Italy, to ascertain the state of other divisions. He met with General Wolff's chief of staff, who noted Otto's idea of a restoration of the 'k.u.k.', the *kaiserlich und königlich*, a reference to the Austro-Hungarian empire.

On 29 April, Hitler signed his last will and testament. He named Admiral Dönitz as his successor, and Arthur Seyss-Inquart, who had fled Holland, as foreign minister. The following day Hitler committed suicide, as Otto made his way to Italy, a brief visit to ascertain the prospects of a Cossack Reserve. There he was reportedly spotted, with Globočnik, by two colleagues, in the village of Timau. There was a suggestion that he may have given a significant donation to the local priest, for the construction of a new church.

On 3 May, Otto attended a modest Ukrainian Easter celebration, for the Ukrainian army general staff. General Shandruk expressed gratitude to Otto, for his presence and courtesies. Privately, however, he expressed the belief that Otto's support was self-serving, intended to exonerate himself and other Germans in the eyes of Ukrainians.

As Allied troops approached Thumersbach, Charlotte grew concerned about the family situation. 'If the Russians come, they'll hang you as the wife of SS-Obergruppenführer Wächter,' she was told, so she should flee. She claimed not to fear death, but was concerned about the children. 'I was very worried about them, they were still so small.'

She took Horst and Heide to safety in Brixen (now Bressanone), to the home of a former nanny. The young woman, to whom she also entrusted some money and jewellery for safekeeping, promised to look after the little ones. Then she took Linde, not yet a year old, to the daughter of her midwife, halfway up a mountain, for safekeeping. 'It was terrible to leave this little worm alone up there, my heart broke just thinking when and if we'd see each other again.'

On 8 May the war ended in Austria. 'The big day of victory for the enemies', Charlotte recorded. 'I am speechless in the face of this fact. Is this really the end of everything we wanted to build?'

The arrival of the Americans at Lake Zell was imminent. A military friend visited to check on the situation of the Wächter family. The Americans liked money and jewellery, he advised, she should hide everything. She buried the remaining jewellery and other possessions in a ditch, near a small wood.

Charlotte received a call from Otto on the last day of Nazi rule. He would try to make his way to Carinthia, to the mountains, but offered no details. She asked what to do with the special boxes he kept in the bicycle shed, his archives. Destroy them, he instructed, and she acted without delay. 'I burned some and threw the rest in the lake, along with the guns one wasn't allowed to have.'

The US Army entered Zell-am-See and Thumersbach on the morning of 9 May. Charlotte was told to stay in the farmhouse, which would be commandeered. When the American soldiers arrived, she asked what to do with the family, including her father-in-law Josef, the 83-year-old general. 'That's your problem,' they told her.

The house was requisitioned. 'They slept in our beds,' Charlotte recorded, yet she felt a sense of relief. 'I had assumed that they would hang us all.' She found another house, a farm building owned by the Schiffereggers, their tenants, higher up the mountain. They arrived with such provisions as they could gather.

Information slowly filtered through, one terrible piece of news after the other. Military collapse. The suicide of the Führer in Berlin, with Eva Braun. Bormann's escape. Goebbels poisoning himself, his wife and all six of their children. Göring caught near Zell, in the village of Bruck-Fusch.

Charlotte tried to be pragmatic, always stronger in adversity, it seemed, and recorded what followed.

I was a fatalist, and thought it best to make contact with the Americans. I went down to the house and asked modestly if I could speak with the boss. He was a young officer and, after we explained in English what was troubling us, and if it was possible to set up a room in the house for the old *k.u.k.* general, because he was so old, his heart softened and, after he'd thought about it for an hour, he let me leave Papa in the house, an exceptional case. That was a big first step. Papa had spent a night up the mountain and was happy to have a room to himself, without a draught. He radiated formality, kept saying: 'wonderful, wonderful'. After that we stayed in close contact. As the Americans could communicate to us in English, we would sit together in the evenings and speak like old friends. Their first question:

'Have you been a Nazi?'

I thought quickly and decided there was no point denying it: 'Of course, I was a very happy Nazi.' Mouths gaped open, astonishment, outcry.

'You have really been a Nazi?' I saw from their astonished eyes that they were completely overwhelmed and I said, 'Naturally, why not?'

'You know, we've been marching through Germany for four weeks and we haven't met a single Nazi. What do you think of that? You're the first. It's a miracle.'

I laughed aloud, as I had no idea they'd be so astonished and thrilled that I acknowledged everything so openly.

I was examined like a mysterious, unusual creature. The discussions started and I told them, as I say to this day, that it was a great, wonderful time, but unfortunately Hitler had the madness of the Caesars and went beyond what was reasonable. I was given tea, coffee, sugar and anything I wanted for the children, chocolate. They were so easily pleased, like children. They really took to me, I had a lovely time.

A few weeks later the Americans returned the farmhouse to the Wächters. An American officer explained he had trouble sleeping in her bed, knowing the family was housed so miserably. Charlotte and the children moved back into their home.

As the Americans were friendlier than expected, she returned to the woods to retrieve the buried jewellery. 'There was a hole where

I'd buried it, the moss had been ripped out.' Everything set aside for difficult times ahead was gone. Charlotte wept.

They did not have long at the Thumersbach farmhouse. Former governor Rehrl, the previous owner, from whom it had been confiscated, wanted it back. 'I had been expecting that we'd have to move out,' Charlotte noted, 'but was still very upset when the lawyer who'd been commissioned to deal with the matter arrived one day and said that we'd have to look for somewhere else to live.'

Finding a new place wasn't easy. 'My friends were all locked up, Reitter, Blaschke, etc.'

Eventually they found a place, though it was much smaller, on the other side of the lake, near the Schmittenhöhem cable car.

For the rest of May and into June Charlotte awaited news from Otto. None came.

She didn't know that on 8 May he was with General Shandruk, near Klagenfurt. He told the Ukrainian that Admiral Dönitz had accepted the Allies' terms of surrender, and a ceasefire would take effect on all fronts at midnight, on 9 May. He told Shandruk he was now the central figure in saving the Galicia Division, and the rest of them. As the British approached Klagenfurt, he made a final, hasty telephone call to Charlotte, in the course of which she asked what to do with the boxes of his papers. Should she destroy them? 'Yes,' he said, and she did, although later she expressed regret about her 'panic-stricken' action. Maybe the diaries, in which he recorded 'everything in detail', could have been used to help him 'justify himself', to show that 'he did everything in his power to help so many people'.

In the evening he travelled to Graz to meet Feldmarschall Kesselring, newly appointed as commander-in-chief of German forces in the southern sector, defending southern Germany and what remained under German control in Austria and Yugoslavia, after the surrender of Italy a few days earlier.

Otto met Kesselring on the morning of 9 May. They parted and headed in different directions.

Kesselring surrendered to the US Army's Major General Maxwell Taylor, with a surreal tea party.

Otto headed west, having agreed to meet a comrade in the Stubalm region. He left Graz by car, with a driver, feeling pessimistic. He hoped for a last reunion with the remnants of the Waffen-SS Galicia Division, and then to find a comrade, Lohmann. According to a friend, who wrote to Charlotte, Lohmann waited for hours at the agreed meeting point. 'Your husband never came. Ever since, we have also lost all trace of your husband.'

Otto didn't make the rendezvous. He drove on, beyond the Stubalm, to rejoin General Shandruk and the Ukrainian Division in Judenburg, as a Soviet tank division approached from Bruck. The Ukrainian Division skirmished with the Soviets, retreated, then split. One part remained in the British zone. The other part, with Otto, General Shandruk and General Fritz Freitag, found themselves in the American zone, near Tamsweg, about 130 kilometres south-east of Salzburg.

The following morning, 10 May, General Freitag disappeared. A search party found him on the outskirts of Tamsweg. He asked to be left alone, wandered off, then took his own life.

Otto decided to leave General Shandruk and take his chances alone. He knew the Americans were after him, as well as the British and the Poles, the Jews and the Soviets. He would take the road south, cross the mountains into Italy, join up with unnamed friends.

On the afternoon of 10 May 1945, he was seen heading out of Tamsweg, alone.

That was the last sighting. Otto Wächter, husband and father, lawyer, former governor, SS man indicted for mass murder, including shootings and executions, disappeared. It happened in the summer of 1934, and now, in the spring of 1945, it happened again.

III

FLIGHT

'My husband died in Rome . . . Faced with the horror of his solitary death, and faced with the anguish that preceded his death, I asked myself if this happened to us . . .'

Natalia Ginzburg, *Winter in the Abruzzi*, 1944

21

2015, New York

In the spring of 1945, Otto Wächter disappeared for the second time. Seventy years later, a festival in New York hosted the premiere of the documentary film in which his son played a leading role. One scene in the film, and Horst's reaction to it, catalysed a chain of events that caused Horst to give me access to Charlotte's papers.

It began with the invitation to the premiere, at the Tribeca Film Festival, of *A Nazi Legacy: What Our Fathers Did*, which was sent to Horst. He wrote to say he did not like the title, and thought that *What Our Fathers Did . . . and What They Did Not Do* would be better. He also worried that the film's contents would disappoint him even more than the unfortunate – and, in his view, misleading – title. Nevertheless, positive as ever, he circulated a note to family and friends. 'Invitation to the premiere', he wrote, a film about 'my father, the Castle of Hagenberg, and me'. He did not mention that he had not yet seen the film.

The premiere at Tribeca went well, and the film was bought for a limited release in cinemas in Britain and America. It was made available on Amazon, Netflix and iTunes, joined the festival circuit, and received reviews that were generally positive. 'A film . . . about a difficult conversation', the *Washington Post* reported, and 'the failure of conversation itself'. 'Disturbing', said the *Guardian*. 'Gripping and compelling', wrote the reviewer from the *San Francisco Chronicle/ GATE*. 'Horribly gripping', the *Spectator* judged. I wondered about Horst's reaction. *Variety* thought the film was 'troubling', a study of denial and wartime responsibility, and 'the challenge of dealing with a monster in the family'. The *New York Times* recognised that Niklas and Horst weren't accountable for the actions of their fathers, but suggested that they were 'obligated to recognize the truth of what happened'. To observe Horst – 'an apologist whose excuses are infuriating' – deny that truth was 'difficult to watch, and just as hard to look away from'. One review in the *Daily Beast* referred to 'Horst's deluded idolization of his father'; a second concluded that Horst and I were equally unable to see things from the perspective of the other.

Horst too had now watched the film, and reported back that it was not entirely to his liking. 'It took me a while to get a grip,' he wrote to David. It was thoroughly made, he acknowledged, and some scenes were in his favour, but they were few, no more than 'small blossoms scattered in a sea of brutality, negligence and ignorance'. He was somewhat affected by the reviews. 'When I read the first review in the *Daily Beast* I was hit by severe diarrhoea!'

Yet, as always, Horst found a silver lining. Our contact had caused him to renew his efforts to research his father's history, he explained, and the filming allowed him to find new evidence of his father's decency, which was 'overwhelming'. He was inclined to make a second film, to focus on what his father did not do, and redouble his efforts to restore the schloss, a building which embodied Otto's positive impact on Horst's life.

One scene in the film had an unexpected consequence. I do not recall the precise chain of events, but the catalyst was Horst's discomfort at being characterised by Niklas, on camera, as 'a new Nazi'. I did not share that view, and said so in the film, and Niklas later retracted the suggestion. Nevertheless, Horst was aggrieved by the charge, and wanted to do something more to show his open attitude and essential decency. He wanted to make a positive gesture.

At this point, three years had passed since we first met. I knew of Charlotte's papers, which were kept at the schloss, but had seen no more than a few photograph albums, several pages from his mother's many diaries, and one or two letters. Horst responded positively to requests for individual documents I might be interested in, but I had not asked for, or seen, the whole. Perhaps Horst could make Charlotte's papers available to a larger audience, in particular scholars and researchers? After all, he was convinced the material reflected Otto's essential decency, and revealed no wrongdoing by either of his parents. He was open to the idea, and said he would reflect on it. In due course he enquired about a possible home for the material. I mentioned the US Holocaust Memorial Museum, in Washington DC. He reflected further and a few weeks later got back in touch to say the idea was a good one and he would like to take it forward.

I introduced him to an archivist at the museum, an Austrian who, by happy coincidence, had a family connection with the Wächters. Exchanges took place, a positive note was struck. A team of digital transcribers from Washington DC descended on the schloss, where they took a few days to scan and digitise Charlotte's papers, thousands of pages of documents and photographs, well beyond the scope I imagined. Generously, Horst offered me a complete set of the papers. A few days later a used envelope was posted into the letterbox at my home in London, barely sealed with sticky tape. It contained a pale-blue USB stick.

I placed the stick into my computer and opened the files. It held nearly thirteen gigabytes of digital images, 8,677 pages of letters, postcards, diaries, photographs, news clippings and official documents. They were roughly curated, folders arranged by type, in a vaguely chronological manner.

Five folders contained letters and postcards that Charlotte and Otto sent to each other over a period of twenty years, from May 1929 (a postcard from Charlotte in Rome) to July 1949 (a letter from Charlotte to Otto, in Rome): 1929–1934, 1935–1937, 1938–1943, 1944–1945, 1945–1949.

A folder entitled *Erinnerungen*, four files of 'Memories' written by Charlotte, many years after the events, which she recorded for the information of her six children, reminiscing across four periods of her life with Otto: 1938–1942, 1942–1945, 1945–1947, 1947–1949.

Meine Liebesjahre, Charlotte's love years, an account of the initial encounter and years with Otto.

Meine Kinderjahre, the years of the children, notebooks in which Charlotte recorded the first year of the life of each of the six Wächter children, from the birth of Otto in 1933 to that of Linde in 1944.

Charlotte took care to explain the purpose of her reminiscences, in a regular, sloping handwriting which a friend would tell me was written in an Austrian dialect that was littered with grammatical errors. 'I have been thinking of setting this interesting life down on paper for some time,' she wrote in 1978, 'a gift for my children'. A year later, in another volume, she elaborated on the purpose of her effort:

> Today I have decided to do what I have wanted to do for a very long time. I wanted to write down the years from 1945, at least in a rough manner as far as I can still remember the events. It will be of value for the children to acquire some knowledge about the time that they can barely remember. I hope that they will realise that the relationship with my husband Otto Wächter only survived because

our love was without any limits and even went beyond death, where
we will be reunited one day.

The files were varied, as their titles made clear.

Lebensgeschichte, a short, handwritten memoir.

Fotoalben, photo albums.

Fotos Lemberg, photographs of Lemberg.

Hochaufgelöste, high-resolution images. This comprised two folders, one with the title *Identitätskarten*, which intrigued me so much
that I could not resist opening it immediately. The folders held identity
cards used by Otto in the time of his second disappearance, after May
1945, in the name of Oswald Werner and Alfredo Reinhardt.

Negative, photographic negatives. Twenty-four folders, each with a
title. Papa and Otto, 1934. Summer, 1938. Versailles. Thumersbach,
1944. *Kriegspolizeiauto*, wartime police car. And so on.

Nachlass, estate documents. Eight folders.

Privatdokumente 1901–1961. Thirteen folders of documents identified as 'private', or personal, divided by year: 1938, 1939 and so on,
to 1945 and then beyond.

Stammbuch, the book of the tribe, starting with the entry Charlotte
made on 1 January 1925, New Year's Eve spent with her parents.

Tagebücher, Charlotte's diaries, twenty-nine folders, one for each
year, mostly divided by year: 1927, 1929, 1930, up to 1945. Some years
were missing, 1928, not so important, but also 1933 and 1939, two
crucial years in their lives. Did she not write a diary in those years, or
were they lost, or destroyed, as part of an exercise in cleansing?

There was only one diary for Otto, a *Kalender* for 1949, the year
entered in pencil, in his angular writing, with a stained cover. This
contained information on Otto's life on the run, after the war, and the
time in Rome, the last months of his life.

Zeitungen 1949, newspaper clippings from the year.

Tonbänder, sound recordings. Fourteen folders, each with two sides
of an old cassette tape, digitised. I opened cassette one, side one, and
heard Charlotte's voice for the first time, methodical and rhythmic,
in German, high-pitched, anxious. 'December 1966 . . .' the tape
began. I listened to a second cassette, with the title 'Conversation with
Melitta Wiedemann', an exchange with the journalist. It took place in
April 1977 in the café of the Four Seasons Hotel, in Munich. Glasses
were clinked, a toast offered, then an account of interesting people

Charlotte met, like Sir Oswald Mosley, founder of the British Union of Fascists. A 'real personality', Charlotte told her dining companion. 'Politics is splendid.'

'I was an enthusiastic Nazi,' a female voice said.

'So was I,' the other replied. 'Still am.'

'Great times,' said the first voice. 'Hitler was our saviour.' Although, the voice added, she did not agree with everything the Führer did. The transgressions, whatever they might have been, were not specified.

The material was voluminous. Over the weeks and months that followed I dipped in and out of the folders. The photographs were accessible, but the written material was more difficult, mostly in German, handwritten not typed. That meant thousands of pages of handwriting to decipher. Charlotte's became easier to read, especially the letters, although the diaries were harder because phrases were often truncated, or words abbreviated. Many entries were mundane, like the time of daily occurrences – awaking, eating, napping, sleeping – or simple facts related to one of the children, such as their weight, or the nature of a fever. She liked to grade aspects of her life – things were '*ganz nett*' (quite nice), or '*sehr schön*' (very nice), or '*schrecklich*' (awful), or '*nicht sehr gut*' (not very good). Individuals received a comment too: '*recht nett*' (really nice), or '*leider beide so sehr unintelligent & dumm*' (unfortunately both so very unintelligent and dumb).

Otto's writing was more difficult to decipher. It was neat and controlled, but I found the angular, tiny and precise words difficult to read, almost incomprehensible. My eye tended to be drawn to that which could more easily be understood: like a pronounced number or letter, or a drawing, of which there were a few.

Nevertheless, in the most general of terms, I was able to gain a sense of the nature of the material. Hundreds of letters and postcards that passed between Charlotte and Otto over two decades, with dates and addresses that allowed their lives to be traced, in a geographic sense. A birth certificate. A school report. A university document. A tram pass, from Vienna, 1929. Three documents, each with a swastika. An SS personnel file. Staff reports. A paper issued by the Vienna Bar Association. A page of testimony from the Nuremberg trials. An academic article on the 1934 July Putsch. Otto's *curriculum vitae*, from 1935. A lunch menu, December 1939. A decree signed by Otto, in Kraków. A letter from Lemberg. A page from the *New York Times*. A handwritten note from Bishop Alois Hudal in Rome. An article clipped from *L'Unità* newspaper. A child's drawing. A cartoon. A poem by Goethe. A typed manuscript with the title *Quo Vadis Germania?*.

Charlotte's papers lingered in my mind. On a summer's evening my wife and I invited a few friends for dinner. One of the guests was an academic colleague at my university, a historian who directed its Centre for Editing Lives and Letters. Professor Lisa Jardine had recently given an inaugural lecture with the enticing title 'Temptation in the Archives'. She posed questions of interest and complexity: What are the different ways to assess archival material of a personal nature? How is such material to be integrated into a broader historical context? How do we deal with surprises? What is the essential value of personal documents, if any?

Over dinner the conversation turned to Charlotte's papers. Lisa was curious to know more and invited me to visit, even though she was ill with an incurable cancer. 'Let me see some of the documents,' she suggested, to assuage her curiosity. A few days later, we met at her home, near the British Museum, where she lay on a large sofa, her husband John close by. She invited James Everest to join us, her last doctoral student, and my editor at *Vanity Fair* came with his wife, as they happened to be in London.

I arrived with a handful of documents that I printed out, thinking they might be of interest to Lisa, some letters and photographs. As we talked over several hours, Lisa gravitated towards the more personal documents, letters that passed between Otto and Charlotte, two decades of correspondence, and diaries.

She was struck in particular by the number of letters written in the last months of Otto's life.

'Why would a husband and wife write to each other so often, at such length and detail?' she asked.

'Because they loved each other?' I ventured.

Lisa's eyes were lively and excited. She was several steps ahead of us.

'No.' She spoke the word emphatically, with a knowing smile, and shook her head. She had been here before.

'There's more there, a code maybe, a communication between the two of them, sharing things they don't want others to see.' We should try to find out what was really there, between the lines and the words. 'Let's see if we can find out what really happened to Otto Wächter, what Charlotte knew, if she helped.'

A seed was sown. Within a few days we agreed on the outlines of a research project, without thinking much about its scope or ambition, or the time it would take. James would lead a group of three German-speaking assistants from among my graduate students. The task was to decipher the letters and diaries from the last period of the shared lives of Charlotte and Otto.

We adopted a methodical approach. Letters and diaries would first be transcribed in the original German language, then digitised, then translated into English. We would search for patterns, names and places that recurred, and seek to decipher those entries which appeared in obvious code. We would try to place the anecdotes and items of information on which Otto and Charlotte wrote into a broader histor-ical and political context. We understood this to be slow and metic-ulous work. It would take time, yet it was important, as the material seemed unique, the private papers of a couple, the husband indicted and on the run, seeking to escape. This would be a painstaking act of reconstruction and interpretation, work that could not be rushed.

We would start with the period between 1945 and 1949, from the end of the war, when Otto disappeared, until the moment he died in bed nine of the Sala Baglivi at the Santo Spirito Hospital.

22

1945, Hagener Hütte

The end of the war, and the disappearance of Otto, turned Charlotte's world upside down. Karl Renner, newly appointed head of a provisional government packed with communists, declared Austria's immediate independence from Germany. Occupied by the four Allied powers, Austria and Vienna were each divided into four zones, with the capital's inner city declared an international area. Thumersbach, where Charlotte lived with the children, and Salzburg, where she visited the family, were in the American zone. Mürzzuschlag was in the Soviet zone.

Charlotte described 1945 as the year of 'The Collapse', and the shock lasted a lifetime. With six children to look after, however, there was no time for introspection. Horst and Heide were retrieved from the safety of the mountains, along with the jewellery Charlotte had left with them there, although that required a struggle with the 'shameless' guardian who tried to keep the valuables.

The older children were enrolled at schools in Zell, where the situation was chaotic. 'Nazi teachers were in part interned in the concentration camp at Glasenbach,' Charlotte noted wistfully, and many who weren't party members were too old to teach. Hoping that Otto junior could continue at his Nazi-inclined school in Kreuzberg, she was disappointed when it was closed down. So she turned to the *Realgymnasium* in Salzburg, where she encountered an unpleasant new reality – the Wächter name, which until recently opened doors, now closed them. 'Unfortunately, we cannot take your son,' the new headmaster, a priest, informed her. She was left to imagine the reason. 'Didn't the Bible say that one should help widows and orphans?' she enquired. An intervention by Bishop Pawlikowski, who would object to the replacement of three hundred imprisoned Nazi doctors with recently liberated Jewish counterparts ('the Catholic views the Jew consistently as an opponent of its ancestral faith'), did not assist.

The family was soon forced out of the farmhouse in Thumersbach, which was returned to its previous owner, former Governor Rehrl. 'An unjust estate never prospers,' Charlotte recognised, but only many years later. Her archive passed in total silence over criminal proceedings brought against Otto in the local courts – 'the accused's current whereabouts are unknown', a court document noted – and the decisions that declared him guilty of property crimes. The farmhouse was seized, and Charlotte kept no clipping of the report of the US military government, or the article in the *Wiener Zeitung*. Evicted from the happy home, she found four rooms in a guesthouse near Zell-am-See's lower station cable car, where the family lived with grandfather Josef and aunt Ilse.

The 'Thousand Year Reich' ended early, as the enemy invaded too fast, Charlotte recorded. She was horrified by the 'army of refugees' that streamed in from the east, pursued by Russians who were 'worse than Vandals or Huns'. Widespread allegations of rape and pillage caused friends in Vienna to hide in cellars, as fearful as chickens. Her parents fled the family apartment, saved by brother Heini, who piled furniture into two old army trucks. Charlotte's brothers lost their homes, 'simply because they were party members'. So unfair, she complained, how the Viennese *Obernazis* lost everything. Still, she recovered some property from a nameless 'plunderer' identified only as a 'concentration camp criminal'.

The family flat in Vienna was confiscated, an ignominy made worse when she learned it was being used as the office of a 'concentration camp association'. Charlotte acted to recover the home, which was no easy task as she needed permissions to cross the Soviet zone to reach Vienna. Being a 'Nazi wife' didn't assist, she reported. The apartment door was opened by an elderly man, friendly and polite. 'I entered, invited him to sit down, and presented myself as the daughter of the Bleckmanns, the owners.' She did not mention the Wächter name. 'How could the concentration camp association take a stranger's flat, and everything in it, without asking?' she enquired. 'It's worse than under Hitler, a regime you condemn.'

She sensed the old man's embarrassment. 'My parents weren't in the party,' she told him, they were decent folk, and the confiscation of the home was illegitimate. She demanded the occupiers leave within four weeks, which they did. The flat was recovered, then sold for a decent sum. 'I got my share,' Charlotte recorded.

Villa Mendl was also forfeited. 'Maybe we shouldn't have taken it,' Charlotte conceded, but only forty years after the event. Maybe the 'flush of victory', seduced by the chance to escape a poor, mostly happy life, to go back to the heights, led them to a path they never should have taken. 'Maybe we did not really understand the impact of our wrong decisions.'

She sought to justify her actions on the grounds that the property was empty when they were given it, and its owner, a 'rich Jew', had chosen to emigrate. Was Charlotte to blame for that? No more than Herr Lippert, she believed, the architect who administered the property and passed it to his friends, the Wächters. 'I never really wanted the villa,' she confided, but there was so little else available, and in such a situation, with three small children, Lippert persuaded her to take it. He was more responsible. If Charlotte had qualms, this was how she overcame them.

Other losses were passed in silence, including the family steel mill in Mürzzuschlag. A friendly archivist in the town's winter sports museum found documents that traced the history of the time, from the issue of the *Schoeller-Bleckmann Werkszeitung* that celebrated the Anschluss with photographs of the steelworks bedecked in swastikas, to the post-war letters that described the approach of the Soviets, the flight of the owners, and the nationalisation of the mill. A new director thwarted efforts by Walther Bleckmann, Charlotte's father – the only one who wasn't a member of the party – to recover the property. The Bleckmann connection was severed.

Faced with the loss, the Bleckmann brothers regrouped in St Gilgen, near Salzburg, and set up a new business. Charlotte visited regularly, and a friend who worked nearby as a milkmaid provided her with a steady supply of eggs, butter, flour and bacon. To pay, Charlotte bartered ballgowns and traded in small quantities of sugar.

As spring turned to summer, newspapers started to report on the fate of senior Nazis, a litany of indictments, arrests, suicides and disappearances. 'Austrian War Criminals Indicted' was a familiar headline. A United Nations commission published a list of three hundred 'particularly grave' cases, with many names from Charlotte's address book. 'Blaschke, former Mayor of Vienna . . . Dr Hans Fischböck, Minister of Commerce in the Government which negotiated the Anschluss . . . Odilo Globotschnick, former Gauleiter of Vienna . . . S.S. Gen. Dr Ernst Kaltenbrunner . . . Seyss-Inquart . . . Dr Otto Waechter'. In December the *Oberösterreichische Nachrichten* ran a front-page story – 'Austria

Accuses!' – which identified Otto as one of the worst war criminals. Such lists and clippings did not make it into Charlotte's papers.

Nor did Charlotte mention the fate of comrades and friends whose lives were overwhelmed by the speed of the changes. At the end of May, 'dear Globus' was discovered by the British while hiding in a hut near the Weissensee. He was taken to Schloss Paternion, south of Salzburg, in the courtyard of which he committed suicide.

Otto's nemesis in the Government General, Friedrich-Wilhelm Krüger, also took his own life, in an American camp near Linz. Heinrich Himmler, caught by the British, took a cyanide capsule. Soon after, his wife Margarete, and daughter Gudrun, were caught near Bolzano. 'Local soldier helps locate Frau Himmler', the *Jersey Journal* declared.

LT. THOMAS A. LUCID

Local Soldier Helps Locate Frau Himmler

Hans Frank was caught in Bavaria, with thirty-eight volumes of diaries and a fine collection of artwork. Ernst Kaltenbrunner, Otto's closest friend in the SS, was found hiding in the Wildensee Hütte in the Altaussee municipality, near Salzburg, posing as a Wehrmacht doctor. The Canadians tracked down Horst's godfather, Arthur Seyss-Inquart, hiding in Holland. The three comrades made it onto the list of 'prominents', twenty-two leading Nazis chosen to face trial at Nuremberg's Palace of Justice, charged with 'crimes against humanity' and genocide. The trials opened on 20 November 1945, with vivid accounts of the killings in the territories governed by Otto, the killings of more than 130,000 people, including more than 8,000 children, during the first year of Otto's reign in Lemberg. Such matters were reported in the newspapers, but I found no mention of the most famous case in history anywhere in Charlotte's diary or letters. A year later, on 1 October 1946, Frank, Seyss-Inquart and Kaltenbrunner, Otto's closest colleagues, were convicted and sentenced to death. Two weeks after that photographs of their hanged bodies were published in newspapers around the world. Their remains were cremated and disposed of in a river.

Josef Bühler, State Secretary of the Government General, hoped to save himself by giving testimony at Nuremberg, but then he too was charged. Convicted of 'crimes against humanity' by the Supreme

National Tribunal of Poland, he was hanged in Kraków, close to his office at the Wawel Castle. Rudolf Pavlu was caught in April 1949, and committed suicide to avoid extradition to Poland and a similar fate. Georg von Ettingshausen disappeared, as did Hans Fischböck, who changed his name to Juan and fled to Argentina, from where he wrote two letters to Charlotte. Fritz Katzmann, Otto's SS colleague from Lemberg, vanished, to reappear in 1957 in a hospital in Darmstadt, revealing his real identity to a hospital chaplain shortly before he died.

As the list of comrades in free circulation diminished, Charlotte feared greatly for Otto, her disappeared husband, knowing he was hunted by many different enemies. The Jews were said to have formed hit squads, and the Soviets set up military tribunals to eliminate Nazi perpetrators in occupied zones. The Poles wanted justice, and the Americans established themselves in Gmunden, only an hour from Salzburg, where the 430th Detachment of the US Army Counter Intelligence Corps (CIC) was leading the search for Nazi criminals. This went on as Winston Churchill declared in a speech in Fulton, Missouri, that 'an iron curtain' had descended across the continent of Europe. In a Cold War context, Charlotte became aware of the presence of the CIC, their efforts to find her husband, and the surveillance she was subjected to.

In 1947, after Josef Wächter and Otto's sister Ilse returned to Vienna, Charlotte moved the family to Salzburg, where her brothers had started their new company. She worked for them as a housekeeper, drawing a much-needed salary. With the proceeds from the sale of porcelain acquired in Vienna, Kraków and Lemberg, she bought a small house at 2 Anton-Hall-Strasse. My hut, she called it, with five bedrooms, a small garden, and views over the Untersberg woods.

She supplemented her income by renting out bedrooms during the summer, when the children were with friends or at camps run by Caritas, the Catholic relief organisation. Richard Woksch, who managed the brothers' business, rented a room two nights a week. Circumstances gradually improved and she was soon able to retain domestic help, a fifteen-year-old girl with 'gypsy blood, wild and stubborn'. Lilly stayed with the family for a year, until Charlotte found her a husband from Texas, an Indian with 'slit eyes'.

The year was characterised by food shortages and riots in Vienna, the end of a denazification programme for Austria's half a million Nazis, and mounting Cold War tensions. The Americans feared a Berlin-style blockade of Vienna, or, less likely, a Soviet invasion of

Austria. At the end of the year the Marshall Plan was agreed, to provide financial aid from the United States. The first tranche of funds brought a degree of economic stability.

By 1948 the situation of the Wächters had stabilised. The family had a home, Charlotte had a regular job, and the children were at school. Yet the fate of Otto remained unknown. In October 1948 a letter arrived from Fritz Ostheim, an engineer who served with him. He provided Charlotte with a brief account of her husband's activities in the last days before the war ended, in Austria in the company of Feldmarschall Albert Kesselring. Since May 1945, Ostheim wrote, 'we as well have lost every trace' of your husband. He wished for better news, but there was none to share.

'We as well . . .'

Herr Ostheim's letter was buried in Charlotte's papers, and I read it carefully, several times. The words chosen suggested he may have written in response to a letter from Charlotte, one in which she told him she had no trace of her husband. If so, it was an act of deception, intended perhaps for those who were watching her and hoping through her to find Otto.

The truth was that in October 1948, when she received Herr Ostheim's letter, she knew exactly where Otto was: en route to the family home in Salzburg, after three years hidden nearby in the mountains of Austria. For all this period, without telling anyone except her sister-in-law Ilse, Charlotte was in close contact with Otto, seeing him every two or three weeks. The truth was that, after May 1945, Otto never strayed far from Zell-am-See or Salzburg.

It took many years for the details to emerge. In a lengthy reminiscence written for the children, buried in her papers, Charlotte described how, at the end of May 1945, as the family gathered for a meal at the farmhouse in Thumersbach, an unknown girl turned up at the house. 'She asked to speak to me.' The girl carried Otto's wedding ring, as proof, and a note which proposed a rendezvous in nearby St Johann, Pongau. At a specified time, the note instructed, Charlotte was to walk along the main street of the town in the direction away from Grossarl. She gave the girl some money, a pair of shoes and a box of cigars, to be passed on to Otto.

A few days later, Charlotte travelled by bus to St Johann. She carried a backpack filled with food, clothing and shoes. As she walked along the specified street, her heart raced, anxious lest she had been followed.

'Suddenly a whistle came from a small barn, I saw Otto waving . . .'
They hugged and cried, spent the night together, talked about the
children, the work diaries which had been destroyed ('everything
was written down, to justify his actions, which were aimed at helping
as many people as possible'), their parents, the new home, Austria's
future, the fate of the Waffen-SS Galicia Division, and the items the
girl never delivered.

On parting they arranged a second rendezvous, two weeks later.
The location was precisely identified on a hiking map of the mountainous region. As she made her way home, the image that stayed in
Charlotte's mind was of Otto barefoot, walking on stony ground, a
man hunted as 'a criminal and persecuted'.

Each rendezvous was based on a precise meeting point. In the early
days she hitched a lift, then took a bus. Later, when they were running,
she could go by train. Each time her nerves were racked with anxiety;

she was unfamiliar with the meeting points, fearful she was being followed, or simply worried that they'd miss each other and lose contact forever. On one occasion they did fail to meet, in the Rauris valley, at a point where two roads forked into the valley, one to the left, the other to the right. She waited for a whistle but it never came. Was he arrested, or ill? She returned the next day, afraid that if she didn't find him their connection would be lost. This time she heard the whistle.

This continued every two or three weeks for three years, until the summer of 1948. Each rendezvous was in a different place. It might be at a hill farm on the mountain, or outside a small town, or near a tiny village, or at a secluded mountain hut. She kept listed some of the locations. Radtstädter Tauern ('frequently'). Vogelalm and Gnadenalm ('where a dairymaid liked him, and supplied food'). Altenmarkt ('in the mountains'). Flachau. St Johann in Pongau ('in the direction away from Wagrain and Grossarl'). Lend. Bad Gastein. Hagereralm. Mallnitz. Rauris ('frequently'). Lofer. Grossarl. Gröbming. At the Hagener Hütte.

Charlotte helped with food and clothing, and in other ways. On the run, Otto needed a new identity, and he took the name Oswald Werner. She explained how she met a friendly 'concentration camp guy', a nice man called Kuno Hoynigg, imprisoned at Dachau for his monarchist views, a follower of Otto von Habsburg, who once served under General Josef Wächter. He worshipped Otto's father, and wanted to assist the son, as a Catholic and a man concerned that the new regime – unlike the Nazis – took insufficient care of mothers in need, like Charlotte. At Dachau he knew an inmate who died there, and it was his identity – Oswald Werner – that Otto apparently took.

Otto obtained a membership card for the *Freies Österreich* (Free Austria), an underground organisation that was illegal in the Nazi period. Undated, it carried the name of Dr Werner, a teacher of languages from Vienna. The photograph, however, was of young Otto in uniform, taken in the 1930s, on the run after the July Putsch. He had a second identity card in Werner's name, issued by police headquarters in Vienna on 4 February 1946. The photograph was more recent, a side view of Otto in civilian

clothes, looking downward. The card was stamped by the police in Vienna and Salzburg, in the four control languages, German, English, French, Russian. Oswald was 1.78 metres tall – four centimetres less than the height referred to in Otto's SS file – with fair hair, blue eyes, 'oval' face, without distinguishing features. This card offered proof of Austrian citizenship, but was 'Valid only in Austria'.

These cards, and Charlotte's determined assistance, helped Otto to survive in the Austrian Alps, for more than three years.

'Death followed him', Charlotte noted, so 'he never stayed in one place for more than three or four days'. He broke into mountain huts, where shepherds might have left cheese or bread or other supplies, a few days there, then on to the next place. The former Nazi governor was now a 'poacher of sheep', a man who buried meat in the snow and hoped it would still be there on his return. Instead of decrees, he wrote poems to his wife, with pencil drawings that described her difficult journeys ('First came a bus . . .') but ended on a note of optimism ('it will again be nice and warm and light!!').

Charlotte brought supplies, based on Otto's list of needs – a basket, rubber shoes, a raincoat, a hat – 'little notes' usually handed over as they parted, which Charlotte kept in her papers. 'I brought nice things, like bacon and non-perishable foods, eaten with great pleasure.' In the autumn she brought winter equipment, like pants, pullovers, under-garments and skis. In the spring, she carried summer items.

Believing herself to be under surveillance, she took precautions. 'I was spied on day and night by the CIC, who were trying to identify a connection to my dear husband Otto.' She relied on a network of friends, leaving home on a bicycle, early in the morning, at five, 'empty-handed, so as not to be conspicuous'. She'd pick up food and other essentials left with a friend, someone like Lukas Hansel, in nearby Bruck-Fusch, where Hermann Göring was caught. Then she might take a local train to St Johann in Pongau, half an hour away, or further up the mountain to Bad Gastein, an hour and a half distant. From there a bus, for a ride that could be as long as twenty-five miles, to the foot of a mountain. Then a hike up the mountain to the Hagener Hütte, 2,450 metres above the sea. A postcard from the time showed the isolation.

'Sometimes, when I arrived I was so exhausted I could barely speak.' She would often go straight to sleep. The next day there was

laundry, if there was a well, and repairs to Otto's clothes. She cooked
and he devoured the food. If she missed the last train back she'd find
somewhere to sleep.

Charlotte's assistance was not, however, the only reason he was able
to survive. Otto was not alone.

23

Buko

For three years Otto's companion in the mountains was a young man Charlotte met at the first rendezvous, in St Johann in Pongau. His name was Burkhardt Rathmann. Buko, as she called him, was a 'younger SS-man, with an adventurous spirit', who she liked very much. 'Simple, honest, a stellar companion', she recorded, Otto was 'in good hands'. Buko was practical, able to pick locks, break into mountain huts and find places of refuge and safety. He knew how to gather food and kill animals, avoid avalanches and survive in bitter alpine conditions.

It was only long after Horst and I first met that I learned about this story. Drinking schnapps, seated around the fireplace in the upstairs living room of the schloss, Horst mused about Otto's escape to the mountains. The archive contained a handful of letters, and a small number of photographs from those years. There were gaps and my questions were plentiful, especially about Buko. What did he do during the war? What was he like? Why did he help Otto?

'You want to know about Buko?' Horst asked. I nodded.

'I could answer your questions and tell you about Buko,' he continued. 'Or we could telephone him.'

The words surprised me: Buko was alive and well, aged ninety-two, and living in Germany. Horst wandered into another room and dialled a telephone number, a direct line to the past. He spoke in German for a few minutes, then returned. Buko would be pleased to receive us in a month's time, at his home.

In January 2017, James Everest and I met Horst at Hanover airport. I brought a copy of *Trouble Follows Me*, as Horst requested, a spy thriller about an unexpected death, by Ross Macdonald (real name Kenneth Millar), one of his favourite writers. We rented a car and drove to Reinhardshagen, a small town on the banks of the River Weser, crossing with a tiny ferry. Buko's house, on the floodplain, was small and well-kept, lined with bookshelves and photographs. Ute, his daughter, kept a watchful eye as her father settled into a wheelchair. I admired Buko's jowls, the abundance of white hair, the bushy eyebrows, the bright, plaid shirt.

Ute hovered, ready to enforce one condition Buko imposed, for the only interview he ever gave: no question was to be asked about anything he did before 9 May 1945. If we asked, the interview was over. For seventy years, it seemed, he worried about being arrested, for his role in tracking down partisans in Italy and Yugoslavia, then dispatching them. He never wanted to talk about the past, Ute told us, not until Horst turned up. The housekeeper offered tea served with slices of rich, flourless chocolate cake.

Buko, born in 1924, was twenty-one when he encountered Otto, in May 1945, in southern Austria. He came from Italy, after service with the 24th Waffen Mountain Division of the SS Karstjäger, a division which, I later learned, was formed in 1944 by Odilo Globočnik. After the 24th Division surrendered to the British in May, Buko fled north, crossing the mountains into Austria with three comrades who wanted to return home. Fearing arrest as an SS man, Buko decided to accompany them part of the way but not to go home.

'We crossed high, as the Americans or English were down below,' he explained. At the Lungau's Lower Tauern area, the highest mountains in Austria, he left his companions. 'That is where I met Otto Wächter.' He couldn't recall the name of the village. Horst had brought Charlotte's maps, with many green pencil markings. We spread them on the table, peered at the underlinings; Horst placed his finger near Mariapfarr. Buko nodded. 'That's the place,' he said, in front of the church.

Was the meeting accidental, or arranged? Buko was evasive. 'Wächter was in Italy, like me, but I was small, insignificant.' No, they didn't know each other, he suggested. 'I agreed to walk around with him for a while. He didn't say who he was, just that he wanted to go home, but needed to stay in the mountains for a little while. So that's what we did.'

And then?

'After ten or fifteen days he met his wife. He sent her a note – that's how I met Frau von Wächter – then we continued to walk around the Lower Tauern, from one place to the next . . .'

'Did you know who my father was?' Horst enquired.

'Neither knew who the other one was,' Buko replied. 'We were both cautious, but he was more cautious.' Buko paused, then said, without a prompt: 'He was a wanted war criminal.' Within a week each knew the other's identity. 'I looked at him and said: "You are either this one or that one."' Otto confirmed. 'From our conversations I knew he was either Wächter or Wächtler.' Fritz Wächtler, SS Gauleiter in Bayreuth, executed at the end of the war for desertion, although Buko wouldn't have known that.

It wasn't difficult to work out Otto's identity. 'He'd tell me, "This and that person would say 'My dear W'." Never the name, but I'm not stupid. I told him straight to his face who he could be, and then he told me who he was.' Buko knew the name Wächter.

'You were a very young SS man,' Horst said, surprised by his father's notoriety.

'Yes, but I wasn't one of the stupid ones.'

Everyone knew Otto Wächter, who he was and what he did. Buko relaxed, a large smile across his face.

'Was my father evil or good-natured?' Horst enquired, a gently leading question. 'He wasn't evil,' Buko said, with another warm smile.

'So he wasn't a bad man?' Horst wanted more.

'We were together and very comradely. In the beginning, he was reserved, but always friendly.'

'Did you know he was hunted?' I asked. Buko nodded. By who? Everyone. Especially the English and the Americans, but the Soviets too, although they were far away. The greatest fear was generated by the Soviets, because Otto had been 'active' as a governor in their territory.

Did he know why he was wanted, what he was accused of?

'That didn't matter. He had a high rank, SS-Gruppenführer, and most of all he was governor of Galicia and Kraków.' Another pause. 'The Austrians were looking for him too, because he led the July Putsch.'

'And the Jews?' Horst asked, gingerly.

'I assumed they were looking for him, although, as far as I know, he treated the Jews humanely.' This brought a knowing smile to Horst's face, and a glance towards me. 'There wasn't much he could do,' Buko continued. 'Jews from other areas were collected and brought into his territory.'

Horst added his own gloss. 'He acted humanely, as far as he could; the thing with the Jews, he was not responsible, he tried to help them.'

Buko moved seamlessly on to the three years spent with Otto. Fearing capture, they moved frequently, from one place to the next, high in the mountains, between huts, where they were safe. They avoided the valleys. 'The Americans and the English were mostly too lazy to go up into the mountains.'

Did news reach them? 'Yes, of course.' Charlotte brought newspapers, so they heard about the Nuremberg trials and the outcome, the hanging of Frank, Seyss-Inquart and Kaltenbrunner.

'How did Otto react to news of the hangings?' Sanguine. He knew Frank and the others well. '*Vae victis*,' he said, a Latin adage, offered with a shrug of the shoulders. Buko looked at us knowingly. Woe to the vanquished, to the victor the spoils. The news increased Otto's sense of anxiety.

'Was my father angry?' Horst asked.

'Can't you imagine?' Buko replied.

He liked Frau Wächter. 'I have nothing bad to say about your mother, a well-liked acquaintance.' For many years they stayed in touch, exchanged cards at Christmas. Over three years in the mountains she met them every two or three weeks, with food and clothing. Buko was the cook, milk thickened with flour and salt. 'We had no eggs,' Buko said, when Horst asked if his father knew how to boil one.

'Whatever he cooked, I wouldn't have eaten,' he added. 'He learned how to cook from me.' Buko grinned. They got milk from the pretty milkmaids, who didn't offer anything else.

'No ladies?' Horst enquired. 'My father worshipped beautiful women.'

No, an 'unnecessary burden'. When she came, his wife stayed for a night or two. They found a place to be alone. 'On the alps, there was always space.'

'I have nothing bad to say about Otto Wächter,' Buko said firmly. 'Why should I? We got along well. We had common interests.'

Buko led, Otto followed. 'He should have been the one to order me around, but that wouldn't have worked.' Buko gave him tasks, and over time Otto learned how to get by. He might have survived a short period alone, but not long, even if he was healthy and strong. He was never ill, Buko said, except for an occasional bout of flu. 'Look at a photo of him, you can see for yourselves.' When they parted Otto was 'in good health'.

In solitude, the two men entertained each other with conversation. They talked about politics, current events, past times, the war. There was no discussion of religion, and they never tried to go to church. 'I am not Catholic, although we were both anti-communists,' Buko added. A shared hatred of communism bonded them, and there was plenty to discuss, as Otto liked to talk about his career. Did Otto ever express any regrets? 'Not something one talks about, but he talked a lot about those times.'

They sang, without instruments. Not even a harmonica, Buko said, as every little gram of weight mattered, while they wandered around the mountains.

'Did he whistle?' Horst asked.

'Very little – your father was not musically talented.'

Were there tensions? 'I can't remember ever having fought with him. You don't fight in a situation like that, when you depend on one another.' The fear of capture was constant, and that made them close. 'The mountain is where freedom lies,' Buko explained. He feared internment. 'Mostly, we felt safe at two thousand metres, with little fear that anyone followed us.'

Over the course of the afternoon other memories emerged, an account of survival during brutal winter conditions.

There was an occasional visitor, but never with a name.

A local might sometimes offer them shelter.

They appreciated places like the Hagener Hütte, a nineteenth-century mountain-top refuge. This prompted Ute to bring out a photograph.

There were avalanches. 'One day we triggered twelve . . . at the top of the mountain we would hop about, until it grumbled, and then the slope would start moving, which brought an avalanche on the opposite side.' He recalled one in particular. 'He was covered up to here.' Buko pointed to his shoulder. 'He could look at his surroundings, but nothing else. If not for me he would have died there. He couldn't move his arm. Once an avalanche solidifies, it's over . . .'

In the summer of 1948 they decided to descend from the mountains, when Buko's mother turned up unexpectedly. 'She said it was time to come home.' Alone, Otto decided he would try to head south, into Italy, the Vatican. 'That was the plan all along, because that's where the Reich migratory route was,' Buko says. The form of words – the Reich migratory route – was new to me. It was better known as the

'Ratline', an escape route used by Nazis to flee from Europe to South America, identified as a place of safety governed by sympathetic leaders like President Juan Perón, in Argentina. Had Otto always intended to head for South America?

'At first he didn't know about it, but later he did.' Maybe Charlotte provided information.

'Did he tell you that he wanted to emigrate to South America?' Horst enquired.

'I don't know if he told me, or his wife Charlotte did.'

Farewells were exchanged in the small town of Gröbming, located between Mariapfarr and Salzburg. 'I was happy to go home, but a goodbye is always sad. We were together for three years, day and night. When you finally go home, you are never sad.'

Did he expect to see Otto again?

'That was the plan.' They stayed in touch via Charlotte.

As the conversation drew to a close, Horst touched briefly on the wartime years. 'You were with the Karstjäger, right?' Buko nodded. There was a large book on the shelf, with that title, a history of the 24th Waffen Mountain Division of the SS Karstjäger.

'It was supposed to be published in German,' Buko said, 'but they ran out of money, so it's in Italian.'

Later, as I thumbed through the pages, Buko said: 'I am in some of the photos.' He chased partisans, an explorer of caves and other places of hiding. He was proud of his work. 'Your brigade?' I asked. 'Yes.' Ute intervened. Nothing about the war, remember?

'Buko hunted communist partisans,' Horst explained after we had left. I found a copy of the book, with photographs of young Buko, details of his activities in the Karstjäger, his rank (*Rottenführer*, a corporal) and the award of a silver *Bandenkampfabzeichen* (Bandit Warfare Badge) presented by SS Gruppenführer Odilo Globočnik, who had established the division in his capacity as 'Higher SS and Police Leader for the Operational Zone of the Adriatic Littoral'. The book was silent as to the division's involvement in war crimes, the killing of large numbers of Italian civilians as a reprisal for partisan attacks.

Among the books, Buko had placed mementos. I opened a small black box, which held a bronze cross with a swastika in the middle.

Along the shelf, in front of a copy of *The Golden Treasury of German Fairy Tales*, stood a wooden frame, small and round. I noticed it behind Buko, as we spoke, but from a distance could not make out who it portrayed.

Standing at the bookshelf, I picked up the frame and looked closely at the image. It was a small black and white photograph. A seated man, pensive, wearing an armband.

24

1948, Salzburg

Otto and Buko came down from the mountain and separated because Charlotte felt a pang of maternal responsibility. 'I was suddenly plagued by a guilty conscience, for not having told Buko's mother that her son was alive.' She contacted Frau Rathmann, who requested to be taken to her son. 'Maybe I shouldn't have done that, but I put myself in her shoes and thought she should know.'

Putting herself in the shoes of others was not something Charlotte appeared to do very often, but it brought much happiness to Frau Rathmann. 'She desired her son's quickest possible return.' Charlotte accompanied her to the mountains. Frau Rathmann, thinking her young SS boy was dead, left the mountain a happy mother.

After the departure of Buko, Charlotte felt a renewed concern about Otto. 'He couldn't wander the mountains on his own,' so she stayed with him for part of the summer. She rented a modest hut, on a farm, where they were joined by the older children. Horst remained in Salzburg. They spent four weeks together, an unexpected vacation, a rare moment of relative peace, harmony and togetherness. Charlotte was anxious. 'We were high up, but we continued to worry that the enemy, the police, could appear at any moment.' The other development was that she became pregnant, for the ninth time. Later that summer, Dr Oberascher performed another abortion, Charlotte's third. Vienna, 1935. Lemberg, 1943. Salzburg, 1948. She had too much on her plate, she calculated; her energies should be directed to the salvation of Otto, and for that she would 'sacrifice' the child.

Otto descended from the mountains to a place of safety, near Going am Wilden Kaiser, a small Tyrolean town at the foot of the Kaiser Mountains. He stayed at the farmhouse of Georg Ettingshausen, a fellow lawyer and former Nazi comrade, a member of the *Deutsche Klub* who was implicated in the July Putsch. After the Anschluss, as head of the Vienna Bar Association, he oversaw the removal of 1,775 of its 2,541 members. Later, he served as legal adviser with the Hungarian mission in Austria and, in May 1945, disappeared. Or, as Charlotte preferred to put it, found himself 'expelled'.

Otto spent a few weeks under the care of 'dear' Helga Ettingshausen and her children, Christian and Irmgard, enjoying mountain hikes in the company of the eight-year-old boy, who took a shine to 'Uncle Ossi'. Charlotte visited, they spent a 'lovely few days together', photographs were taken. When she left, he accompanied her to the station at nearby, familiar St Johann in Pongau. At Christmas he recorded his debt to Helga in a poem. 'May divine powers always preserve the sincerity of your heart,' he wrote. 'May fate turn and bring about better times – Love always reaps love!'

By the end of 1948, with Otto feeling lonely and sad, Charlotte decided to take a risk: she would bring him home to Salzburg for Christmas, to the house on Anton-Hall-Strasse. When he arrived Horst didn't recognise him, not having seen him for nearly four years. Introduced as an uncle, a visitor from a distant land, Otto spent most of the period hidden in Charlotte's bedroom, as Otto junior and the other children bred turkeys and fished for crabs to sell to the Goldene Hirsch, the historic Salzburg hotel.

'A lovely, harmonious time, my Otto able to celebrate Christmas with us, in secret.' Four weeks together was a rare treat, recorded in a few photographs. Charlotte sat outside the wooden house, on a bench under a window, in heavy walking shoes, turned towards her husband, who remained inside the house, leaning on the sill, looking into the camera, caught between anxiety and comfort, in a pale suit. To be photographed was dangerous.

Horst stood on the wooden bench, one foot pushed against the wall, a happy boy. Linde sat between her mother and Traute, with a light-hearted air. Did they know that the man behind them was their father? Horst would tell me he had no memory of this moment. He remembered only the arrival of a man with a moustache, who would sometimes come to his room in the evening and give him a goodnight kiss. An uncle from a faraway place, he recalled, maybe South America.

The arrangement worked for a few weeks until trouble struck, when one of Charlotte's brothers visited and encountered Otto, a matter of considerable surprise. An 'unfortunate first strike', she called it. This was how the Bleckmann brothers learned he was alive and in Salzburg, more than three years after the end of the war. The secret might have been manageable had it stayed in the family, but it didn't. A neighbour visited, an elderly lady accompanied by a grandson who held her hand, a detail that remained in Charlotte's recollection. 'Watch out,' the neighbour warned, 'there are Soviet spies around.' 'It is being said that your husband supposedly lives with you,' another neighbour told her.

Otto had to leave. 'Our joy is over, pack your things, head to Bolzano,' Charlotte instructed. Albert Schnez, formerly of the Wehrmacht, who served with Otto during the last days of the war, visited. 'The astonishment in his eyes was unique,' Charlotte recalled, when he encountered Otto. Schnez told him it wasn't safe in Austria and, if he didn't want to go to Germany, he should head south, to Rome, then abroad. 'He wanted to emigrate to Argentina,' Charlotte noted, but she would not accompany him. 'I have six small children, how are they going to get to Argentina?' He should follow his instincts, head to Bolzano, a place of trusted friends and contacts, like the family of Baldur von Schirach, and Rafelsberger, the Aryaniser and fellow state commissioner in 1938. Riedel the journalist, and Neubacher, recently released from prison, were also in or around Bolzano.

25

1949, Bolzano

For Charlotte, 1949 was the 'terrible year', one that began badly, with Otto having been spotted by neighbours and forced to leave. The twin sister of Charlotte's mother, Aunt Else, died, and a few weeks later Charlotte's niece, the youngest child of her brother Richard, caught pneumonia and also died.

After he left Anton-Hall-Strasse, Otto hid with Richard Woksch for a few days. He left Salzburg by train on 4 February, stopping briefly in the resort town of Saalbach-Hinterglemm. He kept Charlotte informed of progress with notes delivered by hand, or messages communicated by word of mouth, offering coded reassurance. Do not send letters by post, Charlotte told him, they were dangerous and liable to be intercepted. The indelible mark of the military censors, stamped at the bottom of many letters, was too familiar.

He arrived in Innsbruck on 12 February, recorded with an 'I' written in a newly acquired 1949 diary. 'Everything coming together quite well, touch wood!' he wrote to her, as he came across familiar and friendly faces. An 'old acquaintance' from the Hammerschmiede area welcomed him at one place of rest, where he lay in a bathtub, 'naked as a babe'. At a railway station, however, he had a close encounter with a 'monopolistic crook', who passed close by but fortunately did not recognise him.

A couple of days later he left Innsbruck and made his way towards Sölden, intending to cross into Italy, perhaps through the Valler Tal, although the actual route was not detailed. On 16 February he started the difficult trek across the Dolomites and into Italy. He started off at three o'clock in the morning, to avoid being spotted, a climb across a mountainous terrain that was particularly treacherous in midwinter, a journey that took twenty-four hours, described in a coded letter to Charlotte. The 'little lights of Sölden' were one of his last sights of Austria.

Not much snow, so you have to carry your skis a lot, but above all the ice – sheer, green ice cascading over mountainsides, covering slopes, cliffs, boulders and making them impassable. You keep having to go round, climb up or down etc., to go forwards. Often the glaciers have open fissures and fractures – it looks like in high summer, blue ice everywhere. Good that the weather is nice and an advantage there's no danger of avalanches. The snow is rock-hard, so it's safe but hard work, as you're constantly fighting not to slip sideways. All these difficulties eat up your time, hence this 24-hour trip, even at 3 a.m. in the moonlight.

Occasionally he stopped to take shelter by an old stone wall, struggling to stay warm in the winter clothes Charlotte sent him, waiting for a 'much-longed-for' moon to break through to allow him to continue. The trip was nice but 'extremely arduous', he added, hoping that 'your husband doesn't get hold of this letter!' His heart full, his pen could 'not remain still any longer'.

He reached Merano on 17 February, and the next day scribbled 'M-B' in the diary, an indication of the journey to Bolzano and relative safety. From here he sent word to Charlotte. 'Journey completed, relieved to have arrived safely.' He asked her to send clothing and shoes to Albert Schnez in Innsbruck, care of the Arlberger Hof Hotel, from where they would be sent on.

In Bolzano, Frau Oberauch von Hösslin, an acquaintance, offered a bed and a haven for the month that followed. 'Dear Nora', Charlotte called her, a charming, wealthy divorcee who owned an apartment in town and a fine summer house in the mountains. Nora's presence lessened the 'burden' of worrying about Otto's well-being, although it gave rise to other concerns and tensions.

From the base in Bolzano, Otto visited old comrades in other parts of the South Tyrol. On 18 March he sent a postcard to Richard Woksch from the small town of Toblach, where Gustav Mahler composed *Das Lied von der Erde*. A place to 'set your soul and body at ease', the composer wrote. 'Cold, blue, wonderful', was Otto's take, in the shadow of the Dolomites.

He wrote regularly, letters that were careful not to reveal the identity of the comrades he spent time with. 'The monk' came for a meal. He had decided to postpone the 'spiritual journey', sometimes referred to as 'project Riccardo', a reference to Rome, until after Easter.

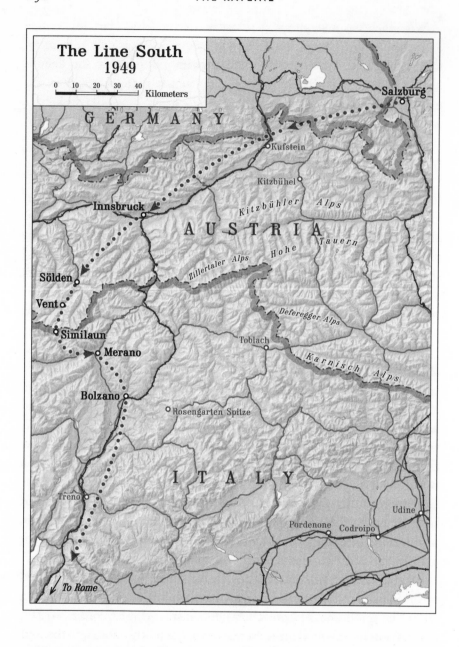

He spent time with 'funny Franz', whose identity, I later established, on the basis of an obscure archive that held two photographs, was Franz Riedl, a journalist with distinct Nazi sympathies, like many in that region. 'With Otto Wächter, summer 1949', Riedl wrote on one of them. The photographs showed Otto with Riedl and a third man, whose identity I did not know.

With the assistance of an acquaintance from Innsbruck, I was able to locate where the photograph was taken. In the Ritten area, he thought, near Bolzano, as the snow-capped mountain in the distant background was the Rosengartenspitze, which rises to nearly 3,000 metres. The wooden structures were used to trail vines, another clue that suggested the location was below 800 metres, which is the upper limit for vines to grow. It might be the village of Unterinn, another correspondent confirmed, an academic in Vienna. A second photograph in the Riedl archive showed Otto tanned and lean, in a clean white shirt and ordinary city shoes. He was seated in the sun, at a wooden table set for two, with wine.

Two days after arriving in Bolzano, as he told Charlotte, Otto decided to postpone the 'R-journey' – a reference to Rome – until after Easter. He would wait for necessities to be delivered, including a pair of slippers, a small suitcase, toiletries and copies of the *Salzburger Nachrichten* newspaper. As spring arrived, he begged Charlotte to visit, in time for the deep-blue sky, as the blossom broke out and young greenery emerged. But, he wrote, she should not travel to Bolzano with too many family members, as it was a time for utmost discretion. They could stay on the Schlern, visit the Seiser Alm, cycle across the blossoming Etschtal to Merano. Perhaps Charlotte might even accompany him to Rome? If so, she should bring all necessary clothes for a journey south. Black was best for Italy, 'for hat, coat, suit and so on'.

Otto's need for money was now urgent. Bring a few items of art, or antiquities, he wrote, which could be sold to raise funds. Prints would be good, as they were easy to carry and sell. Other 'artistic objects' might, however, raise more money, like 'the clock' or the 'old landscape paintings'. Charlotte sent a 'catalogue', a list of prints that could attract interest, more than the carpets, which would be difficult to transport. Of the various items mentioned in the correspondence, which were apparently acquired in Kraków or Lemberg, only one was identified with precision. 'We'd surely be able to get more for the Dürer' in Bolzano, Otto wrote, a reference to a valuable print. 'The clock' arrived in Bolzano in early April, and was quickly sold.

Charlotte agreed to visit, and arrived in Bolzano in time for Easter, on Friday 15 April. She travelled by train from Salzburg accompanied by Liesl and Traute, and Otto met them at the station. The four spent a few days alone in Bolzano, then visited Nora at Villa Oberauch, the mountain house at Völs am Schlern ('a divine area', Charlotte noted, although she was 'unable to obtain any deep, inner calm' because she was too consumed by thoughts of Tchaikovsky's music). Otto introduced Charlotte to 'old friends', Franz Riedl, the journalist, and Walter Rafelsberger. They rode bicycles and made a day trip to Merano, where they 'unexpectedly' met the Küfferles, Charlotte's sister and brother-in-law. Charlotte wrote home to the lady who looked after Horst and the other children in Salzburg, to say she'd be back on Friday, 29 April.

They spent two days with Nora at the summer house. Charlotte was suspicious, imagining what had passed between Nora and Otto. 'It was a strange time together,' she recalled. 'I wondered whether, in spite of her friendly disposition, Nora was jealous of our great love, maybe hoping for a loving friendship with Otto.' Something did happen between Nora and Otto, although Charlotte only ever alluded to it indirectly. 'I told Otto he was free to escape with another woman,' she recalled. 'His life was too dear and precious for me not to give him complete freedom, which I told him. I thought we were so united that nothing could separate us . . .'

On the evening of Wednesday, 27 April, as Otto packed his bags to prepare for the journey to Rome, Charlotte pleaded with him to delay the departure by a day. Travel overnight on the Thursday, she implored, so you arrive in Rome on the Friday morning. The plea fell on deaf ears. 'He wanted to leave in the morning, arrive in the evening.'

'The departure was terribly hard and painful.' She accompanied him to the station, with its distinct clock tower, and they stood on the platform for a long while. 'It tore my heart out to say goodbye, in the

last carriage of a train at Bolzano station.' She had a sense of foreboding, a fear that their farewell would last forever.

With a heavy heart, Charlotte took the two girls north, to Salzburg. Otto headed south, to Rome.

26

2016, Warsaw

As Charlotte and Otto parted at Bolzano train station, they harboured a deep fear that he might be caught by the Americans or Soviets, or the Poles on whose territory so many of his actions were committed and whose trials continued to be reported in the press. They were right to worry, as I learned from a folder of documents that lay untouched for many years in a Warsaw archive, until 2016, when I found it. At the very moment of parting, the Polish authorities recorded that they had encountered a 'trace' of Otto, and a criminal prosecutor redoubled efforts to catch him.

The folder in the archive bore the title 'Files Regarding Dr Otto Gustaw Waechter'. It held forty-one pages of legal documents, gathered by the Central Commission for the Investigation of War Crimes in Poland, a Polish government body charged with tracking down Nazis alleged to have committed crimes on the territory of occupied Poland. The Central Commission was established  at the end of the war, and its documents were mostly in Polish, which meant they needed to be translated into English.

Among the few pages in English, however, was a document with the title 'Request for Delivery of a Person Desired for Trial for a War Crime'. The 'Person Desired' was Otto, who was the subject of a request communicated by the Polish authorities to the military governor of the United States Zone in Germany, on 28 September 1946. The request concerned crimes committed in Lwów between 1942 and 1945, the particulars of which were brief but clear:

Subject is responsible for mass-murder (shooting and executions). Under his command as Governor of District Galicia, more than 100 thousand Polish citizens lost their lives.

The request for extradition to Poland was based on the erroneous belief that Otto was being held in a prison in Vienna.

This was the document I showed to Horst when we were together in Lviv, in the aula of the university, the one that caused me to lose my temper. His response was immediate, and premised on the innocence of his father. 'All the guilty ones have been judged,' he told me. As far as he was concerned, the names of those responsible for crimes had been fully documented, and since none of the lists included Otto's name, he was innocent. Everything else was 'imagination'.

I showed him a copy of the extradition request. 'A Polish document?' he asked. We read it together, aloud, with occasional pauses for reflection, as he digested the words. 'Yes,' he said. Silence. 'Of course.' A longer silence, followed by a sigh. He wasn't aware of this document, but the allegation of shootings and executions were mere 'general suppositions'. Otto was not responsible for the mass murders or killings that took place on his territory, they were *Geheime Reichssache*, Reich secrets. Otto knew nothing about these acts, and had no involvement in any of them. Moreover, he continued, the document was produced by the Soviets, who had a dim view of his father.

It was a Polish and American document, I countered.

'Poland was under Soviet rule at that time,' he retorted. He could not accept what he was reading. 'I have so many documents from people who knew him personally, who said he had a decent character, that he tried everything he could to prevent the things that happened. It could not be him. I want to know what really was going on, the details . . .'

It took some time to translate all the documents from the archive in Warsaw from Polish into English. They offered multiple narratives, but the one I was most interested in was the story of Poland's efforts to locate Otto, from the time the war ended to the moment he headed for Rome, in April 1949.

The trail began with a statement written by a Polish dentist in early 1946. He was prompted to write to the Polish embassy in Prague after he heard a report on Austrian radio, which included the names of several war criminals scheduled to appear before the Austrian courts. One of the names was Dr Wächter who, the dentist asserted, was responsible for the murder of more than 100,000 Jews, Poles and

Ukrainians, including members of his family. The dentist's account made its way into the folder.

A few months later, a Polish officer seconded to the US Army's War Crimes Group reported to the Central Commission in Warsaw that information on Dr Wächter had dried up. This caused the Polish government to seek fresh information, and the matter was passed to the Polish Mission in Berlin, then to the Supreme National Tribunal of Poland. On 12 September 1947, as Otto was in the mountains of Austria, with Buko, the chief prosecutor of the tribunal told the Central Commission he was not aware of 'the current location' of Dr Wächter, although he knew he was not interned in any British camp, or in Germany. There was information that the Americans were hunting for him, and according to the International Military Tribunal in Nuremberg, Otto went 'missing in action'.

Through most of 1948 the trail of Otto remained cold. Then, in December, as Otto took refuge in Charlotte's bedroom in Salzburg, the dossier flickered into life. For reasons unknown, the Polish authorities suddenly ordered all documents in 'The Wächter Case' to be gathered and sent urgently to the Central Commission, in Warsaw. A month later, in January 1949, the Polish embassy in Vienna passed important new information to the Polish Ministry of Foreign Affairs and the Central Commission in Warsaw. 'Dr Wächter's trace has been encountered.' No details were given, but this may have been a reference to his having been spotted in Salzburg.

The Polish Foreign Ministry requested the Central Commission to gather all 'incriminating documents', and to draw up a fresh order for Otto's arrest. The director of the Central Commission wrote three letters, to gather details on Otto's actions in Kraków and Lwów, and his responsibilities. One letter went to the Polish Mission in Berlin, and a second to Kraków, to the Regional Commission Investigating German Crimes. The third letter invited the Jewish Historical Institute in Warsaw to provide assistance, including names and addresses of individuals willing to testify against Otto. The possibility of 'finding and catching' the former governor was real, the letters suggested.

The Jewish Historical Institute sent six incriminating documents to the Polish government, which included four decrees signed by Otto between 1939 and 1941. One ordered the Jews of Kraków to wear armbands, with a Star of David; two ordered the removal of Jews from Kraków; and the fourth decreed the creation of the Kraków ghetto. The institute also passed on the names of six people who lived under Otto's rule, each of whom was able to testify on 'the actions of Governor Wächter'. Three names were known to me, from my research on *East West Street*. Dr David Kahane, whose *Lvov Ghetto Diary* described in detail the *Grosse Aktion* of August 1942, when the families of Hersch Lauterpacht and my grandfather Leon Buchholz were rounded up. Michał Hofman, a journalist who graduated from Lwów University's law faculty and was a member of the Polish government's Central Commission for war crimes. And Professor Tadeusz Zaderecki, whose book, *Lwów under the Swastika*, contained much terrible detail.

In February 1949, the chief of the Polish Military Mission in Berlin located a copy of Otto's SS file, the same one that I would dig up seven decades later in the German national archives. The entire dossier was sent to the prosecutor at the central court in Warsaw. On 19 March 1949, while Otto was in Toblach, Polish prosecutor Julian Menderer informed the Polish government that his investigation of Dr Wächter, for crimes committed in Lwów, was active once more. He had established a jurisdiction based on the decree of 31 August 1944, on 'The punishment of Fascist-Hitlerite criminals guilty of murder and ill-treatment of the civilian population and of prisoners of war, and the punishment of traitors to the Polish Nation'. 'I kindly ask you to send me incriminating materials relating to his criminal activity,' the prosecutor wrote.

As Otto prepared to part from Charlotte and travel from Bolzano to Rome, the Polish authorities were actively seized of his case. A new order for his arrest was prepared.

I shared the information with Horst, who interpreted the documents differently. No more than general suppositions, he concluded, with no hard evidence. His position did not surprise me, as he had, some time earlier, after the trip to Lviv, written to family and friends about the veneration of his father in the region. 'I was honoured as the son,' he wrote.

In accordance with his practice, Horst sent the letter far and wide, to family and friends, and to other contacts who jumped out of his address book. One recipient of the letter was Dieter Schenk, a former director of the *Bundeskriminalamt*, the German Federal Criminal Police. An acknowledged expert on the crimes of the General Government, he was the author of several books on German crimes in occupied Europe and a biography of Hans Frank.

Schenk responded courteously, to thank Horst for the communication. He understood that a son might wish to find a way to exonerate the father. Nevertheless, Horst had to accept that Otto was a 'Nazi criminal', and he restated the bare facts. Under Otto's rule in the District of Galicia, more than 525,000 people lost their lives, between 1942 and July 1944. No more than 15,000 Jews survived, less than 3 per cent of the pre-war population.

The crimes were monstrous, Schenk continued, and were organised with the 'energetic support of the civil administration', headed by Otto. He identified three different arms of his father's government which were actively involved in the mass killings.

Otto's office for population and welfare worked with the SS, to draw up lists of Jews. It identified ghettos and collection points for Jews, and established the transit camps.

Otto's labour division selected the Jews, either for work as skilled labourers or for transportation to extermination camps.

Otto's resettlement division confiscated the property of the Jews.

'As Governor, your father bore the lead role and the responsibility for actions taken.' There was no ambiguity, nothing to discuss, and all the facts and proof lay in the archives.

Dr Schenk ended his letter with a simple request: 'Please erase me from your address-book.'

27

May 1949, Vigna Pia

Otto left Bolzano station on a train to Rome on the morning of Thursday, 28 April. It was a fine spring day, and he carried with him the tiny diary, which doubled up as an address book, into which he scribbled necessary details. As the train passed along the Etschtal valley and past Salorno, he felt optimistic, the views 'truly wonderful'. The calm offered a contrast to the political ferment of Rome and Italy, following national elections which were won clearly, and somewhat unexpectedly, by an effort of the Christian Democrats supported by the Vatican, with the Americans playing a supporting role to cement the anti-communist (and Soviet) sentiments.

Otto travelled with a new name, inscribed in an Italian *carta d'identità* 'issued' in 1946, in the small town of Appiano (Eppan, in German), near Bolzano. He was now Alfredo Reinhardt, an engineer, born on 6 June 1910, the son of Carolina Roithmeier, who was married and lived at number 20 Via Stazione in Appiano. The original photograph of Reinhardt was removed and replaced with a photograph of Otto with a moustache, and the stamp of the Commune filled in by hand.

Otto expected to be met at Rome central station by a man named 'Bauer', but the journey, and Alfredo Reinhardt's peaceful state of mind, were disrupted by the conductor. He was told to change trains at Trento, unless he purchased a first-class ticket. Since he could not afford that, he changed to the slow train, which was then subject to a delay. He arrived late at Rome's Termini station, and 'Bauer' wasn't there to meet him. 'The reception party, dinner in pleasant company and accommodation, all cancelled', he wrote to Charlotte, the first of many letters sent regularly from Rome. Arrived 'alone and abandoned', he wrote to 'Walter Ladurner', apparently a pseudonym, so he found accommodation in the early hours of the morning, a ramshackle bedstead in a dark hallway that cost 350 lire for the night. His neighbours included a bare-chested man who smoked heavily, and a lady who banged on the door of her room through the night, screaming to be let out. Someone eventually liberated the screamer, on payment of rent. 'It was very romantic!' Otto noted.

Dog-tired, Otto fell asleep in a state of anxiety about his meagre possessions. In the morning, as he washed, 'a young sloven with ornate eyebrows and painted nails' offered to help him pack. My language is love, she suggested. He left promptly for a hotel that he thought might offer free accommodation, but the room cost 1,000 lire. The price was high but worthwhile, if only for the hot water and a much-needed scrub.

Friday, 29 April was Otto's first full day in Rome. In the diary he noted in code the two people he met, careful also to avoid naming either in the first letter to Charlotte. One was a sympathetic friend of Nora's, who explained to Otto 'the hopelessness' of his undertaking. The other was a 'religious gentleman', initially reserved, then 'very positive' – Otto's emphasis – as soon as he realised who exactly Otto was. The former governor's situation was well-known, the 'religious gentleman' told him, and he would offer full assistance, including on the 'most problematic question' of overseas travel.

'Bauer' was nowhere to be found that first day. Otto waited at the overpriced hotel, somewhat desperate. Later that morning he met up with 'the second man', who invited him to lunch. Worried his money would last only a few days, in the diary Otto recorded each item of expenditure as he searched for cheap lodgings. He wandered aimlessly around Rome, visiting familiar sites – St Peter's Basilica, Castel Sant'Angelo, the square with the Bernini colonnade – and appreciated the bustle, beggars, hauling and trading. He was thrilled when someone mistook him for an American and asked for black-market dollars he didn't have. 'Old and new, all piled up next to and on top of each other, extraordinary activity.'

It took two days to find 'Bauer', who welcomed him and introduced him to Rome's German community, a sympathetic group. Over drinks, he was introduced to a 'pure-blooded Prussian', a lady married to an Italian academic. Never named in his letters, the Prussian lady would look after him like a mother during his time in Rome, offering assistance on accommodation and work, sewing and repairing worn clothes, and offering her address as a *poste restante*.

'He didn't speak much on that first evening,' the Prussian lady would recall, noting that he gave the impression of being stuck in the alpine air of the mountains he'd left, overwhelmed by the city. She noticed his attention to details, and offered him a bed for the night at her family home, 25 Via Giulio Cesare, which he accepted. It was to this address that Charlotte would, in due course, send letters and parcels. Otto met the family, a husband and two sons, and bonded on the frequent visits, once or twice a week, where he picked up his mail, received advice, had a button replaced, or just came for a chat. He liked to converse about Charlotte and the children, his work in Kraków and Lemberg, the years in the mountains, the need for work. He never talked with the Prussian lady about 'emigration'.

'Bauer' and the 'Prussian lady' acted expeditiously to find permanent lodgings for Otto. His new home was at Vigna Pia, a monastic establishment in a southern suburb of the city, a place that offered company and a space for reflection and, most important, absolute security. Otto described the place to Charlotte:

> A quaint building . . . half ruin, half Roman bath, half prison, unbelievably grimy, yet also incredibly romantic . . . well situated, just in the greenery outside the city, on one side a view over wide open spaces, on the other the city, laid out majestically.

He had a room of his own, a monk's cell with a vaulted roof, on the

top floor. Facing the city, rather than open country, the cell was stuffy and without a breeze. It came with a small desk, a single bed, a coconut bedside rug ('from the time of Nero'), one chair, a chest of drawers, a tiny wash basin, and an ancient and worm-eaten prayer bench. The mortar was falling off the walls, the brick floor was damaged, and everything covered in a fine layer of dust. But, he told Charlotte, it was safe and free, and with a modest financial investment it could be made homely.

From his cell he could hear the monks pray, and listen to the chatter of other residents, who included a few *padres*. Italian was the only language spoken by the residents, 'nice, friendly, incredibly poor'.

Dinner was served every evening at half past eight, rural Italian food, generous portions of pasta, vegetables and fish. 'Just the way I like it' – with plenty of decent red table wine. After a week at Vigna Pia, Otto started to feel more secure and optimistic about the future, although the bothersome ten o'clock curfew ruled out evening visits to the city. Occasionally he attended Mass.

Charlotte was shaken by the initial accounts of Otto's life in Rome, but relieved he had a roof over his head. 'Hopefully this time will pass, so we can be together again,' she wrote, and requested at least one letter a week. Otto complied with the instruction, and in the first month sent eight long letters, and received nine in return. On a sheet of paper he recorded each letter received or sent, and every meeting held, all neatly typed out.

Ten days after arriving, Otto's mood began to dip. The food – a half-litre of milky coffee for breakfast, pasta with *pomodoro* sauce at every meal – was monotonous. He developed an aversion to the warm vegetables fried in oil, with a distressing odour that didn't blend well with other local smells – the gas works, oil containers, petrol stores. He missed the pure, fresh air of the mountains, the 'fragrant forests of the cool North'. The place is like a prison, he wrote to 'Ladurner', the curfew non-negotiable. He struggled with the dirt, and running water didn't reach his room on the top floor. To clean or wash meant carrying water up two flights of stairs, to fill a small metal wash basin with a spittoon.

Still, Vigna Pia had advantages. It was close to the countryside, which allowed early morning runs. 'The fog dissipated over the Tiber, the hills and villas, and in the background the Alban Hills came through. Outside the city, you find the beautiful and the ugly mixed together. Old ruined towers and bits of wall, people living in miserable conditions, modern manufacturing, old picturesque chapels, mansions in beautiful scenery, vineyards and wheat fields.'

The proximity of the Tiber was enticing, even if its 'horrible dirtiness' gave pause for thought about the possibility of swimming, a beloved activity. Not a good idea, he was warned, as this stretch of the river carried much of the city's sewage. As the weeks passed, and spring turned to summer, the temperature rose and Otto succumbed to temptation. On 23 May, three weeks after he arrived, he took a first early morning dip in the Tiber. It refreshed him and elevated his spirits. 'I will do it more often, even if it doesn't look very appealing.'

He learned more about the previous occupant of his cell, a former comrade, who wrote him a lengthy, typewritten letter. 'I was aware that somebody had succeeded me at Vigna Pia,' Walter Rauff wrote to 'dear comrade Reinhardt', but he was unable to work out the Austrian's identity, until a note from the Prussian lady allowed him to understand that 'Reinhardt' was Otto Wächter. Rauff served with Otto in Italy in late 1944, as head of the SS Gruppe Oberitalien-West, based in Milan. He provided an address in Syria (*P.O. Box 95, Damaskus*), and offered advice on life on the run in Rome. Not easy, he warned. Accept your situation, maintain an 'unshakable toughness', take on any work you can, and do not waste time harking back to earlier times.

Damascus was exciting, but opportunities for Germans were limited, and it probably wasn't a place Otto should aim for. Those who did come tended to be 'adventurers and low-life flotsam and jetsam', chancers who damaged the reputation of Germans across the Arab world. Rauff expressed the hope that 'good forces' might yet reassemble, to allow real men to gradually come together again. Within a year of writing Rauff would leave Syria and make his way to South America and, eventually, Chile. A declassified CIA file offered more details about Herr Rauff, an SS man who 'designed gas vans used to murder Jews and persons with disabilities'. From another source I learned that he was rumoured to have worked for the German intelligence service between 1958 and 1962, and later served as a senior adviser to the government of President Pinochet, living in freedom and avoiding extradition. He died in 1984.

Otto settled into a daily routine, which began early each morning with exercises on the roof of the monastery, in front of a large window. 'I've given up running,' he told Charlotte, 'it wears out my shoes.' Breakfast was at 8.30, followed by writing and Italian-language work, then sock repair and shoe cleaning. Lunch was served at 12.30, followed by an afternoon siesta, then trips into town, to the post office or a rendezvous. No details were given about the identity of those he met, or the purpose of meetings. Otto was anxious about surveillance, worried his letters were being opened. To save money, and for exercise, he walked into the city for meetings, which allowed him to discover different parts of Rome. In the evening he'd rush back for dinner, 'mostly at a canter, along the tram tracks', along a palm-lined avenue.

Money was scarce. By mid-May he only had one 5,000-lira note left, about US$8, and needed to economise. It wasn't just the bus (sixty lire to the city centre) or basics, like newspapers and stamps, but the high cost of the documents and tickets to join the Reich migratory route. The need for paid work was urgent. One contact – 'Detering' – thought it would take months to get something, while another said Austria offered greater prospects. An Italian suggested he might try to sell pharmaceutical products, even if it required 'significant quantities of dollars' which he didn't have. With no official papers, the only real option was casual employment, but he found none in May.

Charlotte shared information about the family, Josef's health, news about her parents, his sisters, the children. Perhaps Otto junior, now sixteen, could visit him in Rome, Otto suggested, 'there's plenty of good food and accommodation', and Vigna Pia had an orphanage, with seventy boys training to be farmers. Discipline was light, prayer occasional, a Mediterranean easiness prevailed. Young Otto could learn Italian, and they could swim together in the Tiber, dirty but real, a happy combination of 'sunshine and water'.

In her letters Charlotte often complained of feeling miserable, upset, tired and weary. 'The last four years have really ground me down.' Her mood was unpredictable; she felt a nervous wreck, 'like an over-stretched elastic band', and life in Salzburg wasn't easy. Bed bugs in the boys' bedroom caused her to postpone a trip to Vienna, so Otto and Charlotte discussed the relative merits of 'gassing' and DDT, a new wonder chemical that was cheap, didn't smell, and wasn't harm-ful to humans. Go for it, Otto thought, cheaper than the alternative. 'Gassing will cost at least 500 schillings,' Charlotte worried. Otto faced problems of his own, his cell plagued with 'zanzare', mosquitoes.

Nora from Bolzano featured in the correspondence. A week after arriving in Rome, Otto sent her a poem to express appreciation for her benevolence, for the table and bed she offered. He thanked her warmly, 'with a heart beating with longing'. When Nora visited him in Rome, he assured Charlotte that he 'played it cool', and all talk of 'various unpleasant subjects' was avoided, a reference to a run-in between Charlotte and Nora in Bolzano, in April. 'The adventure with us seems to have aged Nora somewhat,' Otto mused. Charlotte responded that she was no longer angry with him, but nonetheless returned to the subject in a later letter. Nora still had a thing for him, but 'nothing can come between us'. 'I have nothing to blame you for,' she added, and authorised him to 'have some fun'. 'What chutzpah, as the Jew would say,' he replied. His excesses with women were limited to tea with 65-year-olds, and there was no one around to concern her. 'I am handicapped by empty pockets, a newly discovered sense of religious belief, and my great love for you,' he wrote.

Charlotte kept herself busy. She took a rare trip to Vienna, to the theatre and *Julius Caesar* at the Staatsoper. In Salzburg she attended the Festspielhaus for a performance of Beethoven's Ninth and Schubert, conducted by Josef Krips, one of the few Austrians allowed to perform because he had a Jewish father and so hadn't been able to work under the Nazis. She enjoyed a performance of Goethe's *Egmont*, with music by Beethoven. Truly a play for our times, she told Otto, one that reminded her of his love for his old job, which he had never wanted to give up.

Otto took short trips, by bicycle. He visited Mussolini's model city on the Campagna hills, south-west of Rome – 'a reminder of the grand buildings in Nuremberg!' – which had become a ghost town, inhabited by a few refugees from Istria. He and 'Leit', another unnamed old comrade, climbed Monte Cavo, where an old Roman temple to Jupiter had been transformed into an inn. They sat in the garden, enjoyed views over the Campagna and Rome to the sea and, in the other direction, Lake Albano and Castel Gandolfo, the Pope's summer residence. 'Leit stood and watched mournfully' as diplomatic cars passed, a remembrance of times past, reminiscing about the July Putsch, work at the German embassy in Rome, and life as an SS Sturmbannführer. On the terrace of a little trattoria they shared half a bottle of 'amber yellow wine', then made their way back to the city. The only thing that spoiled the day was the sound of 'The Internationale', blaring from loudspeakers, from a festival of peace run by the detested communists.

Charlotte sent items as requested. A cooking plate and an immersion heater, a gift to Vigna Pia. Blue shirts. White shorts, for the morning run. A couple of short-sleeved shirts. Short socks. A sewing kit. An old swimming costume. Shoes and sandals. The weekend edition of the *Salzburger Nachrichten* newspaper, or the *Neue Front*. A *Baedeker* guide to Rome, 'with a map of tram and bus routes!' A small spoon, so Otto didn't have to stir his lemonade with a toothbrush ('my only small treat'). A big-bladed knife, a can opener, a corkscrew, a screwdriver. The addresses of old comrades ('Hö and P and Fi'). Reading glasses. Everything was sent to the Prussian lady. 'Be sure to get my name right, <u>Alfredo</u> (not Alberto)', with a 't' at the end of 'Reinhardt', or the letters would end up at the Central Post Office where he would have to show identification, which was dangerous.

Charlotte offered snippets about former colleagues. Pavlu was ill, and Frau Bauer, whose husband was assassinated by the Soviets in Lemberg, had remarried, ran a shop and hoped to move to Switzerland. As to her own situation, Charlotte worried she'd lost her looks and 'become a crippled old hag'. Not true, Otto replied, 'you're still a very attractive woman', as the behaviour of various 'interested parties' made clear, apparently a reference to her tenant, Richard Woksch. As for him, she should not waste time worrying about what he got up to. There were no acquaintances, not male or female, with whom to take a day trip to the sea. 'Sometimes I feel very lonely, with no one here I can really talk to.' Meeting Italians was difficult.

She missed him. 'I can't quite believe that we can't be together,' she wrote sadly. 'We just have to keep hoping that one day the sun will shine again.'

As May came to an end, Charlotte worried about Otto's safety and freedom, about surveillance, about the Soviets, who were now in league with the Poles. Take care, she wrote.

Otto did take care, describing to Charlotte what he was up to but only in general terms. There was no detail in the letters, about people, prospects or the future path. There were references to 'Bauer' and 'Detering', to the 'religious gentleman', 'the second man', the Prussian lady, and hints about the 'strange people' from across Europe who 'washed up' in Rome after the war. His circle, once small, was growing. Really nice people, but never any names.

A 'Ukrainian bishop', who received him kindly.

A meeting with the 'Fü Bi', Fürst Bishop Pawlikowski, who married them in 1932 and took motoring holidays around Europe with Charlotte.

A rendezvous with 'another man', known from 'before'.

An encounter with 'several birds migrating overseas, stuck in Rome for the moment'. One was a personal friend, the rest individuals 'in our situation'. All were desperate, waiting for passage, struggling to get by. Some were overly qualified, like the aeronautical engineer who lived off the earnings of his eleven-year-old daughter, who worked in a kitchen.

A man referred to as 'Gü', who offered a 'bridge' to people abroad.

A 'Dr March' who proved to be 'helpful', after initial reluctance.

'Detering', who was 'very active'.

A friend of Nora's who offered 'hospitality', a nice but unhappy business lady who owned a decent hotel but was consumed by an extremely negative impression of humanity, and lacked all feelings of sentimentality.

A 'Tridentine friend', with a musical daughter ('eighteen, I think, but don't worry, I didn't find out').

A 'talkative' representative of the Austria Press Agency in Rome, who offered to introduce Otto to Mussolini's press agent.

Several 'German locals', struggling in Rome.

Elderly German ladies, who offered little by way of temptation.

'Native women', Italian ladies imbued with a 'very different etiquette'. In Rome, he explained, to avoid eye contact was considered to be 'an expression of dignity', although everyone liked to 'take a peek'.

A 65-year-old baroness, very nice, who invited him to tea ('I was the only man, three elderly ladies with thick glasses who sat around me like owls').

A lawyer, 'kind and able', who proffered sensible advice.

A 'sophisticated man' from the old German Foreign Office, who made useful introductions to Italians.

'Correspondents' from overseas, including Syria and Argentina.

Gündel, to whom he wrote in Bolzano, describing his difficult situation and the need for better documents, and asking 'how I can best reach Karl', who could be his 'last hope'.

He would leave no stone unturned.

Otto's activity had a central aim, to open the door that would allow him to make his way onto the Reich migratory route, to Argentina or some other place.

Such a journey required new papers. 'A sure thing' to be able to get them, he was told when he first arrived. Yet after a couple of weeks Charlotte picked up on a sense of anxiety. 'I'll pursue everything,' he promised.

I need a better identity card, he told 'Ladurner'. The problem was that it would cost a lot of money, in dollars, which he didn't have.

And, throughout the month, a constant stream of ideas and rumours.

A correspondent from Bolzano – probably 'Gü' – raised hopes. He was leaving, and sent Otto a Red Cross passport and a visa for Argentina, to be returned to Fräulein Luise.

A person who thought the Red Cross would only issue passports until the end of May, when the Vatican would take over.

Another contact believed Vatican documents would have 'less impact', but 'Detering' disagreed.

A third man learned that travel documents would only be issued to those who had 'proof of statelessness'. Such documents could be obtained from 'Hu', but only in the applicant's true name.

An unnamed gentleman told Otto that the *'embarcó libre* option' (a right of free boarding) had been suspended. The best option for escape was a tourist visa, a Red Cross passport and cash ('approximately 150,000 lire').

A group of 'candidates for Argentina' told Otto they had switched focus to Brazil. Better prospects, even if the Brazilian consulate in Rome didn't issue *embarcó libres*, as its other consulates might. A list of necessary documents was listed: a passport (Red Cross would do, so long as it was 'combined with an older document with a photo, dating to before the upheaval', such as membership of an alpine association); a birth certificate; a marriage certificate; a professional certificate ('evidence that you've worked in a technical job for two years'); evidence that 'you're not a communist'.

A fifth man told him that the Brazilians 'would be content with an Austrian passport or ID card', so long as you could 'prove you're a Protestant (that's right: Protestant!)'.

Rumours circulated about the dangers of being caught. 'I know of two cases – after four years! – of proceedings initiated against decent, harmless people.' That was what 'Ladurner' told Otto.

At the end of May, Otto received a hint of good news. The Argentine Emigration Office was about to reopen, and an *embarcó libre* could be obtained from the consulate in Venice.

'The best option is to make your way over the water,' a colleague wrote from Merano. There was nothing for them in Europe, no one was helping, not even relatives. He sent an address in Argentina, his namesake 'Dr A.R.', the name not spelled out, who lived at Pasaje-Arteaga 1188, in the city of Salta.

Otto told Charlotte he would stay in Rome a little longer, where waiting was easier than Austria, and cheaper.

Charlotte's nerves were on edge. Josef Wächter's health was visibly deteriorating, she wrote.

Ilse sent a note of encouragement. You are a 'modern romantic hero', she told her brother.

On the last day of May, Charlotte told him she was preparing for 'the worst'. Inevitably, she was getting used to the idea of taking care of herself, of being on her own.

Otto was now penniless and desperate for money.

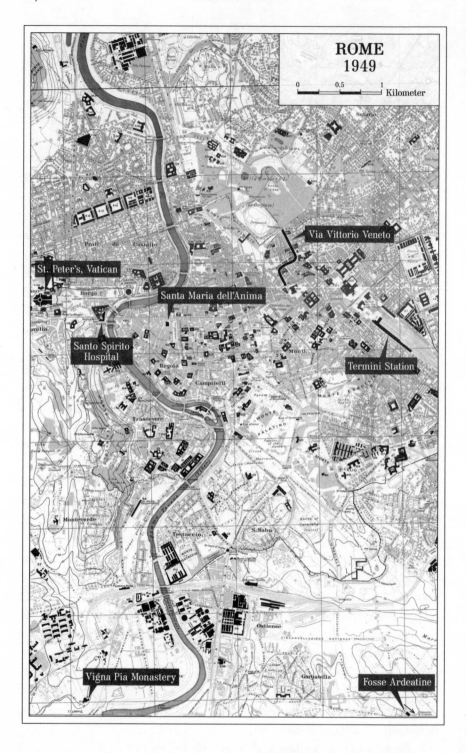

ROME
1949

0   0.5   1
                    Kilometer

Via Vittorio Veneto

St. Peter's, Vatican

Santa Maria dell'Anima

Santo Spirito
Hospital

Termini Station

Vigna Pia Monastery

Fosse Ardeatine

28

Art

Otto's need for money was assuaged by sums regularly sent by Charlotte to the home of the Prussian lady. The moneys were raised, I came to understand, in part from the sale of items acquired in Kraków and Lemberg. The screening of our documentary at the Viennale film festival in Vienna, at a fine movie house, the Gartenbaukino, in the presence of Horst and Niklas, was the catalyst for more information.

Horst's sister-in-law turned up, to call for the screening to be halted, but when it wasn't she decided to stay on to watch the film.

The projection was followed by an intense question-and-answer session, which ran for several hours. A recurrent theme was the extent of Austria's engagement – or non-engagement – with its Nazi past. The next day, Horst and I visited the Kunsthistorisches Museum, and the gallery that held paintings by Pieter Bruegel the Elder. Horst invited a retired curator from the museum, along with Osman, a genial Turkish hairdresser who doubled up as Horst's bodyguard, and his daughter Magdalena. Together, we stood admiringly before *The Fight Between Carnival and Lent*, and discussed its provenance. That we should do so was a consequence of a previous conversation about two mementos from Kraków that Horst kept in his bedroom, an eighteenth-century print of the city and an old map, deeply stained.

Charlotte obtained these objects in Kraków, and later passed them to her son. 'My mother also gave me a painting,' Horst told me, but it was no longer at the schloss. He travelled to Kraków to return it to the original owners, descendants of the Lubomirski family, but the visit ended badly. 'The owners decided at the last minute they did not want to see me.' He left the painting in Poland.

I knew from the *Stammbuch* and her earliest diary entries that Charlotte had an eye for fine objects. In London in 1925, during the Christmas holidays, she visited the city's finest galleries and museums, where she was attracted to the 'vases' and 'Egyptians' at the British Museum. By contrast, the letters and diaries from her time in Kraków made no mention of the city's impressive galleries and museums.

I was interested, therefore, to be sent a copy of an academic article in Polish, on Kraków's looted art. The communication, prompted by a screening of the documentary film, was another reminder that every act, even the screening of a film, is capable of producing unintended consequences. The article was written by a curator at the National Museum of Poland in Kraków, famed for its Cloth Hall (*Sukiennice*). It described the looting of the museum's art in the weeks and months after October 1939. The expropriations were carried out under the watchful eye of Kajetan Mühlmann, an Austrian SS officer and art historian, who wrote a doctoral thesis on the baroque fountains of Salzburg. Kai, as he was known, worked tirelessly to assist Governors Frank and Wächter in their efforts to gather local art.

Charlotte was a willing helper. 'With a lot of ceremony,' the writer of the article explained, 'Frau Wächter sailed into the gallery in the Cloth Hall.' Alarmed by her unexpected arrival, Professor Kopera of the Jagiellonian University, the director of the museum, sensed danger. '*Wir sind keine Räuber*,' Charlotte told him. 'We are not robbers.' She made her way around the rooms of the museum, identifying the items she desired, which were duly gathered by Otto's comrades.

More details were set out in a letter Professor Kopera sent to the Polish authorities after the war, in March 1946. 'The Museum suffered major, irretrievable losses at the hands of the wife of the governor of the Kraków Distrikt,' he wrote. The perpetrator was 'Frau Wächter, a Viennese woman aged about thirty-five, with chestnut brown hair'. According to Professor Kopera, her act of looting, which covered every department of the museum, was intended to furnish the governor's home at the nearby Potocki Palace. She helped herself to 'the most exquisite paintings and the most beautiful items of antique furniture', including Gothic and Renaissance chests, armour, bowls, furniture and paintings, as the director's protests were brushed aside. 'Items that went missing included . . . Bruegel's *The Fight Between Carnival and Lent*, [Julian] Fałat's *The Hunter's Courtship*, and others.' Some objects were returned after the war, a few 'extremely damaged'.

Professor Kopera's letter made its way to the Polish Military Mission for Research into German War Crimes, at Bad Salzuflen. It was followed by another, along with a suggestion. 'I do not know whether the list of war criminals includes Lora Wächter, wife of the Kraków governor,' he wrote. 'She caused us great harm by taking away works to decorate the Wächter residence, including masterpieces by [Fałat and Bruegel], which were lost.' The director gave her name to the local courts, which apparently sought further information about the looting. 'Not knowing if Frau Wächter's name had been entered on the list, I am hereby reporting her harmful activity on behalf of the Museum.'

Seventy-five years after the acts described by Professor Kopera, I mentioned the article to Horst. The events were not mentioned in the diaries or letters. However, Horst did direct me to a document Charlotte wrote in 1984, the last year of her life, after her grandson, Otto junior's son Otto, enquired about the provenance of a carpet in her home. She described it to the young man as a final gift to Otto, from colleagues in Lemberg. 'Did you take it?' the grandson asked. Charlotte responded testily that her faithful servant Wladislaw advised her to take the beautiful carpets and Chinese vases, 'otherwise they would fall into the hands of the Russians'. Against her own instincts, she followed his advice.

My conversation with Horst apparently caused him to renew his efforts to return items to Kraków. Within a year, three objects were handed back to Polish officials, a story that made it into the Polish and international press. He returned the seventeenth-century print of Kraków, and the stained map that lay for many years under a sheet of glass, together with a third item which I had not seen but to which Horst once made reference.

'Wächter, 78, returned three works that his mother stole,' the *Guardian* reported, including 'a painting of the Potocki Palace'. Those were the words Charlotte inscribed on the back of the Biedermeier gouache, Horst explained, painted by countess Julia Potocki, in about 1830. The work depicted Artur Potocki bidding farewell to his relatives, from the balcony of Otto's office. 'My mother liked the painting very much,' Horst noted, on the day he returned the artwork. Acquired in Kraków, it hung in Otto's office until he left for Lemberg, when Charlotte took it to the farmhouse in Thumersbach. 'I am not especially proud of my deeds,' Horst said, of the act of return. 'I did it for the sake of my mother.'

Horst said he knew nothing about Professor Kopera's allegations about other paintings, including the Bruegel and Fałat. The allegations made their way into the public domain, initially in the Polish media and then in an article in the *Financial Times*. That newspaper reported the matter with great care: 'a masterpiece' by Renaissance artist Pieter Bruegel the Elder, *The Fight Between Carnival and Lent*, which hung in Vienna's Kunsthistorisches Museum, was the subject of an 'ownership tussle' between Austria and Poland. 'If it was taken unlawfully from Kraków to Vienna it would be a huge story for the art world – as big as it gets,' an art historian from Cambridge University told the newspaper. Her use of the word 'if' was important: the original painting by Bruegel the Elder existed alongside no fewer than ten other versions of the work said to have been painted by his son, Bruegel the Younger, and it may have been one of these that Charlotte took. The Kunsthistorisches Museum insisted it had owned the painting on display in its gallery for over two centuries. The National Museum in Kraków was only able to confirm that a copy of the painting was in its possession in 1939, but it could not determine which version. Shortly after Horst and I visited the Kunsthistorisches Museum, the painting was removed from public display, for a short period. It is now back.

Charlotte's love of art, and the instinct for possession, would have a continuing legacy. On the occasion of the marriage of each of her six children, she offered as a gift an item from her acquisitions. Horst mentioned a wooden sculpture, given to one of his siblings, and sent a tiny photograph, an object of faded colour.

St George killing the dragon was still in the possession of a family member, who did not intend to part with it. Horst wondered if it might be by Veit Stoss, possibly taken from Kraków's museum or cathedral, or some other place in the city. He hoped the 'original location' and owner might be established 'as soon as possible', so it could be returned. He told me that his own actions, in returning various items, elicited strongly negative reactions from some family members. His sister-in-law was said to be 'completely knocked down' by his actions, and one sister told him he was a Judas, who had betrayed the family. Another fell into a 'deep depression'.

As for Horst, he told me he declined Charlotte's offers of property, or other gifts, because she always wanted something 'in exchange'. Best to avoid the *quid pro quo*, he thought. Yet when she died it was to him that she left her estate, and to whom many papers passed. 'I owe everything to her,' Horst would often tell me. The castle was bought with an inheritance from her, and she passed on the papers, the letters and diaries. Charlotte didn't want to part with them while she lived, so the 'beloved son' took possession when she died.

29

June 1949, Rome

Charlotte spent the opening day of June in bed. Unspeakably tired, she told Otto, in the first of nine letters written that month. The previous evening was spent at a political rally in Salzburg, for a new political party, the *Verband der Unabhängigen* (Federation of Independents), the VDU. 'A reminder of times past,' she wrote, as the VDU included many disenfranchised former Nazis among its supporters and asserted that no country in the world pursued a crueller persecution of ex-Nazis than Austria. The VDU has long disappeared, folded into the Freedom Party (FPÖ), which came to be a part of the Austrian government in more recent times. Deflated and feeling wrecked, everyone and everything got on Charlotte's nerves, but not the VDU.

In Rome, Otto struggled with the heat. 'The sun strikes like a sword at nine in the morning, in the afternoon the room is so oppressively muggy that I have to lie down.' In need of fresh clothing, he asked Charlotte to send shirts and vests. He hoped for a light, single-coloured jacket, made of Lanz flannel, a reference to the Salzburg store whose customers included Herbert von Karajan and Marlene Dietrich. Yellow would be good for the shirts, a colour that went with everything. Checked patterns were fine too, as they didn't show the dirt.

Otto continued to assure his wife that he would leave no stone unturned in his efforts to find work, and obtain documents for travel abroad. The dangers were real, however, and he reminded Charlotte to continue to exercise great care in writing. He warned of a censorship mark on one of her letters, and the dangers that might be occasioned by a momentary lapse.

During June he wrote to Charlotte twice a week, letters that offered details on daily life, and his physical and emotional state. He picked up a minor stomach ailment, and the early morning runs were over, for lack of footwear. 'Dog-tired', he wrote on 9 June, his trouble sleeping caused by the nocturnal clatterings of his monastic neighbours. Even the nuns complained about the noise.

He continued to encounter old acquaintances. On the 12th he again met 'Leit', who now represented German and Austrian businesses in Rome. This allowed him to stay at an expensive hotel and eat real meals, so the two men shared a fine dinner – starters then asparagus and crab, served with a wonderful Soave, just like old times. Conversation touched on future prospects, but not much ensued, as ladies were present. 'Leit's' wife had stayed in the South Tyrol, selling high-class kitsch, but the husband was tempted to emigrate, as he worried about another war in Europe, as did the Italian newspapers.

'I have such a desire for you,' Charlotte wrote in mid-June, but also a 'terrible fear' they would not see each other again. 'Beyond broken', she felt overcome by despair at the hopelessness of the situation, hoping he might yet one day be at her side, so she could feel his positivity wash over her. She was thinking a lot about the old days, Lemberg in particular. Did he ever think about them, she enquired, did he feel lost in sadness?

Occasionally, a glimmer of light pierced the gloom and touched the correspondence. Horst, now ten, attended a first music concert, attentive as a hawk, his mother's pride and joy. On 22 June he would take the entrance exam for a new school. 'Please cross your fingers, at 8 a.m.'

Otto found ways to fill the long hours. He attended the canonisation of a nineteenth-century nun, at a ceremony conducted by Pope Pius XII, in St Peter's Square. In the company of 'L', or 'Pezzo Grosso', the big fish, and his wife, he enjoyed the pageantry, the medieval uniforms and colours. He was less enthused by the idea of 'Pezzo Grosso' that Syria might be a good option, if he could resolve the difficulties obtaining documents.

He started work on a large translation project, from German into Italian, assisted by the Prussian lady and an Italian lawyer she introduced him to. The work didn't pay but could lead to 'possibilities', although the hope was vague and the prospects less than concrete. The task was demanding, so he gave up swimming for a week, and missed the large military parade on 1 June, as planes roared over Rome.

He prepared a manuscript of his own, typing up numerous drafts, to which he gave the title *Quo Vadis Germania?*. It offered a moment for reflection, following the 'exceptional catastrophe' of 1945, and the casting aside by the victors of principles of fair treatment and a 'belief in law and justice' for Germans. 'Law still yields to power,' he surmised, and the victors had no 'moral right to sit in judgement on the German people' or decry the 'sins of German race politics', given their own acts of 'brutal extermination' and 'current treatment of dark-skinned citizens'. Neverthless, Germans would turn to the West and reject Bolshevism, and the Church would play an important role, having rejected 'the idea of blanket guilt of the German people' and offered assistance to all. 'Their support of condemned National Socialists and SS men has left a deep impression,' he typed, but offered no hint of regret for Germany's actions across occupied Europe, or his own, even if terms like 'master race' and 'subhumans' had been recognised for their 'absurdity and passivity' and had been 'mostly rejected'. Most Germans, and the young, envisioned a future in 'a European community', one that was 'united, free, social'. This was 'owed to the millions of dead comrades', Otto concluded.

Such activity did not, however, produce income, which was a problem. 'There's a chance – only small, by no means certain – that in one fell swoop I could earn some money,' Otto wrote on the 18th. Charlotte too felt more positive that day, allowing herself to imagine a summer holiday in the south, in Italy. She asked for more letters.

The search for paid work meant hours trudging around Rome in the heat. Work as an independent salesman might be an option, perhaps for a German business. The problem was the absence of capital, experience or connections. The possibility of work in the hotel industry also seemed bleak, given his lack of contacts, without which he was 'out in the cold'. 'I continue to try to make connections, but things don't look very promising,' he added. He had hope, but not expectations.

Then, unexpectedly, six weeks after arriving in Rome, he finally got a break, with help from the Prussian lady. 'I was able to get him a job with a film,' she later told Charlotte. This made him 'exceptionally happy', and for the first time, burned by the sun, he seemed more 'lively'.

'I earned my first money as a film extra,' Otto wrote, '10,000 lire in three days!' He hoped for more, maybe even to establish himself in the film world. The film, *La Forza del Destino*, was based on the opera by Giuseppe Verdi, with famed opera singer Tito Gobbi in the central role. Gobbi could not have been aware that one of the extras was a man indicted for mass murder, for shootings and executions.

I found a copy of the film and watched it three times, looking for Otto among the hundreds of extras. The director, Carmine Gallone, liked to make historical epics with casts of thousands, films like *Scipione l'Africano*, partly funded by Mussolini to promote Fascist

Italy's colonial activities in North Africa. I didn't find Otto.

Otto thought a better wardrobe might bring more work, so he asked for his tuxedo to be sent to Rome, imagining himself as a 'distinguished gentleman' in the next film. Send more clothes, Otto wrote to Charlotte. 'Send the military boots I left with you in Bolzano,' he told Nora, as film people wanted military types with the 'right equipment'. The Prussian lady noticed he was even more restless than usual until the parcels arrived.

The new wardrobe worked. He picked up a second job, two days as an extra in *Donne Senza Nome* (*Women Without Names*), directed by a Hungarian, Géza von Radványi.
His brother Sándor Márai, exiled in Italy, would achieve fame many decades later with a novel, published during the war, *Embers*. A journalist in Rome sent me the film, thinking he may have spotted Otto. Horst thought it was Otto, in the part of an American military policeman, although we were not sure. He is the one on the right in a still, rounding up  the inhabitants of an apartment in Rome, with a speaking role – '*Tutti nelle stanze!*' bellowed the man who could be Otto, 'Everyone into the rooms!' He was paid 20,000 lire, a generous sum, which would help with the purchase of documents for travel abroad. It brought other benefits, including a first visit to the sea, and, he confessed, a new pair of flannel trousers and two pairs of ankle socks. He felt lucky to penetrate the world of film, an 'unbelievable clique'.

The walk-on parts catalysed other ideas. Journalist Franz Riedl introduced him to Luis Trenker, the well-known Austrian film director who was working in Rome. Trenker specialised in mountain films. 'I cosied up to him,' Otto reported, and they met. 'Success thus far? Zero.' 'He's a pig,' Charlotte responded, he should forget him.

So Otto developed another idea, to write a film script, a romance involving four women. '*Bergluft macht frei*' was the idea he came up with for the title, apparently without irony – *Mountain Air Makes You Free*. He wrote several scenes, with three female parts named after daughters Liesl, Traute and Heide. The fourth was called Lilo, possibly a reference to Charlotte, or maybe Luise Ebner, another love interest in Bolzano, who occasionally sent a box of cigars. Set in a ski hotel, the hero – named Otto – is a poor skier besotted with Lilo, a haughty champion. Otto persuades Toni, a chemist, to concoct a wonder drug, to strengthen his will and transform him into an '*Übermensch*'. It worked! Otto is transformed into a fine skier, and wins over the lady.

Despite the positive developments, at the end of the month Charlotte's mood darkened once more. The cause was a single, terrifying line in one of Otto's letters. 'A few days ago a friend was caught,' he wrote, and all contact with that person was lost.

The fear prompted a change of approach. Their letters now referred to Otto as a third person, a woman called 'Franzi'. 'It would be terrible for Franzi if her cover was blown in some way,' Charlotte wrote. Otto offered reassurance, that he would take all necessary steps to make sure that 'Franzi' didn't become the talk of the town, although it wasn't easy, as certain things couldn't be kept secret from some people. To obtain documents, for example, it was necessary for 'Franzi' to provide basic information, to show that the requirements of a lawful status in Italy were met.

Otto raised a specific concern for the first time. 'From my experience here, the *A* will eventually find out where Franzi is staying (if they don't already know), and the same is true for the *R*. You can't avoid it.' The reference was to the Americans and the Russians, both known to be hunting for Nazis. Both sides, in opposition in the new Cold War, had eyes and ears on the ground, she warned.

The warning coincided with worrisome news received from 'Ladurner', in Bolzano. He informed Otto that a former SS comrade, Wilhelm Höttl, had been turned by the Americans. Höttl, one-time head of the intelligence service of the SD in Vienna after the Anschluss, later in Italy as right-hand man to Ernst Kaltenbrunner, had been recruited by the US Army Counter Intelligence Corps, to use his counter-espionage skills against the Soviets. 'Ladurner' may also have known that three years earlier it was Höttl who offered evidence against former comrades in the Nuremberg trials, including Kaltenbrunner: it was his affidavit that served as the main source for the number of six million murdered Jews, four million killed in 'various concentration camps', the rest shot by 'operational squads' during the Russian campaign.

Alerted, Otto worried about the trustworthiness of fellow Germans in Rome. Until now he had not been spotted, but some were in contact with the Allies, he told Charlotte at the end of the month, and some were said to be in contact with the 'east'. Who could he trust? His comrades had information on the Reich migratory route to South America, and to cut them out might undermine the possibility of escape. Information about new arrivals got around, so 'interested parties' could 'get you in their sights'. He intended to adopt a sensible approach in dealing with compatriots, some of whom may be dangerous.

The situation dampened his spirits. '*È troppo tardi*,' crooned local star Luciano Tajoli, 'it's too late'. He was at a low ebb, he told Charlotte. 'If you flirt, you never know where it might lead.' Be very careful with your letters, he warned. Rumours about 'Franzi' were certain to circulate eventually.

Nevertheless, against this background of increased risk, he renewed efforts to explore all options. Argentina had gone quiet, even if 'Ladurner' was optimistic that new *embarcó libres* would soon be available, as the situation in Argentina relaxed. 'Ladurner' asked him for a photograph, and possible dates for travel.

An unexpected letter arrived from Anton Höller, possibly a relative of someone Otto knew in Bolzano. He wrote from Argentina ('c/o Pablo Gindra, Belgrano 458, Buenos Aires') to congratulate comrade Reinhardt on his transfer to Italy, and to offer advice. Entry into Argentina was increasingly difficult, as Red Cross passports were no longer being accepted, but the situation was about to improve, perhaps within the next three months. Even then, the economic situation in Argentina was dire, so Otto should also explore other options. Höller suggested the Union of South Africa, where 'reliably anti-British' immigrants were being encouraged.

Rome was awash with rumours about other options, including Brazil and Chile, but the ideas were not particularly concrete. An acquaintance urged the Middle East, but this was of little interest to Otto. Everything he'd heard about the region, including from Rauff, was thoroughly negative.

In the last days of June, he assured Charlotte he was trying to be optimistic. She should send a shoehorn and a bootjack, rosaries and a pair of swimming trunks. Zeiss glasses would be a real hit, as they were extraordinarily expensive in Rome.

'Something will turn up in July,' he assured his wife. He would continue to search for cheap options for travel to South America by sea, and would not return to Austria. 'The mountains nearby are too small, and they get too hot (in summer),' a reference to the dangers of being caught. Something else would bear fruit, and the question was not if but when. It was only a matter of luck, of timing, of getting used to the situation. To bumble around and make new connections, which wasn't difficult, was where progress lay. He had several hopeful telephone conversations, which justified trips from the monastery into town. 'A meeting with a church dignitary, or with a man about potential film opportunities, or with the Arab about other prospects for the future etc.' That's how it was, every day.

To make money, Otto continued to generate ideas, and to meet others who might help.

Journalism was a possibility. He reached out to Lothar Rübelt, the photographer who helped him back in July 1934, in Vienna, when he was first on the run. 'Let's re-establish our age-old connection,' he wrote, suggesting they develop a business connection. He could place Lothar's photographs in Italian publications, which liked sensational articles. 'The best would be a series of images with text', on the private lives of big political characters of the kind that Lothar photographed, the old hierarchy. Be discreet, he told the photographer, he didn't want his artistic activities to become common knowledge.

He visited the widow of a former minister, who was shot with Mussolini. She lived well, inhabiting the servants' quarters and renting out her ten-room apartment.

He met with 'G', with whom he was once close but who now seemed a bit cold. Maybe 'G' was unhappy that Otto had a foothold in his circle of friends. The chances of getting something through 'G' were minimal.

He dined regularly with a middle-aged Arab, who was fond of Germans. Don't laugh, he wrote, but the Arab offered the most enjoyable company.

He made contact with Dr Ruggero Vasari, an Italian futurist poet, to explore possible work on 'press affairs'.

And, he wrote to Charlotte, he met a 'süddeutscher meiner Couleur', a south German of my colour, a 'kind old comrade' who might be able to help. No name was mentioned, but Charlotte would have understood the reference as being to the SD. He was Otto's 'sort of chap', married to an Italian, likeable, although not the sharpest tool in the box. They got together now and then for a spot of job-hunting. He would spend the first weekend in July with this kind old comrade, someone with more experience of Italy than Otto.

30

July 1949, Santo Spirito

On the morning of Saturday, 2 July, the sky above Rome was a deep blue. Otto awoke a little earlier than usual, on the top floor of the monastery, then followed the daily routine. Up the stone stairs to the roof, exercises, down three flights to the refectory, breakfast with milky coffee. He left Vigna Pia, made his way to the terminal and caught a local bus. Readers of *Il Tempo* learned of a new European agreement on free trade and the resignation of the British ambassador. They also saw advertisements for steamers across the Atlantic, and the films being shown at Rome's many cinemas, like *The Story of G.I. Joe* (starring Robert Mitchum) and *The Trial*, an Austrian story of anti-Semitism that won awards at the Venice Film Festival.

Half an hour later the bus pulled into a small hamlet near Lake Albano. Otto alighted and walked the short distance to the home of the unnamed 'kind old comrade' who might be helpful. In a letter to Charlotte, written two days later, on Monday, he offered a few details. The 'kind old comrade' had a little girl, 'maybe four weeks' old. The family lived in a tiny two-bedroom apartment, 'near Castel Gandolfo, where the Pope has his summer residence', one floor of a villa with many terraces. From the area there were fine views of the Roman Campagna and distant Alban Hills, and the deep lake that occupied the old volcanic crater, about half the size of Lake Zell. On a sunny day you could see the sea and Cape Circeo, in the distance.

From the apartment they took a local bus, then walked to Lake Albano. They swam and 'ate heartily', a picnic of roast chicken, ham, vegetables and wine. Otto spent the night, and the next day, a Sunday, they went shopping in a nearby village – 'typically Italian' – and shared 'a terrific lunch'. In the afternoon Otto began to feel unwell, so he took to bed in the apartment, shaken by a fever: '41–42 degrees, I've never had anything so bad,' he wrote.

By Sunday evening his blood felt as though it was boiling and he missed his *Hümmchen*, who would have prepared cold compresses.

In the evening, the 'kind old comrade' obtained pills from a nearby monastery, quinine-like, with a strong, bitter taste. They lowered his temperature, to 39.5 degrees. He stayed a second night, with much vomiting. On Monday morning, feeling no better, he gingerly made his way back to Rome, with an uncomfortable half-hour standing in a crowded bus.

'I went straight to a German doctor,' he told Charlotte, one he'd known for a long time, again unnamed. The doctor examined him, found his lungs and all else to be fine. Probably a cold, the doctor thought, of the kind easily picked up around Rome, more unpleasant than northern Italy. Otto returned to Vigna Pia in the midday heat, feeling sorry for himself. He washed himself with cold water, then took to bed. A local doctor – 'very Italian' – visited at the end of the day. No need to worry, he was told, although his temperature remained high. Drink tea, hopefully the next day he'd feel 'A-okay'. The doctor prescribed a *limonade purgative de Rogé*.

Health really was the most important thing, he wrote to Charlotte. He was cheered by the arrival of early birthday greetings from Traute – 'all the very best and another 55 years . . . 10,000,000,000,000 kisses'. 'I'd love to be with you,' Charlotte added. 'If we could be together again at long last, that would be wonderful.' His father Josef was 'on his last legs', she wrote, but a wind of change was sweeping across Austrian politics. 'Franzi should sit tight and make sure nothing happens to her before September,' Charlotte wrote. Really good news was coming, with talk of a general amnesty.

By Tuesday, 5 July, Otto's temperature had risen and fallen. Overnight the fever was high, but in the morning it dropped to 38.5, then 'right down', then 'up again a bit'. Perhaps the worst was behind him, as he was on anti-flu medicine and quinine. He felt weak, barely able to get to the toilet. Five more days of fever, the doctor predicted. Everyone was nice, the *padres* visited, he wasn't doing too badly. He sent a poem:

. . . poor *Hümmi* lies
Here in a bare cell
Where many devils torment him,
Where it's lonely and hot.

Feeling 'like a child', he imagined her 'tender hands', and expressed his gratitude that Charlotte hadn't abandoned him, 'in spite of all the difficulties'. Maybe one day they would 'again enjoy good fortune'. 'Him', he signed off.

Tuesday night was terrible, and on Wednesday morning, 6 July, Otto summoned all his strength to write. His hand was so shaky that the letter was barely legible. He was visited by two doctors, the Italian and the German, both at a loss as to what had stricken him. 'Typhus or something gastric', perhaps, with a 'possibility of jaundice' that could not be confirmed, as there were no telltale yellow spots. A strong purgative made things easier, although his breath had a strange smell, and his tongue and gums felt 'furred'. The afternoon brought a relapse, more vomiting and retching. Nothing positive to report, all very unpleasant.

After three nights with little sleep, Otto lost his appetite. Unable to take more than a bowl of milk, he felt weak. There was talk of an 'American wonder drug' – penicillin – but the Italian doctor, who made enquiries, said it wasn't appropriate. The doctor was a good man, Otto told Charlotte, and 'with the fascists'. He now gave her the name of the German doctor, Dr Willi Marchesani, just in case, and an address and telephone number.

The letter offered scant detail. By eleven o'clock that morning he had 'kept quiet', and the situation seemed to improve. Temperature 38.5. No headache, 'completely clear-headed, and thinking about the strangest things!' The Italian doctor found him restless. Charlotte hadn't written 'for a long time', Otto complained, a sad way to celebrate a birthday. Separately, Dr Marchesani added a few words of his own, confirming the high fever, possibly due to a bowel infection. He couldn't yet say how long the illness would last, but hoped to send good news 'soon'. Later, he added a few more anxious lines. Otto desired her presence, and needed care and attention beyond the basics available at Vigna Pia. 'Your husband would be glad if you were able to come soon.' If she travelled from Salzburg she should send a telegram in advance and Dr Marchesani would arrange for her to be collected at the station. 'The car will be small and dark, driven by a priest with a plump, healthy face.' He would arrange basic accommodation, with the nuns. She should telephone him, Rome 35265 was the number. Between seven and nine in the morning.

On Friday, 8 July, Otto celebrated his forty-eighth birthday. His condition deteriorated, and early the next morning Brother Gabriele and another Italian monk decided to take him from Vigna Pia to a hospital. The *Ospedale di Santo Spirito*, a Vatican-supported institution, was located on the banks of the River Tiber, within sight of St Peter's Basilica. Otto was admitted to the Sala Baglivi, bed number nine.

Dr Marchesani sent a telegram to Salzburg. 'Franzi is in hospital, waiting for mother at the train station, with a taxi.'

On Sunday, 10th, Charlotte tried to telephone Rome, without success, much worried by the telegram. Having not received a letter for some time, she was 'in a state of constant anxiety', surprised by the turn of events. 'I was afraid you'd been discovered.' The news that he was in hospital was 'like a bomb going off'. Until that moment she was doing better, feeling happier.

Charlotte did not, however, understand the situation to be grave. She couldn't travel immediately, she wrote, as the children needed attention. She could not 'just drop everything', so she'd travel to Rome in a week's time, if he still needed her. She had to take care of herself, and her nerves were stretched to breaking point.

As she wrote the letter she was interrupted by a telephone call from Rome – Dr Marchesani, to tell her that the fever was down but Otto seemed to have 'poisoning and jaundice'. Be patient, Charlotte wrote, she would cancel the visit to her sister and be with Otto in a week, to take care of him. 'Get well soon for me, then I'll take over.'

She wrote a second letter that Sunday, on a typewriter. You're made of strong stuff, you must get better. She sent money to 'Frau D', to enjoy his birthday, and would send a parcel with pyjamas and the other items he asked for. She planned to arrive on 20 July, if he still wanted her to come, unless it was no longer necessary. 'I've got nowhere to stay and would rather avoid the expense, but I'll do it if you want. I had jaundice once,' she reminded him, 'it was horrible but I never lost hope. Just remember, *Hümmi* has often been very ill, thought she was at death's door, and she didn't have a *Hümmsten* to call on, because she couldn't get hold of him.'

And, she added, she would be more useful with the aftercare. While he was in hospital she'd only be able to come during visiting hours. 'What would I do in the heat?' Who was taking care of him, she asked, and where did the illness, 'this evil foe', come from?

On Monday, the 11th, she grew increasingly worried. She received the letter he wrote on the 5th, the one with the poem, which raised her spirits, but she remained confused about what to do. If he was contagious she wouldn't be able to see or speak to him. Best to wait for the diagnosis. Could it be malaria? It must be an infection. 'You have to keep telling yourself that I need you desperately, that I can't live without you.' She would come to Rome, but again a sense of reprimand crept in. 'My God, how ill have I been in the past and *Hümmi* didn't come and see me. I had to get by on my own. That was hard. I was so miserable back in Lemberg as well, and *Hümmi* didn't believe me.' Horst's medical check-up that day showed he was eight kilos too light, she added, just skin and bone. Maybe she should send the children to Rome, to see Otto and the Pope.

She wrote again on Tuesday, the 12th. Otto junior fell off his bike, quite badly. The children made money selling crabs. She was anxious, but didn't want to travel all the way to Rome in the heat and then find she couldn't help. 'Please be determined, get well soon.'

Her letter crossed with another from Dr Marchesani, on his old

headed notepaper, the words 'Medical Doctor of the German Embassy' crossed out with ink. 'Have just left "Franzi",' he wrote, who was 'very, very weak', being taken care of in the *Ospedale di Santo Spirito*, housed in 'a large, high-ceilinged room' that was 'pleasantly cool'. He brought everything the doctors allowed, and a 'kind lady' visited each day. 'Our bishop' was also with her, almost every day. No names were mentioned. He shared such information as he had. 'Franzi' was . . .

suffering from a severe infection, which has caused severe inflammation of the liver. She has had a high fever for several days, which made it necessary to transfer her to hospital. The hospital examination is not yet done. Everything will be done to get Franzi back on her feet. Although she is very, very weak, we remain hopeful that she will pull through. We are, however, not out of the woods yet. In my opinion, you need not make a journey that would be expensive and with no influence on the course of events.

He would keep her informed of developments. He read one of Charlotte's letters to 'Franzi', and intended to read the more recent ones, written on the 10th and 11th. As he wrote, Dr Marchesani was interrupted by an urgent telephone call. He returned and wrote in a different pen: 'I have just had a call from Frau Dupré, who was just with Franzi. She has had a complete collapse and we fear the worst. I leave it to you, of course, whether or not you want to come. I know how difficult it is for you to come.' If she decided to travel, she should call Frau Dupré immediately upon her arrival at Rome's train station.

On Wednesday, the 13th, Charlotte received Otto's letter of the 6th. The writing was almost illegible, she couldn't make things out. Desperate to hear from him, she hoped for a call at the end of the week, to set her mind at rest. All the children except Otto were away. 'Please do write, even if it's brief, but make it legible, and draw a little.'

Later that evening, at about half past seven, Dr Marchesani sent a short, urgent telegram to Salzburg, two words and a name: 'CONDITION SERIOUS – MARCHESANI'. The next morning, 14 July, Charlotte wrote again. She was sitting by the telephone, waiting for a call from Graz, to be sure the children were taken care of, so she could travel to Rome. She would go by train, via Trieste, and call Marchesani. She signed with 'a thousand kisses'.

Later that day Charlotte went to Salzburg train station and caught a train for Trieste, and from there another to Rome. The journey took more than twelve hours, without news. On the morning of 15 July, Charlotte arrived at Rome's Termini station. She was met by an older man, rather short, with glasses.

'Baroness W?' he enquired.

'Yes, and you?'

'Dr Marchesani, with whom you have talked on the phone. We will drive to Grete Thiele, who owns a big hotel in the centre and would like to invite you to stay.'

'How is Otto?' Charlotte asked. 'Can we not see him immediately?'

Dr Marchesani didn't answer; Charlotte pressed him.

'It is too late, he passed away during the night of Wednesday 13th, in the arms of Bishop Hudal.'

'My whole world collapsed,' Charlotte recalled. 'I sat there, like a corpse.'

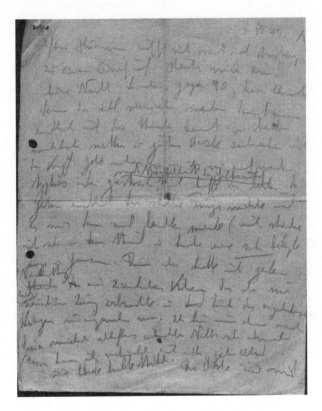

REQUEST FOR DELIVERY OF A PERSON DESIRED
FOR TRIAL FOR A WAR CRIME

Place **Wiesbaden**

Date **28.9.46**

To the Military Governor
United States Zone, Germany

483 2/10.46

I, being the authorized representative of the Government of
_____**Poland**_____, request on behalf of my
government that **NAECHTER, Dr. Gustav**___, who is believed to be at
(give exact location)_____, Germany, be delivered
to____**Poland**_____at____**Warsaw**_____for trial
for the hereinafter described offense.

My government has evidence that the person requested did, at
_____**LWOW (Poland)**_____, on or about_____**1942**_____, 19**45**,
commit the following war crime. (Here give a concise description of
the acts which constitute the war crime.)

      1.) Subject is responsible for mass-murder (shooting and
          executions). Under his command as Governor of District-
          Galicia, more than 100 thousand Polish citizens lost
          their life.

      2.) Subject is listed as War-Criminal on CROWCASS list
          File 78416 page 449.

      3.) Subject is believed to be in Jail at Vienna (Austria).
Nationality of person requested:

                                Austrian

Nationality of victim   :

                                Polish

My government agrees that if the person is not tried and convicted within six months from the date he is so delivered, he will be
returned upon request. It is understood that other conditions may be
imposed by the Military Governor, United States Zone, upon the delivery of the person requested. If my government accepts delivery
subject to such conditions, it agrees to abide by them.

(Name) **Dr. Henry Gielb** /capt.

(Title) **Chief-Extradition**

Description of person desired will be entered upon the attached SHAEF
CROWCASS "Wanted Report" Form

1 Incl: "Wanted Report" Form.

INCL 1

1750-16

IV

DEATH

'Are you a spy and if so, would you not prefer to spy for us?
Or are you merely a criminal?'

John le Carré, A Perfect Spy, 1986

31

The Five Burials of O.W.

Otto's life ended on the evening of 13 July 1949. Two days later, Charlotte arrived in Rome, and the following morning, 16 July, she met the man in whose arms her husband died. He gave her a note, on official letterhead, with his crest – *Ecclesiæ et Nationi*, 'For Church and Nation' – an address and a stamp, *Assistenza Austriaca*. 'I confirm, that Dr Otto Gustav, Freiherr von Wächter on 13 July at 23 hours in the Santo Spirito Hospital departed this life, in my arms and at peace with the Lord.' He signed it Bishop Alois Hudal, in a confident, expansive hand.

Charlotte kept the note in a folder of related documents. They included notes of condolence, including one from the mayor of Vienna, and letters from correspondents, including Albert Schnez, General Kesselring, and Hans – now Juan – Fischböck, who lived in Buenos Aires on Avenue Belgrano. The folder also held newspaper clippings, including one from an Austrian newspaper, the *Arbeiter-Zeitung*, from March 1951, with an intriguing headline. 'Is the July putschist Wächter still alive?' the article asked. It reported on an Austrian court decision to order the forfeiture of Otto's assets, including the house in Thumersbach and shares in the Schoeller-Bleckmann firm worth more than 46,000 Austrian schillings. The whereabouts of other stolen properties – including 'boxes of furs' taken in Poland, and valuable furnishings from the Villa Mendl in Vienna – were said to be 'unknown'. During the court proceedings a question had been raised as to whether Otto was really dead, or had merely faked his death to avoid prosecution. The Austrian court suggested that Otto's death 'was not established beyond doubt'.

As I have mentioned, Charlotte's papers included a number of cassette tapes, and it was from these that I was able to work out what happened in Rome after Otto died. One recorded a conversation Charlotte had in 1984, with Hansjakob Stehle, a German historian, which touched on the meeting with Bishop Hudal. In a firm, high-pitched voice, she told Stehle that Dr Marchesani met her at Rome train station, and accompanied her to see Bishop Hudal.

'I would like to see my husband again,' she told the bishop. 'I still cannot believe that he is really dead.' He accompanied her to the Campo Verano cemetery, where Otto was laid out in the mortuary. She was shocked by what she saw, the discoloration of his corpse. 'He lay as black as wood, all burnt inside,' she told Stehle, 'like a Negro.' More than three decades after Otto's death, in the last year of her life, the recording made clear the lasting impact of that moment.

In Rome's central state archives I found a document that stated that

Otto's body was taken from the Santo Spirito Hospital to the cemetery on 16 July. At the cemetery, a handwritten document recorded that the interment of an Otto Wächter took place on 16 July. He was buried in the area reserved for foreigners of German and Catholic origin, section 38, row 4, plot 13. Bishop Hudal conducted the funeral service at the Campo Verano cemetery later that day. About twenty people attended, including Dr Marchesani and the kind Prussian lady mentioned in Otto's letters. Charlotte learned that her name was Hedwig Dupré, known as Hedi. Charlotte spent two more days in Rome and returned to Salzburg by train on 18 July.

Many decades later, I visited the sprawling, monumental cemetery, on a brutally hot summer's day, with plenty of mosquitoes around. I passed the graves of well-known Italians, like the actor Vittorio Gassman, with a smiling photograph, and the mortuary building where Charlotte would have seen Otto's body. Section 38 was nearby, a few rows of faded headstones, but none bearing Otto's name, not in row 4, not in any other row. He was removed, long ago.

The circumstances emerged from another clipping in Charlotte's papers, a short article published in a German newspaper on 27 April 1961, which offered an arresting headline: 'Interpol searches for a body, the trail leads to Berlin'. The article described the efforts of

Italian police and Interpol to locate 'the mortal remains of Freiherr Otto von Wächter', described as 'a Nazi era war criminal who was never brought to justice'. According to the article, Otto's coffin was removed from the Campo Verano cemetery a few weeks earlier, at the request of his widow, so the remains could be transferred to a mausoleum in Palermo, Sicily. Approval was given by the Italian authorities, the coffin lifted out of the ground, loaded into a car, and driven away. The authorised destination was Sicily, but the remains never arrived. Italian police suspected that Frau Wächter drove the car and the remains to Berlin, for reburial. The German authorities rebutted the claim: the necessary approvals were not sought or obtained, so it was impossible for Otto to have been buried in Germany.

This was Otto's third act of disappearance, after 1934 and 1945. Horst explained what happened, after Bishop Hudal reminded his mother of her husband's dying wish to be buried in Austria. Charlotte requested permission from the Italian authorities to take the remains to Austria, but after this was refused – remains could not be taken out of the country – she applied to transport them to Palermo, where daughter Liesl lived. Charlotte drove to Rome, collected the body, but never took it south. 'Mother drove him to Austria,' Horst said, with a large grin. In her old, dark-green Siemens car, someone later told me.

The disappearance caused a scandal. 'A story circulated that he could be still alive,' Horst explained. An Italian newspaper reported that Otto never actually died, and the body in section 38 was a fake. The idea that his father might have eloped and not stayed in contact with the family was, for Horst, unthinkable. When I revisited the possibility some time later, he asked me, with moist eyes, never again to say this in his presence. He knew what happened. 'Mother brought the remains to the house in Salzburg.'

This was a reference to Haus Wartenberg, at number 2 Riedenburger Strasse, which Charlotte bought in the 1950s. This was where the family lived, after Anton-Hall-Strasse, in a property christened in memory of the false name Otto used while on the run in 1934, and where Charlotte ran a German language school. The student lodgers were unaware that Otto's remains rested in the garden, 'in a small box made of lead', Horst said, near the watchful eye of a stone saint. He described its shape with his hands. 'I don't remember that I looked inside, but it must have contained his head, the skull, bones, arms and . . .' The voice trailed off.

Otto remained in the garden at Haus Wartenberg for a few years until he was moved to the garden of another property bought by Charlotte, outside Fieberbrunn, a small town seventy kilometres south-west of Salzburg. What happened next was described in a cassette, on the label of which Charlotte wrote: 'Burial of Father, Fieberbrunn, 4th January 1974'. This was tape number twelve in Charlotte's papers. In the recording, Charlotte described the first burial of Otto, in 1949 at Campo Verano, and explained how Bishop Hudal ordered her to bring Otto's remains back to Austria. That was around 1960. Fourteen years later, another voice came to her, which said it was time to bury Otto properly. She visited the mayor of Fieberbrunn to request a burial plot, but he was uncomfortable, despite her persistence. So she and her son Otto found a local gravedigger who, for a fee of 2,000 Austrian schillings, overcame various objections and the frozen ground. She was not delighted with the plot but accepted it in the absence of other options.

At four o'clock on the afternoon of 4 January 1974, the family gathered at Charlotte's home in Fieberbrunn. They strapped a large cross to the roof of her car, decorated with a wreath, and placed various 'bits and pieces' into a small suitcase, to be buried with the coffin, then drove to the cemetery, a few kilometres away. On a day of brilliant blue sky, a modest ceremony was conducted by a priest from nearby St Johann, assisted by a youthful chaplain from Vienna. Two of their children – Otto and Traute – were present, with their spouses and the grandchildren. Otto's small coffin was lowered slowly into the grave, along with the items removed from the suitcase. Earth and pine branches were scattered into the grave.

'We bury the body of our brother Gustav Otto, here in the ground. We ask you to liberate his soul from the fetters of all sins.' Charlotte recorded the priest on her tape recorder, so I was able to listen to his deliberate, sonorous voice proclaim that man deviated from God's commandments and, in so doing, brought death into the world. There was no hint of a suggestion of any wrongdoing on the part of Otto. 'You promised paradise to the repentant thief, we ask you to welcome our brother into eternal bliss,' the priest said.

When Charlotte died eleven years later, in 1985, she was buried at the same cemetery, but in a different spot. Otto was disinterred once more, and his remains placed on top of her coffin, the fifth burial of Otto Wächter.

32

2016, Hagenberg

Otto's death in Rome, and the numerous reburials, was not something Horst mentioned when we first met, or for some years after. That changed in 2016, three years after the article in the *Financial Times*, a year after the documentary film. *East West Street* was published in the spring, and a few weeks later Horst wrote to say that Jacqueline, who was ill with cancer, had died. When we spoke he sounded sad, but also detached, and said that their daughter Magdalena was more deeply affected. In the course of the conversation, he enquired about our work on the papers, and I told him progress was interrupted, as Lisa Jardine had also died, a few months earlier.

In due course, we resumed work on Charlotte's papers, to honour Lisa. Not long after the conversation with Horst, I had a meeting at the BBC to explore a possible radio programme on international law and its future, during which the commissioning editor asked if I was working on anything else. I mentioned Charlotte's papers, our quest to decipher the life of a man on the run and his wife's efforts to help him. 'It's a sort of Nazi love story,' I told the editor, whose interest was piqued. That led to another meeting, and an invitation to pitch for a radio series and a podcast on the story of Charlotte and Otto, a tale of love and death, of disappearance and a Nazi in the Vatican.

Charlotte's papers were publicly available in Washington DC, at the US Holocaust Memorial Museum. We could have proceeded on that basis, yet I felt it important to ask Horst if he wanted to be involved. He thought about it, said yes – it offered a fresh chance to persuade, to explain the essential decency of his father. The radio project was commissioned and a producer chosen, Gemma Newby.

Thus, in December 2016, on an extraordinarily cold day, I travelled to Horst's castle for the fifth time, in the company of Gemma, our producer, and James, Lisa's last PhD student, and Lea, a German law graduate who worked as my assistant. Horst welcomed us warmly. The dog, the musty smell, the roaring fire, the kitchen, tea, everything was as it had always been, except that Jacqueline was absent. What was new was a home-baked cake.

This time the focus was different, a conversation about Charlotte's papers, thousands of pages of letters and diaries and reminiscences which I was becoming familiar with. James, Lea and I, with three other law students, had spent a year going through the material and digesting it. We had a basic chronology – the first thing I do on any case on which I am working is to prepare a detailed timeline – so we knew what was there, as well as the gaps in the documents and our comprehension.

For the first time, Charlotte was centre stage. I had come to understand that Horst's defence of Otto was largely inspired not by feelings towards his father, but by the love of his mother. During earlier visits, the focus was always on Otto, but now we were interested in a powerful and resolute personality, someone who 'always succeeded' in what she wanted, as Horst put it. He spoke with warmth about his mother, a person of energy and engagement, opinionated and strong, someone who was capable of love in her own way. 'She was really pretty when she was young, a very attractive person.' He paused. 'Not beautiful, but attractive.' He paused again. 'A special personality.'

Horst described the modest language school she ran in Salzburg at Haus Wartenberg, a place for young people to learn German. Students came from across Europe, the English ones especially fond of her, and she used her handsome son Horst to linger outside the building, to help attract female students. 'She was friendly,' Horst recounted, 'and so was I.' On her better days, he added, she also had a sense of humour.

This information about the language school was not entirely new. After the documentary film was broadcast, I received a number of communications from former students. One wrote to say he had lodged with Charlotte in Salzburg in January 1961, with his sister, but only learned about the family history, and Otto's Nazi role, with the documentary, five decades later. The baroness, or Tante Lotte, as Charlotte wished to be addressed, spoke little of the past, a dominant matriarch who once reduced his sister to tears, as recorded in a diary entry from the time. 'Tante Lotte says unpleasant things . . . about John and me and I feel furious and think that I should leave immediately,' the sister wrote. Charlotte apologised, a 'bit two-faced', the sister recorded, but did not leave. The reason for the dispute was forgotten, although the brother thought it may have been related to the fact that one of their parents was Jewish.

By then, Horst said, Charlotte was deeply religious, active in a Catholic religious community. She travelled to the Holy Land with a friend, a local priest, and hoped Horst might yet become a bishop or someone important. It never happened. Indeed, none of her children became important, a disappointment. 'My mother was very strong, and they had this problem with my father, in the background.'

Horst believed that his mother loved Otto immensely, even if the sense of jealousy and anxiety about his many affairs lasted throughout their relationship. Some letters were missing, perhaps because they contained intimate material, but several documents made clear she entertained the possibility of leaving him. 'I can't go on, you have this other lady . . .' She stayed with *mein Mann* – my man – because he radiated energy, was liked by all and was an impressive person. 'Himmler liked him too,' Horst added. 'He really was a big, great personality . . .'

Charlotte stayed with him while he was alive, and didn't let go after he died. 'My father was everything to my mother, she never said a word against him.' She never remarried, devoting the rest of her life to the defence of his reputation. Although Horst and Charlotte rarely talked about Otto, he recalled that whenever somebody wrote against him she became agitated, 'very upset'. Stories about Jews, for example, for whose deaths he was said to be responsible, annoyed her greatly. 'This is impossible,' she'd say. 'It's wrong, it's a lie.' She searched for people connected to his past, found them, talked to them, recorded their conversations. 'You have all the tapes,' Horst said. There was nothing to hide.

The collected papers of Charlotte Wächter were a private act of memory, but also an expression of advocacy, an effort to cleanse Otto's reputation. By now I knew that many documents – his work files – were missing, deposited by Charlotte, or perhaps her son Otto, as other accounts suggested, into Lake Zell. I suspected, too, that the letters and diaries were filleted, something Horst occasionally alluded to. His approach, I understood, followed Charlotte's path, a son's variation on the theme of the mother, with a different emphasis or nuance. 'There exists no document he signed to show that he ordered any death sentence,' Horst would say. He recognised that his attitude was motivated by feelings for Charlotte, that he never really knew his father. 'I love my mother, I have to do this, because of her.'

His position caused difficulties with other family members. They disapproved strongly of his contact with me, did not appreciate the article in the *Financial Times*, and disliked the documentary. Increasingly, he was excluded from family gatherings, or ignored when he attended them. Three of his siblings were dead, which left two sisters. Heide lived in Paris with her English husband. 'He hates everything I do . . .' Horst said, with an odd smile, as their son hoped to be a Conservative Member of Parliament. 'I might damage his future,' Horst added. Linde, the youngest of the six Wächter children, lived near Hagenberg. The next generation, Horst's twenty-one nephews and nieces, was 'dominated' by nephew Otto, a lawyer, the son of his only brother, Otto junior. 'Keep away from Uncle Horst' seemed to be a mantra.

Otto's side of the family was no less forgiving of Horst's stance, and desire to engage. Horst's Aunt Ilse, who appeared frequently in Charlotte's letters and diaries, was shocked when she learned that Horst worked with the artist Hundertwasser. 'Impossible,' she proclaimed, 'you can't work for a Jew.' As a Wächter, what was he thinking? Horst described Aunt Ilse as openly and fanatically anti-Semitic, which had the merit of making Charlotte appear more reasonable. 'My mother was never like this, not a fanatic Nazi,' although he accepted she was a Nazi. That, however, was 'only because of my father'.

At the castle, on that frozen day, we gathered Otto's final letters, the ones written after the weekend spent at Lake Albano in the company of a person whose name we did not know. Horst was sure the letters would have caused Charlotte tremendous distress, especially the one written on 6 July, in the shaky handwriting.

Together we read the last letters of Otto Wächter, and Charlotte's, and the two letters written by the Prussian lady, sent to Salzburg after his death. Horst showed us the originals, kept in the glass-fronted cabinet opposite his bed, near the photograph of Otto in his SS uniform, and godfather Seyss-Inquart. He placed one of the letters on the wooden table, picked it up, read aloud. 'From him I learned about you, the children, everything he held dear in life.' As Horst read the words he wept, gently and quietly.

'It's not true,' he said.

'What's not true?'

'That my father died from an illness.'

This was the first time Horst suggested his father may have been killed.

What happened?

'It is best to start at the beginning,' he said.

'Time for a schnapps?' James suggested.

'Already poured,' Horst replied, on the rebound.

33

Testament

The reburial of Otto Wächter, in 1974, took place twenty-five years after Charlotte returned to Salzburg from Rome. She travelled with a broken heart and papers Otto left behind at the Santo Spirito Hospital and the Vigna Pia monastery: a diary for 1949, a list of contacts in Rome, and notes on people met and correspondence sent and received over seventy-six days spent in Rome. Charlotte retained the papers, which passed to Horst after her death.

The papers included a one-page letter written by Otto, his testament, signed as 'Alfredo Reinhardt'. 'Rome, date as postmark', he typed, a document addressed to a 'Dear Doctor'. The name 'Marchesani' was added in pencil, in the hand of another, instructed to notify two people if Otto fell ill: the writer's unnamed wife, to be reached 'care of' Richard Woksch, in St Gilgen, Austria; and Fräulein Luise Ebner, in Bolzano, who was in turn to inform three friends in the South Tyrol, namely Riedl, Schnez and 'Ladurner'. 'Maintain links with them,' Otto instructed.

Dr Marchesani was also asked to notify a lawyer, Professor Giangaleazzo Bettoni in Rome – phone number provided – who would assess whether a 'legal intervention' was needed. The lawyer worked at the Italian embassy in Berlin until 1945, Otto explained in the letter, spoke German and had a German wife.

If the situation was 'serious', Dr Marchesani should consult Dr Hudal – the bishop – and also consider involving another bishop, Jan Bucko, of the Greek Unionist Church. 'Bucko knows a governor, Dr W, from his activity in his homeland,' Otto wrote, and had good relations with the Vatican and Western allies. However, this step was only a last resort, to be taken if the situation was 'critical', as matters should not be pushed to the 'international level'.

Dr Marchesani should inform Dr Puccio Pucci, another 'good friend' during the writer's stay in Italy, with whom they should discuss the 'activation' of Otto's comrades. Finally, the notes and papers kept in the cell at Vigna Pia should be tidied away.

The letter ended with an expression of thanks, and various personal details.

Otto's letter of instruction, in the event of incapacity or death, identified trusted contacts in Rome. The inner circle comprised seven people, none of whom was mentioned by name in the letters that passed between Otto and Charlotte. The names offered clues, a web of secret contacts that allowed Otto to survive in Rome and might, possibly, assist in efforts to reach South America. The seven people came from Germany, Italy, Austria and Ukraine. Who were they?

Three of the seven lived in Rome.

Puccio Pucci, described as a 'good acquaintance', was a lawyer and an athlete who once ran the 800 metres for Italy, at the 1924 Paris Olympics, and served briefly as president of the Italian Olympic Committee. He was a close associate of Alessandro Pavolini, secretary of the *Partito Fascista Repubblicano*, shot and then hung by the feet with Mussolini on 28 April 1945. Puccio Pucci, a committed fascist, founded the Black Brigades, a paramilitary organisation active in the Republic of Salò, where he worked closely with the Germans. It must have been then that Otto met him.

The second name on the list was Bishop Jan (Ivan) Bucko (or Buchko), an ardent Ukrainian nationalist who served in Lemberg as an auxiliary bishop with the Ukrainian Catholic Church, when Otto was governor in the city. After the war he moved to Rome to represent the Greek Catholic Church in the Vatican. It was said he played a key role – at the request of General Shandruk – in persuading Pope Pius XII to prevent members of Otto's Waffen-SS Galicia Division being extradited to the Soviet Union.

The third name was Giangalezzo Bettoni, a lawyer. Otto described him as a kind man who offered 'good advice', helping to translate Otto's long article, *Quo Vadis Germania?* From 1943 to 1945, Bettoni worked in Berlin as an aide to the Republic of Salò's ambassador to Germany. The family law firm in Rome still exists, run today by his son Manfredi, who I contacted to see if he could check the archives. He responded graciously and helpfully, but said he found nothing on Otto Wächter or Alfredo Reinhardt in the law firm's records.

The four other names in Otto's letter were based in Bolzano, in South Tyrol.

Luise Ebner, or 'Lilo', ran a shop. She often sent food parcels to Otto, offerings of tea, coffee, honey, sardines and fish paste. 'Everything a young man could desire,' Otto told Charlotte.

Franz Hieronymus Riedl was a journalist. It was in his archive that I found the photographs of Otto taken in the spring of 1949, near Bolzano. He worked as culture editor for *Dolomiten*, a German language newspaper, and acted as Otto's *poste restante* in Bolzano. Otto met him in the 1930s, and Riedl made numerous introductions in Rome, keeping Otto informed on Nora, Lilo and Schnez, and others referred to in code, including 'the monk' and 'Bauer'.

Albert Schnez was a former colonel in the Wehrmacht. In 1949 he worked to create a secret army of former officers – veterans of the Nazi-era Wehrmacht and the Waffen-SS – to defend West Germany against communism. Later, he joined the Bundeswehr, where he became one of its highest-ranking officers.

'Ladurner' was also referred to in several of Otto's letters to Charlotte, an old family name from the South Tyrol. I was unable to find anyone with that name who was active in Rome or South Tyrol in 1949, although I noticed that Buko had a young comrade of that name in the Karstjäger. Armed with Charlotte's papers, it was possible to compare the handwriting of 'Ladurner' with others, and it bore an uncanny similarity to that of Walter Raffelsberger, Otto's old comrade and fellow State Commissioner after the Anschluss. I concluded that 'Ladurner' was, most probably, Raffelsberger.

The seven shared a common sympathy, for fascism or Nazism, or both. Each of them also appeared to have a connection to Bishop Hudal, who, as I discovered in Charlotte's papers, became the subject of unwanted attention, in September 1949, just six weeks after Otto died.

This attention seemed like a good place to start, in the search for the circumstances of Otto's life in Rome, and the unexpected manner of his death.

34

September 1949

Beyond the note he gave to Charlotte on 16 July 1949, Bishop Alois Hudal's name appeared in several clippings kept in Charlotte's papers, articles published after Otto's death. Charlotte did not keep them in any apparent order, but with a chronological rearrangement the outlines of a story emerged.

It began on 1 September, which happened to be the day of the world gala premiere of *The Third Man*, at the Ritz Cinema in Hastings, East Sussex. *Il Giornale d'Italia* published an article about Otto's time in Rome, a Viennese Nazi on the run, said to be protected by the Vatican. The next day the fact of Otto's death was reported

OTTO WAECHTER DIES

Former Nazi Official Planned Assassination of Dollfuss

Special to THE NEW YORK TIMES.

in the *New York Times*, as other Italian newspapers picked up the story.

'The Vatican protects the fascist criminals,' declared *L'Unità*, a communist newspaper. Wächter's body was 'like an Arabian phoenix', the article reported, one that existed although no one knew where it was, reporting that Otto died in bed number nine of the Sala Baglivi of the Santo Spirito Hospital, and that Monsignor Hudal 'dispensed the sacraments'. Such facts were alleged to provide evidence of collusion between fascists, Nazis and the Catholic hierarchy. Wächter was said to have lived undisturbed at the Anima Institute, which enjoyed 'generous subsidies' from the Vatican, and eaten meals with his hosts.

Other newspapers jumped in with a mix of rumour and fact. *Il Quotidiano* claimed that Wächter spent three years in Rome, and 'repented' for his crimes before his death. *Il Paese* declared that Gauleiter Wächter was responsible for the deaths of thousands of Polish Jews in Leopolis (Lviv) and Galicia, and his death confirmed the presence of many 'shady characters' in Rome, welcomed by Vatican institutions.

'Who is this Monsignor Hudal?' *L'Unità* asked, as others defended the bishop. For *L'Osservatore Romano*, the Vatican's semi-official daily newspaper, the articles about Wächter and Hudal were written solely to allow communists and others on the left to attack the Church.

DOPO IL CASO WAECHTER

— MONS. HUDAL: E' Adolfo Hitler; ha mal d fegato...
— L'AGENTE: Passi pure!

L'Unità published a cartoon with the headline 'After the Wächter case', showing Bishop Hudal pushing Hitler into the Santo Spirito. 'It's Adolf; he's got liver trouble.' 'Go ahead,' the guard responds. *Il Giornale d'Italia* reported Otto's false name, Reinhardt, and offered a quote from Bishop Hudal. 'Wächter came to me like many others,' the bishop stated, and offered corrections to earlier articles. 'It is not true that he lived inside the walls of the Anima College, or that he had lived in Rome for three years.'

Il Gazzettino reported Otto's 'calm and undisturbed' time in Rome. Under the name 'Reinhardt', the 'tall, robust and blond' German-Austrian type with a military bearing spent many afternoons wandering along the Via Veneto, chatting with friends. 'He lived in a Roman convent and penetrated the Vatican's highest spheres,' the newspaper claimed, and his wife Charlotte was with him in Rome when he died, 'to embrace him before death'. He was said to have left behind a 'huge German typescript' – presumably a reference to a typed manuscript in Charlotte's papers, *Quo Vadis Germania?* – that was said to justify torture and other Nazi horrors, and imagine Germany's future 'under the spiritual control of Catholicism'.

Several newspapers identified the cause of death as liver disease. He bathed in an establishment close to the Mussolini forum, one reported, ignoring 'categorical orders' not to swim in the River Tiber. Death by swimming, from icteric hepatitis, worsened by the polluted waters of the river, another newspaper concluded.

L'Unità offered details of the funeral, attended by the 'finest of the SS'. It mentioned two names, neither of which appeared in the letters I had now read: Major Wilhelm Friede, a senior SS officer, and a German named Lauterbacher, reported to be living in a 'religious institute' in Rome. That was the name of the deputy to the head of the Hitler Youth, Baldur von Schirach, Otto's former comrade, who was tried at Nuremberg and spent twenty years in Spandau prison.

The effect of the media attention was dramatic.

The police were forced to respond immediately, and defensively. Documents in Italy's central state archives indicated the steps they took, led by Saverio Pòlito, the long-serving chief of police, or *questore*, who had interacted closely with Mussolini and his wife Rachele. Pòlito said the reporting was sensational, that Wächter's presence in Rome was not known to the police, and the files available to them made no mention of Otto Wächter being wanted 'for any crime or war crime'.

The *questore* sought to calm the situation with more details. Wächter succumbed to 'severe jaundice and uraemia'. The bishop visited only 'at the point of death', in the company of 'a woman named Lotte Pfob, who presented herself as the wife of the deceased'. Only after his death did the bishop identify the deceased as Otto Wächter, a 'political fugitive' who arrived in Rome with a false name. Otto's body was taken to Campo Verano cemetery on 16 July, by the Piermattei undertakers. There it was cremated and the ashes 'transported to the cemetery for foreigners at Testaccio'. This, I learned, was not true, as the cemetery records made clear he was buried at Verano.

A week after the first intervention, the *questore* was forced to respond again. The Austrian consulate confirmed Otto's name, identity, parentage and marital situation, and his role in organising the attack on Chancellor Dollfuss in 1934. The *questore* provided a copy of the death certificate, and declared categorically that police research in Austria 'did not show that he was a war criminal'.

Nevertheless, the pressure on Bishop Hudal did not abate, and he reacted. On Sunday, 11 September, ten days after the first article appeared, he dedicated a sermon at the Anima to the 'Wächter matter', as he called it. He sent a typewritten copy of the words he spoke to Charlotte in Salzburg, and two years later the text was published in *Anima Stimmen*, the magazine of the Anima, with a picture of the chapel on the cover. The bishop mounted a classic defence, in the form of an attack. The newspaper articles were driven by the left and foreigners, offering a 'net of lies, slander and revenge'. The real target was not Wächter but the Catholic Church and

the bishop himself, attacked because of his uncompromising approach to the threat of 'communism'. He offered several corrections: Wächter did not live at the Anima, 'not even for an hour'; he did not eat at the bishop's table; he carried 'proper documents', even if they were 'issued under a false name'; and his wife never was in an Italian concentration camp.

'I looked after the gravely ill General Wächter with pleasure,' the bishop told the congregants, and he would do the same again if he could, but with even greater devotion, love and bravery. He was motivated purely by instincts of love, reconciliation and mercy, and would risk his life to protect Germans, a group vilified by *Kollektivschuld*, a collective responsibility for the actions of the Nazis. Otto was entitled to receive help, as a matter of Christian charity.

The bishop went further. He would never surrender those under his care and protection to any secular court, since none was 'completely neutral'. Nor would he ever ask to see their papers or residence permits. 'The Catholic Church does not recognise the term *Kriegsverbrechen*' – 'war crimes' – except for specific offences set out in the Geneva Conventions. This seemed to be a swipe at two new crimes invented in 1945, 'genocide' and 'crimes against humanity', intended to protect groups and individuals, applied for the first time at Nuremberg to twenty-one defendants, including Otto's comrades Frank and Kaltenbrunner, and Horst's godfather Seyss-Inquart.

It is time to draw a 'thick line' across the past, Bishop Hudal concluded. Where were the defenders of human rights for those who languished in the prisons of France, Germany or the Soviet occupation zone, or Buchenwald, where conditions were now worse than during the Nazi period? With such fighting words did the bishop end his sermon, hoping the Wächter matter would be closed.

It was not. Two weeks later he was visited by the *questore*, who asked questions about Charlotte's visit. Two years later Bishop Hudal resigned because of the Wächter matter.

Who was Bishop Hudal, and what exactly was his relationship to Otto? It was to that question that I would now turn.

35

The Bishop

The documents Otto left behind contained numerous references to Bishop Hudal. Some were explicit, others were coded.

In his diary, on Friday, 29 April, at '13h' he wrote 'Excell.', a word underlined. This was most likely a reference to His Excellency Bishop Hudal. Separately, he maintained a list of addresses and contacts in Rome, with thirty-five names typed out across four sheets of yellow paper. There were two entries for Bishop Hudal, with the address at 20 Via della Pace of the Anima Institute, and a phone number, 51130. On a third document Otto listed every person he met in Rome, from the day he arrived on 29 April. Bishop Hudal's name appeared several times, and after his name Otto typed 'B.29.IV., B.30.IV., B.9.V.', etc. With Otto's diary, the code was not hard to crack. 'B' was short for *Besuch*, which meant 'meeting/ visit'; the Arabic number referred to a day; and the Roman number to a month. So 'B.29.IV' meant a meeting on 29 April. Bishop Hudal was the 'religious gentleman' about whom Otto wrote to Charlotte, the one who offered a '<u>very</u> positive' greeting once he realised who Otto was, as though he expected him.

The 'religious gentleman' was sixty-three years old when he met Otto in Rome. Born in the spring of 1885, in Graz, Austria, the son of a shoemaker, at twenty-three he was ordained as a priest, then earned a doctorate in theology at the University of Graz. He moved to Rome to be chaplain at the Anima, a theological seminary for German and Austrian priests. During the First World War he served as a military chaplain, and in 1923 was appointed rector of the Anima. Ten years later he was ordained as titular bishop of Aela by Cardinal Pacelli – later Pope Pius XII – and, surely no coincidence, Bishop Pawlikowski, the Bleckmann family friend who married Otto and Charlotte. Perhaps he was the one who made the introduction to Bishop Hudal?

In the 1930s, as rector of the Anima, Bishop Hudal wrote widely. He addressed matters of race, relations between Church and State and the fate of the German people. In 1936 he published *Die Grundlagen des Nationalsozialismus* (*The Foundations of National Socialism*), a paean to Hitler that proposed a close relationship between the Catholic Church and National Socialism. Two years later, he tried to organise a ballot at the Anima to support the Anschluss, but this was blocked by higher powers in the Vatican. He persisted, forcing a vote to be held on a German naval vessel, the *Admiral Scheer*, docked in the Italian port of Gaeta, but was much disappointed when colleagues at the Anima voted overwhelmingly against the German takeover of Austria.

During the war he offered the Anima as a place of refuge for Germans and Austrians. In 1944 he was made head of the Austrian section of the newly established Pontifical Commission for Assistance, created by Pope Pius XII to help refugees. This organisation appeared in Otto's list of addresses, along with a name – Carlo Bayer – which I recognised: the writer Gitta Sereny interviewed Karl Bayer in her book about Franz Stangl, commandant of the Treblinka extermination camp, present on the rail platform, on 23 September 1942, for the arrival of the three elderly sisters of Sigmund Freud and my great-grandmother Amalia. Odilo Globočnik told Himmler that Stangl was 'the best camp Kommandant in Poland'.

Stangl was caught by the Americans, but in 1948 Bishop Hudal helped him escape to Syria. Within three years he was in Brazil, working at a Volkswagen plant, where he was tracked down by Austrian Nazi hunter Simon Wiesenthal. Extradited to Germany in 1967, Stangl was tried, convicted of murder and other crimes, and sentenced to life imprisonment. In 1971, while an appeal was pending, he died of heart failure. Sereny interviewed him in Düsseldorf prison, shortly before his death. They talked about Bishop Hudal, and she later interviewed Monsignor Karl Bayer, who was living in Vienna, touching on his work at the Papal Commission in Rome. Sereny described Bayer as tall, slim and fair, perfumed with an agreeable scent of after-shave lotion, a man who drove a 'sporty car with an Italian number-plate'.

Otto noted merely that he was a Vatican priest from Breslau, 'politically interested, knows a lot of people'.

Bayer told Sereny he knew Bishop Hudal, but denied they were close. Yes, he confirmed, Hudal provided assistance to a 'comparatively small' number of Nazis and SS personnel, a part of his obligation to those 'in need of help'. Assistance included money – it 'most certainly came from the Vatican' – and other means. Bayer claimed that Hudal assisted refugees of many denominations, including Jews, but despite a concerted effort I was not able to find a single example of a Jew or communist helped by the bishop.

Questions were asked about the background of those who came to them but, Bayer said, they 'hadn't an earthly chance of checking on the answers'. In Rome, in 1949, papers and information of all kinds were easy to buy, and thousands passed through the city. 'How could we have known what they had done? After all, they didn't tell us; they weren't that stupid. And they weren't famous, you know.' Only later did names become notorious, people like Adolf Eichmann and Josef Mengele, the doctor who carried out experiments on twins at Auschwitz. They came to be known only in the 1970s. 'Even so, we tried to question them; we asked everyone questions.'

Bishop Hudal provided money and helped Stangl with a Red Cross passport, an entrance visa to Syria, a boat ticket and a job at a textile mill in Damascus. Yes, Bayer confirmed, the bishop probably did obtain 'batches of passports' for SS men, and supplied money. And yes, he added, Pope Pius XII 'did provide money for this; in driblets sometimes, but it did come . . .'

It was not difficult to find details about the others who were helped by Bishop Hudal. In September 1948, he obtained a Red Cross passport for Erich Priebke, an SS officer involved in the killing of 335 Italian civilians at the Fosse Ardeatine, with Karl Hass and Herbert Kappler. Arrested by the Americans in 1945, Priebke claimed the killings were justified 'reprisals', of the kind 'permitted to all armies' during the war. He escaped by boat from Genoa to Argentina.

In the spring of 1949, Bishop Hudal helped Walter Rauff, the previous occupant of Otto's cell at Vigna Pia, to make his way to Syria.

In July 1949, he helped Josef Mengele obtain a passport with the false name that allowed him to get to Argentina.

The reports in the Italian newspapers of the bishop's assistance to Otto – incendiary, as the first such account – caused him and the

Vatican great difficulty, because of the suspicion that he helped many others. The Wächter story, and other rumours, came to be a final straw, the catalyst that caused the bishop to be removed as rector of the Anima, in 1952. Under irresistible pressure from Austrian and German bishops, he retired to a house at Grottaferrata, near Lake Albano, to tend to a garden of cherry trees and primroses.

In 1960, the abduction of Adolf Eichmann from Argentina gave rise to renewed interest in Hudal's role, and caused a flurry of interest in Otto. Charlotte's papers included a newspaper article reporting that Bishop Hudal had known Josef Wächter, and another which suggested that Otto's death was caused by poisoning, that it was an act of murder. The same article raised another possibility, namely that Otto Wächter wasn't actually dead, that a body double was used to allow him to escape. When I mentioned this to Horst, he wept.

Bishop Hudal died in May 1963, his death reported in the Austrian press. Charlotte kept the articles. *Die Presse* noted that the requiem for Bishop Hudal was celebrated by the auxiliary bishop of Vienna, his successor as rector of the Anima. Another noted – erroneously – that the bishop's funeral was attended by Cardinal Pizzardo, who negotiated the concordat signed between the Vatican and the German Reich on 20 July 1933, on which the bishop worked. He was buried in the Vatican.

Thirteen years passed. In 1976 Bishop Hudal's posthumous memoir was published in Austria. *The Roman Diaries: Confession of an Old Bishop* set out a litany of complaints about Pope Pius XI and Pope Pius XII.

They also offered a surprise.

Roman Diaries was published in Graz, by Leopold Stocker Verlag. A small publishing firm founded at the end of the First World War, in the 1930s it adopted a strongly pro-Nazi stance, and still today continues to be associated with right-wing and extremist publications. Hansjakob Stehle, the historian with whom Charlotte conversed, reviewed Hudal's memoir in *Die Zeit*, emphasising the bishop's sense of embitterment at having been cut adrift by Pope Pius XII. Stehle also identified Bishop Hudal as an important source for *The Deputy*, a controversial play by Rolf Hochhuth, first performed in 1963, which highlighted the Pope's failure to protect the Jews.

Hudal's *Roman Diaries* made a number of references to Otto, the

most interesting in the final pages. He mentioned his role in the killing of Dollfuss, and asserted that shortly before his death the former
governor and SS man expressed regret that National Socialism hadn't
reached an understanding with the Church, to constrain Bolshevism.
The bishop recorded how, hunted by Allied and Jewish authorities,
after 'his superior Frank was hanged at Nuremberg', Otto lived in
Rome for months under an assumed name, assisted by a 'touchingly
selfless' group of Italian monks. He 'died in my arms', the bishop
wrote, and 'I protected him until the end'.

Then came a revelation. As the former governor lay dying, Bishop
Hudal wrote, he told him that he had been poisoned, an act Wächter
'personally attributed to the American secret service'. In Bishop
Hudal's account, Otto identified the culprit as 'a former German
major working in Rome', but he did not name him.

This came out of the blue. There was no hint in Charlotte's papers
of any act of poisoning, and it was not a claim that Horst had mentioned. I returned to the correspondence, to check the note Hudal gave
to Charlotte on 16 July, just two days after Otto died in the bishop's
arms. It contained no hint of foul play. Charlotte's letter of response,
sent three days later, was also silent as to the possibility. 'You were with
him in his final hour, to help his "final passage",' Charlotte wrote, and
she hoped to bring him home and bury him in his own country. The
letter was silent as to the cause of death.

No act of poisoning was hinted at in the two letters that Hedi Dupré
wrote to Charlotte a few days later. The first, on 25 July, mentioned
the cause of death identified by Dr Marchesani, 'acute liver atrophy,
caused by internal poisoning', possibly caused by food or water. If
murder was mentioned, by Bishop Hudal or anyone else, Hedi Dupré
said nothing to Charlotte. Frau Dupré's second letter did not address
the cause of death.

I found no indication in the papers that Charlotte ever mentioned
the possibility of poison to anyone else. There was no hint in her
papers for 1949, and the death certificate made no mention of foul
play. There was no indication of police involvement, or of an autopsy
that gave rise to concerns.

In the months and years that followed Otto's death, Charlotte made
no mention of any suspicious cause of death.

Decades later she wrote a series of reminiscences for the children.
None mentioned poison or foul play.

In all Charlotte's papers and recordings, there was only a single reference to foul play. It was made more than two decades after the death of Bishop Hudal, and eight years after his memoir was published, during a conversation with historian Hansjakob Stehle, in September 1984, a few months before Charlotte died. It took time to go through the tapes, to transcribe and translate them. Eventually I found the reference on cassette number three. When Dr Marchesani met her at the train station, Charlotte told Stehle, she expressed a desire to see his body. The doctor introduced her to the bishop, who accompanied her to the mortuary at the Campo Verano cemetery. She was surprised by what she saw.

'There he was,' she told Stehle. 'He lay as black as this wood, all burnt inside, like a Negro.'

'Poisoning?' Stehle asked.

'Poisoning,' Charlotte says.

The reply to Stehle's suggestion was firm and clear, but it offered no further detail.

36

Cold War

'Do you think Otto Wächter could have been poisoned?'

I put the question to Professor David Kertzer, in whose office at Brown University in Providence, Rhode Island, I sat. An anthropologist and historian, with a deep knowledge of Italian history in the years around the war, I was directed to him by a friend, having read his book on Mussolini and Pope Pius XI, which won a Pulitzer Prize. Context is important, and I hoped to learn more about the political situation in Rome in the spring of 1949, to understand Otto's situation, including the dangers he faced and who could and could not be relied on. To unlock the mystery of what he did over the last three months of his life, and the circumstances of his unexpected death, it might be useful to begin with the people he spent time with, and their connections.

Tall and elegant, in his late sixties, Professor Kertzer is a reflective academic who speaks with care and deliberation. He prepared for our meeting by reaching out to a colleague in Rome, a specialist on the German occupation of Italy. Yes, the colleague confirmed, the Wächter matter was well-known, and Otto was recognised to be a 'serious figure'.

In broad strokes, Professor Kertzer described the context of Otto's arrival in Rome. The country was recovering from a war that left it deeply scarred, in physical, economic and moral terms. Italy was struggling to come to terms with the humiliation of the *ventennio*, the years of fascism that began with Mussolini's ascent to power, in 1922, until he was overthrown on 25 July 1943. There followed a de facto civil war, between supporters and opponents of fascism and the alliance with Nazi Germany, from the creation of the Republic of Salò in September 1943, with which Otto worked closely when he arrived at Lake Garda in the autumn of 1944, until 25 April 1945.

Four years later, Otto arrived in Rome as the country was pulled in opposite directions, west towards the United States, east towards the

Soviet Union. Two forces had emerged from the war with some cred-ibility: on one side the Vatican, led by Pope Pius XII, which sought to reinvent itself by burying the association with Mussolini and fascism; on the other, the Italian Communist Party, with two million members and a leader, Palmiro Togliatti, back from exile in Moscow.

The United States and its allies were concerned by the prospect that Togliatti's communists might gain a foothold in the government of Italy, to establish a perch from which the Soviet Union could influ-ence western Europe, as the other side of the Iron Curtain. A new constitution was adopted, after a national plebiscite that replaced the monarchy with a republic. In April 1948, the first post-war national elections were won by the right-leaning Christian Democrats, backed by the Vatican and the Americans. The national margin was larger than expected, but in some regions, and in certain large cities, the communists took control. The Catholic Church was deeply involved in the election, Professor Kertzer explained, an effort to resist the com-munists. From the upper echelons of the Vatican down to local parish priests, the Vatican backed the Christian Democrats. It was a Cold War election, and that was the context in which Otto arrived in Rome.

'In 1949, in Rome, if you were a communist, you had nothing to do with the Church,' Professor Kertzer explained. 'If you were a Catholic, and a Christian Democrat, you had nothing to do with the commu-nists or their organisations.' The divide foretold the sharp difference adopted by newspapers in reporting Otto's death and the assistance said to have been given to him by Bishop Hudal.

Otto's background was pertinent too. As a Catholic, and a virulent anti-communist, he would be able to count on support from parts of the Vatican. As a senior Nazi, a governor and SS officer who was close to Himmler and who worked with the Republic of Salò, he could count on the support of former fascists, even if the party had been banned. Yet his Nazi past could not be worn openly: just a few months before he arrived in Rome, a military tribunal in the city sentenced Herbert Kappler, the SS chief of the security police and security service in Rome, to a term of life imprisonment for his role in the murder of 335 Italians in Rome's Ardeatine Caves. The reprisal order was implemented with the assistance of senior colleagues, including Captain Erich Priebke, who was also charged but acquitted. Several of Otto's contacts were implicated in the story, including Feldmarschall Kesselring, who received the order from Berlin, and SS Obergruppenführer Karl Wolff.

As Otto arrived in Rome, the artist Mirko Basaldella was working on a design for the gates to the memorial that would shortly be installed as a monument to the victims.

Otto arrived in Rome knowing he had to take care. He could not be open about his past, as Italy sought to recast itself as a supporter of the Allies rather than Nazi Germany. As a staunch anti-communist, you could not be seen to embrace the Nazis. Otto engaged in a 'most delicate dance'.

His main card was the fear of communism, which led him to people who were right-leaning, anti-communist, and close to the Church. 'Of these there were many,' Professor Kertzer said with a smile. One among them was Bishop Hudal, known to offer refuge to Nazis. On the other hand, Otto also had to avoid overt liaison with fascists, or those who retained a nostalgia for the Republic of Salò, including the nucleus of the *Movimento Sociale Italiano* ('basically a nostalgic neo-fascist party', Professor Kertzer explained, even as Italy's new constitution prohibited fascism). 'In Rome in 1949 you could only embrace fascism subterraneously.'

The mention of fascists offered a moment to review the thirty-five names in Otto's address book. Putting aside the two bishops – Hudal and Buchko – and Messrs Bettoni, the lawyer, and Marchesani, the doctor, the great majority of names were Italians, Austrians and Germans. There was also a Croat and a Hungarian, the painter Lajos Markos, who later painted Robert Kennedy and Ronald Reagan. 'Formerly an English prisoner', Otto wrote in pencil, next to Markos' address.

Otto's list of Italian contacts was varied. It included several journalists, like Alessandro Gregorian, described by Otto as 'very friendly' and a 'leader of the Vatican press service'. Ezio Maria Gray was '100 per cent trustworthy . . .!', a 'former president of the Italian journalists' union, good orator, anti-Bolshevik'. Other names were connected to the Church. Dr Egger was a prelate from the South Tyrol, helpful 'for emigration'. Monsignor Draganović, a Croat and a Franciscan priest, was associated with the San Girolamo Institute in Rome, and his cardinal protector was Luis Copello, Archbishop of Buenos Aires and a close supporter of Argentine president Juan Perón, who was strongly critical of the Nuremberg trials. 'Croatian, speaks German, can speak completely openly with him!' Otto wrote of Draganović, who was closely associated with the Nazi-supporting regime of Croatia. It was he, I learned, who helped Klaus Barbie flee to South America.

Several of Otto's contacts were identified as fascist sympathisers. He described Counts Clavio and Piero Tagliavia as 'former fascists, good people'. Count Teodorani Fabbri, the 'son-in-law of the Duce's brother', was said to be close to the Vatican, with ties to 'politics, army, police'. Signorina Elena Vitalis was, according to Otto, 'very nice, neo-fascist?!' The list of thirty-five contacts included only one identified by Otto as 'anti-fascist', the engineer Biagio Bogioannini, an officer in the alpine forces, the *Alpini*, nevertheless 'decent and easily influenced'.

The world of diplomacy also featured in Otto's list. His Excellency Camillo Giuriati, a former Italian diplomat, specialised in trade with India. Baron Folco Aloisi, the son of an Italian representative at the League of Nations during the Abyssinian conflict, had to be treated 'with care'. Baroness Sofia Toran de Castro was in her mid-sixties, 'movingly kind', and with a Viennese mother. Marianne Leibl, 'a handwriting expert from the South Tyrol', who later became an actress and appeared in films directed by Luchino Visconti and King Vidor. Her first film credit was Géza von Radványi's *Donne Senza Nome*, which happened to be the one in which Otto appeared.

'Fascinating list,' Professor Kertzer said quietly. The names confirmed his sense of the circles in which Otto would have moved.

We turned to the subject of foul play, in Rome during the post-war years, the acts of killing. 'There was violence in Rome after the war,' he explained, 'but mostly it was against Italians.' Scores were settled, as thousands were killed across Italy, mostly by former members of the resistance. Austrians and Nazis were generally not targets. 'The resistance, such as it was – mythologised, and exaggerated – was largely dominated by the Communist Party.' Revenge killing of Italian opponents was a calling card, long after the war, but by 1949 acts of killing were, as he put it, 'very unusual'.

Otto's real concern, he continued, having been indicted for 'mass murder', would have been the fear of discovery, of being caught and brought to justice before the courts for his role in Nazi 'mass murder'. 'There would have been plenty of people around in Rome, especially on the left, who would have been eager to root out someone like Wächter.'

The Americans were top of the list of those who might be hunting him, but it was unlikely that Otto would have been killed by them. 'The idea that they would have organised a hit squad seems preposterous.'

It wasn't their style, not in Italy. If the Americans found him, he would be arrested, jailed, tried. 'And hanged,' Professor Kertzer added. 'Rome in 1949 was full of people trying to get him, so he had plenty of reasons to be fearful.'

Could Otto have been targeted by the Soviets, or by Italian communists? 'Not inconceivable,' he responded. In 1949 there was still a 'great rage' against the Nazis, on the left. A targeted killing could be possible.

We turned to the German contacts on Otto's list. The first name was Karl-Gustav Wollenweber. A 'former ambassadorial aide', Otto scribbled in his notes. Someone else added a date – January 2000 – and a few words. 'The poisoning on 2nd July happened at his house.' It looked like Horst's handwriting.

'Do you think Otto Wächter was poisoned?' Professor Kertzer asked.

I had no view, I was digesting the material.

'And that's where it could have happened, at Wollenweber's house?'

I explained what was known about the events of the first weekend of July, back in 1949, when Otto visited a 'kind old comrade' near Lake Albano. The word 'comrade' suggested he was German or Austrian and a Nazi, but Otto did not identify the person by name. I wanted to know who he visited when he fell ill, as a name could help work out the circumstances – and cause – of his death.

I would start with Wollenweber, a name that was new.

37

Wollenweber

Information about Dr Karl-Gustav Wollenweber, the first name in Otto's list of contacts, was not hard to find. Otto's papers included an address – Villa San Francesco on the Via dei Monti Parioli, in Rome's II District, a monumental building with a fine garden – and a reference to a visit, on 26 May. Today the villa serves as the headquarters of the General Council of the Servants of Jesus of Charity, and a retirement home for forty-two elderly Catholic ladies. A website offers a smiling portrait of Pope Francis and describes a home that offers a sense of 'true family', where ladies of a certain age will 'feel serene and happy during the last years of their lives'.

Dr Wollenweber trained as a lawyer and joined the Reich foreign service in 1935. He served in Luxembourg and Berlin, then in Rome from 1940 until the end of the war, a Reich representative to the Vatican. He rose to second secretary, number three under Ambassador Ernst von Weizsäcker who, in April 1949, when Otto arrived in Rome, was on trial before a US military tribunal in Nuremberg for crimes against humanity. He was convicted for the crime of deporting French Jews to Auschwitz. One of his defence lawyers was his son Richard, who became president of West Germany.

After the war, Dr Wollenweber worked briefly for the British Control Commission in Berlin, until he was interned at an Allied camp in Sicily. Released after a brief stay, he joined the West German foreign service, to serve in Spain, Mexico, the Dominican Republic and Malta. During this time he married the daughter of a German diplomat who resigned in 1934 in opposition to the Nazis. With the marriage, Wollenweber acquired two stepsons, Michael and Jörg.

Dr Wollenweber apparently had access to Pope Pius XII, as was reflected in various accounts of the events on the morning of 16 October 1943, when the Jews of Rome started to be rounded up for deportation. According to one account, Princess Lorenza Pignatelli, who lived outside Rome, received an urgent telephone call, inviting her to intercede with the Pope, whom she knew as a former teacher. She was told to make her way to the Vatican, as a matter of urgency.

She asked Dr Wollenweber to drive her from Lake Albano to Rome. They first went to the Jewish ghetto, to see what was happening, then to the Vatican and the private chapel of Pope Pius XII. According to Princess Pignatelli, the Pope telephoned the German authorities, in her presence, to ask that the arrests and deportations be halted with immediate effect. They were halted, but not before 1,023 Jews were sent to Auschwitz, of whom just sixteen returned.

Bishop Hudal became involved, writing a letter that set out the dire implications for relations between the Vatican and the Third Reich if the deportations were not stopped. His memoir contained a reference to a 'Dr W', with the idea he might be appointed as a go-between – an 'extraordinary plenipotentiary' – to improve relations between the Third Reich and the Vatican. The bishop wanted a senior diplomat like him, someone who could deal directly with the Pope.

This was the sum of what I learned about Karl-Gustav Wollenweber. Did Otto spend that first weekend of July with him, and was Dr Wollenweber somehow involved in his death? In American archives I found a single reference to Dr Wollenweber, a document from January 1950. Described as the bishop's 'right-hand man', working to 're-establish' the German embassy to the Holy See after the war, he was identified as a 'favourite' of the former German ambassador Diego von Bergen, recalled to Berlin in February 1943 for being insufficiently Nazi. The CIA document described Wollenweber's past as 'shady and corrupt' – without any evidence – and suggested he tried to re-establish himself in Rome by 'exploiting' the influence of a highly intelligent, but unnamed, 'Prince of the Church'.

To be the 'former comrade' with whom Otto spent that July weekend, Dr Wollenweber would have been married to an Italian, with a four-week-old daughter. I found the former wife of one of Wollenweber's two stepchildren, who lives in Connecticut. She was helpful and friendly. She met Karl-Gustav a few times, she told me, but they never discussed the war. 'He was quiet and not active.' Her ex-husband Michael, one of his stepsons, was not close to him. 'We never spoke about him.' The other stepson, Jörg, was not inclined to communicate directly with me, but did pass on some information, which proved to be decisive.

'Wollenweber was our stepfather,' Jörg wrote, when his mother

married him in 1953. He confirmed other details, and added that he
converted from the Protestant faith to Roman Catholicism, and was 'a
very close friend of Pius XII'. At the end of the war the Vatican offered
asylum to him and two other top officials at the German embassy, the
others to be interned in Allied camps. The number four at the embassy
was Sigismund von Braun, a brother of Wernher von Braun, who
helped design the V2 rockets, one of the German scientists recruited
by the United States. Sigismund's wife was pregnant, so Wollenweber,
who was unmarried at the time, took his place in the internment camp
in Sicily.

This limited information – the date of the marriage, the absence of
any other child – made it clear that this was not the 'former comrade'
with whom Otto swam at Lake Albano. Dr Wollenweber was a red
herring, with no suggestion that he ever worked for the Americans.

38

CIC

The existence of a file on Dr Wollenweber in the American archives suggested that they might hold other information that could assist. The archives of the CIA, and other organisations, were voluminous and labyrinthine, so I needed a guide. I turned to Professor Norman Goda of the University of Florida, in Gainesville, who has written extensively on the relationship between the American intelligence services and former Nazis, drawing on declassified US intelligence materials. I read with particular attention one of his books, co-authored, which focused on US recruitment of known SS and Gestapo officers, in particular those with an intelligence background. One such SS officer was Klaus Barbie, the 'Butcher of Lyon', whose escape to South America was assisted by elements in the Vatican.

Professor Goda's book evoked the organisation of American intelligence in western Europe, as Otto arrived in Rome. The most extensive operation was run by the US Army's Counter Intelligence Corps, the CIC. The reference triggered a recollection, to a line in one of Charlotte's reminiscences. 'I was spied on day and night by the CIC, who were looking for how to connect to my dear husband Otto,' Charlotte wrote. This was the only organisation Charlotte mentioned.

The CIC was formed in 1942, with origins in the First World War. Tasked with all aspects of military intelligence, in the US and abroad, after May 1945 its functions were expanded to include the capture of Nazis across Europe. The CIC came to play a leading role in denazification, an

effort to turn former Nazis into decent citizens. In the course of that activity the organisation moved to recruit former Nazis, in the face of the threat said to be posed by the Soviet Union. In this way, the CIC started to focus on senior Nazis who had experience in intelligence, identifying SS and other personnel who knew the communist enemy. Professor Goda's work offered a myriad of details, including the names of people and organisations that appeared in Otto's papers.

Professor Goda was clear about the CIC and its record, as an organisation that made mistakes: it was known to have recruited Nazis who were being hunted for the most serious crimes. He mentioned the story of Hermann Höfle, who served in Kraków with one of Otto's auxiliary police forces and who, by 1942, was reported to be Odilo Globočnik's 'most important subordinate'. Despite this dubious role, and the known desire of Poland to prosecute Höfle for serious crimes committed on its territory, the CIC recruited him as a source.

Professor Goda was familiar with the names of some of Otto's colleagues and contacts in Rome. The CIC worked closely with Bishop Draganović and General Karl Wolff, Otto's commandant in Italy, who negotiated Operation Sunrise with Allen Dulles, an American who worked for the Office of Strategic Services, an intelligence agency that became the CIA. The Americans knew about – and chose to ignore – aspects of Wolff's past, like the document from 1942 in which Wolff recorded his 'particular joy' at a 'population movement' of Jews, the news that 'for two weeks now a train has been carrying, every day, 5,000 members of the Chosen People to Treblinka'. They acted to remove his name from the list of potential 'main war criminals' to be sent for trial at Nuremberg, and subsequently sought to protect him from prosecution.

There was much of interest in Professor Goda's research. He explained that by 1949 the CIC, other American agencies and the British were well aware that many of the supposed 'refugees' who entered Italy were Nazis, or complicit in Nazi crimes. They were aware too of the Nazi escape routes, the use of false identities, how travel documents were obtained, and the role of the Red Cross and certain individuals associated with the Vatican.

I learned that the CIC was active in Rome in 1949.

I learned that General Wolff's subordinate in Operation Sunrise was Eugen Dollmann, sought by the Italians for his role in the killing of 335 Italian civilians in Rome's Ardeatine massacre. In 1947 the Americans had full knowledge of Dollmann's role, but took steps to protect him from prosecution in Italy, then exfiltrated him from Rome.

I learned that in April 1945, Walter Rauff, the previous occupant of

Otto's cell at Vigna Pia, was caught and interrogated by the CIC. He was thought to be so great a 'menace' that 'life-long internment' was recommended, but he escaped.

I learned that the CIC chief in Upper Austria was Thomas A. Lucid, of the CIC's 430th Detachment, who was involved in the arrest of Frau Himmler. Through Norman Goda's work I learned that Lucid recruited Wilhelm Höttl, the Nazi 'turncoat' about whom Raffelsberger (also known as 'Ladurner') warned Otto. Lucid described Höttl as an 'excellent source', with a background in Nazi intelligence that enabled him to evaluate reports on the Soviets with 'complete accuracy'. In 1948, Lucid retained Höttl to run two new CIC intelligence networks, on Soviet influence in Hungary and Austria.

These names – Wolff, Rauff, Höttl and Dollmann – had something else in common: they all worked with Otto during his period of active duty in Italy, after the autumn of 1944. Nevertheless, Professor Goda told me he had not previously come across Otto's name, a senior Nazi who had been blanked out. He offered to search for documents about him in the CIC and CIA archives. Perhaps, he suggested, something would be found to allow the dots around Otto's life to be joined, to connect elements referred to but not explained in Charlotte's papers.

Professor Goda directed me to one document he thought I would be interested in. It was written by Vincent La Vista, a State Department official, in May 1947, a forty-one-page report, marked 'Top Secret'. The La Vista report emerged in the 1980s. It made clear that already by 1947 – two years before Otto arrived in Rome – the Americans were aware of illegal emigration routes that provided passage from Italy to South America. According to La Vista, the 'largest single organisation involved in the illegal movement of emigrants' was the Vatican, and in Rome the CIC had an active role, as did known Soviet agents.

An annex to La Vista's report offered a list of organisations and individuals involved. The first name on the list was Bishop Alois Hudal, who was closely observed by the Americans, who appeared to know who he met and what he was up to. They were also watching 'Monsignor Buchko', the Ukrainian, and 'Padre Bayer', the perfumed cleric who drove an Italian sports car.

La Vista's report suggested that the Americans could have known of Otto's arrival in Rome, from the moment he first met Bishop Hudal. 'Vincent La Vista may have overstated the case a bit,' Professor Goda explained, 'but the general outlines of his report were right.'

*

Professor Goda and I imagined the situation as perceived by Otto on the day he arrived in Rome.

He feared being caught, then extradited to Poland, where he would be tried, convicted and sentenced to death. He also feared surveillance, as was clear from the correspondence with Charlotte. He knew he was hunted by the Americans and the Poles, who had indicted him for 'mass murder', and probably also the Soviets. He knew that Frank, Kaltenbrunner and Seyss-Inquart were caught and then executed at Nuremberg. He likely knew that other colleagues in the General Government – Josef Bühler and Governor Fischer – were handed over to the Polish authorities by the Americans, to be sentenced to death and executed. He did not know that in January 1949 his 'trace had been encountered' by the Polish authorities, and that just a few weeks earlier a Polish prosecutor had requested that 'incriminating materials relating to his criminal activity' be collected, for the purpose of prosecution.

Otto would have been aware – or concerned – that American intelligence was active in Rome, and perhaps keeping an eye on the Vatican. He probably did not know that in the absence of an American ambassador accredited to the Vatican – none was appointed until the Nixon presidency – the Americans gleaned information as best they could by retaining individuals who were, as Professor Goda put it, 'in the know'. Otto did not know who might be an American informant, and who he needed to avoid. He would have assumed, however, that Bishop Hudal was safe, known to the German community in Rome as a sympathiser and a 'main conduit' for Nazis on the run.

On the other hand, Otto was probably not aware that when he arrived in Rome the political situation had changed, that 1949 was a 'pivotal year' in the Cold War, with the Vatican working hand-in-hand with the Americans. Moreover, Poland was now firmly in the Soviet sphere, which meant that the Americans would be less inclined to cooperate with a request from Warsaw for his extradition. The hunt for ex-Nazis was diminishing. 'It's not that there was no Polish interest in Wächter, in 1949,' Professor Goda explained, 'merely that it was less intense than three years earlier.'

These factors meant that the Americans 'were not necessarily after Wächter in 1949, at least not with an eye on handing him to the Poles', although Otto would not have known that. He would have 'believed he was in danger of arrest and punishment, or perhaps assassination'.

Assassination? Possible but unlikely, Professor Goda clarified. The Soviets did sometimes assassinate – he mentioned the case of Stepan Bandera, a Ukrainian nationalist leader poisoned outside his Munich home with the tip of an umbrella – but that happened only many years later. He doubted the Soviets would have poisoned Otto because of his wartime activities, although they may have done so if they thought he was currently 'involved in political machinations'.

In reality, the Soviets preferred to catch former Nazis, to turn them and play them against the West Germans or the Americans. Professor Goda offered the example of SS officer Friedrich Panzinger, who was caught by the Soviets but not put on trial. Instead, they turned him and sent him back to the West, hoping to penetrate the fledgling West German intelligence organisation run by Reinhard Gehlen, a former Wehrmacht general. Panzinger did not deliver: he told the West Germans what the Soviets were doing, then committed suicide. Perhaps he was a decoy, Professor Goda mused, as the Soviets had by then penetrated West German intelligence with other former SS members.

By the time Otto arrived in Rome, the work of the CIC had shifted direction: for two years they hunted Nazis for prosecution, now they were hunting them as recruits. Otto could be a useful ally against the Soviets, to be integrated into the West German intelligence service, as other former members of the SS, SD or Gestapo had been, with the assistance of the CIC. Höttl was an example, recruited by Thomas Lucid, who later tried to work for the West Germans. Professor Goda thought Höttl was, 'in all likelihood', also a Soviet agent.

Like Professor Kertzer, he doubted that Otto would have been killed by the Americans. 'I'm having trouble thinking of a single case where the Americans assassinated a former Nazi.' The Americans discredited them, or gave them their walking papers, but he was unable to pull up an example of one who was killed.

So why did Otto claim he was poisoned by the Americans, as Bishop Hudal's memoir reported? That's a matter of speculation, Professor Goda said. And, he continued, 'the fact that Wächter believed he was poisoned did not mean he was actually poisoned'.

'And the fact that the bishop wrote in his memoir that Otto told him he'd been poisoned, didn't mean that Wächter actually said it,' I added.

'Correct.'

Could Wächter have been poisoned by a German working for the Americans?

'That's a little more interesting,' Professor Goda thought, and raised the possibility of Jewish revenge. There were plenty of conspiracy theories, fuelled by the fact that many of those who interrogated or prosecuted the Nazis were Jewish.

Could he have been poisoned by a German who worked for the Americans and was a double agent for the Soviets?

'That's also interesting,' Professor Goda said.

He had searched for files about Otto in various US archives. There seemed to be no CIA name file on him, but the US National Archives said there was a CIC file. He had ordered a copy. 'It could be there's nothing in it,' he said, 'just a trace card. Or it could be a full file, with details about what other sources were saying about him. Or, it could be a fugitive file, going back to 1946. Or, if Wächter was connected with Höttl, there could be a file that includes his name but is really about Höttl, or others.' He would send me Otto's file as and when it arrived.

The lengthy conversation with Professor Goda prompted him to revisit the declassified files already available to him. Several related to one German in particular, who might be of interest, because he was known to be active while Otto was in Rome. The man was called Hartmann Lauterbacher. The name seemed familiar, although I wasn't sure why. I went back to Charlotte's papers.

Lauterbacher did not feature in Otto's list of addresses or diaries, or the letters to and from Charlotte. The name did, however, appear in one newspaper clipping, which was why I remembered it. *L'Unità* reported that a man named 'Lauterbacher' had attended the first burial of Otto, his funeral at the Campo Verano cemetery. The article described Lauterbacher as one of the 'finest of the SS'.

Professor Goda said he would gather the declassified Lauterbacher files and pass them on. They might include names or other details that could be cross-checked with Otto's contacts.

39

Lauterbacher

As I awaited the arrival of Hartmann Lauterbacher's files, I returned to Charlotte's papers, to check again if his name featured. I found one other mention of him, in a transcript of the conversation that Charlotte recorded with the historian Hansjakob Stehle, tape number ten.

I could hear Horst speaking in the background of that tape, with his sister Traute, two voices affectionately protective of Charlotte. Her conversation with Stehle traversed the entirety of Otto's life in a single hour. The early years, the July Putsch, the killing of Dollfuss, Otto's escape, Kraków, chess with Hans Frank, the visit by Italian writer Curzio Malaparte, Lemberg, Himmler, Italy, Buko and Kaltenbrunner.

Charlotte told the historian that her recollections were limited. 'I was so active in my youth that I slept through this historical period.' She had time only for Otto, and for his work. The conversation turned to the last time they were together, in Bolzano.

He wanted to continue to Rome, Charlotte told Stehle, after staying with the lady 'he had run into'. This was a reference to Nora.

'Why did he want to go to Rome?'

'Because he knew many people there.'

'Who did he know in Rome?' Stehle asked.

'In Rome he knew . . .' Charlotte's voice trailed off, as she gathered her thoughts, or perhaps wondered what she was able to say. 'I cannot say that now, but it must have been someone connected to the Reichsjugendführer.' Herr Stehle understood the reference to be to Baldur von Schirach, head of the Hitler Youth.

'Lauterbacher?' he said, instantly, a reference to von Schirach's deputy.

'Lauterbacher.' Charlotte spoke the name with deliberation. 'Yes, yes, it must have been him.'

Stehle asked who recommended going to Argentina. Charlotte said she couldn't remember. 'We could not officially write,' so real names were kept out of the correspondence.

'He spent time with someone at Lake Albano, at the end, and from there he returned to Rome fatally ill, and that's why Hudal was of the opinion he was poisoned.'

'Who might have poisoned Otto?' Stehle asked.

'I don't know, but it could be in the letters,' she replied, then corrected herself. 'No, he never mentioned names.'

'Supposedly a German officer?'

Charlotte said nothing. Later the conversation returned to 'the assassination', as she described it. She blamed the Soviets, as they knew Otto was 'completely anti-Bolshevik, a real advocate against Russia'.

'But that wouldn't be a reason to poison him?'

'No, no.'

Hartmann Lauterbacher gave witness testimony at the Nuremberg trials, and published an autobiography in 1984. The two sources offered a vivid picture of the man, colourful and duplicitous.

The British arrested Lauterbacher on 30 May 1945 and interned him at Sandbostel camp, near Bremervörde. He remained there for three years, authorised to travel to Nuremberg, having volunteered to testify in the trial of Baldur von Schirach. A personal friend, he told the judges, with whom he worked closely.

He answered questions about his work, including overseas visits. 'I met the leader of the British Boy Scouts,' he testified, but made no mention of a visit to Eton School, in his capacity as deputy leader of the Hitler Youth, in November 1937.

The Nuremberg testimony of Hartmann Lauterbacher was evasive. He told the judges that the Hitler Youth wore a 'national costume', not a uniform, and that they played no role in anti-Jewish activities. The *Yearbook of the Hitler Youth* was not a reliable source of information, as it was not an 'official' document, even if it was published by the Nazi Party's 'Central Publishing House'. An affidavit sworn by a former colleague alleging that he ordered hundreds of inmates at the Hamelin prison to be 'poisoned with prussic acid or strychnine', or shot, was without foundation. 'I never gave any such order.'

Lauterbacher's autobiography offered an equally self-serving narrative. He described his escape from a British camp in February 1948, a summer spent in Bavaria with his wife, then arrival in Italy, illegally, living in Bolzano. He travelled to Rome, where he went straight to his old friend Bishop Alois Hudal. They first met in 1934, at a Hitler

Youth camp, he noted, and when they looked into each other's eyes, an immediate friendship began that lasted until the bishop's death. In Rome the bishop helped him. He lodged with an elderly Italian princess who lived 'a stone's throw' from Castel Gandolfo, and declined the opportunity to emigrate to Argentina, as he wanted to be near his family. He worked for his brother's export agency, and obtained an Italian residency permit and identity papers. The autobiography made no mention of intelligence activities.

That was the official version, a sanitised account.

A somewhat different story was told by the twenty-eight declassified CIC and CIA files on Hartmann Lauterbacher, as sent by Professor Goda, who also reported that the file in the CIC archives on Otto Wächter was missing. The Lauterbacher files covered the period from November 1948 to the early 1960s, confirming that he arrived in Rome in 1948. There he 'associated with neofascist circles', toyed with 'neo-fascist ideals', and enjoyed extensive contact with 'ex-high-ranking Nazi-type friends'. They offered other details. Lauterbacher was five feet seven inches tall and corpulent, and said to have been an 'active homosexual' throughout his life. He was Catholic, trained as a druggist, married with three children, and drank heavily and smoked.

The files reported a 'clandestine' existence in Rome, in which he used several aliases. American intelligence watched him closely, observing frequent contacts with Bishop Hudal (described as a 'nationalist and anti-communist') and former leaders of various Italian fascist groups. The files reported that he declined an offer by the Argentine ambassador in Rome to travel to South America if he helped bring Germans across, and detailed other activities. He unified anti-communist groups in Germany and Austria, helped to establish an 'anti-communist information network with the aid of the Vatican, in collaboration with Bishop Hudal', and worked to 'conserve Germans living in danger by sending them to Syria'.

In 1949 he and Bishop Hudal established an 'International Anti-Bolshevik Organisation' with, Lauterbacher claimed, support from the Allied authorities. In the summer of 1949 he made contact with the CIC, passing on information about Communist Party activity and activists. His contact there was Joseph Luongo, a special agent based in Gmunden, who worked for Thomas Lucid. Lauterbacher was also said to work for Italian intelligence, and to have contacts with 'elements working for the Russians'.

Lauterbacher's files contained other information more closely connected to Otto. In the summer of 1949, the 430th CIC Detachment became aware of a Soviet 'espionage network operating in Italy', comprised of German nationals. The CIC identified a 'roster' of Germans who were active in Rome, and the names included three of Otto's contacts. One was a journalist called Bauer, who worked with the SD in Amt (department) VI) during the war, and was now 'a reporter for the Austrian Press Agency in Rome'. The second was Walter Rauff, who organised travel for German ex-officers to Syria. And the third was Hedi Dupré, the Prussian lady who, I now learned, was more than just a friendly acquaintance: during the war she served as a secretary to the German naval attaché, and also worked with German military intelligence, the Abwehr. After the war, the document reported, she transferred her efforts to the Italian intelligence services.

In 1951, Lauterbacher was imprisoned at the Fraschette di Alatri internment camp, south of Rome. He escaped and returned to Rome, where he developed a 'permanent liaison with the Italian Social Movement'. He also worked for German intelligence, the BND, but was fired in 1953, for being a 'homosexual and suspected eastern agent'. Ten years later, still under American surveillance, he was taken to an American safehouse to be interrogated. Told it was a 'routine review', he fled, fearing that US intelligence 'had something else in mind'. He disappeared, reportedly to Ghana. After a few years in Africa and the Middle East, he returned to Germany, where he died in 1988.

Those were the American files on Hartmann Lauterbacher. There was also a file held by the East German secret police, which offered other possible links to Otto. This Stasi file reported that Lauterbacher's favourite rendezvous was the Café Doney on the Via Veneto, a street frequently mentioned in Otto's diary. Lauterbacher provided 'incriminated Nazis' with Italian residence permits, due to his excellent relations with the Italian police, for whom he was said to be 'an informer'.

There was more. The CIC and Stasi files listed various false names that Lauterbacher used in Rome in the summer of 1949. One name was 'Giovanni Bauer', another was 'Walter Detering'. Both names were instantly recognisable from Otto's diary.

On 29 April, the day of his arrival in Rome, Otto was to be met by 'Bauer'. In this way I learned that Hartmann Lauterbacher was the real name of the man he expected to greet him at Rome's Termini train station, except that he wasn't there when the train arrived late. Otto spent two days looking for Lauterbacher.

'Bauer' was also referred to in numerous entries in Otto's diary, in May and June.

Otto referred to 'Detering' in three of his letters.

Walter Rauff's letter to Otto referred to a 'Giovanni'.

And 'Giovanni' was the name Otto wrote in his diary on 2 July 1949, the day he went to Lake Albano, where he fell ill.

Hartmann Lauterbacher appeared to be Otto's main contact in Rome, although that name was not mentioned in any document in his or Charlotte's papers. Was Lauterbacher the 'old comrade' that Otto visited on 2 July? According to the CIC files, he lived near Lake Albano.

The files did not, however, mention that Lauterbacher was married to an Italian, or that he had an infant child. Rather, he was said to be actively homosexual. This suggested that the 'former comrade' who Otto visited that first weekend in July was probably not Hartmann Lauterbacher.

I went back through each page of the twenty-eight files sent by Professor Goda, looking carefully at every name. One clue jumped out, a reference to a 'former SS major' with whom Lauterbacher was in contact. This chimed with a reference in Bishop Hudal's posthumous memoir, which referred to a former 'SS major', one who worked for the Americans, as the person the bishop identified as the one Otto believed had poisoned him. The 'former SS major' was identified in some of the files as the source of CIC information on Lauterbacher. Separately, Lauterbacher blamed a 'former SS major' for his arrest, in 1951, and believed that the man in question was 'an American spy'.

One of the files identified the 'former SS major' by name: Karl Hass, based in Rome and Parma during the war. Said to be close to many Germans and in touch with Italian neo-fascists, Hass was also reported to be under the protection of the Italian police.

Was Karl Hass the man Otto visited at Lake Albano, one of the characters in the ferment that Otto encountered in Rome?

40

Persilschein

'In a sense, I was a tiny part of the world that Wächter encountered.' The words surprised me, spoken by my neighbour David Cornwell, better known as John le Carré, writer of novels on espionage during the Cold War. I had approached him for insights into the world described by the CIC files, a subject on which I understood he might have some knowledge.

It started with a note I sent, background material on Otto and Charlotte, and a couple of the declassified CIA files on Lauterbacher. He invited me to tea, I arrived with six small cakes, a handful of Otto's letters, a few photographs. We sat in the living room, as the sun streamed in across papers laid out on the sofa and a low table. David had prepared, with written notes on little cards, ideas and reactions to the material.

He explained his interest, that he actually was in Austria in 1949 – something I hadn't known – during his national service, stationed in Graz. As a young second lieutenant, he was attached to a field security team in Austria, interested in the Russian zone. 'We ran small agents, little guys on motorbikes selling pornographic photographs to Russian sentries, that kind of thing,' he said. 'We were also supposedly Nazi hunters, trawling displaced-persons camps, debriefing refugees, wholesale. A pitiful business – I wrote about it in *A Perfect Spy*, which is drawn entirely from that period.'

He suggested I look into it, as it was 'quite a funny period, too'. In due course I did, and found these words spoken by the novel's protagonist, Magnus Pym: 'Are you a spy and if so, would you not prefer to spy for us? Or are you merely a criminal, in which case you would surely like to take up spying, rather than be tossed back across the border by the Austrian police?'

It was not hard to imagine Otto being asked such questions. Pym's – and David's – experience chimed with what I encountered on the trail of Otto's contacts in Rome. Many passed through internment or POW camps, often with false identities. They were interrogated, escaped, caught, escaped again. Some made their way to safety by illicit means, others were recruited. Otto died.

The possibility that David might have questioned one of Otto's contacts amused us. A small world, one that changed dramatically between his second disappearance, in May 1945, and his first burial, in July 1949. A senior Nazi, hunted for mass murder, then just four years later a potential ally against the Soviets. Italy and Austria, I learned, were at the heart of the struggle between east and west, and David was there.

When his team identified a wanted person as a possible recruit, questions arose. 'It was bewildering,' he said. 'I'd been brought up to hate Nazism and that stuff, and all of a sudden, to find that we'd turned on a sixpence and the great new enemy was to be the Soviet Union, it was very perplexing.'

Cases were referred to his group by different organisations. The CIC played a central role, as information about alleged Nazis circu-lated. By 1949, however, American and British interest in prosecuting Nazis was on the wane, and the new objective was to use the valuable ones, to get them out of Europe, maybe into the US or, under cover, South America. The Americans knew about the Ratline, and may have helped create it, David confirmed. He was aware that there was an escape route, and mentioned a figure of 10,000 ex-Nazis making their way to South America, often with the help of the Vatican. 'A time of willing seller, willing buyer,' he called it. 'Perón in Argentina was saying, "Please come here, we're fascists, the Nuremberg trial's a disgrace."'

The Americans gathered German scientists and former Nazi intel-ligence agents, and set them to work. General Reinhard Gehlen, an intelligence officer who served as chief of department 'Fremde Heere Ost' ('Foreign Armies East') at the Führer's HQ – 'with a disgraceful record', according to David – was brought to Washington with his intelligence files to be interviewed and recruited by Allen Dulles, later director of the CIA. The same Allen Dulles who negotiated Operation Sunrise with Otto's boss, General Karl Wolff. 'Comically,' David points out, 'most of the stuff Gehlen had was junk, fed to him by the Soviets, who were better at penetrating his organisation than he was at penetrating theirs.' Yet Dulles fell for Gehlen.

David was curious about Otto, a man who became a senior Nazi in part because of his virulent anti-communism. 'The case of Wächter is interesting. If I came upon him, I would first report the fact. He would be interrogated. If it was by the right people, he would be talent-spotted, identified as a convinced anti-communist. He's a small Austrian nobleman, a Catholic, perfectly equipped to spy on the Soviets, to work for the Western cause.'

I enquired about the Vatican.

David thought Otto would have been 'naturally attractive' to the Vatican. Back in 1949, the Vatican was a useful ally, 'skilful' in recruiting, turning and exporting former Nazis. 'We knew, in a general way, that the Vatican had leaned in favour of fascism, that elements of the Vatican were complicit in running these exfiltration operations, these ratlines.' Other elements, of course, pulled in a different direction.

They knew too that Otto's past record in Vienna, Kraków and Lemberg would not be an impediment to recruitment or escape. He would have been attractive as a 'talent-spotter', identifying former Nazis who might work for the Americans. His past political career meant he had 'standing and influence among certain people'. He could deliver access, with 'his own Rolodex'. 'The incidental fact that he was also a monster would play no part,' David added, with a grim smile. 'If they looked him over and liked the cut of his jib, I'd be surprised if they didn't recruit him.' If they had recruited him, a well-worn path followed: 'destroy his files, or keep them out of circulation, or put in dummy files, or have some kind of notional hearing and pass him through the system'.

The Germans had a term for it: a '*Persilschein*', a reference to a laundry detergent, one that washed whiter than white. 'When you get

such a certificate, you're clear.' I recalled the large metal advertisement for Persil that Horst kept in one of his bathrooms.

'That happened?'

'It happened.'

'Without objection?'

'There were strenuous objections, but they went nowhere.' If someone of David's limited, junior standing raised a concern, and things got heated, as they sometimes did, when he was based in Trieste, he'd be told to 'leave it be'.

'I was a second lieutenant in national service . . . "Don't waste your fucking time," I was told.'

Could a *Persilschein* be applied to someone as senior as Otto Wächter?

'The problem with Wächter was that he was high-profile. He'd done dreadful things, and done them visibly. But there was no justice.'

David wasn't surprised that Otto wasn't apprehended, or that his CIC file was missing. 'The commandants of Treblinka and Sobibór were successfully sent to South America, and credited their escape to Bishop Hudal, who gave Wächter his final unction. If you are a small Austrian nobleman and a Catholic you are naturally attractive to the Vatican. That's exactly where the Vatican is most at home.'

Our conversation turned to the possibility of assassination. 'Take your pick,' David said, a reference to the infinite variety of possible assassins, including Soviets, Jews, Poles or Americans.

'I think . . . certainly I'm sure he was killed. On the whole, reading the material as you've offered it to me, I would imagine that it was basically a Jewish operation, however indirectly.'

The conclusion surprised me. I had only shown him limited materials, and no medical records.

'It's a hunch really, no more than that, as there was a lot of killing of that sort going on. I would have to say I admired it.'

Who might have been looking for Otto?

'The CIC. Maybe to recruit him, but he was so high-profile, that wasn't going to work. Maybe they wanted to debrief him, find out who his comrades were, in the awful work he did. Or maybe they wanted to arrest him, bring him to justice. It was very regional. The different units had different sentiments.'

The British relationship with the Americans wasn't straightforward. 'The issue would be: do we go for him, imprison him and bring him to trial, or is he potentially useful? The Brits would listen to the Americans. Sometimes they objected – they were overruled.'

And the Soviets? Yes, they had agents in and around Rome. 'Soviet, NKVD and Comintern agents, sympathisers, people at arm's length, run by the Soviet military as well. In those days there was a huge sympathetic core of supporters.' And, David added, the Russians had 'a long history of killing and assassination, more so than Western services'.

The Soviets might have had an interest in Otto. 'If he were of use to them, they'd take him to Russia and prosecute him publicly for what he'd done on Soviet territory. Or they'd turn him, then have him reappear in West or East German intelligence.' This confirmed Professor Goda's thesis.

David added another thought. If Otto was approached by the Americans and made an offer – 'as a talent-spotter, a recruiter of people with Nazi pasts who might work for them' – he couldn't see why he would turn it down. After all, he was virulently anti-communist, on the run, in search of safety. If a proposal came from the Americans, 'he would jump at it, I would have thought'.

David paused, then offered a different angle. 'Maybe the proposal came from somebody else. It sounds to me on that evidence more likely that it was an offer from the Soviets.'

This raised the possibility that Otto was made an offer by a German, who worked for the Americans but was also a double agent for the Soviets. Would Otto turn down a proposal from the Soviets? 'Given his Catholic convictions, yes, possibly,' David said. 'But such people have been turned, taken to the Soviet Union to live out a new life, with a new identity perhaps. It's conceivable that he might be reinvented, his past destroyed, given a new name. That was the daily bread of that world.'

The idea of Otto Wächter living quietly in the Soviet Union seemed unlikely. David paused to think about his own idea. 'The trouble with Wächter was that he was so high-profile, so visible.'

I mentioned the CIA files. If he had access to them, what would he look for?

'Evidence of Wächter's intentions, and the Vatican's intentions. If he had some kind of identity document, who issued it? The International Refugee Organization? The Red Cross?'

'The Austrian Automobile Association,' I responded. 'Or the Austrian Skiing Association?'

'Charming,' David said, with a grin. 'It looks to me as though he was on his way to being prepared to be exfiltrated, to finish up in Argentina . . .'

The thing to look for in the files, he continued, was what made Otto Wächter tick, in this period of his life. He would compare all the names in Otto's documents with those in the CIA files, find out what they had in common, try to discern some purpose in his connections. 'Was it social? Was there a logical strain that ran through all of these meetings? Was he putting together some kind of embryonic organisation?'

On the face of it, there was a connection between some of the names in Otto's address book and letters, and those in the CIC or CIA files. A common theme among these names was a connection to extreme nationalists and anti-communists, to former fascists and people who wanted to take up the struggle against the Soviets.

This resonated with David, who has spent a lifetime in Cold War espionage. 'Crazy remnants of the German and Austrian military community believed they could take the war to Russia, roll on, join up with the American military, go east. There were serious elements in British and American circles who said, "Let's do exactly that, let's wrap up this communist thing now, while they're on the back foot."'

And use people like Otto to do it?

'And use the Wächters to do it. It sounds crazy, but it was very much in the battle smoke of the time.'

And use others too, former Nazis, like Karl Hass, whose name did not appear in any document in Charlotte's papers, but which cropped up in one CIA file on Hartmann Lauterbacher.

41

Los Angeles

I gathered the declassified CIA material that was available on Karl Hass. It was voluminous, far greater than that for Lauterbacher, one hundred and twenty-eight files, starting from 1944 and continuing up to the 1960s. They offered a long, slow and fascinating read.

Karl Hass was born in October 1912, in Kiel, northern Germany. He studied at the University of Berlin, and was awarded a doctorate in political science. By then, 1934, he had joined the SS, and that year, Hitler's first as chancellor, he started work at SD headquarters in Berlin. He began in the department of press affairs, known as Office I, then moved to the department for science and research, Office VII, finally ending up in Office VI, which ran intelligence. In 1937, one of his colleagues at the SD was Otto Wächter, although I could not ascertain if they worked together, or knew each other. What was known was that they worked in the same building and walked the same corridors.

In 1940 Hass was posted to Holland, to work for the SD under the direction of Arthur Seyss-Inquart. In 1943 he was transferred to Rome. By then he was an SS Sturmbannführer, or, in its Anglo-American equivalent, a major. In March 1944, when German soldiers sang the 'Horst Wessel Song' as they marched down Rome's Via Rasella, he was chief assistant to Herbert Kappler, head of the German police and security service in the city, working as head of SS intelligence.

Major Hass's work included the recruitment of secret agents to work for the Germans, against partisans and communists. His front was as a press attaché to the German embassy, which offered cover and allowed him to attend many functions. In the summer of 1944 he came under surveillance by the Americans and British, and a CIA file from that year had a photograph of Major Hass seated with Colonel Kappler – who would later be convicted for the killings in the Fosse Ardeatine. It shows a large man in a dark suit and tie, enjoying a glass of red wine.

A CIC file described him as nearly six feet tall, a man of 'robust build' with 'black hair, short, square type face, pallid complexion'. He was 'dynamic' and liked to present himself to Italians as a German officer with 'pro-Allied sympathies'. The CIC considered him to have an original mind, with a good sense of humour, and to be kind-hearted. He liked a drink and drove a Fiat 1100.

Major Hass left Rome on 4 June 1944, the day before American troops occupied the city. He went to Parma, to train agents to penetrate Allied-occupied territory in southern Italy. He worked closely with Italians who supported the Republic of Salò, and the German occupying forces. His network of colleagues included General Wolff, Walter Rauff, Wilhelm Höttl, and Otto.

In April 1945, as the US Army approached, he fled Parma for Bolzano. There, on 15 July, he married Anna Maria Fiorini, who was later known as Angela, an Italian he met in Parma. One file noted his failure to declare a previous marriage, to Ingeborg, in Germany. In due course a news story reported that his first wife took steps to have him pronounced dead.

In November 1945 he was caught by the CIC, with a false name. The Americans handed him over to the British, who interrogated him in Milan. A photograph was taken, placed in the files, grainy and indistinct, frequently copied and recopied. In January 1946 Major Hass escaped. Four months later he was caught in Rome. He escaped again, was caught again. So it went on, at least five times over the space of a year. By June 1947 he was reported to be teaching Italian at a Catholic institute for boys in Ferme, a small town south of Rome. One sixteen-page file, marked confidential, was titled 'Personal Information'. Both sides had tired of the cycle of arrest and escape, so 'a peace pact' was made, by which Major Hass committed to 'devote his talents and energies to the benefit of CIC'. An agreement was approved by the commanding officer of the CIC's  430th Detachment, Thomas A. Lucid, the man who caught Frau Himmler and recruited Wilhelm Höttl.

Major Hass was taken to Austria, where, on 11 November 1947, he was placed under the custody of Thomas Lucid. He was given a reference number, 10/6369. A meeting was held at CIC headquarters in Gmunden, attended by Hass, Lucid and Joseph Luongo. He was judged to be methodical, analytical, logical and conclusive, a man who did not deviate from tasks to which he was assigned. With twelve years of intelligence experience for the SD, he had access to the 'first families' of Rome, Paris, Rotterdam and Berlin, and was said to be adaptable to any group of people or setting.

The CIC recruited Major Hass. He would run a new project, a network of agents codenamed 'Los Angeles'. Based in Rome, he was paid a basic salary of 150 'green dollars' a month, in cash. The CIC gave him a new identity, Giustini, with an Italian identity card, issued in Trieste, in the name of 'Mario Giustini', although he was also known as 'Rodolfo Giustini' and, with an Austrian passport, as 'Rudolf Steiner'. Other documents he carried had the names 'Hans Popp', 'Carlo Ferrari' and 'Carlo Mantelli'. His codename with the CIC was 'Gruesome 201'.

A first operational meeting was held in May 1948, at the Café Mille Luci in Rome, a location where Hass and Luongo would not be recognised. This was around the time that trials of his former colleagues Herbert Kappler and Erich Priebke took place, before an Italian military tribunal, for the reprisal killings in the Ardeatine Caves (in July, Kappler was convicted and sentenced to life imprisonment; Priebke was acquitted).

Hass arrived at the rendezvous with a list of thirteen names, individuals who were willing to work for the Americans. The names included fascists, journalists, Nazis and a Vatican official, although it did not include Walter Rauff, with whom Hass was in contact and who lived at the Vigna Pia monastery. The thirteen agreed to provide Hass with 'raw information' on the activities of the Italian Communist Party and Soviet and other foreign intelligence agencies, as well as other matters of interest to the CIC. The information would be passed directly to Joseph Luongo.

Several of the names that Hass gave Luongo appeared on Otto's list of contacts. Unwittingly, Otto had entered a nest of spies. Several of his contacts in Rome were secret agents, working for the Americans, for something that came to be known as Project Los Angeles.

*

The CIC document on 'Net Project – Los Angeles' was declassified in 2001. The project was activated on 15 December 1947, after Major Hass was hired. It operated for four years, until 1951.

Its goal was to penetrate the Italian Communist Party, engage in counterintelligence against communist threats, and monitor threatening activities in the South Tyrol, including 'partisan formations'. The project was directed by Joseph Luongo, codename 'Gruesome 4', who was based in Gmunden. He reported to Thomas A. Lucid.

The 'chief source' for Project Los Angeles was 'former SD major Karl Hass'. He was considered reliable because of his 'Teutonic rearing' and experience as a 'main cog' in Office VI of the SD, the SS intelligence service. Based in Rome, Hass collected information from seven named sub-sources, each of whom was paid fifty US dollars a month, in cash. Hass was left with extra dollars each month, for expenses and to 'dine with prospective informants'.

The seven sub-sources had a range of backgrounds. Two of them – Ulderico Caputo and Alberto Barletta – were established members of the Italian intelligence service, the Office of Classified Matters.

The five others were identified as 'former Abwehr colleagues, Vatican dignitaries, and the neo-fascist underground movement "Bands of Revolutionary Action".'

Albert Griezzar, a German, lived in Bolzano. Like Hass, he served in Office VI of the SD, for which he gathered intelligence for the Third Reich.

Pino Romualdi, an Italian, was the former secretary general of the Fascist Party in the Republic of Salò. The CIC described him as 'forceful and strong-willed, idealist, extremely intelligent, good tactician'. He was retained as an agent even as he was being held in a prison in Rome.

Ali Hussain, an Arab of unspecified nationality, was the former chief of the Arabian Youth Movement. He worked closely with General Rommel, and was 'wanted by the French', as a German collaborator. The CIC described him as a loyal, crafty opportunist, 'still deeply attached to Nazi philosophy and doctrine'.

Monsignor Federico Fioretti, an Italian, was chief of the Vatican press bureau. He worked directly for Pope Pius XII, and was considered to be 'astute, tactful, charming and gracious'.

The seventh agent who worked for Karl Hass was Bishop Hudal. Described by the CIC as 'Chief of the German Catholics in Italy', Alois

Hudal was paid fifty dollars a month, in cash, by the Americans for his services as an informer. The arrangement was in effect when he met Otto on 29 April 1949, and lasted at least until 1950.

Hunted by the Americans for 'crimes against humanity' and 'genocide', when Otto arrived in Rome he walked straight into the arms of a 'religious gentleman' who was, secretly, an American agent working for Project Los Angeles.

42

Hass

Bishop Hudal reported to Major Karl Hass, the chief source for Project Los Angeles. Was Hass the 'kind old comrade' with whom Otto spent the weekend of 2 and 3 July 1949? The CIC files offered a conclusive answer to that question.

One file from August 1950 identified Hass's home as Villa Emma, an apartment outside Rome. It was located 'on the Rome–Velletri highway', the CIC reported, 'about 5 kilometres before the latter town at the Poggidoro crossroad'. Poggidoro, or Poggi d'Oro, on Lake Nemi, was a few kilometres south of Lake Albano, from where Otto wrote to Charlotte he had travelled by bus, on the morning of Saturday, 2 July.

According to the file, Major Hass lived with a woman. She passed for his wife, but was actually married to another man, whom she had left to live with Hass. A third person lived at Villa Emma, described as 'a child he had by this mistress'.

The mistress and mother was identified as Anna Maria Giustini. The child, a girl called Enrica Erna Giustini, was born on 18 May 1949. When Otto visited, the child was seven weeks old.

Other Italian documents led to the archives of the parish of Santa Maria in Aquiro, and the child Enrica's certificate of baptism. This event took place on 20 July, a week after Otto died, four days after his funeral, at the Chiesa Santa Maria sopra Minerva in Rome, near the Pantheon. The certificate of baptism identified Enrica's father as Rodolfo Giustini – one of Hass's many false identities – and the mother as Anna Maria Fiorini. The godfather was Joseph Luongo, Hass's CIC controller. There was a photograph of the gathering, grainy and indistinct, twelve people in attendance, including Hass and Luongo.

The information coincided with the details Otto shared with Charlotte, in the letter written on the Monday after his visit to Lake Albano, when he described the first symptoms of illness. He mentioned a 'very kind old comrade', but did not name him, who was married to an Italian. He lived near Castel Gandolfo with a little girl, 'maybe four weeks' old. Otto was out by three weeks.

It was clear that Karl Hass was the 'kind old comrade' who invited Otto to spend a weekend with him near Lake Albano. They ate and swam together, then Otto slept at his house, Villa Emma, at Poggi d'Oro. Otto developed a fever on the Sunday after- noon, at the Hass home. Major Hass, or his mistress Anna Maria, obtained medications from a local source.

I continued through the CIC files. One 1950 document raised concerns about the reliability of Major Hass. It suggested he might be a double agent, who worked for the Americans and the Soviets. This file also contained a first reference to Otto, a single, interesting paragraph.

The document reported that Otto Wächter was a contact of Karl Hass. He was known to be living in Rome, under a false name, Reinhardt, with an Italian identity card without a permit. He was 'preparing for emigration' when, in August 1948, he 'suddenly became ill' and died 'a few days later'. The date was wrong – it may have been an innocuous typing error – as was the place of death, identified as 'Rome's Policlinic'. The CIC document stated that the cause of death was left open, that it was 'never established'.

The file offered other details of interest. On the day before Otto fell ill, he was said to have 'eaten a hearty meal' at the home of Karl Hass. 'It is rumoured', the file reported, that Hass 'made certain proposals which Wächter refused'.

The CIC was aware of Otto's funeral, and knew that Hass attended it. 'It is also interesting', the file noted, that during the funeral Hass 'jokingly remarked to those present that he had poisoned Wächter'. Whether the source of the information, who was not identified, treated the remark with levity or gravity was not clear.

From this single paragraph, several points emerged.

By 1950 the CIC knew that Otto had been in Rome, and in contact with Major Hass and Bishop Hudal.

The CIC knew that he was there under a false name, Reinhardt.

They were aware of his death, but not the correct date or place, or its cause.

The possibility that Otto was poisoned was evoked.

The CIC was aware of a rumour that Major Hass put certain proposals to Otto, and that he refused them.

The CIC was concerned that Major Hass was a double agent.

What became of Major Hass?

A few years after Otto died, the CIC dispensed with his services. They did so because of concerns about his reliability, which caused Project Los Angeles to be terminated.

The circumstances were as follows. In August 1950 the CIC learned that Hass had ceased to work on another project, working for 'a Jew attached to IRO', the International Refugee Organization. Hass was said to have been well-paid, a thousand dollars a month, and the rupture followed a quarrel between the two men.

This information coincided with other, troubling information, as the CIC learned that Hass could be 'working for Cominform', the Soviet intelligence network. He was said to be connected to a Soviet agent sought by the Spanish authorities, and his behaviour – a series of contradictory actions – gave rise to suspicions: on the one hand, he denounced as communists people who were known to be staunchly anti-communist, including Hartmann Lauterbacher, who was arrested because of Hass's denunciation; on the other hand, Hass did not denounce individuals who were known to be communist sympathisers or Soviet agents.

The CIC dropped Karl Hass. By the mid-1950s he was adrift, working as an importer of toys from West Germany, a man who was prone to expressing anti-American views. Reports were received which suggested he hoped to work with the Soviets, through commercial networks, and had contacts with a company associated with East German intelligence services.

Hass was allowed to remain in Italy, on condition that he cease all intelligence work. At the end of the 1950s he worked for the German War Graves Service, responsible for the military cemetery at Motta Sant'Anastasia, in Sicily. He also followed in Otto's cinematic footsteps, obtaining work as a film extra. He got a part as an SS prison officer in an Italian low-budget thriller, *The House of Intrigue*, starring Curt Jurgens. Years later he appeared in Luchino Visconti's *The Damned*. He played an SS officer.

Hass and Anna, his Italian companion, moved to Switzerland, to be close to their daughter Enrica. Retired, and living a discreet existence, in the spring of 1994 their lives were turned upside down, following a trip to Argentina by US television journalist Sam Donaldson. He was looking for Erich Priebke, Major Hass's former colleague, in Rome, who was said to be living in Argentina, having left Italy with the assistance of Father Draganović.

Donaldson found Priebke on a street in the town of Bariloche, and accosted him as he was about to get into his car. 'Why did you shoot them, they hadn't done anything,' the journalist asked. The question concerned the reprisal killing of Italian civilians in the Ardeatine Caves.

'That was our order, in the war that kind of thing happened,' Priebke replied, as the camera filmed the encounter.

'You were just following orders?'

'Yes, of course, but I didn't shoot anybody.'

Donaldson continued to ask questions, as Priebke appeared increasingly irritable.

'You killed civilians in the caves?'

'No. I was there, but it was ordered by our command.'

'But orders are not an excuse.'

'In this time an order was an order.'

'And you carried it out?'

'I had to carry it out.'

'And civilians died?'

'Yes, civilians died, yes . . . but we didn't commit a crime, we did what is ordered of us.'

Priebke's words could have been spoken by Otto, in relation to the Bochnia killings. Priebke brought the brief exchange to an end. 'You are not a gentleman,' he told Donaldson, and with that he got into his car and drove off.

The interview was broadcast around the world, and a request from Italy for Priebke's extradition soon followed. He was arrested and sent to Rome, where he was tried for 'crimes against humanity'. In return for immunity from prosecution, his former colleague Karl Hass, now in his eighties, agreed to appear as a witness in the trial. Hass travelled from Switzerland to Rome to give testimony, but the evening before the trial had second thoughts and tried to leave, in the course of which he injured himself and had to be hospitalised. The action caused him to be stripped of his immunity, and he too was charged with 'crimes against humanity', for his role in the killings.

In March 1998, the Appeals Chamber of the Military Court of Rome sentenced Hass and Priebke to life imprisonment, for killings that were not justified and 'unlawful'. Hass admitted his presence in the caves, and confirmed that he personally executed two of the civilians. On appeal, Italy's Supreme Court of Cassation in Rome upheld the convictions but reduced the sentences. Hass was judged to have been 'fully aware of the unprecedented criminality of what was to take place', and to be responsible for the deaths of the two individuals he executed and, by causal contribution, the deaths of all the other 333 victims. His responsibility extended to five victims who were executed simply to prevent them from bearing witness to the atrocity.

The Supreme Court invoked the Nuremberg precedent to rule that the execution of civilians in an occupied territory was a war crime and a 'crime against humanity', for which the limitation periods did not apply. Hass's sentence was reduced to a period of imprisonment for ten years and eight months. Because of his age – eighty-five – he was allowed to serve the term at home in Italy, near Lake Albano, under house arrest.

Karl Hass died in April 2004, at the age of ninety-one. Erich Priebke took his case to the European Court of Human Rights, which he lost, and lived to the age of one hundred.

43

2017, Rome

In the spring of 2017 I shared with Horst all I had ascertained about Hartmann Lauterbacher and Karl Hass. He was pleased to learn of the identity of the 'old comrade' with whom his father spent a weekend at Lake Albano, and also intrigued: that Hass was an American agent, that he worked for a Jew at the International Refugee Office, and that he might be a double agent for the Soviets. The last point was a bonus.

By now Horst had embraced the view that his father's death was caused by an act of poisoning. It seemed that he had come to it as a consequence of the new material I had introduced him to. In any event, he was now firmly attached to the idea, even if the evidence in support of it was thin. He had not mentioned an act of poisoning when we first met in 2012, or when we sat together at the Purcell Room, in 2014. Three years on, as we entertained the possibility of a visit to Rome, a mere possibility had crystallised into an incontrovertible fact. It had the merit of allowing Otto to be seen as a victim rather than a perpetrator.

As to the culprit, with Dr Wollenweber having been discounted as a suspect, Karl Hass ticked Horst's boxes. He encouraged me to dig deeper into the activities of a man who worked in the same building as his father in Berlin in 1937, then in Italy in 1945. For whom Hass might be acting – the Americans, Poles, Jews and Soviets were all in Horst's frame – was also unclear. That Hass was convicted of 'crimes against humanity', for his involvement in reprisal killings that mirrored Otto's actions in Bochnia, was a matter that Horst did not seem to be much concerned with.

Horst thought it might be a good idea to travel to Rome, to visit some of the places mentioned in Otto's papers, and perhaps meet a few acquaintances. We could go to the Vigna Pia monastery, where Otto lived, and the Santo Spirito Hospital, where he died. We might also go to the Campo Verano cemetery, where he was first buried, and try to get access to the Anima, where Bishop Hudal worked, and even see the Ardeatine Caves. We might also go to Lake Albano to see where

Otto swam for the last time. Horst had a few contacts in Rome, who might see us. There was Irmgard, the daughter of the Ettingshausens, and the child of another friend of his parents, a professor who wished to remain anonymous.

Horst and I travelled to Rome in May 2017, in the company of James Everest and Gemma Newby, who was producing the podcast. Horst also brought Osman the hairdresser, for security and companionship.

Irmgard Ettingshausen agreed to meet and give us an interview on condition we gave her a good lunch. I hoped for some colour, or a point of detail, on the Wächters. She was in her eightieth year, yet appeared somewhat younger, resplendent with long black hair and glamorous white trousers. She wore aviator sunglasses, although we met in a basement room with no windows.

The meeting was brief, as Irmgard said she remembered nothing, or was not willing to share what she did know. She seemed to have little interest in what her father Georg and Otto did as Nazi lawyers, or in Otto's sojourn with her mother Helga, after his time in the mountains with Buko was over. She had read things about Otto on the internet, but did not trust the medium. A single moment of recollection flickered when Horst took out a photograph of his parents, one I hadn't seen before, taken at the Ettingshausens', near the small village of Going, in the Tyrol, in 1948. 'Perhaps my father took the photo,' Irmgard said. 'He had a Leica, after all, and liked to take photographs.'

The picture showed Charlotte and Otto on the grass, bathed in sunlight, the Kaiser Mountains looming behind them. Otto grinned, hands clasped around the knees, jacket and trousers hanging loosely. Charlotte looked lovingly towards him, a traditional jacket draped protectively across her shoulders. The photograph prompted Irmgard to speak warmly of Tante Lotte. Always cheerful, always with a gift. 'I remember her voice still ringing in my ears.' She knew nothing of Otto's death. No, she never heard Charlotte suggest that he was poisoned. The words disappointed Horst. 'Maybe she wanted to say something,' Irmgard added hopefully, 'but never did.'

I gave Irmgard a copy of the poem Otto wrote to Helga. Moving, written from the heart, deep emotions. It was not a love poem, she said emphatically. 'That was a poetic time; it was the kind of thing friends wrote back then.'

Later we visited the professor whose parents knew Otto and

Charlotte and who did not want his identity to be revealed. He was intelligent and humane, and curious, as we talked about family and friendship, until it came to his parents' motive in offering assistance to Otto. A sense of Christian kindness, the professor thought, and probably they did not know what he had done during the war.

I told him we had documents that offered a different interpretation.

Did he know what his parents had done during the war?

'Not really,' he said.

Did he want to know?

He looked at me silently, as our eyes fixed for a long while. Eventually he spoke. 'No,' he did not wish to know.

After a decent lunch, as promised to Irmgard, we made our way to the Vigna Pia monastery, a few kilometres south of St Peter's Square, near a bend in the River Tiber. Founded in the mid-nineteenth century by Pope Pius IX to assist children in need, in the 1920s the Sacra Familia organisation acquired the building as a residence for twenty-five boys. When Otto moved in 150 boys were living there. Today the building is home to an international school.

Accompanied by Rocco Baldassari, a local priest involved in running the facility, we stood in a large hall, under a skylight, that had the look of a prison wing, as Otto described it. 'Many films have been made here,' the priest said, guiding us up two flights of stone stairs, to the top floor and the many small rooms that ran around four sides of the building. The monk's cell that might once have been inhabited by Otto had a vaulted ceiling, high and curved, and a single tall, thin window that offered a fine view across the city. 'Impossible to keep clean,' Otto wrote. The ancient furnishings were gone, so we were left to imagine the old desk, the worm-eaten prayer bench and a floor lined with newspaper.

We made our way up to the roof where Otto did his morning exercises, 'with a view of the city and the Campagna', in the space in front of a large, arched window. We could see the Basilica of St John, the park near the Colosseum and the Vittorio Emanuele II Monument, known as 'the typewriter'. The Tiber flowed below, just a short walk away, reached by passing under the railway track, using an underground passage. 'I'm not going to be able to resist,' he wrote to Charlotte, of the spot where he liked to swim. In the distance was the Campagna, where he ran.

As we stood on the roof, seagulls sang and military planes flew

across the city, leaving a trail of red, white and green smoke, a celebration of the Day of the Republic and the end of the monarchy. Seven
decades earlier Otto missed the parade. 'I sat in my cell and only saw
the planes roaring over Rome,' he told Charlotte.

Back on the ground floor, we sat in the refectory where Otto drank
milky coffee in the mornings and red wine in the evening. Our guide
brought out a copy of an old book, the *Annals of Vigna Pia*, and
found the entries for 1949, with a list of residents. The names included
Colonel Walter Rauff, known as Alfonso, with his wife and two children. In black and white, at page 651, was the name of Otto Wächter.

The following day we visited the place where Otto died. We crossed
city streets, and on the Vittorio Emanuele II bridge, close to Castel
Sant'Angelo, Horst took a silent photograph. We passed through the
large doors of a long building of ancient bricks, and found ourselves
in a courtyard of columns and arches, walls of faded ochre dotted
with plaques and frescoes and signs to the library and pharmacy. This
was the fifteenth-century Santo Spirito Hospital, painted in 1480 as
the background to Botticelli's *Temptations of Christ*, a reference to
an institution that embodied the papal power to heal. The operating
room was visited by Michelangelo and Leonardo da Vinci, seeking
inspiration as to the human form. Looking down on us was the famous
old clock, hands formed with the body of a salamander.

With few people around, we ambled across one courtyard and into
the next, to a fountain and a wall with a sign that pointed to the Sala
Baglivi, where Otto spent the last five days of his life. It was Horst's
first visit, he sighed, but he said he
had no special feelings. 'Maybe
that will change if I see the hall
where he actually died, described
in the letter to my mother.' He
recalled the letter, the sense of an
ending. 'When he entered the hospital he knew that he was dying,'

Horst continued, and must have hoped that Charlotte would visit.

Horst reflected on a childhood with an absent father. 'My mother
was the central figure, with authority and power, the centre of my life.'
He wondered how she managed to carry on. 'Maybe what kept her
alive was the children?' Horst felt a sense of responsibility towards her.

'Her greatest wish was to rehabilitate my father as much as possible – and with all these letters and documents she thought to herself, "I can succeed."

'I don't remember anything about my father, because I had no close relationship,' he said, unlike his three older siblings, who spent more time with him. He came to know his father through the documents. 'I was really astonished, the way he more and more put my mother into his central experience . . . he was a womaniser, yet he saw that my mother more or less gave herself up for him, did everything for him, never quit him . . .' His voice trailed off, then he started up again.

'His death was not prescribed, he was young, not forty-nine, this is no age, you know?' He mentioned Hass.

'Why do you bring him up?' I asked.

'Because I think that he murdered my father, and got paid so much and so . . .'

Horst's voice trailed off once more, as another memory propelled him in a direction, towards the gymnasium exam he took that year. 'In the summer I was sent to Switzerland, when mother sent all the children away, so I was not informed about what happened to my father.' He was away from Salzburg on the day his mother left abruptly for Rome.

We arrived at the entrance to the Sala Baglivi, a few metres from where Otto died. We were not able to gain entry to the vast hall, closed to us because of building works.

'This is the room,' I said.

'Ah, this is the room.'

'These are the windows your father described.'

'Yes, yes.'

We counted them, seven along on each side, high up, large and rectangular.

I showed Horst a photograph of the inside as it was in 1950.

'This is how it was when your father was there.'

'Yes, yes, yes.'

Horst was silent. 'It's a great hall, a great place to die, a place of humanity, with all these people around.'

We walked to the end of the building. Horst wanted to see the large door through which his father passed after the end of his life, but a metal railing prevented access, about two metres high. Horst slowly clambered over it, an agile septuagenarian, protectively accompanied by Osman. A guard ran in, armed with a gun, assuming Horst wanted to break in. Only a son who wanted to connect with the place where his father died, we explained, many years earlier.

When the guard left we sat on a bench and read Hedi Dupré's letter to Charlotte. 'I feel close to my mother,' Horst said. 'What she endured was the worst moment in her life, being here, not knowing what to do, broken.'

On the outskirts of Rome, James, Gemma and I visited the Ardeatine Caves. Horst decided instead to pay his respects to those who lost their lives on the Via Rasella, near the Quirinale Palace, where thirty-three marching Tyrolean soldiers were blown up on 23 March 1944, as they sang the 'Horst Wessel Song'. The walls of the street still bear the scars, as I saw for myself when I visited the following year.

To enter the caves, a site of memory, we passed through Basaldella's vast bronze gates, which evoked the twisted and tortured bodies of 335 Italians. The victims came from 'every professional category and social condition of the Roman population', a brochure informed us. Twelve victims were never identified.

We passed along a thin path excavated into the rock, more than a hundred metres long, from light to dark, heat to cool, a chilling place. Deep underground, embedded in the rock, in groups of five they entered, to a place where they knelt and received a single shot to the head. It took a full day, the events so traumatic for the executioners that the nerves of the young had to be steadied with cognac. Here, where the group gathered, came Kappler and Priebke, and Karl Hass, thirty-two years old, following the order from Hitler, passed on to them via Feldmarschall Albert Kesselring and General Karl Wolff.

I left the cave and entered a memorial building that held the remains of the victims, each in an individual grave, numbered from 1 to 335, in rows. Most bore a photograph and a name, some had flowers.

Antonio Pisino, twenty-six, chief of the military zone of the communist movement, arrested in January 1944 on spying charges, sentenced to three years' imprisonment.

Alessandro Portieri, nineteen, mechanic, communist, arrested ten days earlier for taking up arms.

Ettore Ronconi, forty-six, a wine broker, arrested by the SS and Italian police near the Via Rasella on the day of the attack.

A grave with no name, *ignoto*, unknown.

And so on.

Fourteen rows of individuals, Christians and Jews and non-believers, all men, each selected after the events on the Via Rasella, not one of them connected in any way to the attack. Another group brought together because they happened to be in the wrong place at the wrong time.

44

Anima

Our little group met on the Vicolo della Pace, a discreet passageway outside the entrance to the Anima. I rang the bell, a diminutive, sceptical nun opened the door. An appointment with Dr Ickx, the archivist, I said. 'Ah, yes,' she responded. The large wooden door opened slowly and we entered the courtyard, following in the steps of Messrs Rauff, Mengele, Priebke, Stangl and Hass. Otto too must have passed across the well-trodden stone floor.

We arrived at a large room with a vaulted ceiling, with a mother and child painted on one wall, and two reclining marble statues resting on the other side. Dr Ickx floated in, tall, confident and welcoming. '*Guten Tag, guten Tag*,' said the archivist, with enthusiasm. He guided us to his office, up an ancient staircase, past the refectory where Bishop Hudal denied that Otto ever ate. We reached a long, narrow corridor, lined with portraits of the rectors that dated back to the middle of the nineteenth century. One of the Vatican's oldest colleges, Dr Ickx explained, the Anima was a place of serious learning. He emphasised the word 'serious', as we lingered before a portrait of the bishop, painted in 1943, at the height of his powers. For five decades he walked along this corridor, until the case of Wächter undid him.

'A long, good, active rectorate,' Dr Ickx declared. The bishop was a man of 'various capacities', and this portrait showed him at his most formal. Black garb, red cap, large cross, ring, book, coat of arms. *Ecclesiae et nationi* – I recognised the words from the signed note he gave Charlotte – Church and nation. 'Not a big man, rather thin, not tall, rather small,' Dr Ickx said. Blue eyes, prominent brows, rimless glasses, grey hair, stern. The other rectors looked at those who painted them, but not Bishop Hudal. 'He looks faraway,' Dr Ickx thought, 'a man of reflection and ideas, on Europe, Austria, the Church.'

Within minutes of meeting it was apparent that the words 'staunch defender' did not do justice to Dr Ickx's positive feelings for Bishop Hudal. Funny, engaged and beloved, the words tripped off the archivist's tongue, even if the painting offered a more solemn impression. An intellectual, a man of courage, he continued, in a soft and reassuring voice, a man who selflessly hid many and varied individuals. An Italian carabiniere. An Austrian on the run. Two New Zealanders. An Australian assisted by the resistance. Jews and leftists too, he added, as the Vatican was a 'nest of anti-Nazis'. Dr Ickx offered no names or details, only motive. 'I am a priest and must help anyone, that's my duty' – this was the bishop's mantra.

We walked to the medieval section of the Anima and a fine seventeenth-century chamber, atmospheric with faded red walls, lined with ancient books, three windows, a tiled floor, wooden beams, a fresco, archival boxes. A lady, seated at a large desk, observed us like an owl. The room held the remnants of the bishop's activities, and his contact with the Wächters.

The bishop's archive included books, official papers, private correspondence. There was material on Nazis, communists and capitalists. He was the Vatican's resident 'expert', a man who advised the Vatican on three ideologies, and the threats they posed to the Church.

A large framed certificate hung in a corner of the room with red walls. Awarded to the bishop in 1934, with a medal, the paper honoured the assistance he offered in the negotiation of the concordat between the Vatican and the Nazis. On that project he worked with Cardinal Pacelli, the secretary of state who became Pope Pius XII, and Hitler's vice chancellor, Franz von Papen. 'So rare for the medal and certificate to be together,' Dr Ickx whispered, with pride.

Was not the bishop keen on reconciliation between the Nazis and the Vatican? 'True,' Dr Ickx said, but only until 1938, when his position changed. 'He turned the other way, started to organise *against* the National Socialist ideology.' This claim somehow did not sit so easily with his abortive effort, in April 1938, to organise a vote in favour of the Anschluss. I remained silent.

What of his assistance, in later years, to a great number of Nazis? I enquired, as neutrally as possible.

'You say "a great number", but how many?' Dr Ickx was a man of detail.

I mentioned Franz Stangl, the commandant of Treblinka.

Dr Ickx wanted a number. 'Is it five, or ten, or fifteen, or two hundred?' The subject required precision, not whitewash. Horst nodded, warming to this Dr Ickx. Nobody stopped the bishop or Draganović from their activities, the archivist explained. They were tolerated by those who watched them, by the Americans. But, he quickly added, 'I have no agenda on this issue.'

Dr Ickx's version of the facts was straightforward. The Americans and the British knew exactly what the bishop was up to, and turned a knowing blind eye. The proper inference was that they supported his activities. He went further. 'The Americans set up the whole Ratline, they agreed with the bishop's actions.' And then even further. 'The Ratline was an American idea, to allow them to choose the best people to work with.'

Yet, he added briskly, wanting to be clear, the bishop did not know he was a puppet of the Americans, an instrumentality. He was simply someone who helped all and sundry, without asking questions, not before the war, during, or after. 'He even pleaded for the liberation of an Italian communist caught after the Via Rasella attack!' Dr Ickx exclaimed.

Did the bishop know the true identities of those he helped? Some perhaps, like Erich Priebke, were known to him, Dr Ickx recognised, but for others, how could he have known that someone was a mass murderer? 'That's the question,' the archivist mused. For most he didn't know and couldn't know. Anyway, of those he helped the criminals were 'less than one per cent' of the total. Dr Ickx drew an analogy with our times. 'It's like the flood of immigrants entering Europe today; not all are terrorists, but a terrorist can be in the group.'

The archivist was an unequivocal supporter of the bishop, a decent man who acted wisely, who offered assistance without questions.

Was it always wise to help someone who had been indicted for crimes, as a Nazi?

'It could be,' he replied, although that was a difficult question for a priest. If Stalin turned up at the door of the Anima, the bishop would have helped him. 'We all make mistakes', no one should judge.

The furthest he went was to acknowledge that the bishop may, perhaps, have been 'a little naive'. 'The Catholic Church is blamed, Pius XII is blamed, so Hudal becomes the scapegoat.'

We turned to the case of Otto Wächter. I showed Dr Ickx the letter he wrote to Charlotte on 30 April 1949, the one that referred to a first meeting with the 'religious gentleman', who was initially reserved, then 'very positive' when he heard Otto's name. Dr Ickx accepted that Bishop Hudal knew in general terms who Otto was. 'But the real question is, *what* did he know about Otto von Wächter at that moment?' The answer to that question was unknown. Dr Ickx smiled as he spoke.

As to the paragraph in the bishop's posthumous memoir, the one that recounted Otto's death, one had to recognise that it was most carefully drafted. The bishop was prudent, so he made clear that the allegation of poisoning by a German comrade who worked for the Americans was 'Wächter's version'. Unsure about the cause of death, the bishop distanced himself from the allegation.

Why, then, did he put the allegation into the book? Apparently the bishop said nothing about an act of poisoning to Charlotte, who was in Rome within two days of the deathbed revelation. Seemingly, Charlotte only learned of the allegation after Bishop Hudal's memoir was published, in 1976, thirteen years after he died. Dr Ickx was stumped. It was odd, he accepted. Of course, the fact the bishop wrote the words did not mean that Otto spoke them. Perhaps the bishop had his own reason to make the revelation, but what that reason might be he did not know. Nor did he know *when* the allegation made its way into the text. He had the original manuscript, perhaps we should take a look?

I shared what I knew about the German comrade who Otto visited – Karl Hass. Dr Ickx knew the name, like many people in Italy.

I told him about Project Los Angeles, run by the CIC with Hass's help. He appeared genuinely surprised by the information.

The bishop worked for Hass and the Americans, I explained. He was an agent, paid $50 in cash each month, for four years.

If Dr Ickx was surprised by this fact he reacted with agility and did not show it. Instead, he said: 'It fits my theory; it proves Hudal was a puppet in the hands of the Americans.' This was perplexing.

'Did Bishop Hudal know he was working for the Americans?' he asked, rhetorically, then answered his own question. 'I don't think so.'

Dr Ickx did not make much sense, but he did so as a model of sangfroid. Pushed, he said he was bound to accept that he did not know exactly what the bishop was and was not aware of.

Three facts were clear. Bishop Hudal helped Nazis escape to South America. He helped Otto. He was a paid agent of the Americans.

The interpretation of the facts was less clear. This was a cue to look through the bishop's personal papers, the ones that Dr Ickx was able to show us.

*

Dr Ickx gathered a number of boxes and placed them on the long wooden table. I wondered if the bishop's papers had been cleansed and filleted, like Charlotte's papers, and Otto's too, and imagined the exercise of removing the obviously problematical items. I dared not ask the question, but did later find an article by Dr Ickx which confirmed that 'some material has disappeared'.

Horst and I picked our way through hundreds of pages.

Dr Ickx was immersed in a box, a draft of an unpublished article, the bishop as a helper of refugees, as a victim of myth. The Ratline was an invention of others, Dr Ickx concluded, 'the Church was used by the Americans'.

We found the bishop's work diary, the daily activity of births, marriages and deaths. Otto was buried at the Campo Verano cemetery on 16 July 1949, and Bishop Hudal was said to have officiated, so we checked the date. A Mass and a pontifical benediction, but no mention of a funeral on that day, or of a Wächter or a Reinhardt.

'The burial is not in this book,' Dr Ickx said. 'It will be in the archives' – but no, they were not accessible.

A copy of *Avanti*, the daily newspaper of the Socialist Party of Italy, with an article on Otto, 'The Butcher of Lemberg'. Another headline claimed that Otto spent three years at the Anima, next to which someone had written in red pencil '*altra bugia*'. It means 'another lie', Dr Ickx explained. The bishop wrote the words.

He reacted to articles?

'Always.'

A letter from Hartmann Lauterbacher's wife, in December 1948, to thank the bishop for the nice items sent. A letter from Hans Lauterbacher, in April 1950, following his brother Hartmann's arrest, hoping that the bishop might assist in getting him released. A letter, from the bishop to Lauterbacher, enquiring about the case.

A letter addressed to General Karl Wolff, care of Bishop Hudal.

A leaflet, published by the Hitler Youth organisation, from the 1930s, inviting young Catholics to join. The bishop was 'interested' in the Hitler Youth, Dr Ickx said. Nothing untoward, materials gathered merely to be able to advise the Vatican that the Nazis were recruiting children. I was unable to suppress a chuckle, which irritated Dr Ickx. 'It's not a matter to laugh about.'

A clipping of an article by Simon Wiesenthal, 9 September 1949, published in a newsletter, on the stories printed in Italian newspapers that the bishop helped Wächter. It confirmed Wiesenthal's interest in the story, and the bishop's interest in Wiesenthal.

An article from *Avanti*, 21 April 1961, on the opening of Adolf Eichmann's trial in Jerusalem, with the headline: 'Butcher of Leopolis was poisoned and breathed his last breath in the arms of Monsignor Hudal.' It carried a photograph of the bishop, the portrait that hung in the corridor of the Anima, along with a statement in which he denied having helped Eichmann.

'A communist newspaper.' Dr Ickx spoke the words gravely, matter-of-fact, then read aloud: 'In the shadow of the Anima many Nazi butchers found refuge.'

Which was true, no?

'If three thousand people passed through the Anima and five were butchers, then it was only "some" of them, not "many".'

Several letters from South America, correspondents with German names who left Europe. 'He's in contact with them because he helped them to get there, real Nazis who got away.'

A letter from the Ministry of Justice in Rio de Janeiro, Brazil. I thought of Laurence Olivier removing teeth in the torture scene in the film *Marathon Man*. Later I realised I'd conflated it with a different film, *The Boys from Brazil*.

A letter from Nuremberg, December 1948, from the son of Franz von Papen, who worked with the bishop to negotiate the *Reichskonkordat*, the agreement between the Nazis and the Vatican, for which Hudal was awarded a certificate. Acquitted of all charges at Nuremberg but subsequently convicted by a West German court. 'My father is now seventy years, and after four years' imprisonment, a very sick man,' von Papen junior wrote. Von Papen was released on appeal the following year, and lived for another twenty years.

A note from journalist Franz Hieronymus Riedl, who helped Otto across the Dolomites. He expressed appreciation to the bishop for a copy of the sermon on 'the Wächter case', in September 1949. 'I thank you from my heart.'

The links to Otto were numerous.

A photograph of Charlotte Wächter. 'My mother!' Horst exclaimed excitedly.

A letter from Charlotte, 19 July 1949, three days after the funeral: 'let me first of all thank Your Excellency with the utmost gratitude'.

Horst read aloud, then stopped. 'I can't read more.'

'You can't read it?' Dr Ickx asked.

'No, I can't, I'll try another time.' Yet he was unable to stop himself, so he continued silently, until his voice rose to a whisper, then louder. 'My soul is broken . . . your always thankful, Lotte Wächter.'

'That was hard for me,' Horst said, then asked, in German, whether he could take a photograph of the letter.

And, eventually, the original manuscript of the bishop's memoir. A typed text, several hundred pages, with a few handwritten annotations. A date, 1953. Did the bishop add the poisoning allegation at the end of his life, or was it in the original? We skipped through the pages until we came to the section where he wrote about Otto in his arms, the allegation of poisoning, the comrade. The words were identical to those published many years later, long after Hudal died. It seems he wrote the words just four years after Otto died, while he was still in touch with Charlotte, but apparently never told her.

'Life is never simple, never just black and white,' Dr Ickx said. He had no idea why the allegation was not shared.

'Bishop Hudal is not a grey figure in history,' he continued, more quietly. 'He's a dark white figure.' He saved some during the war, and then there was the other part of his life, when he helped save a few 'butchers' who passed through the Anima. 'And probably he didn't know they were butchers,' Dr Ickx added, with a note of optimism. 'Probably he was set up by others, probably he was part of a game that was bigger than he could have known.'

The visit drew to a close. We thanked Dr Ickx, took our leave and departed. Outside the Anima we passed a shop that sold toy soldiers and other figurines. In the window a few figures arranged in the window caught our attention, a remembrance of times past, of then and now.

45

Café Doney

My interest in the Ratline was not original, and I benefited much from the research of others. After leaving the Anima, I met up with Professor Gerald Steinacher, an Austrian academic who now lives in Nebraska, and with whom I was in contact. He has written extensively on the Ratline, and he happened to be in Rome, with his wife.

We met for a drink on the Via Veneto, at the Café Doney, without Horst. This was the establishment mentioned in Otto's letters, and in various CIC files. It was here that Otto would meet Hedi Dupré, and Hartmann Lauterbacher. Revamped, the Doney was a pale shadow of its illustrious and characterful past.

Professor Steinacher had a deep interest in Nazis on the run, the title of his book, which stemmed from a fascination that first arose in childhood. He grew up near the site of a former concentration camp, but no one in the family wished to talk about that place or the past. The silence triggered a curiosity, so he began to excavate the history, and the role of the Vatican during the Nazi period. He prepared a doctorate, which became the book, an examination of the Ratline from a range of different perspectives. He was well-versed in the minutiae, from the points of entry into Italy to the cooperative networks that existed in the South Tyrol, as well as the identities of all the main actors in the Vatican. The fear of communism was the heart that beat at the centre of his narratives, a fear that caused hunters of Nazis to become recruiters, one that engendered an unlikely alliance of clerics, spies, fascists and Americans.

Bishop Hudal was the central character, a hub from which a multitude of spokes emanated. The index to Professor Steinacher's book listed hundreds of names, but not one featured more often than Bishop Hudal. His Austrian roots did not infuse him with the generous spirit of Dr Ickx: in Professor Steinacher's view, the bishop was a German nationalist with Nazi sympathies, motivated by 'Christian anti-Semitism'. He rejected the idea that the bishop helped all and sundry

– 'if he did, it wasn't very well documented' – and thought there was ample evidence the bishop knew exactly who he was helping, and that some were hunted for the most terrible crimes. Bishop Hudal obstructed justice, Professor Steinacher concluded. He did not deliver Christian mercy, he was not simple or naive, and he knew exactly who Otto was and what he had done.

Otto got a brief mention in the book. The revelation that the bishop hid Otto was the 'final straw' that caused him to lose his position as rector of the Anima. Karl Hass made an appearance too, a more fully developed character who served as an intermediary between the Americans and the Vatican, helping dozens of comrades escape to South America. Professor Steinacher was fully aware of Hass's links to Hudal, Luongo, Lucid and the CIC, acting together as an 'invisible front' in the Cold War, an alliance to safeguard 'Christian Europe'. With Italy as the core of the Catholic universe, it had to be protected at any cost.

Professor Steinacher had not, however, homed in on the allegation that Otto was poisoned, although the brief passage at the end of the bishop's memoir stuck in his mind. 'I couldn't make sense of it,' he noted of the moment he first read the passage. It seemed odd, unique even, and he couldn't think of any other case of someone on the Ratline who might have been disposed of in this way.

He was curious, as I was, as to why the bishop wrote what he did, as early as 1953, but apparently said nothing to Charlotte. Perhaps Otto did say it, he mused. Or maybe he didn't, and the bishop just made it up. But why would he do that?

We were in the realm of speculation, seated at a bar on the Via Veneto. Gerald thought he might have an explanation, even a 'theory', as he put it. The Wächter case caused the bishop considerable difficulties, resulting in him being attacked from within the Vatican, and from outside. He must have felt defensive, and a need to justify his actions, in helping Otto and others, including Stangl, Mengele and Priebke. One justification would be to show that a man like Wächter was basically decent, a good Catholic who found himself in danger and in need of protection. One strategy would be to turn a perpetrator into a victim.

'What better way to construct an impression of victimhood than to suggest that a man was poisoned?' he posited. The image of all-powerful Americans hunting an unfortunate and solitary man could make it easier for Bishop Hudal to justify his actions, to make him look like a priest who offered Christian assistance to a hapless victim pursued by a merciless enemy. Another advantage was that he could say he helped to bring Wächter back into the Church, a form of reconciliation of the kind for which the bishop argued in his writings of the 1930s.

Gerald paused and looked at me. 'Still,' he said, 'it is a puzzle, strange and confusing.'

I shared what we had worked out about the identity of the alleged poisoner, of the weekend spent at Lake Albano with an 'old comrade', and his wife and child, of Project Los Angeles and the CIC. Karl Hass, possibly a double agent working for the Soviets. I showed him the CIC document which placed Karl Hass at the burial of Otto at the Campo Verano cemetery, joking that he poisoned Otto. Nothing beats words in black and white.

'Karl Hass.' Gerald spoke the name several times. 'An interesting character.' Yet he was hard put to imagine why Hass would poison Otto, what the motive would be. Why would an agent of the CIC poison one war criminal hiding in Rome, while working with others on the CIC payroll? He was sceptical.

As to the possibility that Hass might have acted as a poisoner on behalf of the Soviets, assuming he was a double agent, I had checked with a leading expert on the Soviets and the Nazis. 'I've never heard of anything resembling hit squads the Soviets would establish for the purpose of killing prominent Nazis,' Dr Anton Weiss-Wendt told me. In years of research involving Soviet war crimes trials and KGB records, he had never once come across anything to suggest that the Soviets ever sought to kill top Nazis on the run, no doubt because they had hundreds of thousands of alleged Nazi collaborators in the territories under their control.

Later that evening Horst joined us for dinner, accompanied by Osman. The meal did not go well, as Horst did not like the ideas of Professor Steinacher. It was unfortunate, in his view, that Gerald, an Austrian, treated his father as a war criminal, and even worse that he was sceptical about the allegation of poisoning.

Horst had downloaded Professor Steinacher's book onto his Kindle, and did not approve of its contents. 'I read what you wrote about my father, and I have a different view.' There are errors, Horst said, irritated. For example, his father was not a Sturmbannführer.

'Higher rank?' Gerald enquired.

Yes, Horst affirmed, and in any event the SS membership was only 'honorary'. Otto was responsible for the civil government and did not work for the other part of the government, the criminal part run by the SS and Katzmann. 'The theory that my father was a criminal, I cannot accept.'

So why was Otto on the run, Gerald asked, calmly, and why was he trying to get out of Europe?

'Because he was an enemy of the Soviets,' Horst replied. 'Stalin would do everything to kill him.'

Gerald's scepticism was well-entrenched. 'How many former Nazi intelligence specialists were murdered by the Soviets?' he asked.

'My father was a key figure in relations between east and west,' Horst replied. 'He was a target *because* he was important.' With limited facts at hand to support either point, Horst referred Gerald to the assassination of Bauer, his father's deputy, by a Soviet agent dressed as a German, in Lemberg in 1943.

Horst also ruled out the possibility his father would have worked for the Americans. 'A matter of honour,' he said, he would never work for the former enemy. If Hass did try to recruit him, as one of the CIC documents suggested, it would have been on behalf of the Soviets. That, at least, was Horst's logic. Otto refused the offer, so he had to be killed. This was Horst's explanation, a consequence, it seems, of our conversations and my inquiries.

Over dinner, Gerald and Horst squabbled. 'Your father left the Catholic Church,' Gerald said, 'he declared himself *gottgläubig*.'

'He never left the Catholic Church,' Horst responded, testily.

The *gottgläubig* declaration was in Otto's SS file, I interjected.

'You must distinguish between form and substance,' Horst replied. 'He may have declared himself *gottgläubig*, but he never left the Church.'

I could show him the document. 'Maybe, it's possible, but the last words Otto spoke were of regret, that he had difficulties with the Catholic Church.'

Gerald had had enough, and made clear he wanted to wrap up the conversation. 'My father was a real, great figure, not just an SS man, running around shooting, killing people,' Horst continued.

Gerald responded bluntly. 'Did your father ever, after the war, in letters or in other ways, express regret for what happened, for the murder of millions of people by a regime he served in a high-ranking position?'

Quiet, respectful James Everest chose this moment to intervene. 'I've been through every single letter exchanged between Otto and Charlotte in 1949 – there is not a single mention of the Holocaust.'

Was there a single expression of regret in any of the material Horst shared? someone else asked.

Horst was certain that Charlotte had regrets. 'She regretted taking the house in Zell-am-See.'

Any regrets beyond that?

'She became religious at the end of her life, so of course she regretted, as I regret.'

46

Lake Albano

After two days in Rome we travelled to Lake Albano, the water-filled crater of a long-extinct volcano. It was less than an hour by taxi to the spot where Otto took his last swim, in the company of Karl Hass.

We went in search of information about Enrica, the infant daughter of Hass and his Italian companion. Born in May 1949, Enrica would be in her late sixties, but I could find almost no trace of her, except for an Italian newspaper article, published in October 2013, an interview with someone who knew her. A priest named Marco Schrott gave an account of how, after the death of Karl Hass in 2004, he agreed to conduct the funeral service, because he had known Enrica since childhood. 'We went to school together; I buried my friend's father, as no one else would.'

We tracked down Marco Schrott and spoke by telephone. He was friendly and open, but sad to report that Enrica died not long after her father. If I happened to be near Lake Albano he would be pleased to meet. So here we were, sitting on the terrace of a restaurant, on a warm June morning, enjoying the view of Lake Albano.

Marco was full of energy, warm, and with a sense of humour and humility. His eyes were blue, his hair white. Nearly seventy, he had spent most of his life in the area, and knew it well. When he was two his parents moved here from Merano, in northern Italy. They ran a small hotel, the Villa Svizzera, a bar and restaurant with dancing at the weekends. He attended a local school and became a priest, initially in Italy and later, for several years, in Sierra Leone. There he learned first-hand about conflict  and horror, and now he was back near Rome, in charge of three small parishes which he ran with a colleague. 'A very old priest,' he said with a wry smile, 'and we have a lot of satisfaction with our work.'

He was ten years old when he met Enrica Giustini, at school. They became friends and, later, neighbours, when her parents Karl and Angela (previously known as Anna Maria), who both used the name Giustini, moved to Via del Pascolaro, in Castel Gandolfo. Marco was at number 8, Enrica at number 12. He didn't know exactly where the Hass family lived before that, in 1949. Not far from the lake, he thought, maybe Poggi d'Oro.

He often visited Enrica's home. He was fond of her mother Angela, a simple, friendly woman, who cooked, tended the garden and lived an ordinary, decent life. 'Maybe to hide the secret work they did in this family,' Marco suggested, with another smile. Enrica loved her father, Karl, because he was successful, had money and contacts in high places, but he was different to Angela. 'Absolutely not friendly', was the way Marco put it. He recalled Hass sitting in an armchair with a newspaper, 'like a statue, an Egyptian mummy', a man who didn't like to speak. Marco sensed he was a man who wished to be absent, who 'tried to hide himself'. He was unable to recall a single conversation with Hass from the days of his childhood.

At that stage, as a young boy, he knew nothing of Hass's past, or his secret life. Only later did he learn of the Nazi years, followed by work for the intelligence services of different countries. 'He was a part of the community, with an ordinary house and life, trying not to disturb anyone.' The home was filled with simple pictures, no images of Hitler or Mussolini, just flowers and mountains. Marco laughed. 'Then one day I read that the Italian government gave him a pension!' He chuckled loudly. The thought of a man convicted of 'crimes against humanity' for the murder of Italians being paid a pension by the Italian state. Crazy world.

At school Enrica used the name Giustini, not Hass. When she asked for an explanation, her father told her that he had several different names to choose from. Marco believed that Enrica knew nothing of her father's past, not as a child, but may have sensed there were difficulties, as a child often does. This caused her to suffer. 'She was good at school, and liked to write poems, but they were often about death.'

The arrest and trial of her father in 1998 was a moment of crisis for Enrica. 'The cost was high,' Marco said sadly, as his childhood friend was overwhelmed by public attention from which she never really recovered. Enrica had the constant support of a loving husband, who helped with lawyers, and did what he could to keep his father-in-law out of jail. Hass was convicted of 'crimes against humanity' for his role in the Fosse Ardeatine killings, and it was a relief that he was allowed to serve the sentence at home, near Lake Albano. 'To rest in peace for the last days of his life,' Marco said, with irony. Enrica worried about her father's health and visited often, from Switzerland, where she lived. 'She was really a good daughter,' Marco said. 'She knew about the past, but we are another generation.'

Marco felt torn. In principle, he welcomed the trial of Karl Hass, a positive development, a sense of justice. 'It was good that the truth came out, that someone who committed a terrible crime was obliged to recognise what he had done.' Yet it caused his childhood friend to suffer greatly, and he spoke tenderly of Enrica, of their contact during that period. 'She asked me to try to bring her father to faith, to convert him to Catholicism.' As a child Hass was baptised Lutheran, Marco explained, so he visited him at his home, to ascertain if he was aware of his responsibilities, and what was happening to him.

'He acknowledged what he had done,' Marco said. 'He said clearly of that period, "I wanted to show to my superiors that I am really a good Nazi at war, to give a good example, so I killed two men in the Fosse Ardeatine." He wanted to show that he could do exactly what he was ordered to do.'

Did Hass accept personal responsibility for his actions?

Marco thought carefully about the question.

'He tried, he wanted to reach the truth, but his mind was blocked by his Nazi ideology, no?'

So, still a Nazi?

'Yes, sure,' Marco said. 'They are all still Nazis.'

And the two of them carried on talking?

'No, it was impossible.'

After the last conversation Marco invited Hass to pray with him, and Hass accepted the invitation. 'I think perhaps he liked this, found a pleasure in praying, a human dignity, something important.' Marco wasn't sure, however, that Hass really believed in the value of prayer.

Hass died in 2004, six years after he was convicted. The local bishop asked Marco to bury him, as a friend of the family, and because the priest spoke German. The funeral was controversial, the communists were on one side ('wanting to throw stones'), the fascists on the other ('wanting to welcome this hero of the Nazis'). The fact that the funeral was held at the cemetery in Castel Gandolfo, where the Pope had a summer residence, added to the febrile atmosphere.

Marco accepted the bishop's request, without hesitation, for Enrica, his friend. The burial took place under conditions of great secrecy. 'Nobody saw us at the cemetery of Castel Gandolfo.' Ten years later, when Erich Priebke died in 2013, there was greater mayhem, after the Vatican prohibited the funeral from being held in any Catholic church in or near Rome. 'It was not possible to give him a funeral,' Marco said. 'To this day nobody knows where Erich Priebke is buried.'

I told Marco what I knew about Hass and Project Los Angeles, and showed him some of the documents. He was surprised, and seemed to have no idea that his friend's father worked for the Americans. 'To treat your enemies as your friends? It's a mistake. The Americans are doing it again today, with Saudi Arabia.'

Together we read the CIC document that listed the names of Hass's sources.

Caputo? 'Old fascist.'

Albert Griezzar? 'Recycled fascist,' Marco chuckled.

Ali Hussain? 'Mama mia.'

Monsignor Fioretti, of the Vatican? He wasn't surprised that a senior Vatican man might be an American agent. 'Even among the religious are those who think it is better to go to the right or left.'

Bishop Hudal? He didn't know the name, it wasn't his world. 'I was a missionary in Africa,' he reminded us. He met Pope Pius XII once, but that was back in 1955, when he was seven. 'I have no relationship with the Vatican,' he added, and didn't know any bishops.

Nor was he familiar with the name Otto Wächter. He knew nothing about him or his death, after a swim with Karl Hass at Lake Albano.

'I was too little to know about such things.'

The poisoning allegation surprised him and he doubted Hass could have had a role. 'Not a serial killer,' Marco said. 'Not a man who would kill on his own account.'

He paused for a while and thought about it more, then offered a caveat. 'Well, maybe,' he said, maybe in some circumstances Hass could have killed. For reasons of ideology, or if someone ordered him to kill. 'I'm sure if somebody gave him the order to do this, he would be able to follow an order he received.' He was of that generation, taught to obey, to believe that obedience was a good thing, for humanity.

A weak man?

'A man without self-direction,' Marco responded without hesitation. A man who was always willing to act in the interests of others.

Horst, whose face lit up as Marco spoke, suddenly interjected sharply. He was unable to stop himself, here at the place where his father swam.

'Karl Hass was a mean, rat figure who killed my father.'

Marco looked surprised, but maintained a calm disposition.

Horst continued with his theory. 'Hass worked for Stalin, for the Soviets. My father was a man of honour, these were his enemies.'

'I thank you and your father for being such good men,' Marco said. It was apparent that he had never heard of Otto Wächter, yet Horst was thrilled with the words he spoke.

'And your father's name?' Marco asked.

'Otto.'

Horst showed him a photograph of Otto with Charlotte, one taken in the summer of 1948, under the mountains.

'They look like a lovely couple,' Marco said, which was exactly what Horst wanted to hear on a fine June morning in a small town near Rome.

We went for lunch to a local fish restaurant. Marco told us about his family, his two brothers, Viktor, a year and a half older, born in 1946, and Sergio, five years younger. As we ate, he said: 'Karl Hass was a part of my family.'

This came out of the blue, with no previous hint. We must have looked confused, so he spoke on.

'My brother Viktor married Enrica, Hass's daughter.' This was even more surprising. They had a long and happy marriage, he continued, and lived in Geneva, where Viktor remained after Enrica died, not long after her father, of pancreatitis. They had one child, a son, who worked for a coffee company in Geneva.

'Like George Clooney,' Marco said of his nephew, beaming and proud. How was their son's relationship with his grandfather, Karl Hass? Marco shrugged and smiled. 'The son is quiet, a real Swiss man, not so many words.'

'And the son was called Schrott?' I asked, apropos of nothing much, assuming he had the same surname as his uncle, the priest.

Marco didn't answer. He looked thoughtful, then said: 'No, not Schrott, Williams.'

We were silent in the face of incomprehension.

'Yes, my brother is not Viktor Schrott, he is Viktor Williams. My mother had a baby during the war.'

Horst coughed.

'So your mother's maiden name was Williams?'

'No. My mother was von Heyking. My brother's father was called Williams.'

'He was Welsh?'

'No, American.'

We talked and in our minds tried to work out the family structure.

'Actually, it is more complicated,' said Marco, the kind, gentle, understated priest.

His brother's father wasn't really called Williams. The name was invented, as their mother had an affair with an American who was well-known around Bolzano, where she lived. She became pregnant and decided to keep the child. The American lover asked that she not give the child his real name, as it would cause a scandal, so they chose the name Williams.

'Who was Williams?'

'A British soldier, killed in the war.'

'So your brother isn't Viktor Schrott, and he's not really Viktor Williams?'

'Correct.'

'Who was the father?'

An American, quite well-known, a politician, or something like that, Marco explained.

I asked for the name. Marco seemed a little reluctant, but eventually said: 'T-o-m-a-s-o, L-u-c-i-t-o.' He spoke the words slowly. 'Something like that.' Tomaso Lucito.

'Thomas Lucid?' I said, startled.

'You know the name?' Marco asked, surprised that the name was familiar.

I nodded and told him what I knew. Thomas Lucid worked for the CIC. He was commanding officer of the 430th Detachment, the unit that hunted Otto and other Nazis, including Hass. Lucid created and then ran Project Los Angeles. It was he who interviewed Karl Hass, then hired him, then made him the chief source for the project, in 1947.

Thomas Lucid, an American intelligence officer, became the controller of Karl Hass, a former SS intelligence officer who became an American agent.

Marco digested the implications. So did Horst. So did I.

Thomas Lucid's son married Karl Hass's daughter.

The controller and the agent, the CIC officer and the former Nazi, connected by the marriage of their children.

'The situation of your brother's son is curious,' I said to Marco, trying to work things out. 'He has two grandfathers. One grandfather was a senior Nazi, then became an American secret agent, who was later convicted of "crimes against humanity" by an Italian court, for his role in the killings at the Ardeatine Caves. The other grandfather was his American controller.'

'So one grandfather controlled the other?'

'Correct.'

It took a little time for all the implications to become apparent. I drew a picture, as I often do when family connections become complicated, as it is easier for my brain to understand facts when they are depicted graphically.

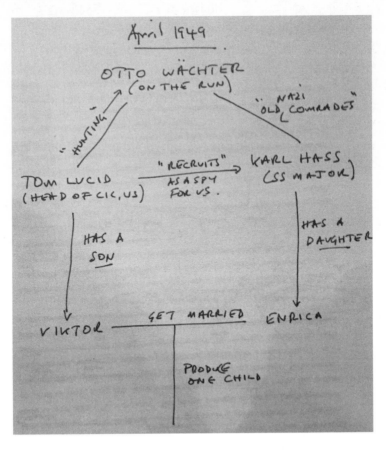

In July 1949, when Otto Wächter was on the run, he accepted an invitation to visit Karl Hass at Lake Albano. At the time, Hass was living with Angela, with whom he had recently had a child called Enrica.

In July 1949, Hass worked secretly for the Americans. He reported to Thomas Lucid of the CIC, the organisation that was hunting Wächter. There was no indication that Otto was aware of Hass's relationship to the Americans. Indeed, he had recently written to Charlotte to warn her that some of his German comrades in Rome were known to be working for the Americans, and they had to be avoided.

Which meant there were two possibilities. Either the Americans knew Wächter was in Rome, because Hass told them, as he was required to do, as chief source of Project Los Angeles. Or the Americans didn't know Wächter was there, because Hass didn't tell them.

Which begged a further question: if Hass didn't report to the Americans that he was in contact with Wächter, why not?

47

Exhumation

Prompted by developments in Rome, Horst thought it might be a good idea to exhume his father's body. He passed along a document. I had seen it before, in Charlotte's papers, two pages, typed, a copy from the file of Otto Wächter, found in an archive in Rome. Horst didn't know where it came from. It was not an official transcript, merely a copy of an original document dated 14 July 1949, with the title: 'Patient File, Ospedale Santo Spirito'.

'On 9 July 1949, a patient by the name of Reinhardt is brought in.' Someone entered the patient's first name, by hand, not quite legible, maybe 'Alfred'.

The document contained personal details, which were contradictory. Page one said the patient was 'single', page two that he was 'married, five children'.

The patient indicates that he has been unable to eat since July 1st; that he developed a high fever on July 2nd, and showed symptoms of jaundice on July 7th. The patient is diabetic, the clinical examination revealed a liver condition: acute yellow liver atrophy (*icterus gravis*).

The document then stated: 'Following the onset of uraemia, the patient dies on 14 July.'

The date of death differed from that given by Bishop Hudal, which was a day earlier, on 13 July. I assumed this was because Otto had died late in the evening. The document continued:

On the same day (as is standard practice for all deaths in the hospital) an autopsy is performed. It reveals a suspicion of Weil's disease (*Leptospirosis ictero haemorragica*).

Horst did not accept the diagnosis. He was convinced it was murder, not by the Americans, he now accepted. He thought it was the Soviets,

or maybe Simon Wiesenthal, the famous Nazi hunter, who he believed
had an animus against his father.

The two-page typed document no longer convinced Horst. Bishop
Hudal's memoir catalysed new theories. So did the conversation
between Charlotte and Hansjakob Stehle, which he was not aware of
until I directed him to it. 'When she arrived in Rome he was dead, and
lying there black as a Negro,' his mother told the historian. 'Corpses
do not turn completely black in a matter of hours,' Horst said. 'You
don't turn black when you die.'

And so, following the trip to Rome, Horst said he was thinking of
raising his father's body from the grave to test it. 'If we make an exhumation of my father's body, it will be quite clear that there is poison
around.' He spoke with the certainty of an apostle.

I was sceptical as to what a further exhumation might offer. Otto
was buried in 1949, exhumed a decade later, spent a few years in
Charlotte's garden in Salzburg, then moved to Fieberbrunn, where he
was then buried for the fourth time, in 1974, in the local cemetery. He
was moved again in 1985, when Charlotte died.

Nevertheless, Horst took steps to ascertain what might be feasible.
He contacted an expert in exhumations in St Johann in Tirol, who
made a preliminary enquiry. This confirmed that an exhumation was
possible, but offered a warning as to what might be found. It reported
that no records were available of Otto's original burial in 1974, that
the grave he was now in was 'lowered' in 1985, when Charlotte was
buried, and that in 1993, as part of a general rearrangement of the
cemetery, the grave was moved by twenty centimetres. All this meant
that it 'cannot be said with certainty that the remains of Mr Otto
Wächter will be found during an exhumation'. If remains were found,
a DNA analysis would have to be carried out, followed by a toxicolog-
ical analysis. The total cost would be between five and eight thousand
euros.

Horst was not put off by the report, but agreed it would be helpful to
obtain more information before engaging in the exercise. 'Perhaps you
could find an expert?' Horst suggested. I was not inclined to do so but
around that time, at a dinner I attended in London, I happened to sit
next to the director of the Royal Society, a scientific academy founded
in the seventeenth century. Over dessert the conversation gravitated to
Otto's story, and one topic led to another, so we eventually came to the

testing of human remains. The director suggested I contact a fellow of the Royal Society, Dame Sue Black, professor of anatomy and forensic anthropology at the University of Dundee, who might offer a view. Professor Black had investigated 'crimes against humanity' and 'genocide' in the former Yugoslavia, Sierra Leone, Iraq and many other places, and was experienced in matters of exhumation. I contacted her, we had two conversations, joined by her colleague, Professor Niamh Nic Daéid, director of the university's centre for forensic science.

They asked me to send the material I had. I passed on the two-page document from the hospital files, various medical bulletins, and the descriptions of the symptoms Otto felt, as shared with Charlotte in his letters.

Over the course of the conversations with Professors Black and Nic Daéid, I learned much about the human body, post mortem. They asked for information on the state of Otto's remains, and details about the original coffin, the shroud and clothes in which he was first buried in 1949. I had little information. He had already been exhumed once, I explained, from a grave in Rome. For many years the remains were kept in a box in Charlotte's garden, then moved to another house, then reburied in a cemetery in the village of Fieberbrunn, in the Tyrol. If my interlocutors were surprised by what I said, they did not show it.

Was it just bones? I didn't know.

Was any hair or nail available? I didn't know.

Was the original coffin lifted out and re-encased in another? Were Otto's remains lifted out and transferred to another vessel? Was an original burial shroud transferred? Do any of these remain? Again, I didn't know.

They explained the purpose of their questions. Several factors combined to affect what happened to a body after burial. The factors included the depth of burial, the nature of the soil, its acidity, levels of water, scavenging by small rodents and insects. Hair tended to be better preserved in warm temperatures, unless the environment was wet. The wooden base of the original coffin, items of clothing, and a burial shroud could offer clues, because body fluids, which might contain measurable elements of a poison, might have seeped into them.

Sue offered a graphic account. 'As the body and tissues decompose, if the fluids don't drain away the body sits in a sort of soup of body fluids. These are slightly acidic, so they break down the soft tissue. The remains are skeletal, only bone, covered in a sort of brown film. It almost looks like a chocolate coating, if that helps to imagine what is left. The body fluids seep into the base of the coffin, the clothes and, if there is one, the burial shroud.'

What was needed, therefore, was more information as to what exactly was in the coffin with Otto Wächter when he was buried for the second time. Horst told me that he never looked inside the box of remains kept in his mother's garden. Even with such information, and its analysis, Sue said she would not wish to speculate on a possible cause of death. That was a matter for a medically qualified person, which she was not. 'We cannot give any opinion as to a cause of death, especially since one possibility – leptospirosis, or Weil's disease – is a clinical condition.'

Nor was she an expert on poisons. For that she needed a toxicologist. Certain poisons did manifest themselves in the tissues of the body, she explained, but if the only available tissue was bone then the prospect of obtaining a definitive result would be limited. This was because bone, unlike hair or nail, had a slow turnover rate of cells. Consequently, bone was unlikely to pick up a poison that passed through the gastrointestinal system in the very short period of time between the introduction of the poison – maybe at a meal eaten with Karl Hass at lunch on Saturday, 2 July – and the moment of death, just eleven days later. 'Bone doesn't turn over that quickly, not in less than two weeks.'

Time was a key factor. If a poison was introduced, was it by a single act, or several acts in the weeks and months before death? 'Was Wächter already ill, and then poisoned?' Professor Black asked. Equally significant would be the passage of time between the moment of death and the analysis of the remains. The more time passed, the less likely it was to be possible to identify a poison. Seventy years was a long time, Sue intimated. The fact that he had already been transferred once, and kept in conditions unknown, further complicated the matter.

A poison introduced over a prolonged period of time, over several months, would increase the chance of identification, depending upon the type of poison. Not all poisons would be picked up in bone, hair or nails. 'Some literally go through the system, without leaving a trace.' Poison introduced a couple of weeks before death would be difficult to pick up. 'I can't say it's not possible, but it's unlikely. Months of poisoning would be easier, but it depends on the poison.'

Sue explained the mechanics, why Otto's bones alone were unlikely to be sufficient. There were basically two types of bone, 'ivory' and 'crunchy'. Ivory bone looked like 'the keys on a piano'. It was compact, the shaft of your thighbone or shinbone, or the bone between elbow and wrist. It had a low turnover of cells, every fifteen years, 'so picking up a poison from compact bone would not happen if the poisoning was just two weeks before death'.

Crunchy bone was cancellous. Think of honeycomb, Sue said, like the inside of a chocolate-covered Malteser sweet. 'Its purpose is to transfer weight in the body, but it's more fragile than the other type.' It's the kind of bone you break when you fall. With a higher turnover of cells – five years – it means that a poison enters this type more quickly than compact bone. Nevertheless, Sue thought 'highly, highly unlikely' that a poison could be identified in cancellous bone if introduced just a week or two before death.

With the passage of more time it was more likely to be picked up, as the poison was distributed across the active surface of a full individual skeleton. It didn't remain in a single bone, or area. Clinical conditions could manifest themselves in bone, she said, 'but because of the slow rate of bone turnover it usually needs to be a long-term, chronic condition'. Sue didn't think Otto's bones were likely to provide answers, certainly not if it was a single act of poisoning, shortly before death. If a small amount of poison has been dispensed over a longer period, months or years, it may be possible to find something, but not with any degree of certainty.

The more useful body tissue would be Otto's hair or nails. 'Each offers a longitudinal laying down of chemical information, as they grow, even in a two-week period.' Even then the information could be very limited.

How much hair or nail was needed for a meaningful analysis? Niamh said that was a matter for a toxicologist. Her job was to collect the samples, to be analysed by a specialist. If she was looking for a particular chemical in nail, she would need the whole nail, because if the poisoning was close to the time of death then she would be interested in the part of the nail that was still growing. 'If you're interested in the hair, then you need the bits closest to the scalp, for the same reason – that's where the chemical is being laid down.'

On the positive side, she wouldn't need ten fingernails, or a full handful of hair. For the nail, she explained, she'd want the little half-moon light-coloured area at the base. 'That's where the poison will be.'

Sue summed up: 'If Otto Wächter was killed by poison, and if it occurred in a single event about two weeks before death, then the only realistic chance of being able to test would be with hair or fingernails, if they have survived.' She was far from convinced that bone alone would add much.

Sue wished to raise another issue, to be addressed before any exhumation took place. Two parties were involved, the deceased and those directly affected by the exhumation, in particular the family. Some people believed that the act of exhumation was intrusive and disturbing of the rest of the deceased, and should only be done for good reason. For those who would be affected – family and friends – there were various factors to take into consideration, and many questions. Was a resolution being sought, and for whom? Was there a mystery to solve, and would it result in someone being held responsible? Was the process being undertaken to achieve some sort of closure? Was this something the exhumed would have wanted? Was it relevant that there has already been an exhumation, many decades ago?

I said I would pass the questions to Horst.

Sue and Niamh made clear they would not take part in any investigation or exhumation unless they were satisfied that all legal requirements had been met. They would want to know that the exhumation was being carried out for the right reasons, and to be satisfied that the families were able to cope with the outcome, whatever it might be.

'In this context, before proceeding, I would want to know the forensic value of an exhumation, for whom and for what purposes,' Sue said. 'There will be legal ramifications.'

Sue concluded bluntly. 'It is unlikely, if it was typhus or leptospirosis, that the skeletal remains would allow you to diagnose either as a condition that killed Otto Wächter. Given the facts you describe, it would be extremely difficult, if indeed possible, to confirm that diagnosis, or an act of poisoning, just from skeletal remains.'

She suggested I needed to find an expert on diseases of the liver.

48

Lucid

As I reflected on the prospects of obtaining anything useful from an exhumation of Otto, Marco Schrott pondered the news of his half-brother's connection to Thomas Lucid. He offered to introduce me to Viktor Williams, the son of Thomas Lucid who married Enrica and became the son-in-law of Karl Hass.

I travelled to Geneva to meet Viktor. He is an industrial chemist who graduated from university in Rome with a doctorate, and worked for much of his life for the DuPont company. Now retired, he invited me to the apartment he shared for many years with Enrica, neat and comfortable. We sat next to each other on a large white sofa in the living room; a low coffee table before us held a vase of red and white flowers, a single red candle, two large glasses of water, and an ashtray which he used during the conversation. He wore a comfortable dark sweater, a short and solid man with white hair and a full beard. His eyes were lively and attentive, behind rimless glasses, his style deliberate. He listened carefully, paid attention to details, chose his words with precision. He reminded me of the Italian writer Primo Levi. I liked him a lot.

He shared his story. He was seven when he met Enrica Giustini, at school, who was three years younger. That was in 1953, near Lake Albano, four years after Otto's visit and death. His stepfather, Falco Schrott, ran a bar and restaurant – with dancing – near where the Hass family lived. Both families were German-speaking, so the children formed part of the same teenage group. 'We grew up together, swam in the lake, danced.' Enrica became engaged to a friend of Viktor's, but when he was nineteen he declared his affections. That was 1966. Eight years later they married, and five years after that, in 1979, their only child was born, a son.

Angela and Karl Hass became his in-laws. Angela was from a good family, in Parma. Karl was a large man, relatively tall, strong, not warm or friendly. 'He had a strange way of showing appreciation, a man of not many words,' Viktor said, choosing his description with care and precision. 'He was difficult, relatively closed, never talked about his past life.' He liked a drink, and after a few glasses, on some occasions, some stories might be told. At some point – Viktor could not recall exactly when – he came to know about his father-in-law's past, as an SS major. But there were no details on offer, and of course nothing about any atrocities.

Viktor had known the man who became his father-in-law for more than forty years when he learned more about his past (he had a photograph of Karl and Angela with their daughter Enrica, from the early 1950s, but that was before he knew them). It was in 1995 that the full story emerged, after Erich Priebke was arrested in Argentina and extradited to Italy for 'crimes against humanity', for his role in the killings in the Ardeatine Caves. Everyone in Italy knew about that horror. It was disastrous for the family, Viktor recalled, a terrible time.

The day before his first interview with an Italian military prosecutor, in hospital recovering from injuries suffered when he tried to abscond, to avoid giving testimony, Hass confessed to Enrica and Viktor about his role. 'He said: "I must tell you something, before I make my witness statement, I was at the Fosse Ardeatine, I killed one person."' Until that moment Karl Hass – patriarch, father and father-in-law – had denied all involvement.

'It was a shock for both of us.' Viktor paused and lit up a cigarette. 'Even more for Enrica, as you can imagine.' She was deeply affected by all that followed: the media circus, a very public trial, conviction, sentence, house arrest at Lake Albano. She had a breakdown and Viktor worried about her well-being, as she was hounded by the media. He stood and walked me through a sliding glass door. 'I worried she might jump from here,' he said, as we stood on the balcony on which he and Enrica once sat with Karl and a journalist from *Il Messaggero*, drinking grappa. 'Karl had more than one glass, so he started coming out with different stories.'

The last years of her father's life took a toll on Enrica. 'They were terrible years, because he wasn't open at all.' Father and daughter loved each other, but he was unable to show his affection. Hass's wife

Angela stood by her husband, as did Enrica and Viktor, who contrib-uted to the costs of a lawyer.

Viktor learned of Karl's post-war activities, including work for the American and Italian intelligence services, which were reported in the press. Yet he had never heard of Project Los Angeles, not until I told him about it, seated on a large white sofa in a Geneva apartment, decades after the network was created and dissolved. The name Joseph Luongo did prompt a vague memory.

'This tells me something,' Viktor said, of the man who was Hass's control agent at the CIC, his wife Enrica's godfather, and who attended her baptism.

Did he know the name of the person to whom Luongo reported? No.

'He reported to the commanding officer of the 430th Detachment of the CIC,' I said. 'His name was Thomas Lucid.' I spoke the words slowly. Viktor looked me in the eye for a long moment, impassive and knowing, and then said, very quietly: 'Ah, okay.'

He recognised the name, and he knew immediately that I knew that Thomas Lucid was his father, but he did not say that, or anything else. There was an extended silence, as the relationship between his father, Thomas Lucid, and his wife's father, Karl Hass, sank in.

Eventually I spoke.

'Thomas Lucid had a son, out of wedlock, who married the daugh-ter of Karl Hass . . .'

'Yes.'

'That's pretty remarkable.'

'Yes, it is.'

'Is it true?'

'It is.' Viktor paused. 'I mean, it's a very strange coincidence, if we can really call it a coincidence.'

He laughed. We were grappling with the reality of the details that tumbled into Viktor's mind, at that moment. His father was not only an American spy, but *the* American spy who recruited and controlled the man who became his father-in-law.

'It seems remarkable that your son has two grandfathers – grand-father number one was an American and the—'

Viktor interrupted.

'. . . controller of grandfather two.' He chuckled as he completed the sentence.

*

Viktor offered a more detailed explanation. 'I was fourteen when I learned the identity of my biological father.' He asked his mother why school documents referred to him as Williams, not Schrott, like his brother Marco. His mother Charlotte told him a story. In April 1945 she was in prison in Bolzano, incarcerated for anti-fascist activity. She was freed when the Americans liberated the town, and, as she spoke English and French, she was hired by a US soldier, Thomas Lucid, to work as his secretary. Lucid was married – to Margaret, known as Peggy – but she was back in America. The affair between Thomas Lucid and Charlotte von Heyking lasted a few months, until September 1945. It was long enough for Charlotte to become pregnant.

'My mother said to me: "I wanted you".' It seemed there was a disagreement about whether his mother should keep the child. She did not end the pregnancy, as Lucid desired, and Viktor was born in March 1946. Following their separation, and the birth, Thomas Lucid made modest financial provision, for a few months, then disappeared from their lives. Viktor never saw him or had any contact. With the passage of time he wanted to know more, especially after Hass died, in 2004. He even tried to change his name from Williams to von Heyking, his mother's maiden name. John Thomas Williams, an Allied soldier from Ireland, was said to have been killed by a land mine crossing the Apennines on a motorbike. Viktor gathered evidence to prove that no such John Thomas Williams ever existed. The population registry in Ireland confirmed this. The Italian commune where the accident occurred informed him that it had no record of the death of a person with this name. Nevertheless, the authorities in Milan refused to change his name. Insufficient evidence, they told him.

For many years he was curious about Thomas Lucid. The internet threw up some basic information – Irish origins, a Catholic family that arrived in the United States in 1879 by boat – and the *Washington Post* carried an obituary of Lucid, who died in May 1985. It offered a brief account of Lucid's work in intelligence – CIA, Gehlen Organization, Vietnam – and his family. He was married to Margaret, together they had six children, three sons and three daughters. The obituary said nothing about Lucid's seventh child, actually his first.

Lucid's second child, but the first with Margaret, was born in the summer of 1947, a year after Viktor. 'He lives in Albuquerque, New Mexico,' I told Viktor.

'Oh.' Viktor had no contact with any member of the Lucid family. 'I have no interest,' he continued, and believed they knew nothing about him, not even his existence. His mother wrote to Lucid in 1963 to ask for financial support, to help Viktor attend university. 'She told me she never received an answer.'

He once saw a picture of Lucid, a father who bore a certain resemblance to his son. I showed him another photograph, from 1961, when Thomas Lucid was in service for the CIA in Vietnam. Lucid and Viktor's son had strong eyebrows. 'I was open and frank with my son; I told him everything, he had a right to know.' Viktor was always open about this story, even with the neighbours.

What his son didn't know was that both grandfathers were spies, and that one, the American, controlled the other, the German.

'He didn't know, because I didn't know.'

Until now.

Did Karl Hass know that his son-in-law's biological father was his former controller?

'He did. He once said to me, "I knew your father."' That was all, no details. Hass said nothing more about the nature of his relationship with Viktor's biological father. He did not say that he once worked for him, and Viktor didn't ask questions.

'Karl said only that he was in a sort of training camp in Austria, where this Thomas Lucid was present. He never said that Lucid was his boss.'

Viktor learned that Hass worked for the Americans, but not that he reported to Lucid, via Luongo.

'I suppose I could have worked it out, because Lucid was the head of the camp, but that he was his direct boss? No.'

I gave Viktor the American archival documents on Project Los Angeles. He was surprised by the detail, especially the vivid account of Karl's character, a man who never deviated from a mission entrusted to him.

'It's a good description.'

He was surprised to read the names of those with whom Karl worked.

'Pino Romualdi! Oh là là,' he said of the well-known fascist politician

who was a member of the European Parliament, a representative of the
Movimento Sociale Italiano, the MSI, who served as vice chair of the
Group of the European Right.

'It's a very well-known name, my God!'

Viktor was even more surprised about a passage that suggested the
Americans severed the connection with Hass in 1951, because they
feared he was a double agent, working for the Soviets.

'This is new,' he said. He shook his head repeatedly, incredulous.
'No, not possible.'

He wanted to know about the weekend his father-in-law spent
with Otto Wächter at Lake Albano, in July 1949. I mentioned Bishop
Hudal's memoir, the account of Otto dying in his arms, the allegation of poisoning by an unnamed SS major, the man we now knew to
be Viktor's father-in-law. I showed Viktor the 1950 CIA file, which
reported Karl Hass's attendance at Wächter's funeral, and the rumour
that he joked about poisoning Otto Wächter.

'Oh my God,' Viktor exclaimed.

Could Hass, his father-in-law, have done such a thing? Like his half-
brother Marco, Viktor thought not.

'In 1949 he was active with the Americans, why would he risk himself? He couldn't stand communists, couldn't stand them.'

You knew that?

'Absolutely. I would be very, very surprised if this is true – very,
very surprised. For a person with his intelligence, to eliminate one
person, to risk everything? I don't see it. How would he have done it?
To poison, how?'

I showed him Otto's letter to Charlotte, written after the visit to
Hass, Angela and Enrica at Lake Albano. Viktor recalled that Hass
lived somewhere between Genzano and Velletri, in a villa on the Via
Appia. They shared it with another German family. The location
chimed with Otto taking a tram or a bus to get to the lake, from
Poggi d'Oro, near Lake Nemi. Viktor hadn't been to the house, but he
knew roughly where it was. 'It is where Enrica grew up, with the two
Dohm daughters.' This was a reference to the children of the other
German family they lived with. He went to a cabinet, to gather a few
photographs. One was in a wooden frame.

Two mothers, three children. Angela and her daughter Enrica, Frau
Dohm with her two daughters, Sybila and Cristina, in Poggi d'Oro.
Sybila was no longer alive, but Viktor spoke with Cristina, who lived

near Rome, just a few days earlier. She called, to find out about his health. 'I have cancer,' Viktor said. He would ask her about the house in Poggi d'Oro, the villa where Otto ate a hearty meal, his last.

I told Viktor that I hoped to visit Thomas Lucid junior, his half-brother, in Albuquerque, New Mexico. I asked if he would be interested to know whether the Lucid children were aware of his existence, but he doubted they were. 'The whole concept of the nature of his character would be destroyed in front of the wife, especially such a Catholic family.'

Thomas Lucid the father could have maintained contact with him, but chose not to. 'That was his decision. Frankly, I don't care. But if I would have Thomas Lucid the father in front of me, I would be very angry. I would really tell him what he did wrong in his life. I have no curiosity to meet his sons.'

We talked about Hass's *Totenkopfring*, the 'death's head ring', awarded to him by Heinrich Himmler, Otto's colleague, as one of the SS's finest. Joseph Luongo took possession of Karl Hass's ring. Many years later, he donated it to the CIA museum, in Washington, where it apparently resides today.

We marvelled at the curiosity of life, the strange and unexpected points of connection, the legacy of actions that took place long ago.

We marvelled too at the idea that Otto Wächter, hunted by the Americans, was befriended in Rome by a former SS comrade who worked for the Americans, and may have been a double agent.

49

2018, Albuquerque

A few weeks after meeting Viktor, I travelled to New Mexico, where I sat in the kitchen of a small, one-storey house, on a neat, suburban street. In Albuquerque, laid out on a kitchen table, were documents and photographs from another age. The house and the papers were owned by a half-brother of Viktor's, but I didn't know if the half-brother was aware of that fact.

When I first met Horst, many years earlier, it never occurred to me that one day I would travel to Albuquerque and drink tea with the son of the American agent whose organisation led the hunt for Otto Wächter, while at the same time running a spy network that might have tried to recruit him to their cause.

The kitchen and the papers belonged to Thomas Lucid junior, the second child of Thomas A. Lucid, commanding officer of the CIC's 430th Detachment. I found his name in a newspaper article, which allowed me to obtain a phone number in Albuquerque. I left a message, he responded promptly. Yes, he'd be happy to meet to discuss his father's wartime experiences.

Tom junior was genial, with warm eyes that twinkled, and a shock of white hair that gave him a resemblance to Viktor Williams. I did not mention this when he met me at the airport, or over a lunch of spicy tacos. Nor did I mention it as we drank coffee in the branch of the Twisters restaurant that was used as the set of Los Pollos Hermanos, from *Breaking Bad*, one of my favourite television series. I remained silent for a simple reason: I did not know what Tom junior knew about his father's first child, the one he left behind in Italy, and I did not know if I had a right to inform him.

Tom junior was born in Austria in 1947, in Gmunden, headquarters of the CIC 430th Detachment. This was where his father worked and interviewed Major Hass, and recruited him as chief source on Project Los Angeles, just a few weeks after the birth of his second child, and his wife's first, but I did not say any of this.

At seventeen, Tom junior joined the army, spent time in the US and Taiwan before enrolling at the University of Maryland in Germany. By the time he graduated in 1972, his father was retired and struck by Parkinson's disease. Tom junior became a schoolteacher, in El Paso, Texas, to where his parents moved, and later he moved to Albuquerque. He married Michelle Lippman, whose father Bruno fled Vienna for Australia after the Anschluss, as Otto and his colleagues targeted Jews. Tom junior served for thirty-two years in the National Guard and Army Reserves, and was called up after 9/11, to be an instructor at the US Army Special Forces School.

Tom spoke affectionately of his parents. 'My father was the life of the party,' he said, 'affable, great sense of humour, a fair and dependable boss, very well liked'. A memoir by a CIA colleague described his father as 'a dedicated professional officer, outgoing, party loving, Irish Catholic with a fine tenor voice and an attractive Irish wife who fit gracefully into his gregarious lifestyle'.

He recalled his father singing at Munich's Oktoberfest, and mixing an 'old-fashioned' – bourbon or Canadian whisky, a touch of water, Angostura bitters, a couple of pieces of fruit. He knew little, however, of his father's job, until the family moved to Saigon and his mother told him that 'Dad worked for the CIA'. There were memories, like the trip across the Atlantic on a liner, when they met the Shah of Iran, who thanked Lucid for the CIA's role in keeping him in power, in 1953, when 'they got rid of the Prime Minister who was a bit leftist'. Tom junior had the Shah's autograph, on a postcard.

The family took a trip to Italy, where they visited the small village of Mondragone, between Naples and Rome. An Italian family recalled a young Lieutenant Thomas Lucid, the liberator. In Rome, he learned, in September 1946, his parents met Pope Pius XII. 'The Pope predicted your birth,' Peggy told him. 'He said, "You will have a son."' Peggy didn't know her husband already had a son. Tom was born nine months later.

His father was born in New Jersey, into an Irish Catholic family. After university he enrolled in the army, to work in counterintelligence. In 1943, he married Margaret Gordon, a Scottish-American, known as Peggy. 'There may have been other girlfriends, before they married,' Tom said, 'but after their marriage they were apparently faithful.' Thomas senior left for North Africa and Italy, where he served with a CIC Detachment that was with the 88th Infantry Division. This was the first American division to enter Rome, on 5 June 1944, the one that caused Karl Hass to flee the city for Parma.

As the war in Europe ended, Lucid was in north Italy. It was here that he arrested Heinrich Himmler's wife and daughter, as reported in the *Jersey Journal* – 'Local soldier helps locate Frau Himmler' – which described the arrest in a well-appointed mountain chalet, fifteen miles south of Bolzano.

Thomas senior helped himself to a few souvenirs from the Himmler household, now in his son's possession. He showed me a black and white photograph of a teenage girl, Himmler's daughter Gudrun ('Confidentially', his father wrote on the back, 'the picture flatters her terrifically'). He also took two Christmas cards from Adolf Hitler to the Himmlers, from 1937 and 1943, with Hitler's signature in dark ink.

In 1946, Thomas senior became commanding officer of the 430th, based in Linz. His brief was counterintelligence, to search for senior

Nazis and interrogate them. 'The focus shifted away from justice,' Tom junior said, 'it became a hunt for information on the Soviets.' Peggy arrived in Europe in the summer of 1946. Tom had a photograph. 'Mum arriving at the train station, July '46,' he says, reunited after three years apart. The sunshine was palpable, so was the happiness. Thomas A. Lucid held a bouquet of flowers, Peggy looked radiant and excited, oblivious that her husband had fathered a son.

In 1947 his father recruited Karl Hass, and in due course he joined the CIA and the family moved to Vietnam. His father became more senior and important. He showed me a photograph:

Thomas A. Lucid with President Lyndon B. Johnson, at a reception. Tom junior gave names to the other faces. 'There's Allen Dulles, there's Richard Helms, there's J. Edgar Hoover, there's the mole hunter James Jesus Angleton.' The voice was matter-of-fact, his father sat at the top table.

Tom junior had a general sense of his father's work, but not the details. He had a vivid memory of Joseph Luongo, who his father used as a translator, and they became close friends. 'A fun guy, friendly, real Italian-looking, talked like an Italian-American, he loved Dad.'

He had never heard of Project Los Angeles, or Karl Hass, although Erich Priebke's name rang a vague bell.

'Dad was involved in interrogating Hass? Hass worked for the Americans? That doesn't mean he *was* working for the Americans, it could simply be that Otto Wächter said he was working for them.'

There was a suggestion that Hass tried to recruit Otto, I explained, as part of Project Los Angeles. Tom junior wanted to know more; I gave a general description. When I finished he said: 'So Wächter might have survived if he'd been recruited!'

I mentioned Horst's theory, that Otto was poisoned by Karl Hass.

'Poisoning isn't an American thing,' Tom said. 'Shooting might be.'

There was too a suspicion that Hass could have been a double agent.

'Oh.' Then he had another thought. 'I think Dad was involved in the arrest of Karl Wolff,' which occurred during his birthday party, on 13 May 1945. He helped himself to Wolff's ceremonial dagger, gave it to his son, who later traded it with a former brother-in-law, for some stamps.

We had now spent several hours together and I had said nothing about Thomas senior's first child. The moment may have come to share what I knew. I reminded Tom junior of the email he wrote, enquiring whether I had a dramatic discovery to share. 'You're not in possession of any bombshells?' he asked. 'You didn't discover, for example, that the Ratline was Dad's brainchild, did you?'

Occasionally his father mentioned the Ratline, and in the early 1980s, after Klaus Barbie was caught in Bolivia and extradited for trial in France, the subject came to the fore, a major political controversy. A letter arrived from Langley, CIA headquarters, some folks wanted to interview him. Tom junior showed me the letter, which asked Lucid to cooperate and share all he knew. 'Maybe there was something that he was sorry he did,' Tom mused. A few years later, the Comptroller General of the United States published a damning report on the recruitment of Nazis, and efforts to help them escape to South America. The rationale was summarised by the words of an unnamed intelligence officer, who could have been Thomas senior. 'The West is fighting a desperate battle with the East – with the Soviets – and we will pick up any man we can who will help us defeat the Soviets – any man no matter what his Nazi record was.'

May I speak openly? I enquired. We had by now been joined by Tom junior's brother, Barney, and his wife. Barney reacted first to my question. 'Oh, yes.'

'Absolutely,' Tom said.

Anything?

'Anything,' Tom said.

I told them the story of Viktor Williams in Geneva. I reached the moment when Marco said: 'The name of the father was not Williams, it was Tomaso Lucito.'

Silence, then: 'Woah!' That was Tom junior.

More silence.

'If that's true, I've got a brother,' Tom junior said.

'Half-brother, right?' Barney interjected.

'Whatever.'

'Wow, this is news, wow, this really is news . . .' Barney spluttered.

The questions poured out. Did Viktor know who his father was? What was Viktor like? What exactly happened in 1945? Their father was far from home and lonely, he had an Italian secretary called Charlotte von Heyking, they had an affair, she became pregnant.

Tom interjected. 'You remember for years I've been saying I know something, a family secret, but I can't tell you because . . .'

Tom junior explained that when his father reached the end of his life he shared the story with one of their brothers, Bill, who, like the father, was deeply religious, a devout Knight of Columbus.

'Dad told Bill in a revealing, commiserative, shameful way, about having a son in Italy, and that Joe Luongo knew everything.'

Thomas senior did not share with his son Bill any details, and asked him to say nothing about the confession to any other member of the family, to protect Peggy. A few years later, after the father died, Bill too became ill, and told Tom junior what he knew. 'Don't tell anyone,' his brother told him, and Tom junior didn't. Bill tracked down Joe Luongo, to get more information, but Luongo didn't want to talk. 'I wish your dad hadn't told you, it was his secret,' Luongo said to Bill. Tom junior tried to find Joe Luongo, without success.

'Where does Viktor live?' Barney asked.

'We have a brother,' Tom said. When I had contacted him he wondered if I was bringing something to share. 'Is this going to clinch it, what little bit I know?' he asked himself. He believed his father sent money; now he learned he didn't, and this troubled him.

They asked to see a photograph of Viktor.

'Wow, looks like Tom,' said Barney.

'Look at his nose, he's got a normal nose, not my button,' said Tom. 'And his head is . . .'

'Has more hair on it,' says Barney. Everyone saw the resemblance.

'I'll be darned,' said Tom. 'Dad with some lady in Italy.'

I showed them a photograph of Karl Hass.

'Looks mean,' Tom said.

I showed them a photograph of Otto Wächter, in SS uniform.

'Looks very mean,' Tom said.

The points of connection slowly sank in.

Lucid. Hass. Wächter.

Tom junior, Viktor, Horst.

'Did Peggy know?' Barney asked.

'Absolutely not,' Tom replied.

We spent the evening with Michelle, Tom's ex-wife, who cooked a very fine meal. She wanted details about Hass and Wächter too, men who inflicted pain on her father and his family, who had themselves fled Vienna after the Anschluss.

'The story could have been different,' Tom said.

As the wine flowed, different thoughts tumbled out.

The story made Tom junior realise how fortunate he was. 'My dad only screwed his secretary,' he exclaimed. 'These other people's dads, they murdered hundreds of thousands of people, or 335 Italians.'

And, said Michelle, if Thomas Lucid hadn't hired Karl Hass, then Karl Hass wouldn't have invited Otto Wächter for lunch, he might not have fallen ill, and he might have made it to South America.

And Horst might have become an Argentinian, I added.

50

Wiesenthal

Horst was now focused on Karl Hass, but he also reserved a small space for another man for whom he felt a high degree of opprobrium, and who was, he was sure, somehow involved in the story of his father's demise.

'Simon Wiesenthal hated my father until the day he died,' he told me, more than once. And, he added, Charlotte gathered clippings of Wiesenthal's activities. In Horst's mind, Wiesenthal, the legendary Nazi hunter, jostled with Karl Hass and the Soviets for the crown of chief suspect for the premature death of his father.

Wiesenthal wanted Otto dead, Horst believed, because he held him responsible for the death of his mother, who was held in the Lemberg ghetto. 'He described my father putting his mother onto the train to Belzec,' Horst explained. 'That is completely wrong, because my father wasn't in Lemberg on the day he mentions, 15 August 1942. He confused my father with Katzmann, of the SS, because they wore the same uniform.'

Horst's belief was driven by a passage in Wiesenthal's memoir, published in 1967. The book described the author's life in Lemberg, including time spent in the ghetto in 1942. Wiesenthal identified Otto Wächter as one of the two 'chief culprits' for the murder of the Jews in Galicia, the other being Friedrich Katzmann. Otto loomed large in a chapter not-so-subtly titled 'The Killers of Galicia'. Here Wiesenthal described his effort, in the late 1950s, to assist a German prosecutor in the 'Lemberg trial' in Stuttgart, fifteen defendants prosecuted for a variety of horrors in the Janowska camp and elsewhere in Lemberg. Genocide was the 'official business', the judge in the case declared. 'Compared to Wächter', Wiesenthal wrote, the fifteen defendants in the Lemberg trial were 'small fry'.

Wiesenthal wanted Otto and Katzmann in the dock, but both were dead. 'I saw him early in 1942, in the ghetto of Lwów,' Wiesenthal wrote of Otto. 'He was personally in charge on August 15, 1942, when

4,000 elderly people were rounded up in the ghetto and sent to the railway station. My mother was among them.'

The words irritated Horst, and he frequently alluded to them. 'My father was not in Lemberg on 15 August,' he explained, 'but in Kraków, with Governor General Hans Frank, at a party meeting.' I found a photograph of Otto and Frank in Kraków on that day, at the Wawel Castle, so Horst was right about that point of detail.

I checked what Wiesenthal actually wrote, as the text was open to interpretation, like many words. He claimed to have seen Otto in the ghetto, 'early in 1942', not on a particular date. His claim for 15 August, the only date specified with precision, referred simply to the fact that Otto was 'personally' in charge of the Lemberg ghetto round-up that occurred that day. Wiesenthal did not write explicitly that Otto was physically present, although the text could certainly be read in that way. As governor of Galicia, however, with overall responsibility for aspects of the round-ups, he was, in a sense, in charge, at least of some of the details if not the whole. The word 'personally' was ambiguous. It could refer to his presence in the ghetto, or his responsibility under a criminal law theory of command responsibility.

Horst's misgivings were multiplied by obvious errors in Wiesenthal's text. He wrote:

> Wächter escaped after the war with the help of ODESSA, and was given refuge in a religious college in Rome by Slovak priests who didn't know his identity. His escape had been well planned; he even took his archives along from Bavaria. In 1949 he became very ill and wasn't expected to live long. He told the people in Rome who he was, asked to see his wife, who lived under the name of 'Lotte Pohl' in a near-by refugee camp. He was given the sacraments by Bishop Alois Hudal, the Austrian rector of the German Catholic Church in Rome, and died. He is buried in Rome. Later, an Austrian aristocrat who occasionally helped me asked Bishop Hudal to release Wächter's files. The bishop refused.

This was different from the facts as I now knew them. There was no indication that Otto's efforts to avoid justice were assisted by an organisation known as ODESSA, codename for a supposed organisation that helped Nazis escape Europe, although John le Carré told me he believed that such an organisation might well have existed. Otto was not given refuge by Slovak priests. He did not have an archive in Rome. Charlotte did not use the name 'Lotte Pohl', or live near Rome in a refugee camp. In 1967 Otto's remains were no longer buried in Rome, they were in Salzburg, in Charlotte's garden at Haus Wartenberg.

I approached the Simon Wiesenthal Institute in Vienna, to access the Wächter files they might hold. The request was granted, and several folders on Otto eventually made their way to me.

There was a copy of Otto's file from the Berlin Documentation Centre, containing documents that I already had.

There were two lengthy affidavits, sworn by Wiesenthal in January 1960 and June 1961, drafted for German prosecutors involved in the Lemberg trial. In them Wiesenthal described his years in Lemberg during the war, with accounts of individual acts of wrongdoing of which he was aware. He gave names, and offered reflections on the role of Otto Wächter.

There was a folder of correspondence, under the handwritten title 'Whereabouts of the Wächter Archive'. This contained several letters. The first, written by hand and dated 16 June 1961, came from a man named Theodor Faber who suggested that Bishop Hudal might have information on Wächter. Wiesenthal passed the information to a German prosecutor involved in the Lemberg trial. For several months nothing happened, then in March 1962 West Germany's Central Office for the Administration of Justice informed Wiesenthal that the bishop had been contacted and denied having seen any Wächter archive. Bishop Hudal claimed that 'he only saw Wächter for the first time after he was poisoned and taken to a hospital in Rome, dying' – a lie – and that he was summoned as rector of the German Church to give Otto the last sacrament. The prosecutor concluded: 'I see no possibility of further investigations, as it is proven by this information that Dr Wächter is no longer alive.' The file on Wächter was closed.

The last document in Wiesenthal's file was received in 1987, a letter from an Italian writer. He asked for a photograph of Otto Wächter.

A few weeks later, more documents arrived from the Wiesenthal archive, in Vienna. One was of particular interest. Ten typed pages, in German, apparently undated. Reading like an affidavit, it was signed by Rosa Stephenson, who lived in Vienna's 14th district. Her brother Carl was, I learned, a writer and publisher.

Miss Stephenson worked as a secretary in Otto's government, first in Kraków, then in Lemberg. 'I have forgotten names, streets and places, due to the shock all of this caused in me, a constant chain of fright and horror.' She had photographs but they were stolen as she returned to Vienna.

She arrived in Kraków in August 1940, to work as a typist in the Department of Economy. She expected to work for the Government General for one year, but stayed for four. 'Dr Wächter was governor,' she recorded, 'the very same Dr Wächter who had initiated the Dollfuss coup.' She offered a description of Charlotte's husband and Horst's father:

> The almost boyish face of Dr Wächter posed a stark contrast to his eyes and his speech. Although he spoke calmly and hardly loud, his voice was like steel and so were his eyes. It was known: what he said was the law. He worked fanatically, required the same from others, and was highly ambitious. He had a tremendous organisational talent and his leadership was immensely rigid. He knew exactly what he wanted.

Otto was one of the 'men in power', the gentlemen under whom she served, the ones who 'worked together throughout the tragedy of the Jews'. Yet, she recorded, 'none of these gentlemen got their hands dirty, they "only" gave the orders'.

She once observed 'a certain *Oberbereichsleiter Studentkowski*' address a group of young boys, members of the Hitler Youth. 'We are not here to think for ourselves,' the man yelled. 'It is the Führer who thinks for us, we simply carry out what he orders. And even if we sometimes believe that something is not right and just – we have to do it nonetheless!' Others observed, approvingly. 'Dr Wächter was present,' she wrote.

In 1941 Rosa Stephenson was transferred to Lemberg. The situation there was bleak, 'a wild mess', a place without order or hygiene. When she arrived Dr Lasch was governor. By her account, it was due to him that no ghetto had been built by February 1942, when he was removed and replaced by Otto. This was 'despite its construction having been ordered many times'. Lasch was replaced by a successor with a track record of building ghettos and emptying them.

'Then came Dr Wächter. The ghetto was built, the persecutions began, the rules became stricter.' Increasingly harsh measures were taken, with raids undertaken in basements, under floorboards, in flats, everywhere, hunting for Jews and those who helped them. 'When Dr Wächter realised that his commands were not being fully obeyed, he called for help. Himmler arrived, known as the "bloodhound", cruelty personified. One look at his eyes was enough to understand that he was abhorrent, a man without feelings. He was like a robot, mercilessly performing his assigned duties.'

Rosa Stephenson observed the killings that followed, and recorded some of the details she encountered.

One Saturday I wanted to get out of town, just to escape from all of this. I randomly cycled around. When I was close to a bridge I saw a group of people, so I got off and started pushing my bike, waiting for the group to pass. [. . .] I was haunted for weeks by their deep-set eyes filled with so much hopelessness, horror, and despair! They were Jews. Out there was Kloparov [I believe this is how the station prior to Lemberg was called; it was some sort of goods yard]. [. . .] most of the wagons of the arriving trains would be uncoupled here – in them were deportees; their hermetically sealed doors would be opened, the bodies of the starved and suffocated would be thrown out, the others would be sent to the compound – and shunted onto a siding. The time of gasifications had begun. A pipe would be pushed through a little opening and gas would be injected. [. . .]

Everyone knew what was going on. 'They all knew, all of them.' Some might not have acted personally, but they passed the commands along, 'all the way down to those who have been blamed'.

Rosa Stephenson left Lemberg in 1944. The cause was the discovery that she had a Jewish grandparent.

Wiesenthal died in 2005.

I did what I could to find support for Horst's belief that Wiesenthal might have been involved in the revenge killing of one or more Nazis. I found nothing, although John le Carré expressed his belief that Jewish vengeance teams did exist, and that they engaged in selective acts of killing. He mentioned a few books and examples, including a notorious attempt to poison the water supply of a small town, used by a million people. He recalled a big, handsome former BBC man who told him he was part of a Jewish assassination group that worked in Latin America. 'Mainly we hanged them,' he told le Carré.

'Nobody quite knows the number of, as you might say, deserving ex-Nazis who were privately assassinated,' le Carré told me. Although Wiesenthal was prone to 'fantasies and boasting', he didn't believe the famed Nazi hunter would have been involved in any act of killing.

'I met Wiesenthal once,' he added, 'in Vienna, in 1962.' He was statesmanlike, seated behind a vast desk, ostentatiously covered with many files. A real spook would have insisted on a bare desk. 'Why do you live in Vienna, the heartland of anti-Semitism?' le Carré asked him. In retelling the response, he adopted a fine middle European accent, one that reminded me of my grandfather.

'If you are studying the disease,' Wiesenthal told le Carré, 'you have to live in the swamp.'

51

Liver

A colleague at my university introduced me to Professor Massimo Pinzani, one of the world's leading experts on the human liver and its diseases. Also based at University College London, he directs the Institute for Liver and Digestive Health, at the Royal Free Hospital, a stone's throw from Hampstead Heath, near to where I live. I had walked below the windows of his office for years.

Professor Pinzani was sturdy and stout, an Italian mastiff in a fine blue suit, with eyes that welcomed, and pronounced eyebrows. In advance of meeting he asked to see the material I had on Otto's medical condition in July 1949. I sent along the two-page 'Patient File', the letters Otto sent to Charlotte after he fell ill, Dr Marchesani's brief account, and Hedi Dupré's two letters to Charlotte.

A man of science, Professor Pinzani proceeded with method and deliberation. He would go forward only on the basis of what was known, he explained. He was not interested in speculation, but happy to gossip and share anecdotes. We went through Otto's letters, chronologically and methodically.

Monday, 4 July 1949, the day on which Otto told Charlotte he had a fever of 41 or 42 degrees. 'At this point it could be anything,' Professor Pinzani said, quite gravely. 'It could be a viral infection, not necessarily connected to a particular meal or a swim.'

The fever rose and fell, Otto vomited, he took quinine. That wasn't because of any thought about malaria, Professor Pinzani explained, simply that aspirin wasn't widely available in those days. Quinine was the old-fashioned way of reducing the temperature of the body.

On Tuesday, 5 July, Otto felt so weak he could barely get to the toilet. 'Getting sicker,' Professor Pinzani interpreted. On Wednesday, 6 July, the fourth day, doctors were speculating about typhus or something 'gastric'. Jaundice was mentioned in a note, for the first time. 'A doctor seeing Wächter's symptoms would focus on what was common in Rome at that time, which explains the reference to typhus.'

There were sewage problems, plenty of rats. Professor Pinzani knew that, because he was Italian. The mention of 'gastric' was a mystery. It's merely an adjective, one that related to matters of the stomach. Perhaps they suspected food poisoning.

As for the mention of jaundice, the doctors must have perceived a yellow aspect to Otto's complexion. The jaundice could be a symptom of one of two things. It could be due to a severe infection, an 'intravascular haemolysis', which would mean that red blood cells were being damaged by the contamination. This would lead to a huge increase of haemoglobin, which was transformed by the liver into biliverdin, then bilirubin. The liver eliminated the bilirubin into the bile, which entered the intestine.

The other possibility, Professor Pinzani explained, was damage to the liver, unable to handle this 'new load'. Without biochemical tests, however, it could not be known if the liver was damaged. 'If you have conjugated bilirubin in circulation, it has escaped into the bile because of damage to the liver.' Modern tests would look at liver enzymes, which would be very high if the liver was damaged.

Professor Pinzani reminded me that in Italy, in 1949, the treatment options would have been very different to those available today. Penicillin had only just been introduced, possibly available for American soldiers, but not someone like Otto, 'a normal person in Europe'.

I enquired about the possibility of poisoning, by human intervention. Professor Pinzani was unwilling to take the bait. He wanted to be methodical, not reach a premature conclusion. Still, he couldn't help himself. 'It doesn't sound like a poisoning, to be honest.'

He offered some reasons. Otto's letters described a high fever, which was a significant indicator that pointed to a strong immune reaction due to an infection. 'With poison you might become yellow and die, but you wouldn't necessarily develop a fever. Poisoning is a toxic event, not one that involves the immune system, which raises the body's temperature.'

Could a poison produce these symptoms? He identified three possibilities. Arsenic, cyanide and, if we were to be banal, rat poison. The last was a crude anti-coagulant, eaten by the rat, which entered the bloodstream and caused internal haematoma. He didn't think that's what happened to Wächter. He may have been on the Ratline, Professor Pinzani said, but he doubted he was exposed to rat poison.

'To me it looks like he has a serious infection.'

He was fit, swam in the Tiber, did daily exercises on the roof of the Vigna Pia monastery. 'The high fever was not inconsistent with his being fit and healthy. A high fever is a positive sign, a healthy body fighting strongly to get rid of a bacteria or parasite.' Buko Rathmann described Otto as fit and healthy. 'These microorganisms cannot withstand a temperature of more than 37, so you basically fry them by keeping your body temperature high.'

We turned to other documents.

Dr Marchesani's letter mentioned a high fever and a possible bowel infection. That meant they were thinking about typhus.

Frau Dupré's letter referred to a possible infection, 'maybe the liver'. 'The liver is mentioned because he was jaundiced, although that could be due to a multiple organ failure.'

As his condition deteriorated, Otto was finally given penicillin, as well as dextrose, to build up his strength. By now he was barely eating. On Wednesday, 13 July, in the last hours, he greeted Frau Dupré. 'It's getting much, much better.'

It wasn't, and he died later that evening. The Santo Spirito Hospital prepared a document which referred to 'yellow liver atrophy' and 'icterus gravis' (severe jaundice), an indication of leptospirosis, a condition more popularly referred to as Weil's disease. This was named in honour of Adolf Weil, a German Jewish physician, who first identified the disease in an article he wrote in 1886 (a year later Dr Weil lost his voice forever, when he caught tuberculosis of the larynx).

The report of the Santo Spirito also mentioned that Otto was diabetic. 'That means he had pancreatic failure,' Professor Pinzani explained. As a result of the infection he lost the beta cells and became instantly diabetic. It didn't mean he had a clinical history of diabetes.

Reading the Santo Spirito document prompted Professor Pinzani to reflect aloud. He thought there were three possible infections.

Typhus. This was unlikely, as symptoms other than fever were lacking.

Fulminant hepatitis, due to hepatitis A, possibly caught while swimming, in the River Tiber or Lake Albano. This too he ruled out, as the clinical picture described in the letters was too complex, and went beyond mere liver failure. Something caused pancreatic failure. 'It's likely he died of lung failure, a cardiovascular arrest.'

Leptospirosis, Weil's disease, was the third possibility. 'It fits everything.' The doctors treating him reached this conclusion, which indicated they were aware of the disease at the Santo Spirito Hospital. Actually, he added, it was endemic in Italy at the time, not rare at all. Ninety per cent of cases were mild, like a bad flu, 10 per cent could be serious, maybe fatal, especially if the patient wasn't protected from potential multi-organ failure.

Weil's disease is caused by contact with contaminated water. It could be river or lake water, contaminated by the urine of a diseased rat or dog. The animal could be a carrier, but it didn't necessarily get sick. Otto could easily have caught it swimming, in a river or lake. He might have swallowed a little water, or it could have come into contact with his conjunctiva, if water splashed on his face. Or he might have had an open wound, which could be as small as a shaving cut. That was all you needed to succumb. Weil's disease was bad luck.

Professor Pinzani did a little research of his own. There was plenty online about the dangers of swimming in the Tiber, or rowing. He mentioned the *Circolo Canottieri Roma*, the city's famous rowing club on the Tiber. 'I've been invited a few times,' he said with a big laugh, 'not the kind of place you go in flip-flops, or to eat pizza.' It was peopled by actors and parliamentarians and other famous names, a lido where you could swim, but in a pool that took water from the river that is then filtered and purified.

Lake Albano had stagnating water, he said, but the river was worse. 'Think of all the rats there may have been in the sewage in Rome, in 1949.'

He returned to another factor. Charlotte described the state of her husband's body as being 'black as a Negro', when she saw him lying in the mortuary at the Campo Verano cemetery. One feature of leptospirosis is a condition called 'intravascular coagulation', a form of subcutaneous haemorrhage. At time of death the patient would have haematomas. As the haemoglobin oxidised, it made the skin look darker. 'It causes a subcutaneous haemorrhage, makes the body look black, and in the days before death it is a terminal event.'

Otto Wächter probably had this when he died, Professor Pinzani said. The summer heat would then have speeded up the process, as the diffusion of the haemorrhage was already fast because the blood vessels were open. It went in stages. 'When you get to this kind of situation, where it is total and affects the internal organs, you are decomposing, you are gone.' And, he added, you are 'gone in black', as the haemorrhaging of blood affects all parts of the body, turning it dark.

Were the symptoms compatible with an act of poisoning by human hand?

It would have to be a very sophisticated act of poisoning, Professor Pinzani said. 'I assume the poisoner doesn't get a sample of *Leptospira japonica* culture and slip it into Wächter's coffee.' He would go with something simpler. On the other hand, he mused, there were crazy people around, so anything was possible. 'But if I was the head of a spy service and wanted to kill Wächter, I would never think of leptospirosis.'

Anyway, he said, 'if Wächter was a Nazi criminal, they'd say, "Let's get him, take him to Nuremberg, hang him", no? Why bother to poison him? Better to catch him, publicly try him, show they'd got a Nazi criminal.'

Professor Pinzani was reasonably certain of his conclusions. With bones, he said, and modern CSI technology, you'd be able to get more information. You might find the DNA or RNA of the bacteria. After all, they'd found DNA and genetic diseases in Egyptian bones from three thousand years ago. Unlike Sue Black, he thought they might find something in a set of bones from 1949.

'If I have to make a bet, I'd say he got leptospirosis, it's the most likely clinical diagnosis.' That fitted too with the sense of the doctors in Rome. 'I doubt very much that a *Leptospira* culture was dropped into his soup.' It could be done, but you'd need a bacteriological laboratory to create a culture in a high concentration, which would have to be swallowed in a liquid that wasn't too hot. 'I have no idea how much you'd need, or what it would taste like.'

The conversation drew to a close. 'I'm hooked on this story,' Professor Pinzani said, 'I'm an Italian.'

It was improbable that Otto was poisoned. He died because he liked to swim. Horst would be disappointed.

52

2018, Hagenberg

I returned to Hagenberg to complete the podcast series. I wanted to share with Horst the materials on Karl Hass, the trip to Albuquerque and the Lucid family and the science lessons obtained. It seemed that there was little point in once more raising the body of his father from the grave. There was something else I wanted to talk about with Horst: in any large collection of documents there is always something you miss, and in this case it was a letter that seemed to have been introduced unintentionally. It was a note, a short email from Horst to his nephew Otto, sent several years before we met.

The castle was in rude health. Dario, a nephew from Palermo in Sicily, the son of Liesl, who expected to receive Otto's remains from Rome after the disinterment from Campo Verano ten years after he was first buried, had moved in and spruced the place up. The Great Hall was tidy, the windows repaired and polished, a large table placed in the centre of the room. It was covered in a fine white tablecloth, laid for four guests. Over lunch we talked.

Horst recognised the trouble with exhumation. 'Thank you for your continued effort to find out the truth about my father's murder,' he wrote in response to the expert report. Unfortunately, it turned out he had no rights in respect of his father's grave, as he didn't contribute to its upkeep. That was taken care of by a niece who inherited Charlotte's farmhouse in Fieberbrunn from her own mother, Horst's sister Traute. He asked her for permission to exhume, but received 'no reaction whatsoever'. The only path to exhumation would be 'to convince the mayor of Fieberbrunn of the importance of my father and his final fate'.

Horst was unmoved by the scientific views of Professor Black and Professor Pinzani, and sceptical that the cause of death was leptospirosis. The idea of a deliberate act of poisoning was more attractive. 'I don't understand why Wiesenthal hated my father so much,' he declared once more, although he seemed to accept it was unlikely that the famed Nazi hunter was also a poisoner. He accepted too that the Americans, in general, didn't go around poisoning people.

By a process of elimination that left the Soviets, with Karl Hass as prime suspect on their behalf. 'He knew he would be killed by the Soviets,' Horst muttered, because he favoured the Ukrainians and was strongly anti-communist. 'I suppose that Karl Hass went to my father to propose him to work for the Americans.' This would have been a proposal for which Otto would have had no problem, he now believed, in contradiction to the views he expressed on a previous occasion.

We returned to the subject of his father's actions, and a comparison of the public execution of fifty Poles in Bochnia in December 1939 and the Fosse Ardeatine killings in March 1944, for which Hass was convicted of 'crimes against humanity'. There was a difference between the two, Horst thought, because the Bochnia act was a 'reprisal killing', of the kind that every army carried out. 'My father didn't decide to kill them, some judge from the Gestapo did.' He was present at the killings, I said, and explained that I hoped to find an album of photographs that was said to exist. 'He *had* to be present,' Horst replied, as the representative of the Kraków government, citing Otto's letter to Charlotte. 'He wrote, "Tomorrow, I have to have 50 Poles publicly shot,"' Horst said. 'Not, "I am glad I have to kill these people" or "I want to kill them" – he writes that he *has* to kill them.' The German text was, he said, very clear.

What about Otto's order to create the ghetto in Kraków, and place Jews there? Horst accepted this was a severe action, one he regretted. However, the action of creating a ghetto did not of itself address the future fate of Jews who happened to be moved there. 'One didn't know what would follow, it was not a pure act of murder.' At this point he mentioned that Charlotte's grandfather, August von Scheindler, may have been Jewish, which was why his mother never got an *Ariernachweis*, the certificate to prove Aryan origins.

The conversation was sharp, our differences stark, yet Horst still felt positive about our relationship, as he considered me to be open-minded. 'I thought you could change your mind, evolve,' he said, 'and there is some progress in our relationship.' He wanted to be positive. 'I'm satisfied that you are still interested in the whole story, it's a good feeling I have.' But, he wished to make clear, he didn't like the documentary film because it sought to show his father as a criminal.

As for the podcast, he hoped it would avoid clichés about the Nazis, and encourage listeners to keep an open mind, to understand why Otto became a Nazi, and inform them as to the great love that existed between his parents. The world needed to know about that. He thought Otto and Charlotte would be happy to see us going over the papers together. After all, Horst said, Charlotte spent the last years of her life trying to persuade journalists and others to look at the materials. 'That was why she kept the documents.' A BBC programme would make her happy, he thought – since she loved England – apparently having forgotten about a letter that Charlotte wrote to Austrian radio, to complain about one of its broadcasts about Otto. 'She wanted to preserve, to explain for their children and grandchildren, to show how it is and how the reality was.' How her reality was, I might have interjected.

Charlotte's reality was reflected in a tape she recorded on the twenty-eighth anniversary of her husband's death, offered to the children as an act of thanksgiving.

'Otto was a sensitive, joyful, optimistic life personified,' she told them.

> He always took pleasure in doing what he thought was the right thing to do. He only became ill when he had to do things – as a soldier, as governor, as the highest functionary in charge of a country, Poland – things he had to do, without wanting to. Till the very end he refused to compromise his conscience, but sometimes he just couldn't do what he thought was right.

And, she continued, there was a broader message. 'Everyone has the light and dark sides. The sun in their heart and the deepest and grisliest darkness. We should only see the good things in everyone.' This struck a chord with Horst, a reminder of his mother's belief that you'd never convince people 'that you never meant to do anything evil'.

Nevertheless, the rest of the family was increasingly unhappy with Horst's efforts at engagement. 'I can understand them,' Horst said. He reminisced about nephew Otto's fight with Charlotte, the one that was prompted by a carpet that she brought home to Austria from Lemberg, towards the end of the war. This was the cue for the document I had brought with me, the one buried in Charlotte's papers, a short email Horst wrote to nephew Otto on 4 December 2007. Maybe I missed it because it was a modern document, or because it was in German, or typed, and I had trained my eye to settle on the older documents or the writing of others. Sometimes we do not see what is immediately before us.

I gave a copy to Horst, which he recognised immediately. 'Yes, I wrote this,' he said.

'*Liebe N.O.!*' he read out. 'Dear Nephew Otto!' He held the sheet close to his face, read it once to himself, then aloud, in German.

Dear N.O.!

Attached are the two letters of your grandfather that I want to compare with Himmler's calendar on Wednesday. They incriminate him more than the documents known to me. It does not help. He knew everything, observed it and consented in principle.

A sad O.H.

'A sad O.H.'– a sad Onkel Horst, a sad Uncle Horst.

The two letters, from Otto to Charlotte in August 1942, attached to the email, were familiar to me. The first letter was written on 16 August, in Kraków. Horst marked up the lines in which Otto reported that there was 'much to do in Lemberg' after Charlotte left, including 'sending of workers to labour camp for the Reich (already 250,000 from the District!) and the current large Jewish operations (*Judenaktionen*)'. Otto ended the letter with a message: 'With Hitler – all or nothing'.

He sent a second letter four days later, to report on Himmler's visit to Lemberg. It went well, he reported, so well that he felt 'almost ashamed' about the many positive things the Reichsführer said of him. 'Everything was very nice and amicable.'

Horst recognised the implications, back in 2007, the significance of what his father was saying. Otto knew everything, observed it, consented. A decade later, the discomfort was palpable, a tension between what he wrote then and the positive gloss he managed to put on the same events when he talked to me, to explain his father's actions.

Yet, once again, Horst dug deep, and did so nimbly, somehow able to conjure up a quick explanation.

'Today I wouldn't say this.' On first reading the letters they caused 'a shock', because Otto was saying he was fine with Himmler. Horst's reaction had evolved. 'It's different today, because I've got so many other things.' He was referring to new material, which didn't show his father as being quite so culpable. Yet, the documents left a trace, total escape was difficult. 'He was really culpable, he was employed, he was acting on . . .' Horst ran out of words.

'I wouldn't say that my father killed 800,000 Jews or something like that. I wouldn't. I wouldn't agree with Wiesenthal.' He reverted to a familiar line, the requirements of filial duty. 'I have to do it for my parents, to find good things.'

The words evoked Charlotte's complaint to Melitta Wiedemann. 'I do not want my children to believe that he is this war criminal, who has murdered hundreds of Jews, a matter that was never within his power, something he didn't promote and was not able to prevent', she told the journalist. Otto declined to visit the 'Jewish camps in Poland', she explained, because, as he told her, 'I cannot help them, and if I cannot help someone when my hands are tied, why should I look at that which I do not see as positive?' That which was not his concern he did not want to know about, Charlotte suggested, adding a gloss of her own: 'One does not look at things if one knows that people are being tortured and murdered.'

Horst could have destroyed the documents back in 2007, when he first saw them, but didn't.

He could have kept the documents to himself, but chose to share them with his nephew Otto, and then with me, although perhaps by inadvertence.

Horst was an open man, in a sense, and for this he paid a price. I remained silent, there was nothing left to say. The documents and tapes spoke for themselves, then and now.

Horst skipped to another subject, the path we had travelled. 'A great journey,' he said, one he had to take, one for which he was thankful. It helped with the castle, allowed him to engage openly with others, to be honest.

'Those who come say, "Oh, you were the Nazi boy and you write about this," but they don't reproach me, they don't say I want to hide things . . .'

EPILOGUE

'There is the condition . . . called the *Idée Fixe*, which may be trifling in character, and accompanied by complete sanity in every other way.'

Arthur Conan Doyle, *The Adventure of the*
Six Napoleons, 1903

Rome, 13 July 2019

The podcast was broadcast in the autumn that followed the visit to Hagenberg. Two episodes a week over the course of a month, it produced responses that were many and, occasionally, unexpected.

From Oregon, a student at Haus Wartenberg from the 1960s wrote with memories of 'The Baroness'. Stern and uncompromising, she recalled, one who claimed to be a good Catholic and knew nothing of Nazis. Another visitor to Salzburg, from England, who was there in the early 1980s and later became a screenwriter, wrote a play about 'Tante Lotte'. He gave it the title *Unrepentant*.

Peter Scharkow, the son of Charlotte's housekeeper in Kraków, who was a few years older than Horst, sent a memory about Otto's return from work each evening. The little boy liked to stand with the guards and click his heels in harmony with them. He sent a photograph, Charlotte and Otto with newborn Horst.

The grandson of a British soldier sent extracts of a diary, along with a photograph that carried an inscription on the back. 'Body of SS General who committed suicide', it said, and showed Odilo Globočnik on the ground, covered by a sheet. The grandfather's regimental record explained that he 'poisoned himself with prussic acid while walking the 150 yards between [Paternion] Castle yard and the prison'.

A woman wrote about her father's return to Hanover, twenty-five years after he fled, in 1934. He recalled the view from his school, a large advertising hoarding on the gable end of a building, and was surprised, when he went back, that the hoarding was still there. '*Persil bleibt Persil*', 'Persil is always Persil'. 'It gave me the horrors and we left Hanover immediately.'

Otto's false identity prompted numerous communications. Why not contact the Red Cross, to see if Alfred (or Alfredo) Reinhardt was issued with documents? I did, and learned that he was, a Red Cross travel pass issued in 1947. It had the same date of birth, family information and signature as the identity card Otto used in Rome. Dr Reinhardt, I would learn, was a member of the Nazi Party in Vienna in 1932, who fled to Munich after the July Putsch. He became an engineer and helped build the *Kehlsteinhaus*, the Eagle's Nest, at Berchtesgaden, near Hitler's retreat at Obersalzberg, where the real Reinhardt served as Martin Bormann's deputy. He fled to Salta in Argentina in 1947, where he lived until his death in 1998.

Several medical doctors wrote about the cause of Otto's death. What about paraquat, one suggested, a herbicide? No, as it produced different symptoms and was not generally available until long after Otto died. Another thought Otto's symptoms could have been caused by *Amanita phalloides*, the death cap mushroom, prevalent in Italy. I contacted an expert in Germany, who explained that *Amanita* poisoning did not generate an early fever. 'The final disease of Wächter was certainly an infection,' he stated, and confirmed Professor Pinzani's assessment of leptospirosis, and that death would have been 'an ordeal'. He felt compelled to add a personal observation: 'I never understood why priests in the Vatican were hiding these persons.'

Tom Lucid wrote from Albuquerque – 'I was thinking of my half-brother' – and enquired about the health of Viktor Williams. He still hoped they might yet be in touch, and wondered if I had a photograph of Charlotte von Heyking, Viktor's mother.

Horst waited for the sixth episode to make contact. He complained that Otto's character was misrepresented, that his father 'was not eager to kill Poles and Jews'. He wrote again after the final broadcast, sanguine but less than delighted. The series reflected the prejudices of others, and failed to acknowledge the reality of the double administration in German-occupied Poland: the civilian government run humanely by Otto, and the murderous SS government run by others. Still, he agreed, it would be good to have a final conversation, to tie up loose ends. This seemed sensible, as I had new material I wanted to share with him.

As spring turned to summer, I returned to Hagenberg, an eighth visit, a few weeks after Horst celebrated his eightieth birthday. A new website welcomed 'connoisseurs of ancient mythology' to the castle. He and his nephew Dario offered food, a bed and the bathroom, the one with the old, metal Persil advertisement.

We talked, as always, in Horst's room, on the first floor. The portrait of Josef was above the bed, near the other photographs, Otto in SS uniform, godfather Seyss-Inquart tucked in beside him, the sad portrait of Charlotte. Little had changed, although I noticed the prints of Kraków were no longer there. 'I've given everything back,' Horst said.

Times were not easy. His sister-in-law, the widow of his brother Otto, had recently died. In her home she kept a torn-up copy of a recent article I'd written, in an Austrian newspaper. Horst should not have been talking with me, a nephew told him. He was *'ein Sargnagler'*, one who puts the nail in the coffin. At the funeral, Horst was received distantly, but maintained a robust attitude. 'You cannot hide things, they have their own rhythm, they come out.'

He regretted our differences of interpretation, but not our engagement, even on the podcast. 'I got so much from you to confirm the importance of the story of my parents.' His views had not shifted, nor had mine. If anything, his had firmed up. Otto was not a part of Nazi brutalism, he continued to insist. He would focus on the castle, a project 'practically sponsored by my father', whom he had succeeded in doing 'something positive'.

I brought along some photographs to Hagenberg, ones not available in Charlotte's papers. 'I am sure she removed some letters, so maybe some photographs too,' he said. There was once one of Horst Stützen, the young soldier she fell in love with, but it disappeared. The absence of photos with Hitler was notable, as they met several times. 'He had no direct access to Hitler, he was not close to him,' Horst said, although he recalled a photo from the early days, also disappeared.

I showed him the large photograph taken by Josef Hoffmann in 1931, the Reichsführerschule group. Horst peered at it, interested, and quickly spotted his father. 'I have not seen that photo,' he said, somewhat wistful. The second photograph was taken three years later, also in Germany, shortly before the July Putsch, standing between Frauenfeld and Hitler. 'It could be him, but I don't think so,' Horst sighed.

Did he want to see photographs of the Bochnia executions? I explained I had finally found a set in a Warsaw archive, after a lengthy search, but the images were distressing. Yes, he said, he wanted to see them. I showed him three. The first showed a line of young men in a field, fear etched across their faces. Selected because they were Polish and in Bochnia, they stood with hands on heads, or before their faces, or behind their backs. A few wept, one lay in the snow, collapsed.

A second photograph captured the moment of death, of soldiers, rifles and smoke. Some victims were already on the ground, others stood with their backs to the executioners, heads bowed. Soldiers observed, and in the background a line of officers watched in coats, one long and black, which reflected the light cast by the snow, a shiny buckle visible. 'I think that's Otto,' I said.

After the killings, officers in peaked caps hanging around. One wore a black coat lined with a fur collar, another held a cigarette holder, a third looked at the camera anxiously, inquisitive or fearful. Otto stood in the middle, a leader with no hint of emotion, arms nonchalant, feet apart, face resolute, an image of authority. 'Tomorrow, I have to have 50 Poles publicly shot,' he wrote to Charlotte. Here he was, in a full-length black leather coat, a white line of reflection running along its length, the buckle prominent, job done.

Horst remained silent. For a time he seemed lost for words, then he spoke, quietly. 'That is for sure an SS coat.' Silence. 'Yes, he was present.' Silence. 'Seyss-Inquart must be there too.' Silence.

Did the image inspire any particular feelings? 'I would say . . . my mother said somewhere that my father was very much against shooting . . . he wouldn't agree . . . he was very much against shooting *Geiseln* . . . hostages . . . yes, this shooting was also remarked in the Nuremberg trial . . . and I of course . . . as governor of course . . . I don't think he felt very happy about that . . .'

Osman arrived to cut Horst's hair. As he was combed and trimmed we talked about the origins of his parents' anti-Semitism, the extended family, and his daughter Magdalena. 'My mother loved her,' he said, but his relationship with her was strained by her conversion to Islam and marriage to Galib. Recently she had displayed a degree of hostility towards Otto, which bothered Horst. 'It shows no respect, after all the work I did.'

As to the cause of Otto's death, Horst maintained the belief that Karl Hass poisoned him. His words reminded me to share a new document, one that emerged only after the broadcast of the podcast. Norman Goda was prompted to return to the US National Archives, to try one more time to find the missing Wächter file. He came across a single document, one missed in previous searches. It was requested, communicated and passed on to me. It required no explanation, and Norman offered none.

The two-paragraph letter was typed on notepaper of the CIC 430th Detachment, signed by Thomas Lucid, and the words 'Los Angeles' stamped on it. The subject line read: 'ITALY – SS General WAECHTER'. It was dated 17 May 1949, just three weeks after Otto arrived in Rome.

The letter reported something passed to the CIC by 'Source 10/6369'. This was a reference to Hass, who had received the information from 'a fairly high-ranking Vatican official who is interested in German refugees residing in Italy'. This was Bishop Hudal, who received the information in 'late April 1949'. Otto met the bishop on 30 April, I reminded Horst, the 'religious gentleman'.

The information that Bishop Hudal passed to Karl Hass was set out in the second paragraph of the letter:

Ex-SS General WAECHTER, onetime Governor of Poland (KRAKAU) during the war has been reported as residing in Rome.

WAECHTER has an International Red Cross passport bearing the name REINHARDT, Karl. WAECHTER alias REINHARDT allegedly has contacted an Italian Intelligence official and has offered his services to the Italians. WAECHTER reportedly asserted that he has organised partisan bands in the mountainous regions of Austria and Germany capable of waging guerrilla warfare against Communist troops when the moment arrives.

Horst digested the words. He read the letter a second time. It confirmed years of detective work, the connections between Hass, Lucid, Hudal and Wächter. It left no doubt that Bishop Hudal shared the news of Otto's arrival immediately, which meant that the Americans were aware of his presence in Rome from the moment he arrived. They even knew his false identity, that he was using the name Reinhardt. It made clear that for nearly three months the Americans took no steps to apprehend a man indicted for mass murder. It also made clear that Otto's fear of the Americans was misplaced. They knew where he was, all along.

Horst said nothing, not even a reaction to the suggestion that Otto had offered to work with the Italians. He wanted to draw a line. 'With you and my father everything is more or less finished'. That was all he said, somewhat abruptly. He had a bigger project, the restoration of the castle, to which he would devote himself. He hoped I might help.

The next morning we shared an early breakfast. As I prepared to leave, I noticed a small colour photograph, recently hung on a wall in the entrance room to the castle. It showed the six children of Charlotte and Otto, taken in the 1970s, standing in a line. Linde, Heide, Horst, Traute, Lieselotte and Otto – left to right, young to old, alive and dead. The six produced twenty-three grandchildren for Charlotte and Otto, but only one seemed to want to engage with me, in any real way. I did not say this to Horst.

I told him I was driving across Austria, to follow in the footsteps of his parents. That was true. I didn't say that I would make the journey in the company of Magdalena and her husband. I said nothing because she wanted to be the one to tell her father, when she was ready.

The trip with Magdalena was the most unexpected consequence of the podcast. We had met twice, first at the Purcell Room, five years earlier, then a few months later at the Kunsthistorisches Museum in Vienna, where we stood together before Bruegel's *The Fight Between*

Carnival and Lent. A few hours after the final episode of the podcast was broadcast, she wrote to me for the first time, an email composed with care. The subject line was: '*Ratline* Podcast and my father Horst and grandparents'.

'I am writing you this email trusting that you will not mention it to my father,' she wrote (later she gave me permission to reproduce the communication). She had recently married and was trying to understand the family's past. She had engaged with a number of different therapies, and some had helped. 'I have come to the conclusion that my grandfather and grandmother were very aware of what they did and somehow never regretted it.'

'For me, this family heritage has been a burden from which I am slowly recovering,' she continued. 'Knowing that I myself am not guilty but still feeling the family's guilt opposite to the rest of my family.' She listened to all the episodes of the *Ratline*, with Horst. 'I want to tell you that I really like the way it is done. I am happy that you portrayed my father fairly.'

Later that day we talked by telephone. She hoped to see the materials referred to in the podcast, the letters and tape recordings – she had not been aware of their existence – and said she would like to meet. A few weeks later we did; a rendezvous near the Hofburg, the site of the *Deutsche Klub* and the July Putsch, where Charlotte and Otto stood with Hitler on the Heldenplatz, where Otto had his office. In the building, accompanied by her husband Galib, we descended the grand marble staircase at the end of which her grandparents agreed that Otto would take the position of state secretary and join the new Nazi government. It was a key moment, a decision that changed the lives of Charlotte and Otto, and those of their children and grandchildren. A short and decisive moment with a lasting and difficult legacy.

Together we drove to the house that Charlotte bought on a hill at Klosterneuburg Weidling, on the outskirts of Vienna. It was in a state of disrepair, but we enjoyed the view and marvelled at the many wallpapers, so old and faded that they might have been hung by Charlotte. At the Villa Mendl, we peered over the wall into the large gardens. Magdalena would tell me that it wasn't quite true that Horst had returned everything, he still had a porcelain service from the villa, one which Charlotte kept. Later, I would suggest to Horst that he ought to return it, and he said he would if I found the heirs, which I did.

Six months after that visit to the Villa Mendl, I left Horst and the castle to meet Magdalena for a second time, on this occasion in the small town of Mariapfarr, in Austria's mountainous Lungau region. This was where Otto met Buko. I drove past signs for Mürzzuschlag and places with familiar names, like Raingut and Wagrain, Flachau and Mallnitz, where Charlotte met Otto, secretly, laden with provisions. Magdalena awaited outside the large wooden doors of the old church, with Galib. We admired a seventeenth-century fresco, learned that 'Silent Night' was composed here, and stood respectfully before a memorial to the dead from two wars which made no mention of Gestapo atrocities committed against locals. Over lunch, Magdalena reminded me she was not only Austrian but also a New Zealander, as she was born there when Hundertwasser's boat, the *Regentag*, visited. 'The artist was my godfather,' she told me, and expressed an admiration for New Zealand's prime minister, for the words and actions that followed a recent attack that killed fifty-one worshippers in a Christchurch mosque.

Along the valley we made our way towards the Higher Tauern mountains, where Buko and Otto wandered for three years. We passed through St Johann in Pongau, where her grandparents were reunited, then Bad Gastein with its fancy hotels, up to the place where Charlotte would start the long hike up the mountain to the Hagener Hütte. As we walked the trail, Magdalena drew an occasional stare from a passer-by. 'Life as a Muslim in Austria,' she said, a reference to her headscarf. 'Can you imagine what my grandparents would think?'

It was little more than an hour by car from there to Thumersbach, to the house the Wächters acquired in April 1940, appropriated from Governor Rehrl with the help of Ernst Kaltenbrunner. Not a large home, it had a fine view over Lake Zell. As we stood there, admiring a wooden carving of Christ, with the date 1931, a neighbour approached. 'My grandfather was a Nazi and he took the house during the war,' Magdalena told him, surprising him with her candour. It is still owned by the Rehrl family, he told us, adding that he knew nothing of a Wächter interlude.

We paused at Schloss Prielau, which Josef Wächter wanted to buy after the First World War. Today it is a luxury hotel and restaurant, owned by the Porsche family, with a website that explains its history but makes no mention of the residency of sculptor Josef Thorack, with whom Charlotte once visited a nearby bird sanctuary.

In Zell-am-See we spent a night at a hotel, halfway up the Schmittenhöhe mountain, close to the cable car station and the home where the family lived after Thumersbach, long ago demolished. Over dinner we conversed with two couples at an adjoining table, visitors from Israel, perplexed to meet an Austrian Muslim who told them her grandfather constructed the Kraków ghetto.

The next morning we drove to Fieberbrunn, another hour away. We visited Charlotte's house on the mountain, also with a fine view, and stood under the balcony outside her room. Carved into it we saw her initials, *CHvW*. Magdalena told me about her decision to convert, an act of escape, from the tight embrace of a 'very Catholic family'. We tried to imagine the moment in January 1974 when Otto's remains were driven from this house, with its wonderful views, to the nearby cemetery of Fieberbrunn, which we later visited. There we stood silently before the fifth and final resting place of the grave. 'Freiherr Otto and Freifrau Charlotte', the headstone declared.

Our final stop was Salzburg. On Riedlenburger Strasse, I admired the sign for *Hauß Wartenberg*, 1686–1954 it told us, now a cluttered hotel. The website described an establishment that was 'Unconventional and Traditional', which seemed right. I entered alone, saw no guests, just a young man in socks, an employee who handed me a visiting card. As I left, passing through the garden once inhabited by Tante Lotte's pupils, I wondered where she placed her husband's remains, after she brought them here illicitly from the Campo Verano cemetery.

On Anton-Hall-Strasse, Charlotte's first home in the city, the site of the 'hut' at number 2 was occupied by a two-storey mid-century modern building, with a rounded balcony and white roses. Here, Magdalena told me about a family member, a psychoanalyst and neurologist, who treated her and Jacqueline, and three of the Wächter daughters. Later, when I spoke to him, at Magdalena's suggestion, he suggested that Charlotte might have had bipolar disorder. It was, he added, a condition believed to have a genetic component, one that could be passed along generations.

In the centre of Salzburg tourists milled around the Landestheater, awaiting a performance of Rodgers and Hammerstein's *The Sound of Music.* We ate nearby, at an Italian restaurant, seated outdoors. We talked about family and legacy, memory and silence, and how decent people with good families and fine educations could become embroiled in terrible things, or turn a blind eye to them. 'All the cousins are affected by the story of our grandparents,' Magdalena said. I mentioned a conversation several years earlier, with the wife of one of the cousins who, by coincidence, was once a student of mine. She chose a moment when her husband was not present to ask a question: could you ensure that the documentary film is never shown in Austria? I expressed surprise. 'To protect our child,' she explained.

Magdalena asked about the book I was writing, and the photographs I might use. Could she see them? Of course, but warned that some were of a distressing nature. Yes, she wanted to see the three photographs taken at Bochnia, the ones I had shown Horst. We homed in on the faces of the victims, lined up, young men, some boys. The image produced a shock and a strong reaction, one of considerable violence from a person of such a gentle disposition.

As we parted, we agreed the trip had been significant for each of us. Magdalena and Galib returned to Vienna. I spent a night in Salzburg, having visited the house of Stefan Zweig, near the Lanz shop that still sells the linen shirts favoured by Otto.

My daughter joined me the next morning, to cross the Dolomites together, on foot, along the path Otto may have taken. We paused in Berchtesgaden to admire Alfred Reinhardt's engineering prowess, an elevator to the top of the mountain and the Eagle's Nest. 'Why would Wächter take the identity of someone who fled to Argentina?' my daughter asked. I had no answer. Hitler's retreat was now a tourist spot, with few references to a dark past, which surprised her.

The next morning we made our way early to the Ötztal valley, past the 'twinkling lights' of Sölden, Otto's last view of Austria, and reached the village of Vent. A lady at the tourist office assured us that the trail over the Dolomites was open and easily walkable, which proved optimistic. The first leg ran for eight kilometres, along a river valley marked with red and white trail posts, upwards past waterfalls and goats, and a stone refuge on which someone had etched their initials and the year, *1949*. The Martin-Hütte offered a first stop, elderflower juice and pasta at 2,500 metres.

The second leg was only four kilometres but rose to an altitude of 3,000 metres. After big snowfalls in April, and the coldest May in years, we found ourselves hiking knee-deep in snow. It was so arduous that we skipped a modest detour to the place where a glacier's retreat uncovered the mummified remains of a man who died five thousand years earlier. The hike was steep, and the snow so deep, that at times I paused every hundred metres, led by my daughter, whose resolve and strength kept me going. The idea of such a crossing in February, as Otto had done, with skis and at night, seemed impossible.

At the summit, the Similaunhütte, we looked back on Austria, and forward to Italy. On the descent, snow gave way to rock, then a path and pastures and a small river, engorged with spring water. Once again, it was my daughter who kept us to the trail, and found a way across. We arrived in the small town of Vernago, exhausted. Several messages awaited.

One was from Horst. The photographs of Bochnia offered no evidence against his father, he wanted to tell me. He sent a photograph of the porcelain service from Villa Mendl. He once tried to return it, he explained, but those who lived there wanted nothing to do with him.

There was also a message from a Spanish friend, a writer of non-fiction novels, as he calls them, which I admire very much. Continue to Rome, he urged, as he had arranged access to the Sala Baglivi, the room at the Santo Spirito Hospital in which Otto died, which I had not yet gained access to.

The next day my daughter and I made our way to Bolzano. The station and clock tower looked much as it did when Charlotte and Otto parted, at the end of its long platform. My daughter left at Verona; I continued to the Termini station, and spent a few days in Rome and Lake Albano.

At Poggi d'Oro, I was, once again, unable to find Villa Emma.

In the Vatican, I visited the Secret Archives and saw the caged papers of Pius XII, not yet public. Later I stood in the garden of the Istituto Teutonico, before Bishop Hudal's impressive grave. The words 'Der Friede Sei Mit Dir' were engraved on the stone. May peace be with you.

In section 38 of the Campo Verano cemetery I finally managed to locate the site of Otto's first burial. I left a few of his documents and photographs on the rectangle, then watched them slowly blow away.

At Castel Sant'Angelo, on a curve of the Tiber, I looked at the postcard that Charlotte sent Otto from Rome in 1929, just a few days after they first met. Curiously, it depicted the place of his death, two decades later.

My friend the Spanish writer wanted to accompany me to the Santo Spirito Hospital. Why are you interested? I asked, as we sat together in the midst of a vibrant crowd of visitors, inside the Vatican. 'It is more important to understand the butcher than the victim'. That was what he said, a pretty phrase, and one that seemed true.

The hospital was a short distance away. In the heat, we made our way through narrow streets to the Via dei Penitenzieri and stood outside the main gate of the Santo Spirito. Inside, we were met by an art historian, who worked in the hospital library. She led us to the Sala Baglivi, vast and impressive beyond anything we might have imagined, a huge space in the final stages of restoration, strikingly empty. From where we stood, between the two rooms, it took a moment to work out that the photograph taken in 1950, the one with which this book opens, was not of the Sala Baglivi, as I had mistakenly believed, but of its neighbour, the Sala Lancisi.

Here, in the centre of this imposing Renaissance space, near the small chapel with the altar by Palladio, it was possible to imagine the patient in bed nine, a man who believed himself to be hunted but who, it turned out, was not quite as hunted as he thought. We gazed upon the objects that surrounded Otto in the last days of his life: the red bricks of the floor, the latticed beams that crossed the ceiling, the papal inscriptions, the windows and many doors, the light and the shadows.

In the distance, painted on the wall that stood between the Sala Baglivi and the waters of the Tiber, high above a locked wooden door, I noticed a series of faded frescoes. They dated to the fifteenth century, telling a story that described the origins of the hospital, three centuries earlier, a place for foundlings. The frescoes were unexpected, with their images of violence and bloodshed. One scene portrayed a child being killed. The panel was once accompanied by lines from the Bible, a verse from Isaiah, but it had been painted over long before Otto arrived. He saw the image but not the words.

> Their bows will slaughter the young men; they will have no mercy on the fruit of the womb; they will not look with pity on the children.

To the north, a child had returned to her home in Vienna, after our journey across Austria. She chose this moment to compose a few words of her own, and display them on her social media page. When her father saw the words, he asked that they be removed. She told him she could not follow his wishes.

Magdalena wrote: 'My grandfather was a mass murderer.'

Acknowledgements

This book is a team effort. Over the past eight years I have been fortunate to work with many remarkable individuals and institutions, and to each and all I acknowledge my debt and thanks. In some cases, the assistance was significant and extended over time; in others, the input was informal or limited, touching upon a reminiscence or, in one case, a single word. I express my deep gratitude to all, with the caveat that such errors or omissions as have crept into the text are my responsibility alone.

I could not have made this journey without the active and engaged support of Horst von Wächter, over many years, to whom I express special thanks. We have not always been in agreement, and on points of factual interpretation we are marked by significant differences, but at all times Horst has been open and transparent, in a way that is rare. I express my thanks also to Jacqueline, his late wife, and their daughter Magdalena, a person of inspiring courage and fortitude, as well as her generous and wise husband, Gerlot Galib Stanfel. Osman Turan (hairdresser and bodyguard) and nephew Dario have also been helpful with time, food and other advice. Other members of the Wächter family with whom I am or have been in touch have shared valuable insights, and whatever differences we may have about the merits of a work such as this, which shines a spotlight on the past, I deeply appreciate and respect their perspectives and integrity. To my dear friend Niklas Frank, who inadvertently set the ball rolling by introducing me to Horst, and to wonderful Hannelore and exceptional Fransziska, I express familial appreciation.

In the round, the project was catalysed by conversations with Liz Jobey, my editor and friend formerly at the *Financial Times*, who commissioned the initial portrait of Horst, with the support of Caroline Daniel. On that first trip, and subsequently, I benefited greatly from the fine eye of Jill Edelstein, and the acuity of Cullen Murphy, now at *The Atlantic*.

The journey has followed a curious and winding path. Unexpected ideas emerged from the documentary film, *My Nazi Legacy*, and the perspectives of David Evans, Amanda Posey, Finola Dwyer, Nick Fraser and David Charap. The *Ratline* podcast then generated new material, with thanks to Hugh Levinson and Mohit Bakaya at the BBC, brilliant producer Gemma Newby, Joel Lovell, Stephen Fry and Laura Linney, and Sandrine Treiner (France Culture), as well as Catrin Finch, Seckou Keita and Tamsin Davies for music that opens the imagination. It was Bea Hemming, my former editor at Weidenfeld, now at Jonathan Cape, who first observed that the podcast should be a book, one that dug deeper, and she was right.

On the academic side, I owe a huge debt to the late, magnificent and much missed Lisa Jardine, my colleague at UCL, and to the active support of her partner John Hare. I have benefited enormously from the work of two diligent and truly outstanding researchers, Dr James Everest and Lea Main-Klingst, my legal assistant, both of whom led the gargantuan effort of transcription, interpretation, translation and understanding, and did so with humour, wisdom and remarkable professionalism.

We were assisted by a fabulous group of dedicated research assistants, mostly from UCL: Felicitas Benziger, Grega Grobovsek, Hannes Joebstl, Benedikt Lucas, Julia Radaszkiewicz, Beatrice Russo, Riccardo Savona Siemens, Bastian Steuwer and Veren Yildiz, as well as Rebecca Leinen (Oxford). My colleagues at University College London – led by my current and former deans, Professors Piet Eekhout and Hazel Genn, and Professor Richard Moorhead, head of research – along with Luis Monteros Vivoya, and my international law colleagues, have been unstinting in their support for a project which might be thought unusual for a law school.

Along the way, I have encountered many remarkable individuals, generous with time, ideas and voice. Particular thanks are due to Professor Norman Goda (University of Florida); Professor David Kertzer (Brown University); Professor Massimo Pinzani (Royal Free); and Professor Gerald Steinacher (University of Nebraska). Bronisława (Niusia) Horowitz (Kraków), and her brother Ryszard Horowitz offered first-hand experiences, as did Michael Katz; Buko Rathmann and his daughter; Herta Ettingshausen; Thomas Lucid and brother Barney; David Cornwell; a friend in Rome who wishes to remain anonymous; Dr Johan Ickx (Anima Institute); Dame Sue Black and Dr Niamh Nic Daéid (University of Dundee); Pamela Putnam Smith;

Friling Tuvia; Stefanie Waske; and Marco Schrott and his brother Viktor Williams.

I have benefited from the generous assistance of a fine community of writers, scholars, librarians, archivists and museum keepers, around the world. I offer special thanks to Harold Stockhammer, a magical lawyer and detective/historian in Innsbruck who contacted me out of the blue, and never let go, and in Rome Mario Tedeschini Lalli has been a remarkable and generous colleague.

In Argentina, Uki Goñi offered insights on the Ratline's endpoint.

In Austria, assistance came from Simon Adler; Gerhard Baumgartner, my old friend from university and Cage aux Folles days in Cambridge, now director of the Dokumentationsarchiv des österreichischen Widerstandes; René Bienert (Vienna Wiesenthal Institute for Holocaust Studies, VWI); Barbara Habermann (WinterSportMuseum, Mürzzuschlag); Andreas Huber and Linda Erker (University of Vienna, on the Deutsche Klub); Ralph Janik (University of Vienna); Klaus Oblin (undertaker); Dr Astrid Reisinger Coracini (University of Vienna); and Kerstin von Lingen (University of Vienna).

In France, Professor Astrid von Busekist, colleague and translator extraordinaire, offered rare insights.

In Germany, Dr Andreas Eichmüller (NS-Dokumentationszentrum, Munich); Hans Christian Jasch (Wannsee Haus); Dieter Pohl; and my wonderful former editor Nina Sillem.

In Italy, Manfredi Bettoni; Massimo Coccia; Gerardo José Fueyo Bros (embassy of Spain to the Holy See), and his wife; Lutz Klinkhammer (Deutsches Historisches Institut in Rome); Ann Pichey, Mauro Canali; Sandro Portelli; Patrizia Ricci (Santo Spirito Hospital); and Bishop Paul Tighe.

In Poland, Dr Agnieszka Bieńczyk-Missala (Instytut Stosunków Międzynarodowych, Uniwersytet Warszawski); Diana Blonska (National Museum, Kraków); Bożena Krawczyk (Archiwum Warszawa); Olga Laskowska (IPN); Magdalena Ogorek; Żanna Słoniowska; my old friend and colleague Dr Adam Redzik, professor at Warsaw University; and Jacek Soszynski, Institute of the History of Science.

On matters Russian, Nanci Adler and Alla Shevelkina, and Anton Weiss-Wendt, of the Norwegian Center for the Study of the Holocaust and Religious Minorities.

In Ukraine, my dear friends Sofia Dyak (Center for Urban History,

Lviv) and Ivan Horodyskyy (Ukrainian Catholic University).

In the United Kingdom, Keith Lowry, on Höttl; my schoolteacher Laurence Impey, and Eddie Reynolds, on translations.

In the United States, special thanks to archivist Anatol Steck at the United States Holocaust Memorial Museum, and colleagues Alla Dvorkin and Alina Skibinska, who found rare documents in a Polish archive; Eli Rosenbaum and David Rich (US Department of Justice); Eric van Slander (NARA).

On matters medical, Dr Allister Vale (Sandwell and West Birmingham Hospitals NHS Trust); Dr Colin Borland, Kevin Moore (UCL) and Professor Dr Thomas Zilker (Technische Universität München).

In relation to the Red Cross, Naomi Cremasco Rolnick and Deborah Mettraux, and Fania Khan at the ICRC Archives.

Dr Jonathan Sklar offered advice on matters psychoanalytical; Laurent Naouri, on matters musical; Vickie Taylor, Scott Edmonds (International Mapping) and Alex Tait (National Geographic) prepared the maps fabulously as ever; Daniel Alexander offered legal advice, with a wry smile.

Unexpected correspondents offered memories of Haus Wartenberg and other matters, including Mark Ballantyne; John Beddington; Deborah Michel; Peter, Melanie, Chris and Erin Westendorf and the Scharkow family; Sue Springer.

A number of friends and colleagues deserve particular mention. Adriana Fabra, our dearest family friend, joined me as an avid detective and companion in Rome and Poggi d'Oro, where we looked and looked, and sometimes found. In deepest Devon, Louise Rands, with whom I have worked for over three decades, decoded my writing and offered careful, scholarly typing and assistance. And Abigail Asher, attentive to nuance, in particular with the Italian language.

I am fortunate to have a wonderful team of literary agents, led in London by Georgia Garrett, at Rogers, Coleridge & White, who is always there and right, with colleagues Laurence Laluyaux and Stephen Edwards; and in New York, Melanie Jackson, of divine patience and acute insights. At Casarotto, Rachel Holroyd is unbeatable for advice of all kinds, and precision, assisted by Sophie-Marie Neal.

I have been fortunate to work with the very finest of editors: at Weidenfeld & Nicolson, Jenny Lord provided detailed thoughts of the kind of which one dreams; at Alfred Knopf, Victoria Wilson continued where she left off on *East West Street*, for which she has my eternal gratitude, with the usual strategic and wonderful guidance. I express my thanks too to Helene Monsacre in France (Albin Michel), Silvia Sese and Jane Pilgrem in Spain (Anagrama), Tanja Hommen in Germany (Fischer), and Luigi Brioschi in Italy (Guanda).

I offer thanks to all my family, for support and nourishment, in particular my dear brother Marc, the best sibling one could imagine; Tante Annie in Paris, who got her hands dirty with research in the Tyrol; Auntie Ita in Devon; and my ever patient parents, Allan and Ruth.

To the other members of the core five, thanks for bearing with me as we (slowly) move beyond Lviv. To Katya, who crossed a mountain for me, knee-deep in snow, a hike I will never forget. To Lara, who keeps me straight on matters of identity and the functioning of the human world. To Leo, who puts my sense of history into a more intelligible context. And, finally, and primarily, and always, to Natalia who keeps it all going, brilliantly, with warmth and humour and forthright thoughts and love and always making sure that feet remain firmly on the earth.

SOURCES

As indicated in the endnotes, this book draws upon a wide and varied range of source materials, including archives, books, articles, news stories and personal interviews (the latter referred to in the text).

Archives

The letters, diaries and other papers of Otto and Charlotte von Wächter are held by their son Horst von Wächter, who has allowed them to be publicly available since 2015 in a digitised version of the originals at the collections of the United States Holocaust Memorial Museum (USHMM) ('Archiv Horst von Wächter', Accession Number 2014.103, RG Number: RG-17.049).

Much of this material has been transcribed and translated into English under the direction of Dr James Everest, with the particular assistance of Lea Main-Klingst. The USHMM material is arranged in eleven series: 1. Correspondence, 1944–5; 2. Letters and postcards, 1929–49; 3. Photo albums, 1920–38; 4. Photographs from Lemberg (Lviv, Ukraine); 5. Miscellaneous photographs of sports in Zakopane (Poland) and photographs from the Warsaw ghetto; 6. Miscellaneous notes and correspondence, 1948–9; 7. Collection of negatives, 1937–65; 8. Private documents, 1901–61; 9. Diaries, 1923–84; 10. Taped conversations between Charlotte von Wächter and friends and associates of Otto von Wächter, 1976–86; 11. Collection of newspapers and clippings, 1949–61.

In addition, Horst von Wächter made a further 480 pages of additional material available to me, which is not yet in the USHMM archives.

Other archives from which I have benefited include the following:

Austria: Dokumentationsarchiv des österreichischen Widerstandes Vienna, DÖW (Documentation Centre of Austrian Resistance);

Wiener Wiesenthal Institut für Holocaust-Studien (Simon Wiesenthal Archive at the Vienna Wiesenthal Institute for Holocaust Studies, VWI) Österreichisches Staatsarchiv (ÖSTA, Austrian State Archives); Suedtiroler Landesarchiv (South Tyrol State Archive); Wiener Stadt und Landesarchiv (Vienna City and State Archive)

Germany: Bundesarchiv ('BArch', German Federal Archives); Institut für Zeitgeschichte (IfZ), Munich

Israel: Yad Vashem Archive, including the Central Database of Shoah Victims' Names

Italy: Archivio Centrale dello Stato (Central State Archive, Rome); Santa Maria dell'Anima; Parish of Santa Maria in Aquiro, Rome

Poland: Instytut Pamięci Narodowej (IPN; Institute of National Remembrance); Archiwum Główne Akt Dawnych (Central Archives of Historical Records in Warsaw)

Ukraine: Government Archive of Lviv Oblast

United States: United States Holocaust Memorial Museum; National Archives and Records Administration; Department of Justice

United Kingdom: National Archives

Internet: www.jewishgen.org

Specific materials relied upon are referenced in the endnotes. Among the many sources, several merit particular reference, and will offer further sources and accounts for interested readers.

On life in Vienna: Carl E. Schorske, *Fin-de-Siècle Vienna: Politics and Culture* (Alfred Knopf, 1979).

On the escape of Nazis through Italy and the Vatican, I returned frequently to Gerald Steinacher, *Nazis on the Run* (OUP, 2011) and Uki Goñi's *The Real Odessa: How Perón Brought the Nazi War Criminals to Argentina* (Granta, 2002).

On the evolving US approach to alleged Nazi perpetrators, three essays by Norman Goda – 'The Nazi Peddler', 'Tracking the Red Orchestra', 'Manhunts' – in Richard Breitman and others, *U.S. Intelligence and the Nazis* (CUP, 2005), as well as Kerstin von Lingen's, *Allen Dulles, the OSS, and Nazi War Criminals* (CUP, 2013).

On the relationship between the Vatican and the Italian state to

1939, David Kertzer's *The Pope and Mussolini* (OUP, 2014).

On the killings in the Fosse Ardeatine, the magnificent oral history by Alessandro Portelli, *The Order Has Been Carried Out: History, Memory and Meaning of a Nazi Massacre in Rome* (Palgrave Macmillan, 2003); Giacomo Debenedetti, *October 16, 1943* (University of Notre Dame Press, 2001), including the preface by Alberto Moravia.

On life under Nazi rule in Kraków and Lemberg: Tadeusz Pankiewicz, *The Kraków Ghetto Pharmacy* (USHMM, 1988); David Kahane's *Lvov Ghetto Diary* (University of Massachusetts Press, 1990).

On the mind of a Nazi commandant, Gitta Sereny's *Into That Darkness* (André Deutsch, 1974).

Personal memoirs which offer especially pertinent insights include:

Allen Dulles, *The Secret Surrender* (Harper & Row, 1966)

Simon Wiesenthal, *The Murderers Among Us* (McGraw-Hill, 1967)

Joy Adamson, *The Searching Spirit* (Harcourt Brace Jovanovich, 1979)

Simon Wiesenthal, *Justice Not Vengeance* (Weidenfeld & Nicolson, 1989)

Herta Reich, *Zwei Tage Zeit – Die Flucht einer Mürzzuschlager Jüdin 1938–1944* (Clio, 1998)

James Milano and Patrick Brogan, *Soldiers, Spies and the Rat Line* (Brassey's, 2001)

Phyllis McDuff, *A Story Dreamt Long Ago* (Bantam, 2003)

Martin Pollack, *The Dead Man in the Bunker: Discovering My Father* (Faber & Faber, 2006)

Aleksander B. Skotnicki, *Bronisława (Niusia) Horowtiz-Karakulska* (Stradomskie Centrum Dialogu, 2012).

Works of history on which I have drawn include:

Steven Beller, *A Concise History of Austria* (CUP, 2006)

Kurt Bauer, *Hitlers Zweiter Putsch – Dollfuss, die Nazis und der 25. Juli 1934* (Residenz Verlag, 2014)

Evan Burr Bukey, *Hitler's Austria* (University of North Carolina Press, 2000)

Christopher Duggan, *A Concise History of Italy* (CUP, 2nd edn, 2014)

Hans-Christian Jasch and Christoph Kreutzmüller (eds.), *The Participants: The Men of the Wannsee Conference* (Berghahn, 2018)

Robert Katz, *Death in Rome* (Jonathan Cape, 1967) (later filmed as *Massacre in Rome*)

Peter Longerich, *Heinrich Himmler* (OUP, 2011)

Marta Marková, *Auf Knopfdruck: Vienna Postwar Flair* (LIT Verlag, 2018)

Johannes Sachslehner, *Hitlers Mann im Vatikan: Bischof Alois Hudal* (Molden Verlag, 2019)

Michael Salter, *Nazi War Crimes, US Intelligence and Selective Prosecution at Nuremberg* (Routledge, 2007)

Adrian Weale, *The SS: A New History* (Little Brown, 2010)

Martin Winstone, *The Dark Heart of Hilter's Europe* (I.B. Tauris, 2015)

Finally, a number of novels offered insight, detail and colour on the period I have confronted:

Curzio Malaparte, *Kaputt* (Casella, 1944)

Alberto Moravia, *The Woman of Rome* (Secker & Warburg, 1949)

Herbert Zand, *The Last Sortie* (*Letzte Ausfahrt*) (Rupert Hart-Davis, 1955)

Elsa Morante, *History* (Giulio Einaudi Editore, 1974)

Thomas Keneally, *Schindler's Ark* (Hodder & Stoughton, 1982)

Wolfgang Koeppen, *Death in Rome* (Granta, 2004)

Graham Greene, *The Third Man* (Vintage, 2005)

NOTES

b.:   born
d.:   died
D: diaries
L: letters
P: CW papers
R: reminiscence
T: cassette tape
EM: email

CB: Charlotte Bleckmann (until September 1932)

JE: James Everet
EF: Eduard Fischer
HH: Heinrich Himmler
LMK: Lea Main-Klingst
LR: Lothar Rübelt
PS: Philippe Sands
HJS: Hansjakob Stehle
CW: Charlotte Wächter (after September 1932)
HW: Horst Wächter
JW: Josef Wächter
OW: Otto Wächter

3   'On July 9th 1949': P, Nachlass, Abschnitt 1, p. 66.
4   'The patient indicates': Ibid.
4   'Like a church': L, Hedi Dupré to CW, 25.07.1949, p. 7.
5   'If Lo can't come now': L, Hedi Dupré to CW, 25.07.1949, pp. 8–9.
5   'I am in good hands': L, Hedi Dupré to CW, 25.07.1949, p. 9.
6   'From him I learned about you': L, Hedi Dupré to CW, 25.07.1949, p. 1.
6   'It is especially that brave cheerfulness': L, Hedi Dupré to CW, 25.07.1949, p. 10.
12   'I'll dance with you': Leonard Cohen, 'Take This Waltz' (1988).
13   Born in Vienna on 14 April 1939: Horst Wessel, b. 9 October 1907, Bielefeld, Germany; d. 14 January 1930, Berlin, Germany, Sturmführer

in SA. He wrote the 'Horst Wessel Song', which after his assassination, allegedly by a member of the KPD (Communist Party of Germany), became the official hymn of the NSDAP, part of the German national anthem (1933–45).

13   His parents chose Arthur as his middle name: Arthur Seyss-Inquart, b. 2 July 1892, Stannern, Moravia; d. 16 October 1946, Nuremberg, Germany. Reichskommissar of the Netherlands 1940–5.

15   *Dr Goebbels* it said: Joseph Goebbels, b. 29 October 1897, Rheydt, Germany; d. 1 May 1945, Berlin. Reichsminister for Propaganda 1933–45.

15   This was a reference to the head of the Hitler Youth: Baldur Benedikt von Schirach, b. 9 May 1907, Berlin; d. 8 August 1974, Kröv an der Mosel, Germany. Head of the Hitler Youth 1931–40, Governor of Reichsgau Vienna 1940–5.

15   'Dear Papa, I've picked you some flowers': L, CW to OW, 30.10.1944.

16   a painter, Friedensreich Hundertwasser: Friedrich Stowasser (Friedensreich Hundertwasser), b. 15 December 1928, Vienna; d. 19 February 2000 aboard the *Queen Elizabeth II* off Brisbane, Australia. Painter, architect, environmentalist.

18   An early image of the family: KuK Hof-Atelier Fritz Knozer.

18   Otto spent his early years in Vienna: Carl E. Schorske, *Fin-de-Siècle Vienna: Politics and Culture* (Alfred Knopf, 1979).

19   As a major in the *kaiserlich und königlich (k.u.k.)*: Richard Lein, *Pflichterfüllung oder Hochverrat? Die tschechischen Soldaten Österreich-Ungarns im Ersten Weltkrieg* (LIT Verlag, 2011), pp. 279–81.

19   He had, however, been awarded: The Military Order of Maria Theresa was the highest military order of the Austrian empire; *Die Dekorierung der Theresienritter* (1918); JW may be seen at http://europeanfilmgate way.eu/de/detail/die%20dekorierung%20der%20theresienritter/ofm::-933c8187a0b58e80e6260cd76e933e90 (at 4'40").

19   Among the refugees: Steven Beller, *A Concise History of Austria* (CUP, 2006), p. 208 ff; Schorske, *Fin-de-Siècle Vienna.*

19   with which his fellow student would become embroiled: Philippe Sands, *East West Street – On the Origins of Genocide and Crimes against Humanity* (W&N, 2016), p. 75 ff.

20   with renowned professors, including Hans Kelsen: Hans Kelsen, b. 11 October 1891, Prague, Czech Republic; d. 19 April 1973, Berkeley, USA. Austrian jurist, legal and political philosopher, professor.

20   Alexander Hold-Ferneck, a virulent nationalist: Antonino Scalone, 'Alexander Hold von Ferneck', in Enrico Pattaro, Corrado Roversi (eds.), *A Treatise of Legal Philosophy and General Jurisprudence: Volume 12* (Springer, 2016), p. 129.

20   Stephan Brassloff, specialist in Roman law: Stephan Brassloff, b. 18 June 1875, Vienna; d. 25 February 1943, Theresienstadt. Professor of Roman law.

20 Josef Hupka, expert in trade and exchanges: Josef Hupka, b. 22 February 1875, Vienna; d. 23 April 1944, Theresienstadt. Professor of trade and exchange law.

20 'very successful, very popular': Wiener Ruderverein Donauhort, 1867–2017.

20 'Buy Only from Aryan Businesses!': Linda Erker, Andreas Huber, Klaus Taschwer, *Deutscher Klub: Austro-Nazis in der Hofburg* (Czernin, 2019).

20 In March 1921: *Antisemitenbund*, 'The Antisemite League', 1918–38, Austrian movement founded by Anton Jerzabek, dissolved after the Anschluss.

20 Jewish shops and streetcar passengers: Bruce Pauley, *From Prejudice to Persecution: A History of Austrian Anti-Semitism* (University of North Carolina Press, 1992), p. 82.

20 Otto was arrested, charged and tried: P, Miscellaneous, Abschnitt 1, p. 11.

21 In an archive in Vienna: *Deutsche Nationalsozialistische Arbeiterpartei* (DNSAP) (German National Socialist Workers' Party), founded 1918, banned by Chancellor Engelbert Dollfuss in 1933, part of German Nazi Party after the Anschluss.

21 In December 1925: P, Miscellaneous, Abschnitt 1, p. 28: *Amtszeugnis, Präsidium des Oberlandesgerichts in Wien* (14.12.1925).

22 the last stop on the Semmering railway line: The Semmering Railway listed as a UNESCO World Heritage Site in 1998: https://whc.unesco.org/en/list/785.

22 Nearby Villa Luisa: Helmut Brenner, *Im Schatten des Phönix: Höhen und Tiefen eines dominierenden Industriebetriebes und deren Auswirkungen auf die Region* (Weishaupt Verlag, 1993).

23 In 1916, the firm of Orenstein & Koppel: On file with the author; *Industriebahnen, Waldbahnen, Touristikbahnen, Landwirtschaftsbahnen usw*, p. 7.

23 Chancellor Karl Renner told the Austrian parliament: Rolf Steininger et al., *Austria in the Twentieth Century (Studies in Austrian and Central European History and Culture)* (Transaction Publishers, 2002), p. 88.

23 Instead, the treaty of Saint-Germain-en-Laye: Margaret MacMillan, *Peacemakers: The Paris Peace Conference of 1919 and Its Attempt to End War* (John Murray, 2001).

24 'Gala Peter': Gala Peter chocolate, first sold by Swiss chocolatier Daniel Peter in 1887.

24 'all's love, yet all's law': Robert Browning, 'Saul', in *Men and Women* (Ticknor and Fields, 1855).

24 August von Scheindler, a classical philologist: August Scheindler, *Ilias: Text aus der Überlieferung hergestellt und mit Vorrede von August Scheindler* (Wien: Österreichischer Bundesverlag, 1925). See also: https://www.biographien.ac.at/oebl/oebl_S/Scheindler_August_1851_1931.xml.

24 'Yes, this tall, old man, already retired': R, CW, 1932–45, p. 53.

24 'Exchanged glances with a Jew who was quite dashing': D, CW, 1923–6, 26.09.1925.

24 Her parents deposited her: Andrew Lycett, *The Man Who Created Sherlock Holmes – The Life and Times of Sir Arthur Conan Doyle* (Free Press, 2007), p. 436; Anna Lee, *Memoir of a Career on General Hospital and in Film* (McFarland & Company, Inc., 2007), p. 43.

25 Mrs Ida Foley, the sister of Arthur Conan Doyle: Jane Adelaide Rose (Ida) Foley (née Doyle), b. 16 March 1875, d. 1 July 1937; teacher at Cheltenham Ladies' College 1901–15, then headteacher at Granville House, Eastbourne.

25 She sought out hairdressers: D, CW, 1923–6: 20.10.1925; 22.10.1925; 28.12.1925; 29.12.1925; 04.01.1926; 05.01.1926; 06.01.1926; 11.01.1926.

25 A second trip, to Paris: General Strike was called by the General Council of the Trades Union Congress (TUC) in solidarity with 1.2 million coalminers, 3–12 May 1926; sympathy strikes were banned by the 1927 Trades Disputes Act: https://www.bbc.co.uk/news/uk-13828537.

25 including Mizzi Getreuer: Marie (Mizzi) Fischer (née Getreuer), b. 21 December 1912; d. 9 August 1944, Stutthof: Wolfgang Scheffler und Diana Schulle, *Buch der Erinnerung – Die ins Baltikum deportierten deutschen, österreichischen und tschechoslowakischen Juden* (K.G. Saur, 2003), p. 476.

25 'I could have cried': D, CW, 1923–6, 27.07.1926.

25 enrolled at the *Wiener Frauenakademie*: *Wiener Frauenakademie* founded in 1897, art school for women, originally operated under the name *Kunstschule für Frauen und Mädchen*, when women were not permitted to attend art school. The *Modeschule Wien im Schloss Hetzendorf*, founded in 1946, is seen as its successor.

26 Introduced to the designer Josef Hoffmann: Josef Hoffmann, b. 15 December 1870, Brtnice, Moravia; d. 7 May 1956, Vienna. Architect and designer, established the Wiener Werkstätte with Koloman Moser, 1903.

27 Distantly related to Charlotte: Herma Szabo, b. 22 February 1902, Vienna; d. 7 May 1986, Rottenmann, Austria. Olympic figure skater.

27 'He wore a diamond ring': R, CW, *Meine Liebesjahre* 1929, pp. 8–9, 12.

27 'what no gentleman had done before': Fischerhütte, a ski lodge, 2,049 metres.

28 'I fell in love with good-looking, cheerful Otto': R, CW, *Meine Liebesjahre* 1929, p. 16.

28 'Who knows which girl': L, CB to OW, 04.05.1929; R, CW, *Meine Liebesjahre* 1929, p. 17.

28 'How beautiful was our young and blossoming love': R, CW, *Meine Liebesjahre* 1929, pp. 20–3.

29 She even allowed Viktor Klarwill: Viktor later married Friederike Gessner, who fled Nazi Austria, divorced him, married a game warden in

Kenya, became Joy Adamson, wrote *Born Free*, the story of Elsa the lioness, murdered in 1980.

29 In Barcelona they attended the World Fair: R, CW, *Meine Liebesjahre* 1929, p. 37.

29 In the autumn, when school resumed: R, CW, *Meine Liebesjahre* 1929, pp. 40–2.

30 'His behaviour, hugging girls': R, CW, *Meine Liebesjahre* 1929, p. 47.

30 '1,350 schillings in the first year': R, CW, *Meine Liebesjahre* 1929, p. 51.

31 'I liked that': R, CW, *Meine Liebesjahre* 1929, pp. 64–7.

31 'Marry and bear 10 children': R, CW, *Meine Liebesjahre* 1929, p. 69.

31 encounters with new ones, like the Fischböcks: Hans Fischböck, b. 24 January 1895, Geras, Austria; d. 3 July 1967 in Marburg, Germany. Reichsminister for the Netherlands 1940–5.

31 'Through struggle and love': On file with the author: *'Durch Kampf & Liebe dem Sturme trotz an's Ziel!'*

31 That was 28 May 1931: BArch, R 9361-II/1173907; *Waechter, Lotte – Personenbezogene Unterlagen der NSDAP/Parteikorrespondenz.*

31 Her diary rarely referenced Otto's political activities: BArch, R 9361-III/561695; *Waechter, Otto – Personenbezogene Unterlagen der SS und SA.*

31 As district chief of the Nazi Party: EM, Andreas Huber to PS, 23.12.2018.

31 the writer Franz Hieronymus Riedl: Franz Hieronymus Riedl, b. 2 April 1906, Vienna; d. 2 April 1994, Lana, Italy. Journalist.

31 Ernst Kaltenbrunner: Ernst Kaltenbrunner, b. 4 October 1913, Ried im Inkkreis, Austria; d. 16 October 1946, Nuremberg, Germany. Chief of Reich Main Security Office 1943–5.

31 Hanns Blaschke: Hanns Blaschke, b. 1 April 1896, Vienna; d. 25 October 1971, Salzburg, Austria. Mayor of Vienna 1943–5.

32 Wilhelm Höttl and Charlotte's brother Heinrich Bleckmann: Heinz Fischer, *Einer im Vordergrund: Taras Borodajkewycz* (Europa Verlag, 1966), p. 104.

32 That summer, Otto spent five weeks: Paul Hoser, 'Sturmabteilung (SA), 1921–1923/1925–1945', *Historisches Lexikon Bayerns*, 14.11.2007: https://www.historisches-lexikon-bayerns.de/Lexikon/Stur mabteilung_(SA),_1921-1923/1925-1945.

32 'The whole thing is very interesting': L, OW to CB, 17.08.1931.

32 Taken by Heinrich Hoffmann: Fritz Erler, 'Adolf Hitler in SA uniform' (30.08.1931), German Art Gallery: http://www.germanartgallery.eu/m/ Webshop/0/product/info/Fritz_Erler,_Adolf_Hitler&id=44.

33 Many of its members would: D, CB, 1931, 01.09.1931; D, CB, 1931, 13.09.1931.

33 'soon be going around with a dagger': L, CB to OW, 10.09.1931.

33 'All I hear on Bräunerstrasse': L, CB to OW, 29.09.1931.

33 'a Jewish ploy': L, CB to OW, 24.10.1931.

33 Mr Caswell of the Calico Printers' Association: The Calico Printers'

Association Ltd, British textile company, founded 1899, comprising forty-six textile printing companies and thirteen textile merchants.

33   Many she met were open to ideas: L, CB to OW, 24.10.1931.

33   'join hands under the flag': L, CB to OW, 28.10.1931; L, CB to OW, 07.11.1931.

34   'You could pick me up': L, CB to OW, 04.11.1931.

34   'under the sign of the swastika': R, CW, *Meine Liebesjahre* 1929, p. 85.

34   Otto completed his training: Dr Georg Freiherr von Ettingshausen, b. 16 September 1896, Baden, Austria; d. 1958. President, Bar Council of Vienna, Niederösterreich and Burgenland; legal counsel, Hungarian Consulate General, Vienna.

34   He acted for the photographer: Lothar Rübelt, b. 8 April 1901, Vienna; d. 4 August 1990, Reifnitz, Austria. Sports and press photographer.

34   infringement of his rights by the writer Karl Kraus: Revisionsschrift der klagenden Partei (Eingereicht von Otto Gustav Wächter beim Landesgerichts für Z.R.S. Wien, G.Z.16 CG 552/31), 14.04.1932, at: http://www.kraus.wienbibliothek.at/content/revisionsschrift-der-klagenden-partei-eingereicht-von-otto-gustav-waechter-beim.

34   In April 1932 he joined the *Schutzstaffel*: Adrian Weale, *The SS: A New History* (Hachette Digital, 2010).

34   As a member of the *Verband deutsch-arischer Rechtsanwälte Österreichs*: Peter Melichar, *Otto Ender 1875–1960* (Böhlau Verlag, 2018), pp. 161–2.

34   she attended the thirty-first International Eucharistic Congress: Thirty-first International Eucharistic Congress, Dublin, 22–26 June 1932, on the 1,500th anniversary of St Patrick's arrival in Ireland. The final public mass in Phoenix Park was one of the largest Eucharistic Congresses of the twentieth century.

35   'the biggest secret': R, CW, *Meine Liebesjahre* 1929, p. 113.

35   'I could not wait': R, CW, *Meine Liebesjahre* 1929, p. 102.

36   Horst wrote in detail: Thomas Jorda, 'Horst Wächter – Sagen, wie es ist', Nön, 13 December 2010: https://www.noen.at/ niederoesterreich/ gesellschaft/adel-verpflichtet/sagen-wie-es-ist-4901171.

36   a temple to honour Hermes Trismegistus: Hermes Trismegistus, associated with Greek god Hermes and Egyptian god Thoth, is the supposed author of the sacred texts of hermeticism, considered to have influenced Western esoteric tradition.

36   the Waffen-SS 'Galicia' Division: Michael James Melnyk, *The History of the Galician Division of the Waffen SS – On the Eastern Front, April 1943 to July 1944* (Vol. I), and *Stalin's Nemesis* (Vol. II) (Fonthill Media, 2016).

36   At this time, Ukraine was: Andrey Kurkov, *Ukraine Diaries* (Harvill Secker, 2014); 'Ukraine's revolution: Making sense of a year of chaos', *BBC News*, 21 November 2014: https://www.bbc.co.uk/news/world-europe-30131108.

36 A century earlier, in September 1914: 'Austrian Rout in Great Battle', *New York Times*, 2 September 1914: https://timesmachine.nytimes.com/timesmachine/1914/09/02/120283470.pdf.

38 'I never forgot Otto's adjutant Stasny': L, Erwin Axer to HW, 06.09.2006.

39 was 'a leading part of an horrifying machinery': EM, HW to PS, 26.02.2013.

39 He directed me to extracts: Ludwig Losacker, b. 29 July 1906, Mannheim, Germany; d. 23 July 1990, Heidelberg. Vice-governor District Kraków 1943–5, head of main administration General Government 1943–5; Ludwig Losacker, 'Von der Schwierigkeit, ein Deutscher zu sein – Erinnerungen an das besetzte Polen – Schilderung der Erlebnisse als Angehöriger der deutschen Verwaltung im besetzten Polen' (unpublished, c. 1980), extracts on file with author.

39 'Losacker was characterised as': Thomas Sandkuehler, 'Arbeitsgemeinschaft Holocaust', *Die Zeit*, 27 October 1995: https://www.zeit.de/1995/44/Arbeitsgemeinschaft_Holocaust.

39 The real culprit in Lemberg: Friedrich (Fritz) Katzmann, b. 6 May 1906, Bochum, Germany; d. 19 September 1957, Darmstadt, Germany. Higher SS and Police Leader of the District of Galicia 1941–5.

40 A third letter: Note, 13 February 1942, attaching Note on 'Resettlement of the Jews', 9 January 1942; Order, 'On Employment of Jews', 13 March 1942; L, Himmler to Stuckart, 25.08.1942; on file with author.

40 In May 2013: Philippe Sands, 'My Father, the Good Nazi', *Financial Times*, 3 May 2013: https://www.ft.com/content/7d6214f2-b2be-11e2-8540-00144feabdco.

40 The Austrian ambassador in London: EM, HW to PS, 26.02.2013.

40 He said this not to me: EM, HW to PS, 05.05.2013.

42 This changed the status of the Nazi Party: William L. Shirer, *The Rise and Fall of the Third Reich: A History of Nazi Germany* (Secker & Warburg, 1960); Thomas Childers, *The Third Reich: A History of Nazi Germany* (Simon & Schuster, 2018).

42 'inhumane and anti-Christian': Andreas Predikaka, 'Ferdinand Pawlikowski – Ein Realpolitiker der Zwischenkriegszeit?', Master's Thesis, University of Vienna, January 2013, pp. 87–8: http://othes.univie.ac.at/26100/1/2013-01-30_9210170.pdf. Pawlikowski, who expressed opposition to National Socialism in 1931 (ibid., p. 84), recited parts of the letter at the pastoral conference of the military pastorate in Vienna in November 1932 (p. 88).

42 'I always was a bit of a revolutionary': R, CW, *Meine Liebesjahre* 1929, p. 112; T, CW and HJS, Cassette 3, Side 1, 28.09.1984.

42 On 21 March, Otto travelled: L, CW to OW, 30.01.1945.

43 In May, the Austrian chancellor: Steininger et al., *Austria in the Twentieth Century*, p. 139.

43 'Nazi lawyer Otto Wächter': 'Die ausgehobene Nazizentrale', *Der Abend*, 04.08.1933, p. 2, available at: http://anno.onb.ac.at/

cgi-content/anno?aid=abd&datum=19330804&query=%2225+Personen%22+%22Wächter%22&ref=anno-search&seite=2.

43 Convened by his father Josef: Rudolf Weydenhammer, b. 1 May 1890, Wilhelmshaven, Germany; d. 1972. German industrialist.

43 Dertil was sentenced: On file with the author. *Das Kleine Blatt*, 19.11.1933, p. 8.

43 'I was still considered Miss Bleckmann': L, CW to OW, 01.12.1933.

43 'I love everything you do': D, CW, 1934, 10.05.1934.

43 to meet Theodor Habicht: Theodor Habicht, b. 4 April 1898, Wiesbaden, Germany; d. 31 January 1944, Newel, Russia. Mayor of Witten 1937–8, mayor of Koblenz from 1939.

44 where he met Gerhard Köpke: Gerhard Köpke, b. 1873; d. 1953. From 1923 head of department West and Southern Europe of the foreign service, forced to retire in 1935.

44 In 1945 it emerged: Dokument 868-D, 'Aufzeichnung über mündlichen Bericht des Österreichischen Baron Wächter im Auswärtigen Amt Berlin', 31.05.1934, on file with author.

44 In due course, I found a photograph: Erwin Peterseil, *Der Weg in den FASCHISMUS – Österreich 1933–1938* (Antifa-Info, 2003), p. 42; https://www.atheisten-info.at/downloads/WEG.pdf.

44 Fridolin Glass: Fridolin Glass, b. 14 December 1910, Lemberg; d. 21 February 1943, Dniprodserschynsk, Soviet Union. A leader of the July Putsch.

44 Anton Rintelen, Austria's ambassador: Philip Scheriau, *Mediale Reaktionen auf den Juliputsch 1934 in In- und Ausland*, Master's Thesis, University of Vienna, 2014, p.11: http://othes.univie.ac.at/32646/1/2014-04-07_0808067.pdf; citing to: Gerhard Jagschitz, *Der Putsch. Die Nationalsozialisten 1934 in Österreich* (Styria, 1976), p. 80 ff.

45 Matters spiralled out of control: Kurt Bauer, *Hitlers Zweiter Putsch – Dollfuß, die Nazis und der 25. Juli 1934* (Residenz Verlag, 2014).

45 'Ask Mussolini to look after my wife': Howard M. Sachar, *The Assassination of Europe, 1918–1942: A Political History* (University of Toronto Press, 2015), p. 212; Bauer, *Hitlers Zweiter Putsch – Dollfuß, die Nazis und der 25. Juli 1934*.

45 Some of those involved: Sachar, *Assassination of Europe*, p. 214.

45 Some reports suggested he: Sachar, *Assassination of Europe*, p. 212.

45 worked on Leni Riefenstahl's film: Helene Bertha Amalie (Leni) Riefenstahl, b. 22 August 1902, Berlin; d. 8 September 2003, Pöcking, Germany. German film director, producer and actress, including *Der weiße Rausch (The White Ecstasy)* (1931), a German mountain and skiing film.

45 Decades later, she told historian Hansjakob Stehle: T, CW and HJS, Cassette 3, Side 1, 28.09.1983.

46 'If you have a pistol': T, CW and Lola Matsek, Cassette 1, Side 1, 19.12.1976.

47 The police seized the house: T, CW and HJS, Cassette 3, Side 1, 28.09.1983.

47 He was met by a dishevelled journalist: Peter Broucek, *Ein General im Zwielicht: Die Erinnerungen Edmund Glaises von Horstenau*, Vol. 76 (Böhlau, 1998), p. 458.

47 Herr Kornhuber, who helped him: Arthur Kornhuber, b. 22 June 1901; d. 24 March 1993. Journalist.

47 He would rise quickly: BArch, R 9361-III/561695: Dienstlaufbahn.

47 'It seems you are being watched': L, OW to CW, 28.09.1934.

48 Kurt von Schuschnigg, who succeeded Dollfuss: Kurt Alois Josef Johann Schuschnigg, b. 14 December 1897, Riva del Garda, Austria-Hungary; d. 18 November 1977, Mutters, Austria. Chancellor of Austria 1934–8.

48 a supporter of the death penalty: Günter Bischof, Anton Pelinka and Alexander Lassner (eds.), *The Dollfuss/Schuschnigg Era in Austria – A Reassessment* (Transaction Publishers, 2003).

48 'Evening in Berchtesgaden': Geoffrey Moorhouse, 'Hitler's eyrie: a visit to Berchtesgaden', *Guardian*, 21.02.1970: https://www.theguardian.com/world/2017/feb/21/hitler-eyrie-berchtesgaden-nazi-1970.

49 'I had no hint of any plan': 'Das Geheimnis der Putschautos vom 25 Juli', *Illustrierte Kronen Zeitung*, 02.02.1935, p. 9; http://anno.onb.ac.at/cgi-content/anno?aid=krz&datum=19350202&query=%22Gusta-v+Wächter%22&ref=anno-search&seite=9.

49 In Germany, the Nuremberg decrees: Amy Newman, *The Nuremberg Laws: Institutionalized Anti-Semitism* (Lucent Books, 1999).

49 'Ski jumping with Hitler': D, CW, 1936, 13.02.1936.

49 She saw Rudolf Pavlu: Gabriele Volsansky, *Pakt auf Zeit: das Deutsch-Österreichische Juli-Abkommen 1936* (Böhlau, 2011), p. 83 ff.

49 'another colleague of Otto's': Edmund Glaise-Horstenau, b. 27 February 1882, Braunau am Inn, Austria; d. 20 July 1946, Langwasser military camp, near Nuremberg. Vice-Chancellor of Austria 1938 and Federal Minister of the Interior 1936–8. See also: Peter Broucek, *Ein General im Zwielicht: Die Erinnerungen Edmund Glaises von Horstenau* (Böhlau Verlag, 1983), Band (Vol.) 2, p. 445.

50 'I have had close ties with the SS': *Die zwei Wiener Illegale Nazis – Dr Otto Wächter und Rudolf Pavlu* (Haifa: Inst. of Documentation in Israel for the Investigation of Nazi War Crimes, 2002). OW to SS Gruppenführer Alfred Rodenbücher (11.10.1936); SS-Gruppenführer Alfred Rodenbücher to Reichsführer SS Heinrich Himmler (15.10.1936); EM, LMK to PS, 17.12.2018.

50 On multiple occasions, the referee: Ibid., Statement SS Standartenführer Josef Fitzthum (21.09.1936).

50 'At last the family was together': R, CW, 1932–45, pp. 12–13.

50 His character was recorded: Weale, *The SS: A New History*. BArch, R 9361-III/561695; *Personenbezogene Unterlagen der SS und SA – Otto Wächter. Personalbericht & Beurteilung*, undated.

50   'office of spying and surveillance services': R, CW, 1932–45, p. 13.

50   He worked in the SD's Criminal Division: *Schutzstaffel* (SS), originally
     a unit that served as bodyguards to Hitler, later a paramilitary group.
     Sicherheitsdienst (SD), the intelligence and security agency of the SS,
     mainly tasked with intelligence gathering relating to finding and neutral-
     ising opposition, both internal and external to the Nazi Party. *Geheime
     Staatspolizei* (Gestapo) was the secret state police, tasked with identify-
     ing opposition, considered a sister organisation of the SD. The SD and
     the Gestapo were subdivisions of the SS.

50   the orbit of Reinhard Heydrich: Reinhard Tristan Eugen Heydrich, b. 7
     March 1904, Halle (Saale) Germany; d. 4 June 1942, Prague. Director
     Reich Main Security Office 1939–42. Deputy Reich-Protector of Bohe-
     mia and Moravia 1941–2.

50   Heinrich Himmler: Heinrich Luitpold Himmler, b. 7 October 1900,
     Munich; d. 23 May 1945, Lüneburg, Germany. Reichsführer-SS 1929–
     45, and Chief of the German Police 1936–45.

50   In the Berlin federal archive: BArch, R58/7074, *Zeichnung mit Signen
     durch Mitarbeiter des SD-Hauptamts, Signenverzeichnis, 1.1.1937;
     Stabsbefehl Nr. 3/37 vom 15 Jan. 1937.*

50   included SS-Hauptscharführer Adolf Eichmann: Otto Adolf Eichmann,
     b. 19 March 1906, Solingen, Germany; d. 1 June 1962, Ramla, Israel.
     SS-Obersturmbannführer.

50   SS-Unterscharführer Karl Hass: Karl Hass, b. 5 October 1912, Elm-
     schenhagen, Germany; d. 21 April 2004, Castel Gandolfo, Italy.
     SS-Sturmbannführer.

51   'he surely saw things': R, CW, *Lebensgeschichte* 1932–45, p. 13.

51   'Heil Hitler! Wächter': BArch, R 9361-III/561695; *Personenbezogene
     Unterlagen der SS und SA – Otto Wächter. OW an die Personalkanzlei
     RFSS,* 15.04.1937.

51   He declared himself *gottgläubig*: Richard Steigmann-Gall, *The Holy
     Reich – Nazi Conceptions of Christianity, 1919–1945* (CUP, 2003),
     p. 218 ff.

51   Otto spent several months: Rudolf Pavlu, b. 15 July 1902, Vienna; d.
     1949, Römlinghoven, Germany. Mayor of Kraków 1941–3.

51   His personnel file described him: BArch, R 9361-III/561695; *Personen-
     bezogene Unterlagen der SS und SA – Otto Wächter. Personalbericht,*
     16.02.1935.

52   'That should please you': R, CW, 1932–45, p. 17.

52   evoked the 'abyss': Kurt von Schuschnigg, *Austrian Requiem* (Victor
     Gollancz Ltd, 1947), p. 47.

52   now bearing a *Totenkopf*: The skull and crossbones (*Totenkopf*) was the
     insignia of the SS, the Nazi paramilitary organisation.

52   She planned to move in: R, CW, 1932–45, p. 19.

52   On 12 February 1938: Éric Vuillard, *L'ordre du jour* (Actes Sud,
     2017).

53 On 11 March: Von Schuschnigg, *Austrian Requiem*, pp. 44–55.

53 The moment was known as the Anschluss: Bruno Simma and Hans-Peter Folz, *Restitution und Entschädigung im Völkerrecht; Die Verpflichtungen der Republik Österreich nach 1945 im Lichte ihrer außenpolitischen Praxis* (Boehlau, 2004), p. 200.

53 'so the Austrian government': R, CW, 1932–45, p. 22.

57 'Then a single event changed': R, CW, 1932–45, p. 19.

57 'Every Nazi felt such joy': R, CW, 1932–45, pp. 19–21.

57 a journey 'full of excitement': R, CW, 1932–45, p. 21.

58 'The morning after arriving in Vienna': R, CW, 1932–45, pp. 22–9.

60 'the best moment of my life': T, CW and LR, Cassette 1, Side 2, undated.

60 'we will always have enough to eat': R, CW, *Lebensgeschichte 1932–45*, p. 29.

60 comrades from the *Deutsche Klub*: Deutsche Klub (1908–39), founded in Vienna as part of a larger German nationalist movement, many members were involved in the 1934 Putsch and 1938 Anschluss.

60 Odilo Globočnik became Gauleiter of Vienna: Odilo Globočnik, b. 21 April 1904, Trieste, Austria-Hungary; d. 31 May 1945, Paternion, Austria. Gauleiter of Vienna 1938–9 and SS and police chief for Lublin 1939–43.

60 Bishop Pawlikowski, briefly imprisoned: Predikaka, *Ferdinand Pawlikowski*, p. 84.

60 Josef Bürckel: Josef Bürckel, b. 30 March 1895, Lingenfeld, Germany; d. 28 September 1944, Neustadt an der Weinstrasse, Germany. Member of the German Reichstag 1930–44, and Gauleiter of Vienna 1939–40.

60 He established the *Zentralstelle*: Alexandra-Eileen Wenck, Gabriele Anderl, Dirk Rupnow, *Die Zentralstelle für jüdische Auswanderung als Beraubungsinstitution* (Oldenbourg, 2004).

60 One among them was my grandfather: Sands, *East West Street*, p. 30.

60 He was offered a position: 'Der Staatskommissar beim Reichsstatthalter in Österreich', *Völkischer Beobachter – Berliner Ausgabe*, 23.03.1938.

60 'Dr Arthur Seyss-Inquart': 'NAZIS LIST 1,742 JAILED IN AUSTRIA; Public Believes That Total in "Protective Custody" Is Five Times That Number', *New York Times*, 23.03.1938: https://www.nytimes.com/1938/03/23/archives/nazis-list-1742-jailed-in-austria-public-believes-that-total-in.html?searchResultPosition=4.

61 Hitler returned to Vienna: 'Stifter des Neuen Reiches', *Neue Freie Presse*, 09.04.1938: http://anno.onb.ac.at/cgi-content/anno?aid=nfp&datum=19380409&seite=1&zoom=33.

61 'Sat in the second row, marvellous': D, CW, 1938, 09.04.1938.

61 leader of the Social Democrats, Karl Renner: Karl Renner, b. 14 December 1870, Untertannowitz, Moravia; d. 31 December 1950, Vienna. Chancellor of Austria 1918–20 and 1945. President of Austria 1945–50.

61 'the destructive influence of world Judaism': Oskar Veselsky, *Bischof*

und Klerus der Diözese Seckau unter nationalsozialistischer Herrschaft (Dbv-Verlag, 1981), p. 308 f.

61 Otto received other positive news: Records of the Reich Leader of the SS and Chief of the German Police, NARA, RG 242, Microfilm Publication T175, Roll 32. Himmler to Standartenführer Dr Wächter, 09.06.1938.

61 and political leaders Ernst Kaltenbrunner: On Kaltenbrunner's capture and condition at Nuremberg see: https://www.cia.gov/library/center-for-the-study-of-intelligence/kent-csi/vol4no2/html/v04i2a07p_0001.htm.

61 Hermann Neubacher: Hermann Neubacher, b. 24 June 1893, Wels, Austria; d. 1 July 1960, Vienna. Mayor of Vienna 1938–40.

61 Professor Norbert Gürke: Norbert Gürke, b. 14 March 1904, Graz, Austria-Hungary; d. 29 June 1941, Vienna. Professor of international law 1936–9, author of *Der Einfluß jüdischer Theoretiker auf die deutsche Völkerrechtslehre* ('The influence of Jewish theorists on German approaches to international law').

61 'The Führer is here': L, CW to OW, 29.07.1938.

61 'Trude went to see Frau Göbbels': D, CW, 1938, 31.07.1938.

62 'I loved nursing him': R, CW, 1932–45, p. 36.

63 'Everyone to Kiev!': Andrey Kurkov, *Ukraine Diaries: Dispatches from Kiev* (Harvill Secker, 2014), p. 108.

64 Horst's approach was the more difficult: Guy Walters, 'Haunted by the sins of their Nazi fathers', *Daily Telegraph*, 18 February 2014: https://www.telegraph.co.uk/history/world-war-two/10644048/Haunted-by-the-sins-of-their-Nazi-fathers.html.

66 There was a Polish indictment: 'Poland Indicts 10 in 400,000 Deaths; They Head Roster of 3,000 War Criminals to be Brought to Trial After Peace', *New York Times,* 17 October 1942: https://timesmachine.nytimes.com/timesmachine/1942/10/17/85600360.pdf.

68 with the help of Georg Lippert: Georg Lippert, b. 27 January 1908, Vienna; d. 14 October 1992, Vienna, Austria. Austrian architect.

68 the renowned Ankerbrot bakery: Ankerbrot, bakery, founded in 1891 by Fritz and Heinrich Mendl.

68 'obtained the Jewess Bettina Mendl's house': R, CW, 1932–45, p. 31.

68 'become the residence of Dr (Baron) Gustav Otto Wächter': Phyllis McDuff, *A Story Dreamt Long Ago* (Bantam, 2003), p. 191.

68 'In the years after World War II': Ibid.

69 Villa Mendl was no doubt 'very beautiful': R, CW, 1932–45, p. 32.

69 'Today you stand among us': Max Domarus, *Hitler: Speeches and Proclamations Vol. II, 1935–1938* (Bolchazy-Carducci Publishers, 1997), p. 1150 f.

70 'Chamberlain with Führer': Sudetenland was a border region in Czechoslovakia, inhabited by Sudeten Germans who found themselves living in the new country of Czechoslovakia, after the collapse of the Austro-Hungarian empire. Following the Anschluss, Hitler declared himself protector of the Sudeten Germans, pushed for autonomy, and

after negotiations between Hitler, British Prime Minister Chamberlain and French Prime Minister Daladier, the Sudetenland was ceded to the German Reich; D, CW, 1938, 23.09.1938.

70 'strong leadership in the service': W.E. Yates, *Theatre in Vienna: A Critical History, 1776–1995* (CUP, 1996), p. 224.

70 If, on leaving the theatre: Alan E. Steinweis, *Kristallnacht 1938* (HUP, 2009).

70 'I was cross and nasty, again': D, CW, 1938, 09.11.1938; 10.11.1938.

70 'Afterwards home and waited for midnight': R, CW, *Meine Kinderjahre*, p. 63.

71 A special ordinance restructured the Austrian civil service: RGBl I 1938, Nr. 87, p. 607 ff – *Verordnung zur Neuordnung des östereichischen Berufsbeamtentums* (31.05.1938).

71 He removed Viktor Kraft: Victor Kraft, b. 4 July 1880, Vienna; d. 3 January 1975, Vienna. Rehabilitated to his teaching and librarian posts in 1945: https://gedenkbuch.univie.ac.at/index.php?id=435&no_cache=1&L=2&no_cache=1&person_single_id=33353.

71 was once a member of the *Wiener Kreis*: Michael Dippelreiter, 'Beamtenentlassungen in den höchsten Dienstklassen nach der nationalsozialistischen Machtübernahme 1938/39': https://www.univie.ac.at/zeitgeschichte/cms/uploads/Paper-Dippelreiter.pdf; citing *Rot-Weiß Rot-Buch, Gerechtigkeit für Österreich*, Teil 1, Wien 1946, 77.

71 Friedrich König was another target: Friedrich Wilhelm König, b. 1 July 1897, Adlerkosteletz, Bohemia; d. 5 February 1972, Vienna. Lecturer in history: https://gedenkbuch.univie.ac.at/index.php?id=435&no_cache=1&L=2&no_cache=1&person_single_id=33313.

71 'Because you are a *Mischling*': ÖSta/AdR, BKA, BBV, Der Staatskommissar beim Reichsstatthalter, Otto Wächter an König, 05.06.1939.

71 The numbers included: Michael Dippelreiter, 'Beamtenentlassungen in den höchsten Dienstklassen nach der nationalsozialistischen Machtübernahme 1938/39', Teil 1, Wien 1946, 77.

72 'A number of times I tried': Peter Broucek, *Ein General im Zwielicht: Die Erinnerungen des Edmund Glaises von Horstenau – Band 2: Minister im Ständestaat und General im OKW* (Böhlau, 2005), p. 279 (von Horstenau reported Wächter to be 'better than his reputation', and reported having seen documents in which 'Wächter had toned down the wishes of some party member', p. 333).

72 former procurator-general, Robert Winterstein: Robert Winterstein, b. 26 June 1874, Gitschin, Bohemia; d. 13 April 1940, Buchenwald concentration camp. Procurator-General 1932–5, 36–8. Austrian Minister of Justice 1935–6.

72 'In light of § 4 para. 3': Werner Winterstein, *Anmerkung: Prominent – Die Geschichte der Familie Winterstein 1867–1945* (Böhlau, 2008), p. 121.

72 'temporary position': R, CW, 1932–45, p. 33.

72   In other words, to paraphrase: T, CW and LR, Cassette 1, Side 2. R, CW,
      1932–45, p. 33.

73   'The Nazis said he wasn't tough': R, CW, 1932–45, p. 33.

73   Then, unexpectedly, Seyss-Inquart was replaced: 'Peace Key is Held by
      Foes, Nazis Say', New York Times, 1 May 1939: https://timesmachine.
      nytimes.com/timesmachine/1939/05/01/113344548.pdf.

73   'spheres of influence': The Molotov–Ribbentrop Pact, signed by the
      German Reich and the Soviet Union, Moscow, 23 August 1939, commit-
      ting neither to go to war against the other, or ally itself with an enemy
      of the other. Unilaterally terminated by the Reich on 22 June 1941 when
      Germany launched Operation Barbarossa and invaded the Soviet Union.

73   Two weeks later: 'The First Pictures of Germany's Invasion and Bom-
      bardment of Poland', New York Times, 2 September 1939: https://
      timesmachine.nytimes.com/timesmachine/1939/09/02/93952902.pdf.

73   naming Dr Hans Frank: Hans Michael Frank, b. 23 May 1900, Karls-
      ruhe, Germany; d. 16 October 1946, Nuremberg, Governor General of
      Poland 1939–5; Sands, East West Street, p. 216 f.

73   The territory of German-occupied Poland: Martyn Housden, Hans
      Frank: Lebensraum and the Holocaust (Palgrave Macmillan, 2003);
      Dieter Schenk, Hans Frank: Hitlers Kronjurist und Generalgouverneur
      (Fischer, 2006); Karl Baedeker, Das Generalgouvernement: Reisehand-
      buch (Karl Baedeker, 1943).

73   On 17 October: OW CV and Biography, p. 18, provided by HW, on file
      with author.

73   'Full of joy to change posts': R, CW, 1938–42 I, p. 11.

74   'Poland was taken': R, CW, 1932–45, pp. 34–5.

74   Within a month Seyss-Inquart: Paul R. Bartrop and Eve E. Grimm,
      Perpetrating the Holocaust: Leaders, Enablers and Collaborators (ABC-
      CLIO, 2019), p. 301.

74   'humane and sympathetic': R, CW, 1932–45, p. 43.

74   'decent man, of good character': T, CW and EF, former SS-
      Hauptsturmführer, Cassette 8, Side 2, 24.11.1976.

74   The Wächters occupied a large villa: Jodłowa 13, 30-251 Kraków,
      Poland. Known today as Przegoraly castle, built in the 1920s by Polish
      architect Adolf Szyszko-Bohusz as his family residence, taken by the
      German Reich and expanded for the Wächter family, to create 'Schloss
      Wartenberg'. Until 2018 it housed the Jagiellonian University's Institute
      of European Studies and Centre for Holocaust Studies. Today it is a
      restaurant and hotel: http://www.uziyada.pl/#.

74   'Very intelligent': R, CW, 1932–45, p. 45.

75   She enjoyed his parties: Krzeszowice (Kressendorf, during the German
      occupation 1941–5), a town outside Kraków. The local Potocki Palace
      became known as Haus Kressendorf and served as a residence for the
      Frank family.

75   'She had no cause on my account': R, CW, 1932–45, p. 46.

75 'peeped out, with an air of curiosity': R, CW, 1932–45, pp. 47–9.

75 Frank talked animatedly about design: Since 1633, the imperial crypt housed at the Capuchin church is the final resting place for members of the Habsburg House.

75 'A long row of rulers': R, CW, 1932–45, pp. 54–5.

76 'the city in the entire General Government': David M. Crowe, *Oskar Schindler: The Untold Account of His Life, Wartime Activities, and the True Story Behind the List* (Basic Books, 2004), p. 141.

76 Most Jews would be expelled: Doron Rabinovici, *Eichmann's Jews*, trans. Nick Somers (Polity Press, 2011).

76 SS-Obergruppenführer Friedrich-Wilhelm Krüger: Friedrich-Wilhelm Krüger, b. 8 May 1894, Strasbourg; d. 10 May 1945, Gundertshausen, Austria. SS and police chief in the General Government 1939–43.

76 'faced with the guillotine': R, CW, 1932–45, p. 56.

76 'He refused to shoot': R, CW, 1932–45, p. 57.

76 the notorious *Sonderaktion Krakau*: *Sonderaktion Krakau* was the code-name given to the Nazi operation targeting professors and academics at the universities in Kraków.

76 'precautionary measure': Nuremberg Trial Proceedings, Vol. 12, 23 April 1946, morning session, p. 106: https://avalon.law.yale.edu/imt/04-23-46.asp.

77 'brutality': Crowe, *Oskar Schindler*, p. 144.

77 'severe punishment': *Anordnung – Kennzeichnung der Juden im Distrikt Krakau* (18.11.1939).

77 Walther Funk: Walther Funk, b. 18 August 1890, East Prussia; d. 31 May 1960, Düsseldorf, Germany. Reichsminister for economic affairs 1938–45.

77 The Vienna Philharmonic visited: *Wiener Bild*, 10 January 1940, p. 21, reporting the visit under director Hans Knappertsbusch; also Fritz Trümpi, *The Repertoire of the Vienna Philharmonic in the Nazi Era*: http://wphdata.blob.core.windows.net/documents/Documents/pdf/NS/ns_truem_05_repertoire_en_v01a.pdf.

77 'Tomorrow, I have to have': L, OW to CW, 17.12.1939.

78 Two German police officers: Instytut Pamięci Narodowej (Institute of National Remembrance), album of photographs taken at Bochnia on 18 December 1939, order reference BUWa-I-541-277/18, on file with author.

78 'leaning against a well': Broucek, *Ein General im Zwielicht*, p. 445.

78 'Five hours screaming': R, CW, 1932–45, pp. 38–9.

78 Schloss Prielau: Gerti von Hofmannsthal bought Schloss Prielau in 1932; the family was dispossessed during the Second World War, the property acquired by Josef Thorak. After the war the property was returned to the Hofmannsthal family. In 1987 the Porsche family bought the Schloss and converted it into a hotel.

78 inhabited by Josef Thorak: Josef Thorak, b. 7 February 1889, Vienna; d.

25 February 1952, Hartmannsberg, Germany. Sculptor.

79   Dr Franz Rehrl: Franz Rehrl, b. 4 December 1890, Salzburg; d. 23 January 1947, Salzburg. Governor of Salzburg, 1922–38.

79   'how would I get out of Vienna': R, CW, 1932–45, p. 43.

79   'good, healthy, restorative times': R, CW, 1932–45, pp. 43–4.

79   Otto would not allow Jews: R, OW, *Tagebuchblätter Aufenthalt im Sowjetgebiet vom 29.4. bis 2.5.1940 (04.05.1940)* (Visit to Soviet territory, 29 April to 2 May 1940).

79   'Holland capitulates': Antony Beevor, *The Second World War* (Weidenfeld & Nicolson, 2012). D, CW, 1940: 15.05.1940; 18.05.1940; 19.05.1940; 23.06.1940.

79   'huge help in the kitchen': R, CW, 1932–45, pp. 44–5.

79   'sweet, intelligent thing': R, CW, 1932–45, p. 40.

79   'No end in sight': L, OW to CW, 13.11.1940.

80   title of nobility, 'von': BArch, R 9361-III/561695; *Waechter, Otto – Personenbezogene Unterlagen der SS und SA. OW an den Reichsführer SS; Betrifft: Dortiges Schreiben vom 18.III.1940, ZK-ECK/0,* 01.04.1940.

81   All others were to be expelled: 25 November 1940: http://www.holocaustresearchproject.org/ghettos/krakow/krakow.html.

81   On 3 March he signed the decree: *Krakauer Zeitung*, 3 March 1941. See also: Dieter Schenk, *Krakauer Burg: die Machtzentrale des Generalgouverneurs Hans Frank, 1939–1945* (Christoph Links Verlag, 2010), p. 144; Crowe, *Oskar Schindler*, pp. 144–5.

81   Thousands were forced from their homes: Crowe, *Oskar Schindler*, p. 145.

81   The pastor was lucky: Crowe, *Oskar Schindler*, p. 146.

81   'Inhuman deportations': Ibid.

81   'Dinner with Wächter': Curzio Malaparte, *Journal Secret (1941–1944)* (Quai Voltaire, 2019), p. 45 (author's translation).

82   One scene in the novel: Curzio Malaparte, *Kaputt* (NYRB, 2005), pp. 97, 100, 103, 182–3.

82   Malaparte reported: *Corriere della Sera*, 22 March 1942, p. 3; also 17 and 22 February 1942.

83   In the evening she attended: D, CW, 1941, 02.04.1941.

84   In the company of Niklas Frank: Cecilia Gallerani, 1473–1536, mistress of the Duke of Milan, best known as the subject of Leonardo da Vinci's painting *Lady with an Ermine* (c. 1489).

84   I sat on an ancient sofa: The Potocki Palace was built for Alfred II Potosky, former governor of Galicia 1875–83.

84   A friend introduced me to Bronisława Horowitz: Bronisława Horowitz, b. 22 April 1930, Kraków, Poland; prisoner number 76307.

84   'panic, planes and sirens': Hans-Christian Jasch and Christoph Kreutzmüller (eds.), *The Participants: The Men of the Wannsee Conference* (Berghahn, 2018).

85   Otto brought him to Kraków:VWI-SWA Galizien 1_Augenzeugenbe-

richt_Galizien 3729-7, Rosa Stephenson.

85   Later they were transported: Amon Leopold Göth, b. 11 December 1908, Vienna; d. 13 September 1946, Kraków. Commander of the Plaszow concentration camp 1943–4.

85   where he met Oskar Schindler: Oskar Schindler, b. 28 April 1908, Zwittau, Germany; d. 9 October 1974, Hildesheim, Germany. Industrialist.

85   another work camp, Arbeitslager Brünnlitz: KZ-Außenlager Brünnlitz, 1944–5. Site for the pretend armaments factory run by Oskar Schindler, set up to protect the Jews in his workforce from being deported to concentration camps.

87   Might Otto intervene to assist: L, Government of Kraków to Otto Schremmer, 21.04.1941.

87   'special protégé Horsti': L, OW to JW, 22.04.1941.

87   In June 1941: David Stahel, *Operation Barbarossa and Germany's Defeat in the East* (CUP, 2009).

87   Karl Lasch: Karl Lasch, b. 29 December 1904, Kassel, Germany; d. 1 June 1942 in Breslau, or Auschwitz. Governor of the District of Radom 1939–41 and Governor of the District of Galicia 1941–2.

88   'Otto told me about a Waldtraute': D, CW, 1941, 30.05.1941.

88   'very low': D, CW, 1941, 07.06.1941.

88   'All is well': L, CW to OW, 1941, undated.

88   'I have not felt this good': L, CW to OW, 1941, 15.10.1941.

88   'Otto hammered the final nail': D, CW, 1941, 15.11.1941.

88   pianist Elly Ney: Elly Ney, b. 27 September 1882, Düsseldorf, Germany; d. 31 March 1968, Tutzing, Germany. Pianist.

88   'I long for a separate bedroom': D, CW, 1941, 22.11.1941.

88   Conflicts arose: BArch, NS 19/806. *Wächter Differenzen mit dem höheren SS- und Polizeiführer Ost, Krüger*.

89   'ultimately a radical solution': Bogdan Musial, *Deutsche Zivilverwaltung und Judenverfolgung im Generalgouvernement* (Harrassowitz Verlag, 1999), p. 196.

89   On the instruction of Heinrich Himmler: Belzec, Key Dates: https://encyclopedia.ushmm.org/content/en/article/belzec-key-dates.

89   'total elimination of the Jews': Trial of the Major War Criminals Before the International Military Tribunal, Vol. 22 – 1 October 1946 (Nuremberg, 1947), p. 542: https://avalon.law.yale.edu/imt/10-01-46.asp.

89   'It will bring me great joy': L, OW to Hans Frank, 20.12.1941.

89   state secretary of the Government General, Dr Josef Bühler: Josef Bühler, b. 16 February 1904; d. 21 August 1948. State Secretary and Deputy Governor of the General Government 1939–45.

89   'forced emigration': The minutes available on the website of the House of the Wannsee Conference: https://www.ghwk.de/fileadmin/user_upload/pdf-wannsee/engl/protokol.pdf.

90   'from West to East': Sands, *East West Street*, p. 220.

90 The next day, 23 January: 'Dr Waechter Gouverneur von Galizien', 24.01.1942, on file with author.

90 'We need to send our best man: T, CW with EF, Cassette 8, Side 1, Part 1, 24.11.1976.

91 In July 1941 Germany occupied: Sands, *East West Street*, pp. xvii, 68–9.

91 Within a few weeks Otto: P, 5.9, 1942, p. 55: '*Anordnung über den Arbeitseinsatz von Juden*' (Order on labour input of Jews), 13.03.1942, on file with author.

91 the large villa at number 11 Leuthenstrasse: Today it is called 'Ivana Franka Street': https://www.lvivcenter.org/en/streets/Leuthenstrasse/.

91 'enormous joy': R, CW, 1938–42 I, p. 28.

92 He hoped to master the job: L, OW to JW, 12.02.1942.

92 His team included Dr Egon Höller: Egon Ambros Höller, b. 16 July 1907, Kritzendorf, Austria-Hungary; d. 9 August 1991, Kreuth, Germany. Stadthauptmann Lemberg 1942–4.

92 *Abteilungsleiter* Otto Bauer: Otto Bauer, b. 1 April 1888, Ravensburg, Germany; d. 9 February 1944, Lemberg. Abteilungsleiter Innere Verwaltung 1941–44.

92 Theobald Thier as SS-Gruppenführer: Theobald Thier, b. 12 April 1897, Stuttgart; d. 12 July 1949, Kraków. SS-Brigadeführer and police major 1942–5.

92 In the east, Reichskommissar Erich Koch: Erich Koch, b. 19 June 1896, Eberfeld, Germany; d. 12 November 1986, Barczewo, Poland. Gauleiter of East Prussia 1928–45.

92 Metropolitan Andrey Sheptytsky: Andrey Sheptytsky, b. 29 July 1865, Prylbychi, Austrian empire; d. 1 November 1944, Lviv, Ukraine. Metropolitan archbishop of the Ukrainian Greek Catholic Church 1901–44.

93 musical education that appeared in *Das Reich*: *Das Reich* (1940–5), German newspaper founded by propaganda minister Joseph Goebbels.

93 'You can see the hand': L, OW to CW, 20.04.1942.

93 'sacred duty to annihilate': Peter Longerich, *Heinrich Himmler* (OUP, 2011), p. 570.

93 'In my heart': L, OW to CW, 05.06.1942; L, CW to OW, 08.06.1942.

93 'I wore Frank's boots, sloppily': D, CW, 1942, 01.02.1942.

93 'for the Führer's headquarters': D, CW, 1942, 04.03.1942.

93 'he played the piano': D, CW, 1942, 06.03.1942.

93 'I breathed in his air': D, CW, 1942, 07.05.1942.

93 'dreamt of Governor General': D, CW, 1942, 21.06.1942.

94 Hitler stripped Frank of various: Sands, *East West Street*, pp. 233–4.

94 Frank told his wife: Sands, *East West Street*, pp. 234–5, 259–60.

94 'He seems mad, loves another': D, CW, 1942, 23.09.1942.

94 'Did you even try to call': L, CW to OW, 15.06.1942.

94 'For my love': Lemberg, 08.08.1942.

95 'Party comrade Wächter!': Sands, *East West Street*, pp. 239–41.

95 'within half a year': Note of meeting 6 August 1942, Resettlement of the Jews, attended by Losacker, Katzmann, Bauer, Gereis, on file with author.

95 'There was much to do': L, OW to CW, 16.08.1942.

96 'I arrived just in time': L, OW to CW, 20.08.1942.

96 'almost ashamed': L, OW to CW, 20.08.1942.

96 In early September, Martin Bormann: Martin Bormann, b. 17 June 1900, Halberstadt, Germany; d. 2 May 1945, Berlin, Germany. Chief of the Nazi Party chancellery 1941–5.

96 'very capable': Abschrift, Beauftragter des Reichsleiters M Bormann (13.09.1942).

97 It sounded even better: L, CW to OW, 23.08.1942.

97 not least by Herbert von Karajan: 'Karajan: Fast wäre er ein Zeller geworden', *Salzburger Nachrichten*, 23.08.2017: https://www.pressreader. com/austria/salzburger-nachrichten/20170823/282282435421614.

97 'I'll be interested to see': L, CW to OW, 23.08.1942.

97 'unbelievably lovely': L, CW to OW, 27.08.1942.

97 'The Jews are being deported': L, OW to CW, 29.08.1942.

98 'a very positive impression': L, OW to CW, 10.09.1942.

98 'The path of life can be mountainous': L, CW to OW, 15.08.1942.

98 'the beautiful picture from Lemberg': BArch, R 9361-III/561695; Waechter, Otto – *Personenbezogene Unterlagen der SS und SA. Der Reichsführer SS Einschreiben an SS-Brigadeführer Gouverneur Dr. Wächter*, 19.01.1943.

98 his deputy, SS-Obergruppenführer Karl Wolff: Karl Friedrich Otto Wolff, b. 13 May 1900, Darmstadt; d. 15 July 1984, Rosenheim, Germany. Commander SS and police forces in Italy 1943–5.

99 Hans Frank was listed as number one: *New York Times*, 17 October 1942.

100 He recalled the first '*Aktion*': Dieter Pohl, 'Ivan Kalymon, the Ukrainian Auxiliary Police, and the Nazi Anti-Jewish Policy in L'viv, 1941–1944', Report for the Office of Special Investigations, US Department of Justice, 31 May 2005; Dieter Pohl, *Nationalsozialistische Judenverfolgung in Ostgalizien 1941–1944*, 2nd edn (Oldenbourg, 1997).

100 'I was protected by my papers': *Anordnung über den Arbeitseinsatz von Juden*, 13.03.1942, Drohobyz, on file with author.

102 'I should like to know': L, Myron Taylor to Cardinal Maglione, 26.09.1942, NARA, on file with author.

103 produced his *Final Report: Der SS u. Polizeiführer im Distrikt Galizien, Lösung der Judenfrage in Galizien*, 20.06.1943: http://nuremberg.law.harvard.edu/documents/4404-cover-letter-to-ss?q=katzmann#p.1 (in English).

103 Otto took the opportunity: Olesya Khromeychuk, *Undetermined Ukrainians: Post-war narratives of the Waffen SS 'Galicia' Division* (Peter Lang, 2013), p. 3.

103 He wanted a military draft: EM, HCJ to PS, 12.09.2018.

103 'They demanded equal rights': R, CW, 1932–45, p. 66.
103 'One of the saddest days': Geoffrey Roberts, *Victory at Stalingrad* (Routledge, 2013). D, CW, 1943, 03.02.1943.
104 'For every hundred seriously injured': R, CW 1932–45.
104 She came to like Stützen: D, CW, 1943, 07.03.1943.
104 'When can I have the next child?': D, CW, 1943, 05.05.1943.
104 Two weeks later Mussolini: Christopher Duggan, *A Concise History of Italy* (CUP, 2nd edn, 2014).
104 'immeasurable': D, CW, 1943, 28.08.1943.
104 'I like flirting with this child': D, CW, 1943, 28.09.1943; 23.09.1943; 30.09.1943.
105 Rudolf Pavlu was relieved: T, CW and EF, Cassette 2, Side 2, 24.11.1976. See also: 'Law Report of Trials of War Criminals', *The United Nations War Crimes Commission*, Volume VII, 1948, p. 3 – Trial of Haupsturmführer Amon Leopold Goeth; available at: https://www.loc.gov/rr/frd/Military_Law/pdf/Law-Reports_Vol-7.pdf.
106 to mark the Battle of Brody: Battle of Brody (1944), tank battle fought by the Red Army and German forces between the Ukrainian towns of Brody, Dubno and Lutsk.
107 The next day we travelled: Sands, *East West Street*, p. 13.
109 sympathisers from *Svoboda*: Svoboda, Ukrainian nationalist party founded 1995, widely recognised as anti-Semitic.
110 a baroque, sixteenth-century castle: Podhorce castle, located some 80km from Lviv, constructed between 1635 and 1640 as a residential palace for Stanisław Koniecpolski, a wealthy Polish military commander.
111 The assassin was a Soviet agent: Michael James Melnyk, *The History of the Galician Division of the Waffen-SS, Volume I: On the Eastern Front, April 1943 to July 1944* (Fonthill Media, 2016), p. 156.
111 'Despite all difficulties': L, OW to JW, 01.03.1944.
111 closing down the Janowska camp: Janowska concentration camp, Lviv, September 1941 to November 1943. It is estimated that around 100,000 inmates passed through the camp, of whom about 40,000 were killed.
111 'Let me have some fun': R, CW, 1932–45, pp. 70–1.
112 A total of 335 Italians: Alessandro Portelli, *The Order Has Been Carried Out* (Palgrave Macmillan, 2003); Robert Katz, *Death in Rome* (Jonathan Cape, 1967) (filmed as *Massacre in Rome*).
112 'I was strict': R, CW, 1932–45, p. 72.
112 When the Red Army was less: D, CW, 1944, 17.04.1944.
112 'I promote the SS-Brigadeführer Dr Otto Wächter': BArch, R 9361-III/561695; *Waechter, Otto – Personenbezogene Unterlagen der SS und SA. Führerhauptquartier*, 16.05.1944.
112 'I will endeavour to warrant': BArch, R 9361-III/561695; *Waechter, Otto – Personenbezogene Unterlagen der SS und SA. Dr. Otto G Wächter an den Reichsführer-SS und Chef der Deutschen Polizei*, 03.06.1944.
112 On 5 June, the US Army's 88th: Edward Kennedy, 'Nazis Wreck

Area in Front of Rome', *New York Times*, 04.06.1944: https://times
machine.nytimes.com/timesmachine/1944/06/04/85157507.pdf; Milton
Bracker, 'Road to Rome Hard Fought Yet Crowded with Civilians', *New
York Times,* 05.06.1944: https://timesmachine.nytimes.com/timesma-
chine/1944/06/05/86725571.pdf; Herbert L. Matthews, 'Conquerors'
Goal Reached by Allies', *New York Times*, 05.06.1944: https://times
machine.nytimes.com/timesmachine/1944/06/05/86725572.pdf.

112 'I hope that the English': L, CW to OW, 04.07.1944.

113 'Thank God, nothing happened': Hans Royce, *20. Juli 1944* (Berto
Verlag, 1961), pp. 180–1; D, CW, 1944, 20.07.1944; 21.07.1944.

113 'practically lost': *Das Diensttagebuch des deutschen Generalgouverneurs
in Polen* (Deutsche Verlags-Anstalt, 1984), 26 July 1944, p. 890.

113 'A king without a country': L, OW to CW, 27.07.1944.

113 'His greatest wish was': R, CW, 1932–45, p. 74.

114 Himmler transferred him to Italy: *Fernschreiben des SS-Reichsführer
an Gouverneur SS-Gruppenführer Wächter,* 01.08.1944, on file with
author.

114 'He was the liaison man': R, CW, 1932–45, p. 75.

114 the journalist Melitta Wiedemann: Melitta Wiedemann, b. 2 April 1900,
St Petersburg, Russia; d. 13 September 1980, Munich. Journalist, editor
of *Die Aktion* 1939–44.

114 'we had a nice maid': R, CW, 1932–45, pp. 76–7.

114 'I'm swimming as much as possible': L, OW to CW, 20.08.1944.

115 'true German Führerkind': L, CW to OW, 26.08.1944.

115 The Reichsführer enquired: Telegram, HH to OW, 13.10.1944, on file
with author.

115 'Like locusts, by air and by foot': R, CW, 1932–45.

115 'Being despondent and reflective': L, OW to CW, 06.09.1944.

115 'we will stand with him in the future': L, OW to CW, 20.09.1944.

115 In September, somewhat optimistically: Telegram to OW, 02.09.1944, on
file with author.

116 'I've just been with Globus': L, OW to OW jr, 26.08.1944; L, OW to
CW, 10.09.1944. Globočnik transferred most of the men who worked
for him in *Aktion Reinhardt* in the General Government to Trieste,
where they formed *Abteilung R,* with the task of rounding up Jews
and partisans: Stefano di Giusto and Tommaso Chiussi, *Globočnik's
Men in Italy, 1943–45: Abteilung R and the SS-Wachmannschaften
of the Operationszone Adriatisches Küstenland* (Atglen, PA., Schiffer,
2017).

116 General Wolff's chief of staff noted: BArch, R/70/Italien/3 – *Tagebuch
des Führungsstabes.*

116 He wrote most days: L, OW to CW, 17.11.1944; L, OW to CW,
25.11.1944.

116 'I know your husband better': L, CW to Brigitte Frank, 17.11.1944.

117 'very optimistic': L, OW to Hella Jasper-Leithe, 16.12.1944.

117 'good and right against the destructive powers': *Weihnachtsrede des Gruppenführers Dr. Wächter bei der A.O. der NSDAP Ortsgruppe Fasano*, 17.12.1944, on file with author.

117 'the Jews would sing with one voice': L, CW to OW, 09.12.1944.

118 'a difficult time for a great German celebration': L, CW to OW, 06.01.1945; L, OW to CW, 10.01.1945.

118 As Allied bomber squadrons flew: L, CW to OW, 06.01.1945.

118 She welcomed the packets of coffee: L, CW to OW, 14.01.1945.

118 a man on whose shoulders: L, OW to CW, 08.02.1945.

118 Italy too was 'tricky': L, OW to CW, 14.01.1945; L, OW to CW, 19.01.1945; L, OW to CW, 23.01.1945.

118 Yes, he supported her idea: L, OW to CW, 15.01.1945.

118 'Our beautiful Reich is destroyed': L, CW to OW, 24.01.1945.

118 'king without a country:' L, CW to OW, 26.01.1945.

118 The situation today was gloomy: L, CW to OW, 30.01.1945.

118 Listening to another Hitler speech: L, OW to CW, 31.01.1945.

119 'Hundreds of foreign workers': L, CW to OW, 17.02.1945.

119 'a bridge to the family in Zell': L, OW to CW, 11.02.1945.

119 Otto worried about the Allied attacks: L, OW to CW, 09.02.1945.

119 'fate swirls around us': L, OW to CW, 08.02.1945.

119 'It would be too great an injustice': L, OW to CW, 17.02.1945.

119 A work trip revived memories: L, OW to CW, 10.02.1945.

119 the Reichsminister for Bohemia and Moravia, Karl Hermann Frank: Karl Hermann Frank, b. 24 January 1898, Bohemia; d. 22 May 1946 Prague. Reichsminister Bohemia and Moravia 1942–5.

119 Instead, Gottlob Berger: Gottlob Christian Berger, b. 16 July 1896, Gerstetten, Germany; d. 5 January 1975, Stuttgart. Chief SS Main Office 1940–5.

119 a search for an 'outstanding personality': Telegram by Berger to Himmler, dated 28 January 1945, on file with author.

119 'I know that W. is an outstanding employee': Telegram by Himmler to Wolff, dated 30 January 1945, on file with author.

119 The reference was to the small army: The Russian Liberation Army, also referred to as the Vlasov Army, active in 1944–5, composed of Russian defectors, former Soviet prisoners of war and Russian volunteers who enlisted with the German army.

120 With General Wolff's support: L, OW to CW, 28.01.1945.

120 'more ruins, even less traffic': L, OW to CW, 24.03.1945.

120 the leadership of General Pavlo Shandruk: Pavlo Shandruk, b. 28 February 1889, Volhynia; d. 15 February 1979, New Jersey, USA. Head of Ukrainian National Committee, commander of the Ukrainian National Army 1945.

120 At Yalta, in early February: The Yalta Conference was held 4–11 February 1945 between the USA, UK and Soviet Union to decide on Europe's future post-war.

120 'Representatives of the various eastern peoples': L, OW to CW, 19.03.1945.

120 agreed to establish a Ukrainian National Committee: The Ukrainian National Army (UNA), created in March 1945 to unite Ukrainian forces fighting the Soviet army, a sub-organisation of the Ukrainian National Committee (UNC), founded in March 1945 as the sole representation of Ukraine.

121 the two visited General Fritz Freitag: Fritz Freitag, b. 28 April 1894, Allenstein, East Prussia; d. 10 May 1945, Graz, Austria. SS Commander Galicia Division 1943–4.

121 Otto supported Shandruk's proposals: Khromeychuk, *Undetermined Ukrainians*, p. 19.

121 He wanted the UNA to function: Michael Melnyk, *The History of the Galician Division of the Waffen SS, Vol. II: Stalin's Nemesis* (Fonthill Media, 2016).

121 I found no indication: Kerstin von Lingen, *Allen Dulles, the OSS, and Nazi War Criminals: The Dynamics of Selective Prosecution* (CUP, 2013).

121 He met with General Wolff's chief of staff: BArch R 70/Italien/3 – *Tagebuch des Führungsstabes* (Chief of staff diary, around 28 April 1945); EM, JE to PS, 08.04.19.

121 On 29 April, Hitler signed: Marriage Certificate, Private Will and Political Testament, available at: https://catalog.archives.gov/id/6883511.

121 He named Admiral Dönitz: Karl Dönitz, b. 16 September 1891, Grünau, Germany; d. 24 December 1980, Aumühle, Germany. High Command of the Navy 1943–5, Minister of War and President of the German Reich 1943.

121 The following day Hitler committed suicide: 'The End of Hitler', *New York Times*, 2 May 1945: https://timesmachine.nytimes.com/times machine/1945/05/02/313695522.pdf.

121 There he was reportedly spotted: Pavlo Shandruk, *Arms of Valor* (R. Speller, 1959), p. 273; on Otto's presence in Timau, see: Pier Arrigo Carnier, 'Storia della Chiesa di "Christo Re" – Timau', in *Asou Greats*, No. 51, April 2006, 11–14: https://drive.google.com/file/d/0BwYsaQ_4psX7QX-cycWYocDBock1RWE5XMXFCZ3NVMDhzNE5v/view; and 'Storia di una Donazione Tedesca, Verificatasi Durante la Ritirata in Carnia, 2 Maggio 1945' (23 August 2013): http://pierarrigocarnierstoricoe-giornalista.blogspot.com/2013/08/storia-di-una-donazione-tedesca.html (sourced to Dr Franz Hradetsky (SS Hauptsturmführer of the Kommando Waffen SS 'Adria' in Trieste) and Enrst Lerch (SS Sturmbann-führer and former Stabsführer to Odilo Globočnik in Lublin and later in Trieste).

121 Privately, however, he expressed: Shandruk, *Arms of Valor*, pp. 277–80.

122 'I was very worried about them': R, CW, 1932–45, p. 93.

122 'It was terrible to leave': R, CW, 1932–45, p. 94.

122   On 8 May the war ended: Beller, *Concise History of Austria*, p. 245 f.

122   'The big day of victory for the enemies': R, CW, *Geburtsbuch*, p. 174.

122   'I burned some and threw the rest in the lake': R, CW, 1932–45.

122   The US Army entered Zell-am-See: Stephen Ambrose, *Band of Brothers* (Simon & Schuster, 1992), p. 274.

122   'They slept in our beds': R, CW, 1932–45, p. 98.

123   'I was a fatalist, and thought it best': R, CW, 1932–45, pp. 100–102.

123   'There was a hole where I'd buried it': R, CW, 1932–45, p. 103.

124   'My friends were all locked up': R, CW, 1932–45, pp. 104–5.

124   regret about her 'panic-stricken' action: R, CW, 1942–45 II, pp. 32–3; R, CW, 1945–47 III, pp. 5–6.

124   Kesselring surrendered to the US: Kerstin von Lingen, *Kesselring's Last Battle: War Crimes Trials and Cold War Politics, 1945–1960* (University Press of Kansas, 2009).

125   'Your husband never came': L, F. Ostheim to CW, 1948.

125   He asked to be left alone: Shandruk, *Arms of Valor*, Chapter 29.

129   'A film ... about a difficult conversation': Pat Padua, 'What Our Fathers Did: A Nazi Legacy brings up a difficult conversation', *Washington Post*, 12 November 2015: https://www.washingtonpost.com/goingoutguide/movies/what-our-fathers-did-a-nazi-legacy-brings-up-a-difficult-conversation/2015/11/12/e2484c4e-84ab-11e5-a7ca-6ab6ec20f839_story.html?utm_term=.dec177429fdb.

129   'Disturbing': Peter Bradshaw, 'My Nazi Legacy review – the poison of the past lives on', *Guardian*, 19 November 2015: https://www.theguardian.com/film/2015/nov/19/my-nazi-legacy-review-the-poison-of-the-past-lives-on.

129   'Gripping and compelling': Leba Hertz, 'Two sons of Nazi fathers take two views', *SF GATE*, 12 November 2015: https://www.sfgate.com/movies/article/Two-sons-take-two-views-of-their-Nazi-fathers-6625367.php.

129   'Horribly gripping': Deborah Ross, 'What's it like to have a Nazi for a father?', *Spectator*, 21 November 2015: https://www.spectator.co.uk/2015/11/whats-it-like-to-have-a-nazi-for-a-father/.

129   'troubling': Justin Chang, 'Film Review: What Our Fathers Did: My Nazi Legacy', *Variety*, 10 November 2015: https://variety.com/2015/film/reviews/what-our-fathers-did-review-a-nazi-legacy-1201637890/.

129   'obligated to recognize the truth': Ken Jaworowski, 'Review: What Our Fathers Did: My Nazi Legacy', *New York Times*, 5 November 2015: https://www.nytimes.com/2015/11/06/movies/review-what-our-fathers-did-a-nazi-legacy.html.

129   'Horst's deluded idolization of his father': Lizzie Crocker, 'Forgiving my Nazi Father: A Horrific Past Made Present', *Daily Beast*, 17 April 2015:   https://www.thedailybeast.com/forgiving-my-nazi-father-a-horrific-past-made-present; Teo Bugbee, 'What It's Like Growing Up With a Nazi', *Daily Beast*, 8 November 2015: https://www.thedailybeast.com/

what-its-like-growing-up-with-a-nazi.

131 Charlotte took care to explain: EM, Kerstin von Lingen to PS, 23.05.2019.

131 'Today I have decided to do': R, CW, 1938–42 I, p. 2.

132 'December 1966 . . .': T, CW and Melitta Wiedemann, Cassette 2, Side 2, 02.04.1977.

134 She posed questions of interest and complexity: Lisa Jardine, *Temptation in the Archives: Essays in Golden Age Dutch Culture* (UCL Press, 2015), pp. 1–17.

136 Karl Renner, newly appointed head: Beller, *Concise History of Austria*, p. 247 ff.

136 'Nazi teachers were in part interned': R, CW, 1932–45, pp. 109, 113.

136 'the Catholic views the Jew consistently': Predikaka, *Ferdinand Pawlikowski*, p. 91.

137 the article in the *Wiener Zeitung*: S3.1030 ZE Otto and Charlotte Wächter; Military Government – Austria, Property Register, available at: www.fold3.com/image/306459764; 'Ratskammerbeschluss, *Wiener Zeitung*, 29 December 1946: on file.

137 The 'Thousand Year Reich' ended: R, CW, 1932–45, pp. 127–8.

137 'I entered, invited him to sit down': R, CW, 1932–45, pp. 129–36.

137 'Maybe we shouldn't have taken it': R, CW, 1938–42 I, pp. 5–7.

138 A new director thwarted efforts: On file with the author. *Beiligendes Schreiben an Landeshauptmann Machold*, 150/Vw/R/Md, 04.09.1945.

138 'Blaschke, former Mayor of Vienna . . .': *London Information of the Austrain Socialists in Great Britain*, 15 December 1945, pp. 7–8.

138 'Austria Accuses!': 'Österreich klagt an!', *Oberösterreichische Nachrichten*, 4 December 1945: http://anno.onb.ac.at/cgi-content/anno?aid=oon &datum=19451204&seite=1&zoom=33&.

139 At the end of May, 'dear Globus' was discovered: David Lester, *Suicide and the Holocaust* (Nova Science, 2005), p. 11.

139 Otto's nemesis in the Government General: Nicolas Patin, *Krüger: un Bourreau Ordinaire* (Fayard, 2017), p. 207. See also: Lester, *Suicide and the Holocaust*, p. 11.

139 Soon after, his wife Margarete: James MacDonald, 'Arch Criminal Dies', *New York Times*, 25 May 1945: https://timesmachine.nytimes.com/timesmachine/1945/05/25/88233713.pdf; 'Frau Himmler Calm at News of Husband', *New York Times*, 13 July 1945: https://timesmachine.nytimes.com/timesmachine/1945/07/13/94856204.pdf.

139 'Local soldier helps locate Frau Himmler': 'Local Soldier Helps Locate Frau Himmler', *Jersey Journal*, 16.05.1945.

139 Hans Frank was caught in Bavaria: Sands, *East West Street*, pp. 209, 284–5, 331.

139 Ernst Kaltenbrunner, Otto's closest friend: 'The Last Days of Ernst Kaltenbrunner': https://www.cia.gov/library/center-for-the-study-of-intelligence/kent-csi/vol4no2/html/v04i2a07p_0001.htm.

139 The Canadians tracked down Horst's godfather: 'Canadians Arrest

Nazi Trojan Horse', *New York Times*, 9 May 1945: https://times machine.nytimes.com/timesmachine/1945/05/09/88225382.pdf.

139   The three comrades made it onto the list: Telford Taylor, *The Anatomy of the Nuremberg Trials: A Personal Memoir* (Knopf, 1992).

139   A year later, on 1 October 1946: 'Sketches of the 11 Nazi Leaders Who Paid With Their Lives at Nuremberg for War Crimes', *New York Times*, 16.10.1946: https://timesmachine.nytimes.com/times-machine/1946/10/16/107146522.pdf.

139   Their remains were cremated: Thomas Darnstädt, 'Der Zweite Weltkrieg: Ein Glücksfall der Geschichte', *Der Spiegel*, 04.04.2005: https://www.spiegel.de/spiegel/print/d-39916258.html.

139   Convicted of 'crimes against humanity': 'Nazi Hanged in Poland; Buehler Convicted in Killing 2 Million, Vast Deportation', *New York Times*, 23.08.1948: https://timesmachine.nytimes.com/times machine/1948/08/23/96597127.pdf.

140   Rudolf Pavlu was caught in April 1949: Bernd-A. Rusinek, *Der Fall Greifeld, Karlsruhe – Wissenschaftsmanagement und NS-Vergangenheit* (KIT – Scientific Publishing, 2019), p. 311.

140   Georg von Ettingshausen disappeared: See: USHMM, Hans Fischböck Papers, Clippings 1966–7: https://collections.ushmm.org/search/cata log/irn652282#?rsc=187553&cv=2&xywh=-1015%2C0%2C4567%2 C3195&c=0&m=0&s=0.

140   Fritz Katzmann, Otto's SS colleague: Thomas Sandkühler, *'Endlösung' in Galizien. Der Judenmord in Ostpolen und die Rettungsinitiativen von Berthold Beitz 1941–1944* (Dietz, 1996), p. 426 ff.

140   The Jews were said to have formed hit squads: Ronen Bergman, *Rise and Kill First: The Secret History of Israel's Targeted Assassinations* (Random House, 2018); also Ian Black, 'Rise and Kill First: The Secret History of Israel's Targeted Assassinations – review', *Guardian*, 22 July 2018: https://www.theguardian.com/books/2018/jul/22/rise-kill-first-secret-history-israel-targeted-assassinations-ronen-bergman-review-mossad.

140   the Soviets set up military tribunals: Sanye Romeike, 'Transitional Justice in Germany after 1945 and after 1990', *International Nuremberg Academy Principles*, Occasional paper No. 1, 2016, pp. 19–22.

140   The Poles wanted justice: Gabriel N. Finder and Alexander V. Prusin, *Justice Behind the Iron Curtain: Nazis on Trial in Communist Poland* (University of Toronto Press, 2018).

140   the Americans established themselves in Gmunden: Michael Salter, *Nazi War Crimes, US Intelligence and Selective Prosecution at Nuremberg* (Routledge, 2007).

140   Winston Churchill declared in a speech: Winston Churchill, *Sinews of Peace*, 5 March 1946: https://winstonchurchill.org/resources/speeches/1946-1963-elder-statesman/the-sinews-of-peace/.

140   an Indian with 'slit eyes': R, CW, 1932–45, p. 153.

140 The year was characterised by food shortages: Frederick Taylor, *Exorcising Hitler: The Occupation and Denazification of Germany* (Bloomsbury Press, 2011); Perry Biddiscombe, *The Denazification of Germany 1945–48* (The History Press, 2006).

141 The first tranche of funds: John Agnew and J. Nicholas Entrikin (eds.), *The Marshall Plan Today – Model and Metaphor* (Routledge, 2004).

141 'we as well have lost every trace': L, Fritz Ostheim to CW, 1945.

142 'Suddenly a whistle came': R, CW, 1932–45, pp. 106–7.

142 'a criminal and persecuted': R, CW, 1945–47 III, pp. 1–2, 7.

143 Otto obtained a membership card: P, OW, Identitätskarten, pp. 1–2.

144 Oswald was 1.78 metres tall: OW papers, 3.1, p. 2, on file with author.

144 'Valid only in Austria': P, OW, Identitätskarten, pp. 3–4.

144 'poacher of sheep': R, CW, 1932–45, p. 141.

144 'First came a bus . . .': OW, undated, with title 'A gloomy story', on file with author.

144 'I brought nice things': L, OW to CW, undated; P, *Nachlass*, Abschnitt 1.

144 'I was spied on day and night': R, CW, 1932–45, p. 131.

144 someone like Lukas Hansel: Lukas Hansel is also mentioned in R, CW, 1945–47 III, p. 14.

144 Bruck-Fusch, where Hermann Göring was caught: 'Goering Yields to 7th Army', *New York Times*, 10.05.1945: https://timesmachine.nytimes.com/timesmachine/1945/05/10/313716012.pdf.

144 'Sometimes, when I arrived': R, CW, 1932–45, p. 146.

146 Buko, as she called him: For military background see Sergio Corbatti and Marco Nava, *Karstjäger: Du SS-Karstwehr-Bataillon á la 24. Waffen-Gebirgs-Division der SS* (Heimdal, 2009), especially p. 391.

146 'in good hands': R, CW, 1932–45, pp. 107, 140.

147 after service with the 24th Waffen Mountain Division: 24th Waffen Mountain Division of the SS Karstjäger was a mountain infantry division active 1944–5, primarily tasked with fighting partisans along the Karst plateau, spreading along the borders of Austria, Italy and Yugoslavia, established by Odilo Globočnik.

147 'That is where I met Otto Wächter': Buko Interview transcript, 04.01.2017, on file with author.

148 'he was either Wächter or Wächtler': Fritz Wächtler, b. 7 January 1891, Triebes, Germany; d. 19 April 1945, Waldmünchen, Germany. Gauleiter Bayreuth 1935–45.

148 'He'd tell me, "This and that': Buko Interview transcript.

148 'Was my father evil or good-natured?': Buko Interview transcript.

149 'The Americans and the English were mostly too lazy': Buko Interview transcript.

149 'He should have been the one to order me around': Buko Interview transcript.

150 'One day we triggered twelve': Buko Interview transcript.

151 'At first he didn't know about it, but later he did': Buko Interview transcript.

151 'You were with the Karstjäger, right?': Corbatti and Nava, *Karstjäger* (Heimdal, 2009). Burkhard Rathmann appears in photographs at *inter alia* pp. 17, 18, 21, 27, 135, 162, 164, 165, 275, with more information at p. 391.

151 'It was supposed to be published in German': Buko Interview transcript.

151 The book was silent: *Atlante delle Stargi Naziste e Fasciste in Italia*, produced by a Joint Historical German-Italian Commission established in 2009: http://www.straginazifasciste.it/?page_id=297&ricerca=33&lang=en.

152 in front of a copy of *The Golden Treasury of German Fairy Tales*: *Der Goldene Deutsche Märchenschatz* (ADAC Verlag, 2004).

153 'He couldn't wander the mountains on his own': R, CW, 1932–35, p. 150; R, CW, 1947–49, pp. 14, 25–6.

153 she would 'sacrifice' the child: R, CW, 1947–49, p. 18.

153 He stayed at the farmhouse of Georg Ettingshausen: Barbara Sauer and Ilse Reiter-Zatloukal, *Advokaten 1938. Das Schicksal der in Österreich verfolgten jüdischen Rechtsanwälte und Rechtsanwältinnen* (MANZ, 2010). The number of Jewish lawyers removed from the Vienna bar was between 1,775 and 1,834: http://www.erinnern.at/bundeslaender/ oesterreich/e_bibliothek/miscellen/barbara-sauer-ilse-reiter-zatloukal- advokaten-1938-das-schicksal-der-in-den-jahren-1938-bis-1945- verfolgten-osterreichischen-rechtsanwaltinnen-und-rechtsanwalt.

154 'May divine powers always preserve': L, OW to Helga Ettingshausen, Christmas 1948.

154 the Goldene Hirsch, the historic Salzburg hotel: The Goldene Hirsch has been a hotel since 1564; today it's a five-star hotel.

154 'A lovely, harmonious time': R, CW, 1932–45, pp. 151–2.

155 Albert Schnez, formerly of the Wehrmacht: Albert Schnez, b. 30 August 1911, Abtsgmünd, Germany; d. 26 April 2007, Bonn. German army officer.

155 'He wanted to emigrate to Argentina': T, CW and HJS, Cassette 3, Side 2, 28.09.1984.

155 'I have six small children': T, CW and HJS, Cassette 3, Side 2, 28.09.1984.

156 'terrible year': R, CW, 1932–45, p. 154.

156 'Everything coming together quite well': L, OW to CW, 12.02.1949.

157 'Not much snow': L, OW to CW, 18.02.1949.

157 'Journey completed, relieved': L, OW to CW, 20.03.1949.

157 In Bolzano, Frau Oberauch von Hösslin: Eleonore 'Nora' Oberrauch von Hösslin, b. 27 November 1905; date of death unknown.

157 'set your soul and body at ease': L, OW to Richard Woksch, 18.03.1949.

158 He spent time with 'funny Franz': Franz Hieronymus Riedl, journalist.

159 'for hat, coat, suit and so on': L, OW to CW, 24.03.1949.

159 Bring a few items of art, or antiquities, he wrote: L, OW to CW, 24.03.1949; L, OW to CW, 29.03.1949.00 the mountain house at

Völs am Schlern: The house, a blend of Jugendstil and Arts and Crafts, may be seen in Renate Brenn-Rammlmair, *Stadtbaumeister Gustav Nolte: der Heimatstil in Bozen* (Bozen: Verl.-Anst. Athesia, 2007).

160 'It was a strange time together': L, CW to Richard Woksch, 21.04.1949; R, CW, 1932–45, pp. 158–9.

161 The folder in the archive bore the title: 'Investigation against Dr. OTTO, WAECHTER Gustaw, Gauleiter of the Kraków district, then the district of Galizien, accused of giving orders of mass executions and actions directed against the Jewish people', File no. 176, 41 pages, IPN (Institute of National Remembrance, Warsaw), records of investigation and documentation of the main Commission to Investigate Nazi Crimes in Poland (so called B.d. records); USHMM (RG-15.155M); on file with author.

162 they were *Geheime Reichssache*: Günther W. Gellermann, ... *und lauschten für Hitler – Geheime Reichssache: die Abhörzentralen des Dritten Reiches* (Bernard & Graefe, 1991).

162 He was prompted to write to the Polish embassy: L, Edward Tuszkiewicz to Polish Embassy in Prague, 13.12.1945, in File 176, Document 10.

163 'Dr Wächter's trace has been encountered': L, Rzeczpospolita Polska (Poland), Ministry of Foreign Affairs to the Central Commission Investigation War Crimes, 11.01.1949, File 176, Document 21.

164 Professor Tadeusz Zaderecki, whose book, *Lwów under the Swastika*: Tadeusz Zaderecki, *Lwów under the Swastika – The Destruction of the Jewish Community through the Eyes of a Polish Writer* (Yad Vashem, 2018).

164 One recipient of the letter was Dieter Schenk: Dieter Schenk, *Hans Frank: Hitlers Kronjurist und Generalgouverneur* (S. Fischer, 2006).

165 Schenk responded courteously: EM, Dieter Schenk to HW, August 2014.

166 following national elections which were won clearly: On 18 June 1948, elections were held to elect the First Republican Parliament after the end of the war, following a referendum to end the monarchy. The 1948 election was won by the Christian Democratic Party (supported by the Vatican and the US) and the Popular Democratic Front, comprised of the Italian Communist Party and the Italian Socialist Party. The Christian Democratic Party formed a coalition with Liberals, Republicans and Social Democrats, even though the Christian Democratic Party held an absolute majority in both chambers.

166 'The reception party, dinner in pleasant company': L, OW to Walter Ladurner, 06.05.1949; L, OW to CW, 30.04.1949.

167 'Old and new, all piled up': L, OW to CW, 04.05.1949.

168 'He didn't speak much on that first evening,': L, OW to CW, 20.06.1949; L, Hedi Dupré to CW, 25.07.1949.

168 His new home was at Vigna Pia: Vigna Pia, Via Filippo Tajani 50, Rome: http://www.vignapia.com/edificio-storico/. The history is silent on the immediate post-war years.

168 'A quaint building . . . half ruin': L, OW to CW, 05.05.1949.

168 'from the time of Nero': L, OW to CW, 22.05.1949.

168 'nice, friendly, incredibly poor': L, OW to CW, 05.05.1949.

169 'Hopefully this time will pass': L, CW to OW, 09.05.1949.

169 'fragrant forests of the cool North': L, OW to CW, 22.05.1949.

169 'The fog dissipated over the Tiber': L, OW to CW, 05.05.1949.

169 'I will do it more often': L, OW to CW, 29.06.1949; L, OW to CW, 12.05.1949.

170 'I was aware that somebody': Walter Rauff, b. 19 June 1906, Köthen, Germany; d. 14 May 1984, Santiago de Chile, Chile. SS commander.

170 'adventurers and low-life flotsam and jetsam': L, Walter Rauff to OW, 25.05.1949.

170 'designed gas vans': Kevin Freeman, 'Wiesenthal Center Releases Documents Which Link Rauff to Important Figures in the Catholic Church in Italy', *JTA – Daily News Bulletin*, 10.05.1984: http://pdfs.jta.org/1984/1984-05-10_089.pdf?_ga=2.16161555 1.2063636335.1564532125-115840253.1564532105.

170 From another source I learned: Klaus Wiegrefe, 'SS Colonel Walter Rauff – West German Intelligence Protected Fugitive Nazi', *Spiegel Online*, 27.09.2011: https://www.spiegel.de/international/germany/ ss-colonel-walter-rauff-west-german-intelligence-protected-fugitive- nazi-a-788348.html.

170 'I've given up running': L, OW to CW, 22.05.1949.

171 'there's plenty of good food and accommodation': L, OW to Walter Ladurner, 06.05.1949; L, OW to CW, 29.06.1949.

171 the relative merits of 'gassing' and DDT: Dichlorodiphenyltrichloro- ethane (DDT) was initially developed for insecticidal purposes, in 1939; later infamous for adverse environmental effects and largely banned.

171 'Gassing will cost at least 500': L, CW to OW, 07.05.1949; L, CW to OW, 26.05.1949.

171 'with a heart beating with longing': L, OW to Nora Oberrauch von Hösslin, 06.05.1949; L, OW to CW, 12.05.1949; L, CW to OW, 21.05.1949; OW to CW, 27.05.1949.

172 conducted by Josef Krips: Josef Alois Krips, b. 8 April 1902, Vienna; d. 13 October 1974, Geneva. Conductor.

172 Truly a play for our times: *Egmont* (1788), theatrical play by Johann Wolfgang von Goethe, understood as a political manifesto in which the main character, Count Egmont, a Dutch warrior, faces down a Spanish duke to defend national liberty, and is later sentenced to death.

172 'Leit stood and watched mournfully': L, OW to CW, 16.05.1949.

172 life as an SS Sturmbannführer: Leithe's son Manfred, whom I met at the Kunsthistorische Museum in Vienna on 31 October 2015, was director of the museum's treasure chamber: EM, HW to PS, 27.03.17.

172 The weekend edition of the *Salzburger Nachrichten*: *Salzburger Nachrichten*, daily newspaper, established June 1945 by US occupying forces. *Neue Front – Zeitung der Unabhängigen*, newspaper founded in 1945

by the VdU (predecessor of the FPÖ), rebranded in 1973 as *Neue Freie Zeitung.*

172 A *Baedeker* guide to Rome: *Baedeker's Rome and Central Italy* (16th edition), 1930.

172 'Be sure to get my name right': L, OW to CW, 22.05.1949.

173 'I can't quite believe that we can't': L, CW to OW, 28.05.1949; L, CW to OW, 12.06. 1949.

173 'several birds migrating overseas': L, OW to CW, 04.06.1949.

173 A man referred to as 'Gü': L, OW to Herbert Gündel, 08.05.1949; L, OW to CW, 16.04.1949; L, Franz Hieronymus Riedl to OW, 15.05.1949; L, OW to CW, 27.05.1949.

174 'how I can best reach Karl': L, OW to Herbert Gündel, 08.05.1949.

174 'I'll pursue everything': L, OW to CW, 05.05.1949.

174 A person who thought the Red Cross: The International Committee of the Red Cross issues emergency travel documents following humanitarian crises and wars, to enable recipients to travel to seek asylum or return home. Issued in lieu of formally recognised identity papers, they are usually valid only for a one-way trip. After the Second World War many Nazis posed as refugees to obtain such papers: https://www.icrc.org/en/doc/resources/documents/article/other/57jpu5.htm.

175 '*embarcó libre* option': an *embarcó libre* is a form of document used to enter certain South American countries; mentioned in L, OW to Walter Ladurner, 10.05.1949 and L, Sepp Breitenberger to OW, 31.05.1949.

175 'combined with an older document': L, OW to WL, 10.05.1949.

175 'would be content with an Austrian passport': L, OW to Walter Ladurner, 10.05.1949.

175 'I know of two cases': L, Walter Ladurner to OW, 12.05.1949.

175 'The best option': L, Sepp Breitenberger to OW, 31.05.1949.

177 Together, we stood before: *The Fight Between Carnival and Lent* (1559), by Pieter Bruegel the Elder (1525–1569); Hanns Swarzenski, 'The Battle between Carnival and Lent', *Bulletin of the Museum of Fine Arts,* Vol. 49, No. 275 (February 1951), pp. 2–11.

178 The article was written by a curator: Diana Błońska, *O Muzeum Narodowym w Krakowie w czasie drugiej wojny światowej* (Klio. Czasopismo poświęcone dziejom Polski i powszechnym, t. 28 (1)/ 2014), pp. 85–128: http://apcz.umk.pl/czasopisma/index.php/KLIO/ article/view/KLIO.2014.005.

178 under the watchful eye of Kajetan Mühlmann: Kajetan (Kai) Mühlmann, b. 26 June 1898, Uttendorf, Austria-Hungary; d. 2 August 1958, Munich. Special Representative for the Protection and Securing of Artworks in the Occupied Eastern Territories (*Sonderbeauftragter für den Schutz und die Sicherung von Kunstwerken in den besetzten Ostgebieten*) 1939–43.

178 Professor Kopera of the Jagiellonian University: Feliks Kopera, b. 12 May 1871, Kraków; d. 27 March 1952, Kraków. Professor, Jagiellonian University 1910-50; Director, National Museum 1901-1950.

178 More details were set out in a letter: L, Feliks Kopera to the Polish War Crimes Commission, 09.12.1946, on file with author.

179 'otherwise they would fall into the hands of the Russians': R, CW, 1932–45, p. 72.

179 'Wächter, 78, returned three works': Uki Goñi, 'Son of Nazi governor returns art stolen from Poland during second world war', *Guardian*, 26.02.2017: https://www.theguardian.com/artanddesign/2017/feb/26/nazi-art-stolen-poland-returned-horst-waechter.

180 The allegations made their way: Henry Foy, 'Nazi claims spur fight between Vienna and Kraków over Bruegel', *Financial Times*, 21.10. 2015: https://www.ft.com/content/d1eaf34e-7810-11e5-933d-efcdc3c11c89.

180 it might be by Veit Stoss: Veit Stoss (c. 1450–1533). German sculptor.

182 for a new political party, the *Verband der Unabhängigen*: The *Verband der Unabhängigen* (Federation of Independents, VDU), a German nationalist party in Austria (1949–55), predecessor to the FPÖ.

182 'A reminder of times past': Thomas Riegler, 'Wie der US-Geheimdienst Ex-Nazis anheuerte und so die FPÖ-Gründung förderte', *Profil*, 4 December 2013: https://www.profil.at/oesterreich/history/wie-us-geheimdienst-ex-nazis-fpoe-gruendung-370249; L, CW to OW, 01.06.1949.

182 The VDU has long disappeared, folded into: *Freiheitliche Partei Österreichs* (Freedom Party of Austria, FPÖ), a right-wing, conservative political party founded in 1956, part of Austria's governing coalition in late 2017, collapsed in May 2019.

182 a light, single-coloured jacket, made of Lanz flannel: Lanz Trachten, founded 1922, produced high-end traditional clothing in Austria and southern Germany, known as 'Trachten': http://www.lanztrachten.at/lt/geschichte/.

183 'Please cross your fingers, at 8 a.m.': L, CW to OW, 12.06.1949; L, CW to OW, 13.06.1949.

184 'There's a chance – only small': L, OW to CW, 18.06.1949.

184 'out in the cold': L, OW to CW, 04.06.1949.

184 'I was able to get him a job with a film': L, Hedi Dupré to CW, 25.07.1949.

184 'I earned my first money': L, OW to CW, 09.06.1949.

184 The film, *La Forza del Destino*: *La Forza del Destino* (1950), Italian film, based on opera by Giuseppe Verdi.

185 *Donne Senza Nome*: *Women Without Names* (1950), Italian film set in a displaced-persons camp at the end of the Second World War. Director Géza von Radványi, b. 26 September 1907, Kaschau, Austria-Hungary; d. 27 November 1986, Budapest.

185 Journalist Franz Riedl introduced him to Luis Trenker: Alois (Luis) Franz Trenker, b. 4 October 1892, St Ullrich in Gröden, Austria-Hungary; d. 12 April 1990, Bolzano, Italy. Film director, architect, athlete.

185 'I cosied up to him': L, OW to CW, 29.06.1949; L, OW to CW, 09.06.1949; L, CW to OW, 04.07.1949.

186 'A few days ago a friend': L, OW to CW, 04.06.1949.

186 'It would be terrible for Franzi': L, CW to OW, 24.06.1949.

186 'From my experience here': L, OW to CW, 16.06.1949.

186 He informed Otto: L, Walter Ladurner to OW, 23.06.1949.

186 it was his affidavit that served: Affidavit of Willhelm Höttl, available in Nuremberg Trial Proceedings, Vol. 3, 14.12.1945, morning session: https://avalon.law.yale.edu/imt/12-14-45.asp.

187 'If you flirt, you never know': L, OW to CW, 29.06.1949; L, OW to CW, 18.06.1949.

187 'reliably anti-British': L, Egon Höller to OW, 15.06.1949.

187 'Something will turn up in July': L, OW to CW, 29.06.1949; L, OW to CW, 20.06.1949.

188 'Let's re-establish our age-old connection': L, OW to Lothar Rübelt, 30.06.1949.

188 He made contact with Dr Ruggero Vasari: Ruggero Vasari, b. 6 February 1898, Messina, Italy; d. 1968, Messina. Playwright and poet.

189 Readers of *Il Tempo*: *Il Tempo*, 2 July 1949, on file with author.

189 *The Story of G.I. Joe*: *The Story of G.I. Joe* (1945), American war film, follows storyline of American infantrymen through the eyes of Pulitzer Prize-winning correspondent Ernie Pyle. *Der Prozeß* (*The Trial*, 1948), Austrian film based on the Tiszaeszlár affair, depicting the anti-Semitic sentiments in the 1880s, with allegations of blood libel, ritual murder.

189 'kind old comrade': L, OW to CW, 04.07.1949.

190 'I went straight to a German doctor': L, OW to CW, 04.07.1949.

190 The doctor prescribed a *limonade purgative de Rogé*: A purgative (laxative) lemonade, based on a formula using magnesium citrate, invented by pharmacist M. Rogé-Delabarre in 1838; see Armand Trousseau and H. Pidoux, *Traité de thérapeutique et de matière médicale*, Vol. 1 (Bechet Jeune, 1858).

190 'all the very best and another 55 years . . .': L, Traute Wächter to OW, 04.07.1949; L, CW to OW, 04.07.1949.

191 '. . . poor *Hümmi* lies': L, OW to CW, 04.07.1949; L, OW to CW, 05.07.1949.

191 'Typhus or something gastric': L, OW to CW, 06.07.1949.

191 There was talk of an 'American wonder drug': Penicillin, whose discovery in 1928 is ascribed to Scottish scientist Alexander Fleming, only began to be used to treat bacterial infections in 1942.

191 the German doctor, Dr Willi Marchesani: Willi Marchesani, b. 12 November 1896, Trieste; date of death unknown. Medical doctor.

191 By eleven o'clock that morning he had 'kept quiet': L, OW to CW, 06.07.1949.

192 *Ospedale di Santo Spirito*, a Vatican-supported institution: Ospedale di Santo Spirito, oldest hospital in Europe; Sivigliano and Luisa Alloisi, *Santo Spirito in Saxia* (Istituto nazionale di studi romani, 2002).

192 'Get well soon for me': L, CW to OW, 10.07.1949.

192 'I've got nowhere to stay': L, CW to OW, 10.07.1949.

193 'You have to keep telling yourself': L, CW to OW, 11.07.1949.

193 'Please be determined': L, CW to OW, 12.07.1949.

193 'Have just left "Franzi"': L, Willi Marchesani to CW, 12.07.1949.

194 'Please do write': L, CW to OW, 13.07.1949.

194 'a big hotel in the centre': Hotel Victoria: https://www.hotelvictoria roma.com/en/.

194 'Baroness W?' he enquired: T, CW and HJS, Cassette 3, Side 2, 28.09.1984.

199 He signed it Bishop Alois Hudal: Alois Hudal, b. 31 May 1885, Graz; d. 13 May 1963, Rome. Rector of Santa Maria dell'Anima 1923–52; on file with author.

199 one from the mayor of Vienna: L, Theodor Körner to CW, 11.11.1949. Körner was president of Austria from 1951 to 1957.

199 letters from correspondents: L, Hans Fischböck to CW, 11.6.1956 (from Buenos Aires); L, Hans Fischböck to CW, 22.12.1964 (from Essen).

199 'Is the July putschist Wächter still alive?': 'Lebt de Juliputschist Wächter noch?', *Arbeiter Zeitung*, 6 March 1951, p. 4.

200 'He lay as black as wood': T, CW and HJS, Cassette 3, Side 1, 28.09.1984.

200 In Rome's central state archives: Archivio centrale dello Stato (ACS), Ministero dell'Interno (MI), Direzione Generale di Pubblica sicurezza (DGPS), Divisione Affari riservati (AARR), Categorie permanenti, Ctg. O, Stranieri pericolosi per la sicurezza delle istituzioni, fascicoli personali 1949–1965, Busta 108, Fascicolo 'Wächter Otto Gustav fu Josef'.

200 At the cemetery, a handwritten document: EM, Riccardo Savona Siemens to JE, 03.07.2017.

200 'Interpol searches for a body, the trail leads to Berlin': 'Interpol sucht eine Leiche – die Spur führt nach Berlin', *Berliner Zeitung*, 27.04.1961.

201 An Italian newspaper reported that: 'I Nazisti Sono Fra Noi – Waechter "Boia" Di Leopoli veramente sepolto a Testaccio?', *Avanti*, 08.04.1961. Available at: https://avanti.senato.it/avanti/js/pdfjs-dist/web/viewer.html?file=/avanti/files/reader.php?f%3DAvanti%201896-1993%20PDF/Avanti-Lotto2/CFI0422392_19610408_84.pdf.

202 'We bury the body of our brother': T, CW, burial, Cassette 12, Side 1, 04.01.1974.

203 Charlotte's papers were publicly available: USHMM, *Archiv Horst von Wächter 1901–1965* (Accession Number 2014.103; RG Number: RG-17.049).

204 One wrote to say: L, John Beddington to PS, 8.09.2017, with Charlotte Beddington diary, 09.01.1961.

208 a lawyer, Professor Giangalezzo Bettoni: Prof. Dr Giangalezzo Bettoni, d. November 2008: http://studiobettoni.org.

208 another bishop, Jan Bucko: Ivan Bucko, b. 1 October 1891, Hermaniv, Austria-Hungary; d. 21 September 1974, Rome. Apostolic Visitator for the Ukrainians in western Europe 1945–71.

208 Dr Puccio Pucci, another 'good friend': Dr Puccio Pucci, b. 12 April 1904, Florence; d. 1985, Florence. Lawyer and athlete.

209 The letter ended: On file with author.

209 the Black Brigades, a paramilitary organisation: The *Corpo Ausiliario delle Squadre d'azione di Camicie nere*, more commonly known as the Black Brigades Italian paramilitary group, operated in Republic of Salò, 1944–5.

209 After the war he moved to Rome: Richard Breitman and Norman J.W. Goda, *Hitler's Shadow: Nazi War Criminals, U.S. Intelligence, and the Cold War* (United States, National Archives and Records Administration, 2010), p. 77.

209 It was said he played a key role: Christopher Simpson, *Blowback: America's Recruitment of Nazis and its Destructive Impact on our Domestic and Foreign Policy* (Weidenfeld & Nicolson, 1988), Chapter 13.

209 He responded graciously and helpfully: EM, Manfred Bettoni to PS, 20.04.2017.

210 In 1949 he worked to create: Klaus Wiegrefe, 'Files Uncovered: Nazi Veterans Created Illegal Army', *Der Spiegel*, 14 May 2014: http://www.spiegel.de/international/germany/wehrmacht-veterans-created-a-secret-army-in-west-germany-a-969015.html.

211 *Il Giornale d'Italia* published an article: The *Giornale d'Italia* article is referenced in: 'Si Tratta Dell'Attentatore di Dollfussi – Contrastanti ipotesi sul passato di Otto Wächter', *Il Quotidiano*, 03.09.1949. On file with author.

211 The next day the fact of Otto's death was reported: 'Otto Waechter Dies; Former Nazi Official Planned Assassination of Dollfuss', *New York Times*, 02.09.1949: https://www.nytimes.com/1949/09/02/archives/otto-waechter-dies-former-nazi-official-planned-assassination-of.html?searchResultPosition=3.

211 'The Vatican protects the fascist criminals': 'L'assassino di Dollfüss viveva nascosto nell'Istituto Cattolico Teutonico', *L'Unità*, 03.09.1949.

211 *Il Quotidiano* claimed: 'Contrastanti ipotesi sul passato di Otto Wachter', *Il Quotidiano*, 03.09.1949.

211 *Il Paese* declared: 'Il Caso Waechter', *Il Paese*, 03.09.1949.

212 'Who is this Monsignor Hudal?': 'I trascorsi di mons. Hudal protettore del nazista Waechter', *L'Unità*, 06.09.1949.

212 *L'Osservatore Romano*, the Vatican's semi-official daily newspaper: Ibid.

212 *L'Unità* published a cartoon: 'Il partito nazista ricostituito negli istituti religiosi teutonici', *L'Unità*, 04.09.1949.

212 *Il Giornale d'Italia* reported Otto's false name: 'Wächter aveva documenti regolari al nome die Reinhard', *Il Giornale D'Italia*, 06.09.1949.

212 'calm and undisturbed': Aristide Raimondi, 'Come Viveva a Roma Il Capo Degli Assassini di Dollfuss – "Quo vadis, Germany?" ultima fatica di Otto Wächter', *Il Gazzettino*, 12.09.1949.

212 Death by swimming: Ibid.

212 'finest of the SS': 'Il partito nazista ricostituito negli istituti religiosi teutonici', *L'Unità*, 04.09.1949.

212 a German named Lauterbacher: Hartmann Lauterbacher, b. 24 May 1909, Reutte, Austria; d. 12 April 1998, Seebruck, Germany. Gauleiter of South Hanover-Braunschweig 1940–5 and Reich Defence Commissar 1942–5.

213 led by Saverio Pòlito: Saverio Pòlito, b. 1881; d. 12 May 1959. Rome police chief.

213 'for any crime or war crime': Archivio centrale dello Stato (ACS), Ministero dell'Interno (MI), Direzione Generale di Pubblica sicurezza (DGPS), Divisione Affari riservati (AARR), Categorie permanenti, Ctg. O, Stranieri pericolosi per la sicurezza delle istituzioni, fascicoli personali 1949–1965, Busta 108, Fascicolo 'Wächter Otto Gustav fu Josef'. note of 2 September 1949.

213 'severe jaundice and uraemia': Archivio centrale dello Stato (ACS), as ibid.

213 'did not show that he was a war criminal': Archivio centrale dello Stato (ACS), as ibid.

213 two years later the text was published in *Anima Stimmen*: 'Die katholische Caritas in einer Zeitenwende – Predigt, gehalten am 11. September 1949 in der Deutschen Nationalkirche der Anima zu Rom', *Anima Stimmen*, Vol. IV, March 1951, pp. 25–30, on file with author.

213 'net of lies, slander and revenge': Ibid., pp. 25–9.

214 Two weeks later he was visited: EM, Mario Tedeschini to PS, 28.02.2019.

216 In 1936 he published *Die Grundlagen des Nationalsozialismus*: Alois Hudal, *Die Grundlagen des Nationalsozialismus. Eine ideengeschichtliche Untersuchung* (Johannes Günther Verlag, 1937).

216 He persisted, forcing a vote: Anna Pawlikowska, 'Watykański agent III Rzeszy', 14 October 2010: https://www.znak.org. pl/?lang1=pl&page1=people&subpage1=people00&infopassid1=333&scrt1=sn.

216 the newly established Pontifical Commission for Assistance: *Pontificia Commissione di Assistenza* (Pontifical Commission for Assistance), created in April 1944 by Pope Pius XII to provide aid during and after the war, addressing basic needs and identity papers.

216 along with a name – Carlo Bayer: Karl Johannes (Carlo) Bayer, b. 13 February 1915, Obernigk, Poland; d. 16 January 1977, Rome. Secretary General Caritas Internationalis 1951–70.

216 Gitta Sereny interviewed Karl Bayer: Gitta Sereny, *Into That Darkness: From Mercy Killing to Mass Murder, a study of Franz Stangl, the commandant of Treblinka* (André Deutsch, 1974).

216 my great-grandmother Amalia: Sands, *East West Street*, p. 42.

216 'the best camp Kommandant in Poland': Sereny, *Into That Darkness*, pp. 11–12.

216 Austrian Nazi hunter Simon Wiesenthal: Simon Wiesenthal, b. 31

December 1908, Buczacz, Galicia; d. 20 September 2005, Vienna. Nazi hunter.

217 Josef Mengele, the doctor who carried out experiments: Josef Mengele, b. 16 March 1911, Günzburg, Germany; d. 7 February 1979, Bertioga, Brazil. Medical doctor, at Auschwitz concentration camp 1943–5.

217 'did provide money for this': Gitta Sereny, *Into That Darkness*, p. 315.

217 'reprisals': Guy Walters, *Hunting Evil* (Bantam Press, 2009), p. 246.

218 Under irresistible pressure: Gerald Steinacher, *Nazis on the Run* (OUP, 2011), p.128.

218 In 1960, the abduction of Adolf Eichmann: 'I Nazisti Sono Fra Noi – Il "boia" di Leopoli avvelenato spirò fra le braccia di mons. Hudal', *Avanti*, 21.04.1961, p. 2

218 Charlotte's papers included a newspaper article: 'I Nazisti Sono Fra Noi', *Avanti*, 21.04.1961.

218 the auxiliary bishop of Vienna: Jakob Weinbacher, b. 20 December 1901, Vienna; d. 15 June 1985, Vienna. Rector, Santa Maria dell'Anima 1952–61.

218 Another noted – erroneously: James Carroll, *Constantine's Sword* (Houghton Mifflin, 2002), pp. 505, 512, citing Cardinal Faulhaber.

218 *The Roman Diaries: Confession of an Old Bishop*: Alois C. Hudal, *Römische Tagebücher. Lebensbeichte eines alten Bischofs* (Leopold Stocker Verlag, 1976).

218 Hansjakob Stehle, the historian: Hansjakob Stehle, 'Des "braunen Bischofs" Abschied', *Die Zeit*, 24 December 1976: https://www.zeit.de/1976/53/des-braunen-bischofs-abschied.

218 *The Deputy*, a controversial play: Rolf Hochhuth, *Der Stellvertreter. Ein christliches Trauerspiel* (The Deputy, a Christian tragedy) (1963).

218 Hudal's *Roman Diaries* made a number: Hudal, *Römische Tagebücher*, pp. 262–3, 298.

219 'You were with him in his final hour': L, CW to Alois Hudal, 19.07.1949.

219 'acute liver atrophy': L, Hedi Dupré to CW, 25.07.1949.

220 'There he was': T, CW and HJS, Cassette 3, Side 1, 28.09.1984.

221 I put the question to Professor David Kertzer: David Kertzer, b. 1948, professor of anthropology and Italian studies at Brown University, United States.

221 having read his book: David Kertzer, *The Pope and Mussolini: The Secret History of Pius XI and the Rise of Fascism in Europe* (OUP, 2014).

221 'serious figure': Conversation with Dr Lutz Klinkhammer, German Institute in Rome; Lutz Klinkhammer, *Zwischen Bündnis und Besatzung – Das nationalsozialistische Deutschland und die Republik von Salò 1943–1945* (Niemeyer, 1993), p. 94. Wächter is mentioned three times in the book, in the period between the summer of 1944 and early 1945, when he worked under General Wolff, alongside Globočnik.

221 There followed a de facto civil war: Duggan, *Concise History of Italy*.

222 a leader, Palmiro Togliatti: Palmiro Togliatti, b. 26 March 1893, Genoa; d. 21 August 1964, Yalta, Crimea. Founder and leader of the Italian Communist Party 1927–64.

222 Herbert Kappler, the SS chief of: Herbert Kappler, b. 29 September 1907, Stuttgart; d. 9 February 1978, Soltau, Germany. Chief of German police in occupied Rome 1943–5.

222 to a term of life imprisonment: Felix Nikolaus Bohr, 'Flucht aus Rom. Das spektakuläre Ende des "Falles Kappler" im August 1977', *Vierteljahrshefte für Zeitgeschichte* 60 (IFZ, 2012), pp. 111–41: https://www. ifz-muenchen.de/heftarchiv/2012_1_5_bohr.pdf.

222 Captain Erich Priebke: Erich Priebke, b. 29 July 1913, Hennigsdorf, Germany; d. 11 October 2013, Rome, Italy. SS commander.

222 Feldmarschall Kesselring: Albert Kesselring, b. 30 November 1885, Marktsteft, Germany; d. 16 July 1960, Bad Nauheim, Germany. Field Marshal of the Luftwaffe.

223 the artist Mirko Basaldella was working on: 'Jewish Museum of Rome Displays Mirko Basaldella Sketch for Holocaust Remembrance Day', Getty Images: https://www.gettyimages.de/fotos/jewish-museum-of-rome-displays-mirko-basaldella-sketch-for-holocaust-remembrance-da y?sort=mostpopular&mediatype=photography&phrase=jewish%20 museum%20of%20rome%20displays%20mirko%20basaldella%20 sketch%20for%20holocaust%20remembrance%20day. Mirko Basaldella, b. 28 September 1910, Udine, Italy; d. 24 November 1969, Cambridge, Massachusetts. Artist.

223 the nucleus of the *Movimento Sociale Italiano*: The Italian Social Movement (*Movimento Sociale Italiano*, MSI), post-fascist party, founded in 1946 by supporters of Benito Mussolini, disbanded in 1995, succeeded by the AN (National Alliance), which merged into The People of Freedom, launched by Silvio Berlusconi, later dissolved.

223 the painter Lajos Markos: Lajos Markos, b. 1917, Marosvásárhely, Hungary; d. 1993, Houston, Texas. Artist.

223 Ezio Maria Gray: Ezio Maria Gray, b. 9 October 1885, Novara, Italy; d. 8 February 1969, Rome. Fascist politician, journalist and editor of journal *Il Pensiero di Benito Mussolini*.

223 Monsignor Draganović, a Croat: Krunoslav Stjepan Draganović, b. 30 October 1903, Matići, Austria-Hungary; d. 3 June 1983, Sarajevo, Yugoslavia. Roman Catholic priest and a member of Croat fascist organisation, Ustashe.

223 his cardinal protector was Luis Copello: Santiago Luis Copello, b. 7 January 1880, Buenos Aires; d. 9 February 1967, Rome. Archbishop of Buenos Aires, 1932–59.

223 Argentine president Juan Perón: Juan Perón, b. 8 October 1895, Buenos Aires; d. 1 July 1974, Buenos Aires. President of Argentina, 1946–55 and 1973–4.

224 helped Klaus Barbie flee: Nikolaus (Klaus) Barbie, b. 25 October 1913,

Godesberg, Prussia; d. 25 September 1991, Lyon, France. SS and Gestapo officer.

224 Count Teodorani Fabbri: Giovanni (Vanni) Pozzo Teodorani Fabbri, b. 1916; d. 1964. Journalist and politican.

224 Baron Folco Aloisi: Baron Folco Aloisi, b. 1905, Paris; date of death unknown.

224 Marianne Leibl: Marianne Leibl, b. 24 April 1898, Merano, Italy; d. 5 June 1988, Rome. Actress.

226 Otto's papers included an address – Villa San Francesco: Villa Francesco: http://www.villasanfrancesco.org, located at: Via Monti Parioli 64, Rome.

226 a German diplomat who resigned: Rudolf Nadolny, b. 12 July 1873, Groß Stürlack, German empire; d. 18 May 1953, Düsseldorf. Diplomat.

226 Princess Lorenza Pignatelli, who lived outside Rome: Robert Katz, *The Battle for Rome* (Simon & Schuster, 2003), p. 103.

227 According to Princess Pignatelli: Ibid. Fr Dennis McManus, 'A Brief Note on the Significance of the "Graham Archives"': http://legacy.ptwf.org/Downloads/Grahamnotes9%2008.pdf.

227 They were halted: Giacomo Debenedetti, *October 16, 1943*, with a preface by Alberto Moravia (University of Notre Dame Press, 2001).

227 Bishop Hudal became involved: Michael Phayer, *Pius XII, The Holocaust, and the Cold War* (Indiana University Press, 2008), p. 76.

227 His memoir contained a reference: Hudal, *Römische Tagebücher*, p. 261.

227 In American archives I found: CIA, 'Forwarded Italian-Slanted report on Eugene Dollmann', 8 February 1950, p. 7.

227 'He was quiet and not active': EM, Pamela Putnam-Smith to LMK, 04.01.2017.

227 'Wollenweber was our stepfather': EM, ibid.

229 read with particular attention one of his books: Norman Goda et al., *U.S. Intelligence and the Nazis* (CUP, 2005).

229 'I was spied on day and night': R, CW, 1932–45, p. 131.

229 The CIC was formed in 1942: CIC Center, 'History and Mission of the Counter Intelligence Corps in World War II': https://fas.org/irp/agency/army/cic-wwii.pdf.

230 the story of Hermann Höfle: Hermann Julius Höfle, b. 19 June 1911, Salzburg; d. 21 August 1962, Vienna. Deputy to Odilo Globočnik during *Aktion Reinhardt* 1940–5; Goda et al., *U.S. Intelligence and the Nazis*, pp. 450–2.

230 'particular joy': Michael V. Korda, 'Beginning the Cold War', *NYRB*, 29 December 1966: https://www.nybooks.com/articles/1966/12/29/beginning-the-cold-war-1/.

230 They acted to remove his name: Kerstin von Lingen, *Allen Dulles, the ISS, and Nazi War Criminals: the Dynamics of Selected Prosecution* (Cambridge, 2013), pp. 155–98, 287–94.

230 I learned that the CIC was active: Goda et al., *U.S. Intelligence and the Nazis*, p. 456.

230 I learned that General Wolff's subordinate: Goda et al., *U.S. Intelligence and the Nazis*, pp. 317–36.

230 I learned that in April 1945: Goda et al., *U.S. Intelligence and the Nazis*, p. 153.

231 I learned that Lucid recruited: Thomas A. Lucid, b. 1917; d. 1985.

231 In 1948, Lucid retained Höttl: Goda et al., *U.S. Intelligence and the Nazis*, p. 274. See also: CIA, 'Net Project – Mount Vernon' and CIA, 'Net Project – Montgomery'.

231 Professor Goda directed me to one document: CIA, 'Illegal Emigration Movements In and Through Italy', 15.05.1947.

233 organisation run by Reinhard Gehlen: Reinhard Gehlen, b. 3 April 1902, Erfurt, Germany; d. 8 June 1979, Starnberg, Germany. Generalmajor 1944–5. President of German Federal Intelligence Service (BND) 1956–68. Goda et al., *U.S. Intelligence and the Nazis*, pp. 307–8.

233 Höttl was an example: On Höttl, see Norman Goda, 'The Nazi Peddler: Willhelm Höttl and Allied Intelligence', in Goda et al., *U.S. Intelligence and the Nazis*, pp. 265–92.

234 There seemed to be no CIA name file: EM, Norman Goda to PS, 01.02.2017.

235 'I was so active in my youth': T, CW and HJS, Cassette 3, Side 2, 28.09.1983.

236 Hartmann Lauterbacher gave witness testimony: Nuremberg Trial Proceedings, Vol. 14, 139th Day, 27.05.1946: https://avalon.law.yale.edu/imt/05-27-46.asp#lauterbacher.

236 and published an autobiography: Hartmann Lauterbacher, *Erlebt und mitgestaltet. Kronzeuge einer Epoche 1923–1945: zu neuen Ufern nach Kriegsende* (Preussisch Oldendorf : K.W. Schütz, 1984).

236 'I met the leader of the British Boy Scouts'; 'Nazis at Eton', *The Times*, 9 March 2010, letter from Guy Walters: https://www.thetimes.co.uk/article/nazis-at-eton-r8nmqfv5brd.

237 The Lauterbacher files: NARA, IRR Personal Name File Hartmann Lauterbacher, XE008169WJ.

237 Lauterbacher was five feet seven: NARA, IRR Personal Name File Hartmann Lauterbacher, XE008169WJ.

238 His contact there was Joseph Luongo: Joseph Luongo, b. 3 May 1916, New Haven, USA; date of death unknown. CIC and US Army military intelligence.

238 There was also a file: Provided by Stefanie Waske, *Bundeszentrale für die Unterlagen der Staatssicherheit der DDR* (Stasi), AV 2/83 part 1 of 2, p. 155.

239 One clue jumped out: CIA, 'Germans in Italy', 24.08.1950.

240 better known as John le Carré: David John Moore Cornwell (John le

Carré), b. 19 October 1931, Poole, England. British writer of espionage novels.

240 'Are you a spy and if so': John le Carré, *A Perfect Spy* (Hodder & Stoughton, 1986).

242 '*Persilschein*': *Persilschein* is a German idiom akin to a carte blanche, meaning its holder is free to go about their business, despite the questionable morality of the business or the person. The term originates from the washing powder Persil, but acquired a new meaning following the Second World War during the denazification process undertaken by the Allies.

246 one hundred and twenty-eight files: CIA, 'HASS Karl, aka "Carlo" 0006', 28.08.1950.

246 He began in the department of press affairs: Michael Wildt, *Generation des Unbedingten: das Führungskorps des Reichssicherheitshauptamtes* (Hamburger Edition, 2003).

246 In the summer of 1944 he came under surveillance: UK National Archives, WO 204/12798.

247 An agreement was approved: Goda et al., *U.S. Intelligence and the Nazis*, p. 274.

248 The CIC recruited Major Hass: CIA, 'Net Project – Los Angeles' and CIA, 'HASS Karl, aka "Carlo" 0006', 28.08.1950.

249 Two of them – Ulderico Caputo and Alberto Barletta: The *Ufficio Affari Riservati* (UAR; Office of Classified Matters) was restructured following the end of the war, as part of the Ministry of the Interior overseeing the activities of foreigners on Italian territory; Ulderico Caputo, chief of the Office of Classified Matters, 1959–61; Alberto Barletta, b. Naples, chief of the Office of Classified Matters, 1948–58.

249 Albert Griezzar: No other information is available on Albert Griezzar.

249 Pino Romualdi: Giuseppe (Pino) Romualdi, b. 24 July 1913, Predappio, Italy; d. 21 May 1988, Rome. Politician.

249 the Republic of Salò: *Repubblica Sociale Italiana* (commonly known as Republic of Salò) was the German puppet state set up in Fascist Italy from September 1943 until German surrender in May 1945, under the leadership of Benito Mussolini. CIC, 'Net Project – Los Angeles', pp. 2, 6, 7, 10, 21.

249 Monsignor Federico Fioretti: No other information is available on Monsignor Fioretti.

251 One file from August 1950: CIA, 'HASS Karl, aka "Carlo" 0006', 28.08.1950.

251 identified as Anna Maria Giustini: Anna Maria Fiorini, b. 1 May 1914, Parma; date of death unknown (may also have been named Berengere Giglioli, b. 25 April 1914). Married Karl Hass, 15 July 1945.

251 Enrica Erna Giustini: Enrica Erna Williams (née Giustini), b. 18 May 1949; date of death unknown.

251 Enrica's certificate of baptism: On file with author.

251 'very kind old comrade': L, OW to CW, 04.07.1949.

252 This file also contained: CIA, 'HASS Karl, aka "Carlo" 0006', 28.08.1950.

253 the CIC dispensed with his services: Hass was dropped by the CIC on 1 January 1953 (CIA Karl Hass, 0002, 0038).

253 'a Jew attached to IRO': The International Refugee Organization (IRO) was an intergovernmental organisation founded in 1946 to address large-scale refugee movements following the Second World War; replaced by the United Nations High Commissioner for Refugees (UNHCR).

253 'working for Cominform': The Communist Information Bureau (Cominform), founded in 1947 as the official forum of the International Communist Movement.

253 He also followed in Otto's cinematic footsteps: *Londra Chiami Polo Nord* (*The House of Intrigue*) (1956), Italian wartime espionage film on Nazis sending misleading radio signals to undermine British intelligence efforts; *La caduta degli dei* (*The Damned*) (1969) is a film about a wealthy German industrialist family engaging in business with the Nazi Party.

254 Donaldson found Priebke on a street: 'Nazi Capt. Erich Priebke: An Order Was an Order', *ABC News*, 5 May 1994, at 05:48: https://abcnews.go.com/International/video/nazi-captain-erich-priebke-found-abc-news-20575216.

255 In March 1998, the Appeals Chamber: Sentenza della Corte Militare die Appello di Roma, in data 07.03.1998: https://www.difesa.it/Gius tizia_Militare/rassegna/Processi/Priebke/Pagine/11Sentenza070398.aspx (in Italian).

255 On appeal, Italy's Supreme Court: Sentenza della Corte Suprema di Cassazione, in data 16.11.1998: https://www.difesa.it/Giustizia_ Militare/rassegna/Processi/Priebke/Pagine/12Sentenza161198.aspx (in Italian); http://www.internationalcrimesdatabase.org/Case/1104/Hass-and-Priebke/ (English reference).

255 Erich Priebke took his case to: Erich Priebke appealed his war crimes conviction by the Italian courts before the European Courts of Human Rights on the basis of lack of an impartial tribunal and other elements relating to an unfair trial; *Erich Priebke v. Italy* (dec.), no. 48799/99, 5 April 2001.

258 Founded in the mid-nineteenth century: http://www.vignapia.com/ edificio-storico/.

259 a celebration of the Day of the Republic: *Festa della Repubblica* (Day of the Republic) is celebrated on 2 June. It commemorates the formal end of the monarchy, following the 1946 referendum.

259 'I sat in my cell': L, OW to CW, 05.05.1949; L, OW to CW 22.05.1949; L, OW to CW, 04.06.1949.

259 with a list of residents: Photograph of the relevant page is on file with the author.

259 This was the fifteenth-century Santo Spirito Hospital: Carla Keyvan-
ian, *Hospitals and Urbanism in Rome, 1200–1500* (Brill, 2016),
p. 349.

259 The operating room was visited by: Garabed Eknoyan, 'Michelangelo:
Art, anatomy, and the kidney', *Kidney International*, Vol. 57, Issue 3,
March 2000, pp. 1190–1201: https://www.sciencedirect.com/science/
article/pii/S0085253815468516.

261 To enter the caves: The *Mausoleo Fosse Ardeatine* is located on the
outskirts of Rome where, on 24 March 1944, 335 men were killed as
a reprisal for an attack by partisans against German soldiers on Via
Rasella on 23 March 1944.

261 Antonio Pisino: Antonio Pisino, b. 26 May 1917, Maglie, Italy; d. 24
March 1944. Arrested on spying charges.

261 Alessandro Portieri: Alessandro Portieri, b. 17 July 1924, Rome, Italy; d.
24 March 1944. Previously arrested for possession of weapons.

261 Ettore Ronconi: Ettore Ronconi, b. 23 September 1897, Rome; d. 24
March 1944. Picked up by chance.

263 Dr Ickx floated in: Johan Ickx, b. 5 July 1962, Wilrijk, Belgium. Head of
the Historical Archive, Section II for Relations with States of the Secre-
tariat of State, since 2010.

264 the negotiation of the concordat: The *Reichskonkordat* treaty was negotiated between Nazi Germany and the Vatican, signed on 20 July 1933
by Eugenio Pacelli (later Pius XII) and Franz von Papen, to guarantee
rights of the Roman Catholic Church in Germany.

264 Franz von Papen: Franz von Papen, b. 29 October 1879, Werl, German
empire; d. 2 May 1969, Sasbach, Germany. Chancellor of Germany
1932, Vice-Chancellor 1933–4.

267 'some material has disappeared': Johan Ickx, 'The Roman "non pos-
sumus" and the Attitude of Bishop Alois Hudal towards the National
Socialist Ideological Aberrations', fn 2, in: Lieve Gevers and Jan Bank
(eds.), *Religion under Siege – Volume I: The Roman Catholic Church in
Occupied Europe (1939–1950)* (Peeters Publishers, 2007).

267 'The Butcher of Lemberg': 'I Nazisti Sono Fra Noi – Il "boia" di Leopoli
avvelenato spirò fra le braccia di mons. Hudal', *Avanti*, 21.04.1961.

268 'Butcher of Leopolis was poisoned': Ibid.

268 I thought of Laurence Olivier: *Marathon Man* (1976), film based on William Goldman's novel, starring Laurence Olivier as a Nazi war criminal
in hiding in South America, for which he won an Academy Award for
Best Supporting Actor; *The Boys from Brazil* (1978), based on the novel
by Ira Levin, featured Laurence Olivier as a Nazi hunter on the trail of
Dr Josef Mengele.

268 'My father is now seventy years': L, Franz von Papen Jr to Alois Hudal,
12.12.1948.

268 'I thank you from my heart': L, Franz Hiernoymus Riedl to Alois Hudal,
02.10.1949.

268 'let me first of all thank Your Excellency': L, CW to Alois Hudal, 19.07.1949.

269 the original manuscript of the bishop's memoir: Alois Hudal, *Römische Tagebücher* (manuscript, 1953); extracts on file with author.

270 He has written extensively on the Ratline: Steinacher, *Nazis on the Run*.

271 'final straw': Ibid., p. 127.

272 'I've never heard of anything': EM, Anton Weiss-Wendt to PS, 14.02.2019.

273 The *gottgläubig* declaration was in: BArch, R 9361-III/561695; *Waechter, Otto – Personenbezogene Unterlagen der SS und SA: Otto von Wächter an die Personalkanzlei RFSS*, 15.04.1937.

275 except for an Italian newspaper article: 'Così depistai tutti ai funerali di Hass', *Il Tempo*, 20.10.2013: https://www.iltempo.it/cronache/2013/10/20/news/cosi-depistai-tutti-ai-funerali-di-hass-911504/.

283 He passed along a document: On file with author.

283 *Leptospirosis ictero haemorragica*: Leptospirosis is an infection transmitted by animals, usually rodents, through water or soil containing animal urine.

284 He contacted an expert: L, Bestattung Helmuth Treffer to HW, 28.02.2017.

285 Dame Sue Black: Dame Susan Margaret Black, b. 7 May 1961, Inverness, Scotland. Forensic anthropologist.

285 Professor Niamh Nic Daéid: Professor Niamh Nic Daéid, forensic scientist.

292 the *Washington Post* carried an obituary: 'Obituaries – Thomas A. Lucid', *Washington Post*, 28.05.1985, on file with author.

295 where it apparently resides today: Kevin Ruffner, 'World War II Artifacts Donated to Exhibit Centre', in *Centre for the Study of Intelligence Bulletin*, Spring 1999, Issue No. 9, article available at: https://forum.axishistory.com/viewtopic.php?t=33217.

296 the set of Los Pollos Hermanos, from *Breaking Bad*: *Breaking Bad* (2008–13), US television series in which main character Walter White, a high-school chemistry teacher, manufactures and sells crystal meth, after he learns about his cancer diagnosis.

297 the Shah of Iran: Mohammad Reza Pahlavi, b. 26 October 1919, Tehran; d. 27 July 1980, Cairo. Shah of Iran 1941–79.

298 as reported in the *Jersey Journal*: 'Local soldier helps locate Frau Himmler', *Jersey Journal*, 16.05.1945.

298 He also took two Christmas cards: Berlin, December 1937, on file with author.

298 'There's Allen Dulles': Allen Welsh Dulles, b. 7 April 1893, Watertown, USA; d. 29 January 1969, Washington DC. Director, Central Intelligence for the CIA 1953–61; Richard McGarrah Helms, b. 30 March 1913, St Davids, USA; d. 23 October 2002, Washington DC. CIA Director, 1966–73; John Edgar Hoover, b. 1 January 1895, Washington DC, d. 2 May 1972, Washington DC. FBI Director, 1924–72.

299 'Oh.': Kerstin von Lingen, *SS und Secret Service: „Verschwörung des Schweigens": die Akte Karl Wolff* (Schöningh, 2010), Chapter 1, fn. 14.

299 A letter arrived from Langley: L, Charles A. Briggs to Thomas A. Lucid, 30.08.1983, on file with author.

299 A few years later, the Comptroller General: Report by the Comptroller General of the United States, 'Nazis and Axis Collaborators Were Used to Further U.S. Anti-Communist Objectives in Europe', 28 June 1985: https://www.cia.gov/library/readingroom/docs/CIA-RDP87M01152R000300410001-8.pdf.

299 'The West is fighting a desperate battle': Ibid., p. 24.

300 a devout Knight of Columbus: The Knights of Columbus, named in honour of Christopher Columbus, founded in Connecticut in 1882 to aid working-class and immigrant Catholic communities in the US; today it has some 2 million members.

302 Wiesenthal's memoir, published in 1967: Simon Wiesenthal, *The Murderers Among Us* (McGraw-Hill, 1967).

302 Here Wiesenthal described: Wendy Lower, *Diary of Samuel Golfard and the Holocaust in Galicia* (AltaMira, 2011), p. 119, citing to: R.W. Kempner, '"Genocide as Official Business": The Judgment in the Lemberg Trial', *Aufbau* (New York), 10 May 1968, p. 7 (translated from German).

302 'He was personally in charge': Wiesenthal, *The Murderers Among Us*, p. 236.

303 'Wächter escaped after the war': Ibid., pp. 236–7.

303 an organisation known as ODESSA: Uki Goñi, *The Real Odessa: How Perón Brought the Nazi War Criminals to Argentina* (Granta, 2002); John Cornwell, *Hitler's Pope* (Viking, 1999), p. 267

304 There were two lengthy affidavits: VWI-SWA, Ritschek Viktor,_Zeugenaussage Wiesenthal_7249.

304 There was a folder of correspondence: VWI-SWA, Waechter Otto, Korresp Verbleib Archiv 8193.

304 Ten typed pages: VWI-SWA, Galizien_1_Augenzeugenbericht_Galizien3729, Rosa Stephenson.

308 Professor Massimo Pinzani: Professor Massimo Pinzani, Director of University College London's Institute for Liver and Digestive Health since 2012.

311 *Circolo Canottieri Roma*: The Rowing Club Rome, founded 1919.

313 'Thank you for your continued effort': EM, HW to Klaus Oblin, 05.05.2018.

315 'He always took pleasure': T, CW, 12.07.1977 (tape 10).

316 '*Dear N.O.!*': EM, HW to OW Jr, 04.12.2007.

316 'much to do in Lemberg': L, OW to CW, 16.08.1942.

316 'Everything was very nice and amicable': L, OW to CW, 20.08.1942.

317 The words evoked: T, CW and Melitta Wiedemann, Cassette 2, Side 2, 02.04.1977.

321 Stern and uncompromising: EM, Sue Springer to PS, 12.11.2018.

321 to which he gave the title *Unrepentant*: Simon van der Borgh, *Unrepentant* (play), 2018.

321 The grandson of a British soldier sent extracts: EM, Charlie Barne to PS, 13.11.2018; Transcript of War Diary of the 4th Hussars, 31 May 1945 ('The man suspected of being Glovocnik [sp] was trapped into acknowledging his name by a slight movement of the head when Major Ramsey shouted his name across the courtyard'; Diary of Lieutenant Colonel Anthony Barne, 30 May 1945; see Anthony Barne, *Churchill's Colonel* (Pen and Sword Books, 2019).

321 A woman wrote about her father's return: EM, Deborah Michel to PS, 15.10.2018 (citing the words of her father Frank Michel). See also Ernst Klee, *Persilscheine und falsche Pässe – Wie die Kirchen den Nazis halfen* (Fischer, 1991).

322 I did, and learned that he was: Information received from Harald Stockhammer; Florian Beierl, *Hitlers Berg* (Verlag Beierl, 2004), pp. 47, 260. Through an intermediary, contact was made with Peter Reinhardt, son of Alfred Reinhardt, who indicated that, at the age of eighty-three, he was not familiar with the Wächter name and had no interest in learning more.

322 'The final disease of Wächter': EM, Professor Dr Thomas Zilker to PS, 23.04.2019, 25.04.2019.

323 a recent article I'd written: Gabriel Rath, 'Ich rieche die Gefahr', *Die Presse*, 08.12.2018: https://diepresse.com/home/ausland/aussenpolitik/5543143/Ich-rieche-die-Gefahr.

325 came across a single document: Italy-SS General Waechter, NARA, XA205194.

328 We admired a seventeenth-century fresco: Klaus Heitzmann, 'Aspekte der Kriegs- und Frühen Nachkriegsgeschichte im Lungau um 1945', *Salzburg, Geschichte und Politik*, 1999, Vol 2/3, p. 13: http://www.lechner-forschungsgesellschaft.at/files/zeitschrift/1999_2_3A.pdf.

328 It is still owned by the Rehrl family: The local land registry confirmed the Wächters had title over the property from 18 April 1940 to 19 April 1948, when it was transferred to a Restitution Commission and, eventually, Governor Rehrl's daughters, following the death of their father on 21 June 1948; on file with author.

331 the mummified remains of a man: On Ötzi the iceman, see Brenda Fowler, Iceman: Uncovering the Life and Times of a Prehistoric Man found in an Alpine Glacier (University of Chicago Press, 2001).

332 'Their bows will slaughter the young men': Erika Longmuir, *Imagining Childhood* (Yale, 2006), p. 44; see also Diana Bullen Presciutti, 'Dead Infants, Cruel Mothers, and Heroic Popes: The Visual Rhetoric of Foundling Care at the Hospital of Santo Spirito, Rome', *Renaissance Quarterly*, Vol. 64, 2011, pp. 752–99.

ILLUSTRATION AND MAP CREDITS

Sources and permissions (by reference to photo number)
Jill Edelstein: 13
Eunice D. Howe: 76
Ian Sayer Archive: 12
IPN: 45, 78–80
International Mapping, Maps 1–4, pp. 8, 142, 158, 176
Thomas Lucid: 37, 73, 74
NARA: 61, 64
New York Times: 32, 57
Erwin Peterseil: 14
Burkhardt Rathmann: 40
Philippe Sands: 35, 39, 41, 44, 47, 51, 54, 63, 67, 69–71, 81–2
Santo Spirito Hospital: 1
Scharkow family: 77
Mario Tedeschi: 50, 65
United States Holocaust Memorial Museum: 28, 29
University of Vienna: 24, 25
Horst Wächter: 2–12, 15–22, 25–7, 29–31, 34, 36, 38, 42, 46, 48–9, 52–3, 55–6, 58–60, 66, 75
Viktor Williams: 72

INDEX

EAST WEST STREET

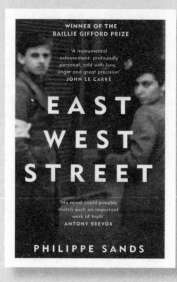

**Winner of the Baillie Gifford Prize, the JQ-Wingate
Literary Prize, Prix du Livre Européen, and Prix Montaigne**

'A monumental achievement: profoundly personal,
told with love, anger and great precision'
John le Carré

'One of the most gripping and powerful books imaginable'
Sunday Times

When he receives an invitation to deliver a lecture in the Ukrainian
city of Lviv, international lawyer Philippe Sands begins a journey on
the trail of his family's secret history that leads him halfway across
the world, to the origins of international law at the Nuremberg trial.
Interweaving the stories of the two prosecutors who invented the
crimes of genocide and crimes against humanity, the Nazi governor
responsible for the murder of thousands, and incredible acts of
wartime bravery, *East West Street* is an unforgettable blend of
memoir and historical detective story, and a powerful meditation on
the way memory, crime and guilt leave scars across generations.